PREFACE FROM USGBC

The built environment has a profound impact on our natural environment, economy, health, and productivity. Breakthroughs in building science, technology, and operations are now available to designers, builders, operators, and owners who want to build green and maximize both economic and environmental performance.

Through the LEED® green building certification program, the U.S. Green Building Council (USGBC) is transforming the built environment. The green building movement offers an unprecedented opportunity to respond to the most important challenges of our time, including global climate change, dependence on unsustainable and expensive sources of energy, and threats to human health. The work of innovative building professionals is a fundamental driving force in the green building moment. Such leadership is a critical component to achieving USGBC's mission of a sustainable built environment for all within a generation.

USGBC MEMBERSHIP

USGBC's greatest strength is the diversity of our membership. USGBC is a balanced, consensus-based nonprofit with more than 16,000 member companies and organizations representing the entire building industry. Since its inception in 1993, USGBC has played a vital role in providing a leadership forum and a unique, integrating force for the building industry. USGBC's programs have three distinguishing characteristics:

Committee-based

The heart of this effective coalition is our committee structure, in which volunteer members design strategies that are implemented by staff and expert consultants. Our committees provide a forum for members to resolve differences, build alliances, and forge cooperative solutions for influencing change in all sectors of the building industry.

Member-driven

Membership is open and balanced and provides a comprehensive platform for carrying out important programs and activities. We target the issues identified by our members as the highest priority. We conduct an annual review of achievements that allows us to set policy, revise strategies, and devise work plans based on members' needs.

Consensus-focused

We work together to promote green buildings, and in doing so, we help foster greater economic vitality and environmental health at lower costs. We work to bridge ideological gaps between industry segments and develop balanced policies that benefit the entire industry.

Contact the U.S. Green Building Council
2101 L Street, NW
Suite 500
Washington, DC 20037
(800) 795-1747 Office
(202) 828-5110 Fax
www.usgbc.org

COPYRIGHT

DISCLAIMER

U.S. Green Building Council
2101 L Street, NW
Suite 500
Washington, DC 20036

TRADEMARKS

USGBC®, U.S. Green Building Council®, GBCI, and LEED® are registered trademarks of the U.S. Green Building Council.

LEED Reference Guide for Green Building Design and Construction
For the Design, Construction and Major Renovations of Commercial and Institutional Buildings
Healthcare Supplement
2011 Edition
ISBN # 978-1-932444-48-3

ACKNOWLEDGMENTS

The LEED 2009 for Healthcare New Construction & Major Renovations rating system has been made possible only through the efforts of many dedicated volunteers, staff members, and others in the USGBC community. The rating system improvement work was managed and implemented by USGBC staff and included review and input by many Technical Advisory Group (TAG) members with oversight by the LEED Steering Committee. We extend our deepest gratitude to all of our LEED committee members who participated in the development of this rating system, for their tireless volunteer efforts and constant support of USGBC's mission:

LEED for Healthcare Committee

Steve Guttman, Chair	Guttman & Blaevoet Consulting Engineers
Carol Antle, Vice-Chair	Kaiser Permanente
Patrick Branch	Branch Engineers
Jason Choyce	DPR Construction, Inc.
Robin Guenther	Perkins + Will
Jean Hansen	HDR , Inc.
Tom Lent	Healthy Building Network
Sholem Prasow	Teknion
Clark Reed	U.S. Environmental Protection Agency
Greg Roberts	WHR Architects
Kim Shinn	TLC Engineering for Architecture
Lance Stewart	Farnsworth Group, Inc.
Gail Vittori, Founding Chair	Center for Maximum Potential Building Systems

LEED Steering Committee

Joel Ann Todd, Chair	Joel Ann Todd
Bryna Dunn, Vice-Chair	Moseley Architects P.C.
Elaine Hsieh	KEMA Services, Inc
Susan Kaplan	Battery Park City Authority
Malcolm Lewis	CTG Energetics, Inc.
Muscoe Martin	M2 Architecture
Lisa Matthiessen	Buro Happold
Brenda Morawa	BVM Engineering, Inc.
Tim Murray	Morris Architects
Dave Sheridan	Aqua Cura
Lynn Simon	Simon and Associates

Implementation Advisory Committee

David Sheridan, Chair	AquaCura
Brenda Morawa, Vice-Chair	BVM Engineering, Inc.
Adam Fransen	CB Richard Ellis
Michelle Malanca	Michelle Malanca Sustainability Consulting, LLC
Brad Pease	Paladino and Co., Inc.
Ken Potts	McGough
Richard Schneider	U.S. Army Engineer Research and Development Center
Greg Shank	CTG Energetics, Inc
Natalie Terrill	Viridian Energy & Environmental, LLC
Bill Worthen	Simon & Associates, Inc.
Max Zahniser	Praxis | Building Solutions, LLC

Market Advisory Committee

Muscoe Martin, Chair	M2 Architecture
Lisa Matthiessen, Vice-Chair	Buro Happold
Liana Berberidou-Kallivoka	City of Austin, Austin Energy Green Building
Jeffrey Cole	Konstrukt
Walter Cuculic	Pulte Homes
Rand Ekman	OWP/P | Canon Design
Holley Henderson	H2 Ecodesign Inc.
Richard Kleinman	LaSalle Investment Management
Craig Kneeland	New York State Energy Research and Development Authority
Cindy Quan	The Goldman Sachs Group, Inc.
Matt Raimi	Raimi + Associates
Rebecca Stafford	University of California, Treasurer's Office
Gary Thomas	CB Richard Ellis
Keith Winn	Catalyst Partners

Technical Committee

Malcolm Lewis, Chair	CTG Energetics, Inc.
Susan Kaplan, Vice-Chair	Battery Park City Authority
Jennifer Atlee	BuildingGreen, LLC
Steve Baer	Five Winds International
Ted Bardacke	Global Green USA
Dan Bruck	BRC Acoustics
Dave Carlson	Columbia University
Mark Frankel	New Buildings Institute
Maureen Mahle	Steven Winter Associates, Inc.
Tom Scarola	Tischman Speyer
Chris Schaffner	The Green Engineer LLP
Sheila Sheridan	Sheridan & Associates
Alfred Vick	University of Georgia

Location and Planning TAG

Ted Bardacke, Chair	Global Green USA
Justin Horner, Vice-Chair	Natural Resources Defense Council
Eliot Allen	Criterion Planners
Laurence Aurbach	Office of Laurence Aurbach

Erin Christensen	Mithun, Inc.
Andy Clarke	League of American Bicyclists
John Dalzell	Boston Redevelopment Authority
Fred Dock	Department of Transportation, City of Pasadena
Reid Ewing	University of Utah
Doug Farr	Farr & Associates
Lois Fisher	Fisher Town Design, Inc.
Tim Frank	Sierra Club
Randy Hansell	Earth Advantage, Inc.
Justin Horner	Natural Resources Defense Council
Ron Kilcoyne	Greater Bridgeport Transit Authority
Todd Litman	Victoria Transport Policy Institute
Art Lomenick	Trammell Crow Company
Jessica Millman	The Agora Group
Steve Mouzon	New Urban Guild
Lynn Richards	U.S. Environmental Protection Agency
Harrison Rue	ICF International
Tony Sease	Civitech, Inc
Laurie Volk	Zimmerman/Volk Associates, Inc.
Trish White	Defenders of Wildlife

Sustainable Sites TAG

Alfred Vick, Chair	University of Georgia
Jenny Carney, Vice-Chair	YRG Sustainability
Michele Adams	Meliora Environmental Design, LLC
Neal Billetdeaux	JJR
Joby Carlson	Global Institute of Sustainability, Arizona State University
Laura Case	BVM Engineering, Inc.
Stephen Cook	The Brickman Group, Ltd.
Richard Heinisch	Acuity Brands, Inc.
Heather Holdridge Lake	Flato Architects
Katrina Rosa	ecoLogicStudio
Kyle Thomas	Natural Systems Engineering, PLLC
Teresa Watkins	St. John's River Water Management District

Water Efficiency TAG

David Carlson, Chair	Columbia University
David Bracciano, Vice-Chair	Alliance for Water Efficiency
Damann Anderson	Hazen and Sawyer
Robert Benazzi	Jaros, Baum & Bolles
Doug Bennett	Southern Nevada Water Authority
Ron Hand	E/FECT. Sustainable Design Solutions
Winston Huff	SSR Engineers
Joanna Kind	Eastern Research Group, Inc.
Shawn Martin	International Code Council
Don Mills	Clivus Multrum, Inc.
Karen Poff	Austin Energy
Shabbir Rawalpindiwala	Kohler Co.
Neil Rosen	North Shore-LIJ Health System
Robert Rubin	McKim & Creed, P.A.

David Viola	International Association of Plumbing and Mechanical Officials
Daniel Yeh	University of South Florida

Energy & Atmosphere TAG

Chris Schaffner, Chair	The Green Engineer, LLP
Gail Hampsmire, Vice-Chair	Low Energy Low Cost
John Adams	U.S. General Services Administration
Allan Daly	Taylor Engineering
Charles Dorgan	University of Wisconsin–Madison
Ellen Franconi	Rocky Mountain Institute
Scott Frank	Jaros, Baum & Bolles
Nathan Gauthier	Jones Lang LaSalle
Rusty Hodapp	Dallas/Fort Worth International Airport, Energy & Transportation Management
Dan Katzenberger	Engineering, Energy, and the Environment, LLC
Bob Maddox	Sterling Planet, Inc.
Michael Rosenberg	Pacific Northwest National Laboratory, U.S. Department of Energy
Gord Shymko	GF Shymko & Associates Inc.
Jorge Torres Coto	MBO Inc.
Tate Walker	Energy Center of Wisconsin

Materials & Resources TAG

Steven Baer, Chair	Five Winds International
Lee Gros, Vice-Chair	Lee Gros Architect and Artisan, Inc
Paul Bertram	Kingspan Insulated Panels Inc.
Paul Bierman-Lytle	iMCC Group
Steve Brauneis	Rocky Mountain Institute
Amy Costello	Armstrong World Industries, Inc.
Chris Geiger	San Francisco Department of the Environment
Avi Golen	Construction Waste Management
Brad Guy	Materials Reuse
Rick Levin	Kahler Slater, Inc.
Joep Meijer	The Right Environment Ltd. Co.
Raymond Smith	U.S. Environmental Protection Agency
Denise Van Valkenburg	MASCO Retail Cabinet Group

Indoor Environmental Quality TAG

Daniel Bruck, Chair	BRC Acoustics & Technology Consulting
John McFarland, Vice-Chair	Working Buildings, LLC
Sahar Abbaszadeh	CTG Energetics, Inc.
Terry Brennan	Camroden Associates, Inc.
Randal Carter	Steelcase, Inc.
Nancy Clanton	Clanton & Associates, Inc.
Dan Dempsey	Carrier RCLS Engineering
Michelle Halle Stern	Perkins + Will
Dan Int-Hout	Krueger
Alexis Kurtz	Ove Arup & Partners
Richard Master	USG Corporation

Reinhard Oppl	Eurofins Product Testing A/S
Ozgem Ornektekin	New York City Department of Education
Charles Salter	Charles Salter Associates
Don Stevens	Panasonic Home & Environment Company
Ellen Tohn	Tohn Environmental Strategies
Prasad Vaidya	The Weidt Group, Inc.

GREEN GUIDE FOR HEALTH CARE

In addition, the rating system and reference guide benefited greatly from the Green Guide for Health Care (GGHC), a joint project of Health Care Without Harm and Center for Maximum Potential Building Systems. GGHC is the first voluntary, self-certifying toolkit of green building best practices customized for the healthcare sector. The LEED for Healthcare Reference Guide Supplement incorporates, with permission, technical expertise and content created for GGHC. GGHC content, not specifically cited, is used in all sections of this reference guide.

A special thanks to the following people without whom this rating system and reference guide would not be possible:

Lead author:

Adele Houghton	Adele Houghton Consulting, LLC

Contributors:

Brianne Copes	Mazzetti + Nash Lipsey Burch
Rachel Dewane	
Dustin Glibert	Mazzetti + Nash Lipsey Burch
Arash Guity	Mazzetti + Nash Lipsey Burch
Amy Jarvis	Mazzetti + Nash Lipsey Burch
Christy Love	Mazzetti + Nash Lipsey Burch
Jerry Smith	Smith\GreenHealth Consulting, LLC

TABLE OF CONTENTS

LEED 2009 for Healthcare New Construction & Major Renovations rating system

100 base points, plus six possible Innovation in Design and four possible Regional Priority points.

Certified	40–49 points
Silver	50–59 points
Gold	60–79 points
Platinum	80 points and above

INTRODUCTION

I. WHY MAKE YOUR BUILDING GREEN?

The environmental impact of the building design, construction, and operations industry is enormous. Buildings annually consume more than 30% of the total energy and more than 60% of the electricity used in the United States. In 2006, the commercial building sector produced more than 1 billion metric tons of carbon dioxide, an increase of more than 30% over 1990 levels.[1] Each day 5 billion gallons of potable water is used solely to flush toilets. A typical North American commercial building generates about 1.6 pounds of solid waste per employee per day[2]; in a building with 1,500 employees, that can amount to 300 tons of waste per year. Development alters land from natural, biologically diverse habitats to hardscape that is impervious and devoid of biodiversity. The far-reaching influence of the built environment necessitates action to reduce its impact.

Healthcare facilities represent an energy-, water-, and personnel-intensive building type. According to the Commercial Buildings Energy Consumption Survey, healthcare is the third most energy intensive commercial building type, after food service and food sales.[3] Furthermore, at nearly 250,000 square feet, the average licensed inpatient healthcare facility is more than six times the average size of the next largest commercial building type, lodging.[4] Hospitals are extremely water intensive, often ranking among the top-10 water consumers in their water utility service areas.[5-6] A personnel-intensive industry, healthcare accounted for 9.5% of total jobs in the United States in 2008, according to the Bureau of Labor Statistics. As the U.S. population ages and treatment shifts from acute care to long-term care of chronic diseases, the need for healthcare personnel is expected to continue to rise. Healthcare is projected to create 3.2 million to 4.0 million new jobs between 2008 and 2018—more than any other sector of the economy.[7]

Healthcare facilities are designed with secondary and tertiary backup systems to ensure that they can function during emergencies; this system redundancy is seen as an asset rather than an expense. Because of the primacy of health and safety regulations, particularly for infection control and utilities, many licensed inpatient healthcare facilities are exempted from energy, water, and other conservation building codes, further exacerbating their tendency to consume large quantities of resources. In addition, many healthcare facilities function 24 hours a day, seven days a week.

Green building practices can substantially reduce or eliminate healthcare facilities' negative environmental effects through high-performance, market-leading design, construction, and operations practices. As an added benefit, green healthcare operations and management reduce operating costs, enhance building marketability, increase workers' productivity, and reduce potential liability resulting from indoor air quality problems.

1 Energy Information Administration, Emissions of Greenhouse Gas Report (DOE/EIA-0573 2006, released November 28, 2007, http://www.eia.doe.gov/oiaf/1605/ggrpt/carbon.html#commercial).

2 Office of the Federal Environmental Executive (http://ofee.gov/wpr/wastestream.asp, modified April 24, 2008).

3 U.S. Energy Information Administration, Commercial Buildings Energy Consumption Survey (CBECS) (http://www.eia.doe.gov/emeu/cbecs/contents.html, accessed October 13, 2010).

4 Ibid.

5 Massachusetts Water Resources Authority, Hospital Information (http://www.mwra.state.ma.us/04water/html/bullet1.htm, accessed October 13, 2010).

6 Pacific Institute, *Waste Not, Want Not: The Potential for Urban Water Conservation in California* (http://www.pacinst.org/reports/urban_usage/waste_not_want_not_full_report.pdf, released November 2003).

7 U.S. Bureau of Labor Statistics (http://www.bls.gov/, accessed October 13, 2010).

Examples of sustainable healthcare projects abound. A strong commitment to energy efficiency and innovative energy strategies, including the use of methane gas as one energy source for its boilers, saves Rockingham Memorial Hospital, Harrisonburg, VA, an estimated $400,000 annually in energy costs. Dell Children's Medical Center of Central Texas, Austin, TX, diverted 92% of construction waste from landfills through recycling and by using the airport runway it is built on as the building's and parking lot's base material.

With a six-story atrium full of greenery, waterfalls, and natural light, Spectrum Health's Lemmen-Holton Cancer Pavilion in Grand Rapids, MI creates a healing environment and a connection with nature intended to reduce the length of patient stays. An on-site wastewater treatment plant at the Oregon Health and Science University's Center for Health and Healing in Portland, OR reduces potable water use by 56% and keeps 30,000 gallons of water a day out of the city's sewer system. The five-story South Pavilion at the Women & Infants Hospital of Rhode Island in Providence, RI, has a mechanical system designed to improve indoor air quality by providing 30% more fresh air than required. By implementing green design, construction, and operations, these healthcare facilities have environmental, economic, and social elements that benefit all building stakeholders, including owners, occupants, and the general public.

II. LEED® GREEN BUILDING RATING SYSTEM

Background on LEED®

Following the formation of the U.S. Green Building Council (USGBC) in 1993, the organization's members quickly realized that the sustainable building industry needed a system to define and measure "green buildings." USGBC began to research existing green building metrics and rating systems. Less than a year after formation, the members acted on the initial findings by establishing a committee to focus solely on this topic. The composition of the committee was diverse; it included architects, real estate agents, a building owner, a lawyer, an environmentalist, and industry representatives. This cross section of people and professions added a richness and depth both to the process and to the ultimate product.

The first LEED Pilot Project Program, also referred to as LEED Version 1.0, was launched at the USGBC Membership Summit in August 1998. After extensive modifications, LEED Green Building rating system Version 2.0 was released in March 2000, with LEED Version 2.1 following in 2002 and LEED Version 2.2 in 2005.

As LEED has evolved and matured, the program has undertaken new initiatives. In addition to a rating system specifically devoted to building operational and maintenance issues (LEED for Existing Buildings: Operations & Maintenance), LEED addresses the different project development and delivery processes that exist in the U.S. building design and construction market through rating systems for specific building typologies, sectors, and project scopes: LEED for Core & Shell, LEED for New Construction, LEED for Schools, LEED for Neighborhood Development, LEED for Retail, LEED for Healthcare, LEED for Homes, and LEED for Commercial Interiors.

Project teams interact with the Green Building Certification Institute (GBCI) for project registration and certification. GBCI was established in 2008 as a separately incorporated entity with the support of the U.S. Green Building Council. GBCI administers credentialing and certification programs related to green building practice. These programs support the application of proven strategies for increasing and measuring the performance of buildings and communities as defined by industry systems such as LEED.

The green building field is growing and changing daily. New technologies and products are being introduced into the marketplace, and innovative designs and practices are proving their effectiveness. The LEED rating systems and reference guides will evolve as well. Project teams must comply with the version of the rating system that is current at the time of their registration.

USGBC will highlight new developments on its website on a continual basis, at www.usgbc.org.

LEED® for Healthcare

The LEED 2009 for Healthcare New Construction & Major Renovations rating system represents a culmination of seven years of dedicated effort by the healthcare community involving the volunteers on the LEED for Healthcare Committee and the LEED TAGs, and close collaboration between the Green Guide for Health Care (GGHC) and USGBC. GGHC helped to streamline the LEED for Healthcare's development schedule by aligning with the LEED for New Construction rating system's organizational structure and conducting a robust pilot program with more than 100 healthcare facilities. The GGHC pilot project informed the development of the LEED for Healthcare. The combined efforts have specifically addressed the usability and verifiability of the draft credits, with feedback solicited from the pilots on their use of the GGHC.

This reference guide supplement, which draws on materials sourced from both USGBC and GGHC, is a natural outgrowth from the memorandum of understanding (MOU) signed by both organizations in 2007, pledging to work together on the development of tools, educational programs, and other activities to support green healthcare building. Also in the spirit of the MOU, USGBC will administer the LEED for Healthcare certification process and the GGHC will continue to act as a change agent dedicated to developing tools that empower the health delivery industry to take a leadership position in green building and operation.

Features of LEED®

The LEED Green Building rating systems are voluntary, consensus-based, and market-driven. Based on existing, proven technology, they evaluate environmental performance from a whole-building perspective over a building's life cycle, providing a definitive standard for what constitutes a green building in design, construction, and operation.

The LEED rating systems are designed for rating new and existing commercial, institutional, and residential buildings, as well as entire neighborhood developments. They are based on accepted energy and environmental principles and strike a balance between known, established practices and emerging concepts. Each rating system is organized into five environmental categories: Sustainable Sites, Water Efficiency, Energy and Atmosphere, Materials and Resources, and Indoor Environmental Quality. A sixth category, Innovation in Design, rewards sustainable building expertise as well as design measures not covered under the five environmental categories. Regional bonus points are another feature of LEED; this addition acknowledges the importance of local conditions in determining best environmental design and construction practices.

The LEED Credit Weightings

In LEED 2009, the allocation of points among credits is based on the potential environmental impacts and human benefits of each credit with respect to a set of impact categories. The impacts are defined as the environmental or human effect of the design, construction, operation, and maintenance of the building, such as greenhouse gas emissions, fossil fuel use, toxins and carcinogens, air and water pollutants, and indoor environmental conditions. A combination of approaches, including energy modeling, life-cycle assessment, and transportation analysis, is used to quantify each type of impact. The resulting allocation of points among credits is called credit weighting.

LEED 2009 uses the U.S. Environmental Protection Agency's TRACI[1] environmental impact categories as the basis for weighting each credit. TRACI was developed to assist with impact evaluation for life-cycle assessment, industrial ecology, process design, and pollution prevention.

LEED 2009 also takes into consideration the weightings developed by the National Institute of Standards and Technology (NIST); these compare impact categories with one another and assign a relative weight to each. Together, the two approaches provide a solid foundation for determining the point value of each credit in LEED 2009.

The LEED 2009 credit weightings process is based on the following parameters, which maintain consistency and usability across rating systems:

- All LEED credits are worth a minimum of one point.
- All LEED credits are positive, whole numbers; there are no fractions or negative values.
- All LEED credits receive a single, static weight in each rating system; there are no individualized scorecards based on project location.
- All LEED rating systems have 100 base points; Innovation in Design (or Operations) and Regional Priority credits provide opportunities for up to 10 bonus points.

Given the above criteria, the LEED 2009 credit weightings process involves three steps:

1. A reference building is used to estimate the environmental impacts in 13 categories associated with a typical building pursuing LEED certification.
2. The relative importance of building impacts in each category is set to reflect values based on the NIST weightings.[2]
3. Data that quantify building impacts on environmental and human health are used to assign points to individual credits.

Each credit is allocated points based on the relative importance of the building-related impacts that it addresses. The result is a weighted average that combines building impacts and the relative value of the impact categories. Credits that most directly address the most important impacts are given the greatest weight, subject to the system design parameters described above. Credit weights also reflect a decision by LEED to recognize the market implications of point allocation. The result is a significant change in allocation of points compared with previous LEED rating systems. Overall, the changes increase the relative emphasis on reducing energy consumption and greenhouse gas emissions associated with building systems, transportation, the embodied energy of water, the embodied energy of materials, and where applicable, solid waste.

The details of the weightings process vary slightly among individual rating systems. For example, LEED for Existing Buildings: Operations & Maintenance includes credits related to solid waste management, but LEED for New Construction does not. This results in a difference in the portion of the environmental footprint addressed by each rating system and the relative allocation of points. The weightings process for each rating system is fully documented in a weightings workbook.

The credit weightings process will be reevaluated over time to incorporate changes in values ascribed to different building impacts and building types, based on both market reality and evolving scientific knowledge related to buildings. A complete explanation of the LEED credit weightings system is available on the USGBC website, at www.usgbc.org.

1 U.S. Environmental Protection Agency, Office of Research and Development, Tools for the Reduction and Assessment of Chemical and Other Environmental Impacts (TRACI) (http://www.epa.gov/nrmrl/std/sab/traci/).

2 Relative impact category weights based on an exercise undertaken by NIST (National Institute of Standards and Technology) for the BEES program (http://www.bfrl.nist.gov/oae/software/bees/).

III. OVERVIEW AND PROCESS

The LEED 2009 for Healthcare New Construction & Major Renovations rating system is a set of performance standards for certifying the design and construction of healthcare buildings of all sizes. The intent is to promote healthful, durable, affordable, and environmentally sound practices in building design and construction.

Prerequisites and credits in the LEED Green Building Rating Systems address seven topics:

- Sustainable Sites (SS)
- Water Efficiency (WE)
- Energy and Atmosphere (EA)
- Materials and Resources (MR)
- Indoor Environmental Quality (IEQ)
- Innovation in Design (ID)
- Regional Priority (RP)

LEED prerequisites and credits have identical structures; see Section XI of this Introduction.

When to Use LEED 2009 for Healthcare

LEED for Healthcare was designed primarily for licensed and federal inpatient and outpatient care facilities and licensed long term care facilities. The rating system may also be used for medical offices, assisted-living facilities, and medical education and research centers. LEED for Healthcare addresses design and construction activities for both new buildings and major renovations of existing buildings. A major renovation involves major HVAC renovation, significant envelope modifications, and major interior rehabilitation. For a major renovation of an existing building, LEED for Healthcare is the appropriate rating system. If the project scope does not involve significant design and construction activities and focuses more on operations and maintenance activities, LEED for Existing Buildings: Operations & Maintenance is more appropriate because it addresses operational and maintenance issues of working buildings.

Some projects are designed and constructed to be partially occupied by the owner or developer and partially occupied by other tenants. In such projects, the owner or developer has direct influence over the portion of the work that he or she will occupy. To pursue LEED for Healthcare certification, the owner or tenant must occupy more than 50% of the building's leasable square footage. Projects in which 50% or less of the building's leasable square footage is occupied by an owner should pursue LEED for Core & Shell certification.

Minimum Program Requirements

A project must adhere to LEED's minimum program requirements (MPRs) to be eligible for certification under LEED 2009. These requirements define the categories and characteristics of buildings that the LEED rating systems were designed to evaluate and serve three goals: (1) to give clear guidance to customers, (2) to protect the integrity of the LEED program, and (3) to reduce challenges that occur during the LEED certification process. The MPRs will evolve over time in tandem with the LEED rating systems. To be eligible for certification under any LEED 2009 rating system, projects must comply with the associated MPRs. The MPRs can be found in the LEED 2009 rating systems. In addition, definitions and more extensive guidance on certain issues are provided in a separate document, titled Supplemental Guidance, available on the USGBC website.

The Green Building Certification Institute (GBCI) reserves the right to revoke LEED certification from any LEED 2009 project upon gaining knowledge of noncompliance with any applicable MPRs. If such a circumstance occurs, no registration or certification fees paid to GBCI will be refunded.

Exceptions to the MPRs will be considered on a case-by-case basis. Direction on the nature of allowable exceptions is given in the Supplemental Guidance Document available on the USGBC website, at www.usgbc.org.

Registration

Project teams interested in earning LEED certification for their buildings must first register with GBCI. Projects can be registered on the GBCI website, www.gbci.org. The website also has information on registration costs for USGBC national members as well as nonmembers. Registration is an important step that establishes contact with GBCI and provides access to software tools, errata, critical communications, and other essential information.

LEED Online

LEED Online is the primary resource for managing the LEED documentation process. From LEED Online, project teams can manage project details, complete documentation requirements for LEED credits and prerequisites, upload supporting files, submit applications for review, receive reviewer feedback, and ultimately earn LEED certification. LEED Online provides a common space where members of a project team can work together to document compliance with the LEED rating system. All project teams pursuing LEED certification are required to use LEED Online and its submittal documentation paths. LEED submittals are instrumental in demonstrating credit compliance because they contain all the documentation requirements for each LEED credit. Additionally, LEED Online contains embedded calculators and tables to ensure that the submittal package delivered to GBCI is complete and accurate.

LEED Online also features several support capabilities. It enables team members to view and submit credit interpretation requests, contact customer service, generate project-specific reports, and consult supplementary LEED resources, such as FAQs, tutorials, offline calculators, and sample documentation. Applicants with multiple projects have access to reporting tools that use data from projects across their entire LEED portfolio. LEED certificates for successful projects are also issued through LEED Online.

Credit Interpretation Requests and Rulings

In some cases, a LEED project team may encounter challenges when interpreting the requirements of a prerequisite or credit for their project, perhaps because the reference guide does not sufficiently address a specific issue or a conflict requires resolution. To address such issues, a credit interpretation ruling process has been established for each LEED rating system. See the GBCI website for more information, at www.gbci.org.

Credit interpretation requests must be submitted online. Provide a brief but clear description of the challenge encountered, refer to the prerequisite or credit information found in the rating system and reference guide, and emphasize the intent of the prerequisite or credit. If possible, the project team should offer potential solutions to the problem or a proposed interpretation. Follow the detailed instructions in LEED Online.

Communications related to credit interpretation requests are in electronic format.

Review and Certification

To earn LEED certification, the applicant project must satisfy all the prerequisites and credits worth the minimum number of points to warrant the desired project rating under LEED for Healthcare.

Projects must comply with the version of the rating system that is current in LEED Online at the time of project registration.

Appeals

Appeals may be filed after the design phase review, the construction phase review, or the full application review. Please see the GBCI website for more information on appeals.

Fees

Information on certification fees can be found on the GBCI website. GBCI will acknowledge receipt of the application and proceed with application review when all project documentation and payments have been received and processed. Registration fees, appeal review fees, and any additional fees required to expedite LEED certification are not refundable.

Updates and Addenda

This is the first edition of the LEED for Healthcare Reference Guide Supplement, 2011. As building science and technology continue to improve and evolve, updates and addenda will be made available. USGBC cannot be held liable for any criteria set forth herein that may not be applicable to later versions of LEED rating systems, and GBCI reserves the right to modify its policies from time to time. Updates and addenda will be accumulated between revisions and will be formally incorporated in major revisions. In the interim, between major revisions, USGBC may issue updates or addenda to clarify criteria. The prerequisites, credits, amendments, and addenda current at the time of project registration will continue to guide the project throughout its certification process.

Project teams are subject to rating system addenda requirements based on registration date. Rating system and reference guide addenda can be found on the USGBC LEED Resources and Tools website, www.usgbc.org/projecttools.

Information Privacy and Policy Guidelines

For more information on the privacy policy of the U.S. Green Building Council, Inc. (USGBC), see the Policies and Guidelines section of the USGBC website, at www.usgbc.org. With the support of its members, volunteers, and other stakeholders, USGBC is the developer of the LEED rating systems.

The Green Building Certification Institute, Inc., implements the LEED rating systems and carries out credentialing programs relating to LEED. For more information on the privacy policy of GBCI, including the privacy policy on documentation submitted through LEED Online, see the Policies and Guidelines section of the GBCI website, at www.gbci.org. Projects whose information should be treated as confidential may select this option during registration; project confidentiality status may be changed at any time through LEED Online. Please review the GBCI privacy policy for further details.

IV. LEED ONLINE DOCUMENTATION REQUIREMENTS

All LEED for Healthcare certification applications must include the required LEED Online documentation: general documentation requirements, documentation requirements for all prerequisites, and documentation requirements for all pursued credits.

General Requirements

LEED certification application requires the submission of an overall project narrative with the completed LEED Online documentation requirements. The project narrative describes the applicant's organization, building, site, and team. This narrative helps the LEED review team understand the major elements of the project and building performance, and it also aids in highlighting projects in future communications efforts. General documentation also requires the basic details pertaining to project site conditions, construction scope and timeline, occupant and usage data, and project team identification. Project teams must address all the elements in the general documentation requirements, providing details and clarifications where appropriate, and they may include any optional elements that are helpful in describing the project.

Credit Substitution

The LEED 2009 rating systems do not allow credit substitution using another version. Currently registered LEED projects that want to use LEED 2009 credits need to switch to the new version in its entirety. USGBC expects that most projects will find this switch feasible and advantageous.

V. CERTIFICATION APPLICATION

To earn LEED certification, the applicant project must satisfy all the prerequisites and qualify for a minimum number of points to attain one of the ratings listed below. Having satisfied the basic prerequisites of the program, applicant projects are then rated according to their degree of compliance within the rating system.

After registration, the project design team should begin to collect information and perform calculations to satisfy the prerequisite and credit documentation requirements. Because documentation should be gathered throughout design and construction, it is helpful to designate a LEED team leader who will be responsible for managing its compilation.

LEED for Healthcare provides the option of splitting a certification application into two phases: design and construction. Documentation for design phase credits, identified in LEED Online, can be submitted for review at the end of the design phase; the submittals for these credits can be fully evaluated based on documentation available during this phase of the project. For example, if a project site meets the requirements of LEED for Commercial Interiors Sustainable Sites Credit 3, Brownfield Redevelopment, the likelihood of credit achievement can be assessed before construction is complete. The LEED credit itself, however, is not awarded at the design review stage.

Design Phase Review

A project team can elect to be reviewed at a preliminary design phase review and a final design phase review. GBCI formally rules on the design phase application by designating each attempted credit as either anticipated or denied. Participating in a design phase review does not guarantee award of any credit and will not result in LEED certification. The intent is to help project teams assess the likelihood of credit achievement; the design must then be executed in the construction phase, according to design specifications, for the credit to be earned.

Construction Phase Review

At the completion of construction, the project team submits all attempted credits for review, including any newly attempted design credits. If the project team has undergone a design phase review and any of the design specifications for anticipated credits have since changed, additional documentation must be submitted to substantiate continued compliance with credit requirements. Upon receipt of the full certification application and fee, a final review will be conducted. Credits that were designated as anticipated in the design phase review and whose specifications have not changed will be awarded. All other credits will be designated as either awarded or denied.

Project teams should refer to LEED Online and the rating system scorecards to get information on credits that can be submitted for design phase review and credits that must be submitted for construction phase review.

LEED for Healthcare certifications are awarded according to the following scale:

Certified	40–49 points
Silver	50–59 points
Gold	60–79 points
Platinum	80 points and above

GBCI recognizes buildings that achieve these rating levels with a formal letter of certification.

Design or Construction Phase Submittal

Healthcare: NC		
Credit		**D/C**
SSp2	Environmental Site Assessment	D
SSc9.1	Connection to the Natural World—Places of Respite	D
SSc9.2	Connection to the Natural World-Direct Access for Patients	D
WEp2	Minimize Potable Water Use for Medical Equipment Cooling	D
WEc2	Water Use Reduction—Measurement and Verification	D
WEc4.1	Water Use Reduction—Building Equipment	D
WEc4.2	Water Use Reduction—Cooling Towers	D
WEc4.3	Water Use Reduction—Food Waste Systems	D
EAc7	Community Contaminant Prevention-Airborne Releases	D
MRp2	PBT Source Reduction—Mercury	D
MRc3	Sustainably Sourced Materials and Products	C
MRc4.1	PBT Source Reduction—Mercury in Lamps	D
MRc4.2	PBT Source Reduction—Lead, Cadmium and Copper	C
MRc5	Furniture and Medical Furnishings	C
MRc6	Resource Use-Design for Flexibility	D
IEQp3	Hazardous Material Removal or Encapsulation (Renovations Only)	C
IEQc2	Acoustic Environment	C
IEQc4	Low-Emitting Materials	C
IDp1	Integrative Project Planning and Design	D
IDc3	Integrative Project Planning and Design	C

VI. CERTIFICATION STRATEGY

Timeline and Project Design Phases

Project teams should study the principles and objectives of LEED as early in the site selection and design process as possible. The project design phases mentioned throughout this reference guide correspond to the architectural design and planning steps commonly used in the construction industry:

1. Predesign entails gathering information, recognizing stakeholder needs, and establishing project goals.

2. Schematic design explores several design options and alternatives, with the intent to establish an agreed-upon project layout and scope of work.

3. Design development begins the process of spatial refinement and usually involves the first design of a project's energy systems.
4. Construction documents carry the design into the level of details for all spaces and systems and materials so that construction can take place.
5. Construction.
6. Substantial completion is a contractual benchmark that usually corresponds to the point at which a client could occupy a nearly completed space.
7. Final completion.
8. Certificate of occupancy is the official recognition by a local building department that a building conforms to applicable building and safety codes.

Related Credits

When pursuing LEED certification, it is important to consider how credits are interconnected and how their synergies and trade-offs will ultimately affect both the project and the other credits the team may consider pursuing. Consult the Related Credits section of each prerequisite and credit to help inform design and construction decisions leading to certification.

Consistent Documentation across Credits

Several kinds of project information are required for consistent LEED documentation across various credits. Pay special attention to overlapping project data; doing so will help the application and review process go smoothly.

Guidance for Multiple Buildings and On-Campus Projects

In the United States, 20% of all healthcare buildings, representing 60% of total healthcare square footage, are located in medical or academic campus settings.1 Hospitals are often surrounded by administration and support buildings, medical office buildings, labs, and increasingly, long term care facilities. As the U.S. population ages, the healthcare industry is shifting from primarily treating acute medical conditions, such as heart attacks, to managing chronic illnesses, such as diabetes and cancer. This shift has increased the demand for long-term care and residential facilities, where patients with chronic illnesses can live while they undergo lengthy treatments.

The 2010 LEED Application Guidance for Multiple Buildings and On-Campus Building Projects (available at www.usgbc.org/campusguidance) helps teams apply the LEED rating systems to multiple-building and on-campus projects that are on a shared site under the control of a single entity, as on a corporate or educational campus or government installation. This guidance encourages a holistic, sustainable approach to project management, captures economies of scale in the certification process through shared credit, and addresses the unique challenges and opportunities inherent in projects on a campus. Particularly valuable to healthcare projects, which are often part of a healthcare organization with existing operational policies and programs, the 2010 LEED Application Guidance for Multiple Buildings and On-Campus Building Projects includes guidance on operations and maintenance as well as guidance on design and construction projects.

The 2010 LEED Application Guidance for Multiple Buildings and On-Campus Building Projects is not a separate rating system. Rather, it applies to the requirements for projects on a campus or shared site that are seeking certification under the Design and Construction, Interior Design and Construction, or Existing Buildings: Operations & Maintenance rating system. The guide will be

1 U.S. Energy Information Administration, Commercial Buildings Energy Consumption Survey (CBECS) (http://www.eia.doe.gov/emeu/cbecs/contents.html, accessed October 13, 2010).

released in two parts. Part 1, released in October 2010, includes opportunities for streamlining documentation and review of on-campus projects. Part 2, coming in 2011, will allow for the certification of multiple projects in one registration.

Operations and Maintenance in LEED for Healthcare Certified Buildings

The LEED for Healthcare Supplement to the LEED Reference Guide for Green Building Design and Construction contains information to help project teams streamline green operations and maintenance (O&M) practices once the LEED design and construction project has been completed. Although not required as part of the LEED certification process, upfront planning for green O&M can help building owners, operators, and maintenance staff ensure that the building continues to operate in a sustainable manner.

Healthcare projects on existing campuses should coordinate with caregivers and facilities staff to design strategies that will improve facilities operations. Both the LEED 2009 Existing Buildings: Operations & Maintenance rating system (available at www.usgbc.org) and the GGHC 2009 Operations section (available at www.gghc.org) provide guidance on greening operations. Healthcare facilities pursuing LEED for Existing Buildings should use the GGHC Operations section as a reference for healthcare-specific practices that are not covered in LEED for Existing Buildings.

This LEED reference guide supplement identifies credits that will most benefit from coordination with operations staff.

VII. EXEMPLARY PERFORMANCE STRATEGIES

Exemplary performance strategies result in performance that greatly exceeds the performance level or expands the scope required by an existing LEED for Healthcare credit. To earn exemplary performance credits, teams must meet the performance level defined by the next step in the threshold progression. For credits with more than one compliance path, an Innovation in Design point can be earned by satisfying more than one compliance path if their benefits are additive. See the Innovation in Design credit section for further details.

The credits for which exemplary performance points are available through expanded performance are noted throughout this reference guide and in LEED Online and identified by this logo:

The exemplary performance points available in LEED for Healthcare are as follows:

Sustainable Sites

SS Credit 2	Development Density and Community Connectivity
SS Credit 4.1	Alternative Transportation—Public Transportation Access
SS Credit 5.1	Site Development—Protect or Restore Habitat
SS Credit 5.2	Site Development—Maximize Open Space
SS Credit 6.1	Stormwater Design—Quantity Control
SS Credit 6.2	Stormwater Design—Quality Control
SS Credit 7.1	Heat Island Effect—Nonroof
SS Credit 7.2	Heat Island Effect—Roof
SS Credit 9.1	Connection to the Natural World—Places of Respite
SS Credit 9.2	Connection to the Natural World—Direct Exterior Access for Patients

Water Efficiency

WE Credit 2	Water Use Reduction—Measurement and Verification
WE Credit 3	Water Use Reduction

Energy and Atmosphere

EA Credit 1	Optimize Energy Performance
EA Credit 2	On-Site Renewable Energy
EA Credit 6	Green Power

Materials and Resources

MR Credit 2	Construction Waste Management
MR Credit 3	Sustainably Sourced Materials and Products
MR Credit 5	Furniture and Medical Furnishings

Indoor Environmental Quality

IEQ Credit 4	Low-Emitting Materials
IEQ Credit 6.2	Controllability of Systems—Thermal Comfort
IEQ Credit 8.1	Daylight and Views—Daylight
IEQ Credit 8.2	Daylight and Views—Views

VIII. REGIONAL PRIORITY

To provide incentive to address geographically specific environmental issues, USGBC regional councils and chapters have identified six credits per rating system that are of particular importance to specific areas. Each Regional Priority credit is worth an additional one point, and a total of four additional points may be earned by achieving Regional Priority credits, with one point earned per credit. Upon project registration, LEED Online automatically determines a project's Regional Priority credits based on its zip code. If the project achieves more than four Regional Priority credits, the team can choose the credits for which these points will apply. The USGBC website (www.usgbc.org) also contains a searchable database of Regional Priority credits.

IX. TOOLS FOR REGISTERED PROJECTS

LEED offers additional resources for LEED project teams on the USGBC website, at www.usgbc.org/projecttools. The Registered Project Tools website provides resources for starting the project, including rating system errata, documentation requirements, and referenced industry standards.

Also consult the website for the following:

Declarant definitions and other definitions. This resource describes the team members who are required to sign off on certain documentation requirements and indicates the prerequisites and credits for which each team member is responsible. The required declarant is noted in the corresponding credit documentation section of LEED Online.

Licensed Professional Exemption Form. The Licensed Professional Exemption Form can be used by a project team's registered professional engineer, registered architect, or registered landscape architect as a streamlined path to certain credits, bypassing otherwise-required submittals. This form is used in conjunction with the declarations in LEED Online to document any exemptions. The form is required for any eligible submittal requirements the project team wishes to waive; the exemption is invalid without a properly executed Licensed Professional Exemption Form. Licensed professional exemptions are noted in the corresponding credit documentation section of LEED Online.

X. HOW TO USE THIS REFERENCE GUIDE

The LEED for Healthcare Reference Guide Supplement is a supporting document to the LEED 2009 for Healthcare New Construction & Major Renovations rating system. The guide helps project teams understand the criteria, the reasons behind them, strategies for implementation, and documentation requirements. It includes examples of strategies that can be used in each category and additional resources. It does not provide an exhaustive list of strategies for meeting the criteria or all the information that a project team needs to determine the applicability of a credit to the project.

The LEED for Healthcare Reference Guide Supplement should be consulted in conjunction with the LEED Reference Guide for Green Building Design and Construction. Information in the LEED reference guide is not repeated in the reference guide supplement. The supplement focuses instead on the following:

1. Information specific to considerations for healthcare projects.
2. New information for new or existing credits.

Prerequisite or credit information in LEED for Healthcare that is derived from multiple credits in LEED for New Construction, LEED for Core & Shell, or LEED for Schools points users to the relevant information in the LEED Reference Guide for Green Building Design and Construction.

IMPORTANT! This reference guide supplement contains only the reference guide sections that pertain to healthcare projects. Use this supplement alongside the LEED Reference Guide for Green Building Design and Construction for complete credit information. For the omitted sections, refer to the main reference guide.

Rating System Pages

The rating system, published in its entirety on the USGBC website, is embedded in this reference guide. Each prerequisite and credit discussion begins with a gray page that repeats the rating systems' Intent and Requirements. This Reference Guide Supplement addresses the Intents and Requirements for the following Rating Systems: LEED 2009 for Healthcare New Construction & Major Renovations.

Prerequisite and Credit Format

Each prerequisite or credit is organized in a standardized format for simplicity and quick reference. The first sections summarize the main points regarding the green measure and includes the intent, requirements, required submittals for certification, and a summary of any referenced industry standard. Subsequent sections provide supporting information to help interpret the measure and offer links to resources and examples. The sections for each credit are described in the following paragraphs:

Intent identifies the main sustainability goal or benefit of the prerequisite or credit.

Requirements specifies the criteria that satisfy the prerequisite or credit and the number of points available. The prerequisites must be achieved; the credits are optional, but each contributes to the overall project score. Some credits have two or more paths with cumulative points. Other credits have several options from which the project team must choose. For example, Energy and Atmosphere Credit 1, Optimize Energy Efficiency Performance, has three options, but a project team can apply for only one, depending on the type of building.

Benefits and Issues to Consider addresses the environmental benefits of the activity encouraged by the prerequisite or credit, and economic considerations related to first costs, life-cycle costs, and estimated savings.

Related Credits acknowledges the trade-offs and synergies within the LEED rating system credit categories. Achieving a particular credit may make it worthwhile and comparatively easy to pursue related credits; the converse is also possible.

The **Summary of Referenced Standards**, where applicable, introduces the required standards used to measure achievement of the credit intent. Teams are strongly encouraged to review the full standard and not rely on the summary.

Implementation discusses specific methods or assemblies that facilitate achievement of the requirements.

Timeline and Team guides the project team by identifying who should lead an effort and when the tasks should begin.

Calculations offers sample formulas or computations that determine achievement of a particular prerequisite or credit. Most calculations are facilitated in LEED Online.

The **Documentation Guidance** section provides the first steps in preparing to complete the LEED Online documentation requirements.

Examples illustrates strategies for credit achievement.

Exemplary Performance, if applicable, details the level of performance needed for the award of points in addition to those for credit achievement.

Regional Variations outlines concerns specific to the geographic location of the building.

Resources offers suggestions for further research and provides examples or illustrations, detailed technical information, or other information relevant to the prerequisite or credit. The resources include websites, online materials, and printed books and articles that can be obtained directly from the organizations listed.

Definitions clarifies the meaning of certain terms relevant to the prerequisite or credit. These may be general terms or terms specific to LEED for Healthcare. A glossary is found at the end of the reference guide supplement.

SUSTAINABLE SITES

OVERVIEW

Healthcare facilities combine a physically demanding and stressful work environment with sensitive patient populations, often in a campus setting. Achieving Sustainable Sites credits can contribute to mitigating such conditions by providing access to nature, reducing emissions from traffic, and remediating contamination on brownfield sites. These considerations are discussed below, and more detail is provided in the reference information for each credit.

Nature has been shown to have a calming effect on all occupants in a healthcare facility.1 By prioritizing habitat conservation and restoration and by providing visual and physical access to natural features, project teams can help create a healing environment. Healthcare institutions can also promote wellness and the healing influence of nature in the surrounding community by connecting to nearby parks, hike-and-bike trails, and nature preserves. This approach is particularly effective in medical campus settings, which often house a concentration of systems-intensive building types such as laboratories and hospitals. Introducing healing gardens, nature trails, and other landscaped areas both encourage staff to engage in outdoor physical activity and integrate the campus into the surrounding neighborhood. Other "good neighbor" policies include reducing light pollution (SS Credit 8), on-site emissions (EA Credit 7), and on-site noise (IEQ Credits 2 and 3.1).

LEED encourages healthcare facilities to take advantage of existing infrastructure by locating on brownfield sites. In many cases, brownfields are near or adjacent to underserved populations; locating a new facility on such sites can increase access to care. However, because of the vulnerabilities of the patient population, project teams should protect future occupants from potential exposure to toxic chemicals by performing an environmental assessment of the site and conducting any necessary remediation.

Establishing a successful alternative transportation program on a medical campus can be a challenge. As population growth has moved away from city centers, new facilities have followed their patient base and located outside the reach of robust public transportation systems with frequent service and convenient locations. Socioeconomically disadvantaged patients and family members may find access to the site a challenge. Staff members often work 12-hour shifts, arriving or leaving the facility at times when public transit options are few, and telecommuting is usually not feasible. The unintended consequences often include large surface parking lots, traffic congestion surrounding healthcare campuses, and public health consequences, such as urban heat island effects, exposure to particulates and ground-level ozone emissions, and traffic accidents. Nevertheless, because of their high occupancy and importance as an economic engine for the region, many healthcare institutions, particularly medical campuses, are in a position to work with regional transit authorities and public works departments to extend bus lines, light rail lines, bicycle paths, and sidewalks to service new facilities.

IMPORTANT! This reference guide supplement contains only the reference guide sections that pertain to healthcare projects. Use this supplement alongside the LEED Reference Guide for Green Building Design and Construction for complete credit information. For the omitted sections, refer to the main reference guide.

1 H. Frumkin, Beyond Toxicity: Human Health and the Natural Environment, American Journal of Preventive Medicine 20(3), 2001 (http://www.ncbi.nlm.nih.gov).

SS OVERVIEW

CREDIT	TITLE	HEALTHCARE
SS Prerequisite 1	Construction Activity Pollution Prevention	Required
SS Prerequisite 2	Environmental Site Assessment	Required
SS Credit 1	Site Selection	1 point
SS Credit 2	Development Density and Community Connectivity	1 point
SS Credit 3	Brownfield Redevelopment	1 point
SS Credit 4.1	Alternative Transportation—Public Transportation Access	3 points
SS Credit 4.2	Alternative Transportation—Bicycle Storage and Changing Rooms	1 point
SS Credit 4.3	Alternative Transportation—Low-Emitting and Fuel-Efficient Vehicles	1 point
SS Credit 4.4	Alternative Transportation—Parking Capacity	1 point
SS Credit 5.1	Site Development—Protect or Restore Habitat	1 point
SS Credit 5.2	Site Development—Maximize Open Space	1 point
SS Credit 6.1	Stormwater Design—Quantity Control	1 point
SS Credit 6.2	Stormwater Design—Quality Control	1 point
SS Credit 7.1	Heat Island Effect—Nonroof	1 point
SS Credit 7.2	Heat Island Effect—Roof	1 point
SS Credit 8	Light Pollution Reduction	1 point
SS Credit 9.1	Connection to the Natural World—Places of Respite	1 point
SS Credit 9.2	Connection to the Natural World—Direct Exterior Access for Patients	1 point

CONSTRUCTION ACTIVITY POLLUTION PREVENTION

	HEALTHCARE: NC
Prerequisite	SS Prerequisite 1
Points	Required

Intent

To reduce pollution from construction activities by controlling soil erosion, waterway sedimentation, and airborne dust generation.

Requirements

Create and implement an erosion and sedimentation control (ESC) plan for all construction activities associated with the project. The ESC plan must conform to the erosion and sedimentation requirements of the 2003 EPA Construction General Permit OR local standards and codes, whichever is more stringent. The plan must describe the measures implemented to accomplish the following objectives:

- Prevent loss of soil during construction by stormwater runoff and/or wind erosion, including protecting topsoil by stockpiling for reuse.
- Prevent sedimentation of storm sewers or receiving streams.
- Prevent pollution of the air with dust and particulate matter.

EPA's construction general permit (CGP) outlines the provisions necessary to comply with Phases I and II of the National Pollutant Discharge Elimination System (NPDES) Program. While the CGP permit only applies to construction sites greater than one acre, the requirements are applied to all projects for the purposes of this prerequisite. Information on the EPA construction general permit is available at http://cfpub.epa.gov/npdes/stormwater/cgp.cfm.

IMPORTANT! This reference guide supplement contains only the reference guide sections that pertain to healthcare projects. Use this supplement alongside the LEED Reference Guide for Green Building Design and Construction for complete credit information. For the omitted sections, refer to the main reference guide.

SS	
HEALTHCARE: NC	Prerequisite 1

1. Benefits and Issues to Consider

Environmental Issues

In the United States, 20% of all healthcare buildings, representing 60% of all healthcare square footage, are located in campus settings, either medical or higher education.1 Hospitals are often surrounded by administration and support buildings, medical office buildings, labs, and increasingly, long-term care facilities. Airborne dust from construction activity can enter airways and lungs. Fine particulates such as dust have been linked to numerous health problems, including asthma, decreased lung function, and breathing difficulties. It is important to minimize site disturbance in healthcare projects, both on and adjacent to the construction site, to avoid harming immunocompromised patients.

2. Related Credits

On existing healthcare campuses, address potential sources of construction pollution, such as dust, water, and noise, in the hazardous material management program and infection control risk assessment, as required under the following prerequisite and credit:

- IEQ Prerequisite 3, Hazardous Material Removal or Encapsulation
- IEQ Credit 3.1, Construction Indoor Air Quality Management Plan—During Construction

Minimizing site disturbance during construction and carrying out site restoration efforts to prevent erosion and sedimentation will also contribute to achievement of the following credits:

- SS Credit 9.1, Connection to the Natural World—Places of Respite
- SS Credit 9.2, Connection to the Natural World—Direct Exterior Access for Patients
- IEQ Credit 3.1, Construction Indoor Air Quality Management Plan—During Construction

5. Timeline and Team

On existing healthcare campuses, engage infection control staff early in the design process to ensure that the erosion and sedimentation control plan aligns with infection control policies.

11. Operations and Maintenance Considerations

Coordinate with infection control staff to ensure that any future construction activities are addressed by facility infection control policies.

12. Resources

Websites

Green Guide for Health Care Low Impact Construction Practices Technical Brief, by Jim Moler
http://www.gghc.org/tools.technical.php
Construction best practices for a green healthcare facility, including waste reduction and recycling, site and materials management, infection control, and utility and emissions control.

13. Definitions

infection control policies and procedures to minimize the risk of spreading infections through cross-contamination.

infection control risk assessment (ICRA) an evaluation that anticipates the potential risks of infection transmission associated with construction and renovation projects.

1 U.S. Energy Information Administration, Commercial Buildings Energy Consumption Survey (CBECS) (http://www.eia.doe.gov/emeu/cbecs/contents.html, accessed October 13, 2010).

ENVIRONMENTAL SITE ASSESSMENT

	HEALTHCARE: NC
Prerequisite	SS Prerequisite 2
Points	Required

Intent

To ensure that the site is assessed for environmental contamination and, if contaminated, that the environmental contamination has been remediated to protect occupant health.

Requirements

Conduct a Phase I Environmental Site Assessment (as described in ASTM E1527-05) to determine if environmental contamination exists at the site. If contamination is suspected, conduct a Phase II Environmental Site Assessment [as described in ASTM E1903-97 (2002)].

AND

Sites that are contaminated due to the past existence of a landfill on the site are prohibited. If the site is otherwise contaminated, then it must be remediated to meet local, state or federal EPA region residential (unrestricted) standards, whichever is the most stringent. Documentation from the authority must be provided, such as EPA's Ready for Reuse document, to prove "safe" levels of contamination have been achieved. As the remediation process leads to significant environmental benefit, one point (in SS Credit 3, Brownfield Redevelopment) will be given for successful documented remediation of the site.

IMPORTANT! This reference guide supplement contains only the reference guide sections that pertain to healthcare projects. Use this supplement alongside the LEED Reference Guide for Green Building Design and Construction for complete credit information. For the omitted sections, refer to the main reference guide.

SS	
HEALTHCARE: NC	Prerequisite 2

1. Benefits and Issues to Consider

Environmental Issues

Remediating a brownfield site to the local, state, or federal EPA residential standard demonstrates community stewardship by asserting a healthcare project's fundamental role in safeguarding the health of the general public. Cumulative exposure to environmental pollutants may lead to the development of serious health problems, such as chronic and acute respiratory diseases, cancer, and damage to the nervous system. Healthcare patients are at greater risk from environmental hazards because of their increased sensitivity to environmental stressors during illness and treatment. Some patients' illnesses have been directly or indirectly linked to the environmental contamination on hospital sites. Identifying any contaminants and remediating the site can help make the healthcare facility safe for all occupants. Additionally, remediation activities that remove or encapsulate the contamination can benefit the surrounding community by preventing ongoing contamination via groundwater leaching or windblown dust.

Economic Issues

Remediation to the residential standard exceeds the commercial-level remediation required by law in many jurisdictions and increase upfront costs. However, it will greatly reduce liability associated with the real and perceived health risks related to redeveloping a brownfield.

2. Related Credits

Address potential sources of construction pollution, such as dust and water, in the hazardous material management program and infection control risk assessment, as required under the following prerequisite and credit:

- IEQ Prerequisite 3, Hazardous Material Removal or Encapsulation
- IEQ Credit 3.1, Construction Indoor Air Quality Management Plan—During Construction

11. Operations and Maintenance Considerations

Consider addressing exposure risks by developing educational materials for patients and staff describing the sources of contamination, the remediation process, and any ongoing testing procedures.

12. Resources

Websites

Green Guide for Health Care Brownfield Redevelopment Technical Brief, by Walt Vernon
http://www.gghc.org/tools.technical.php
Brownfield remediation considerations and best practices for a green healthcare facility, including how to evaluate brownfield sites, levels of remediation, and common remediation strategies.

13. Definitions

infection control policies and procedures to minimize the risk of spreading infections through cross-contamination.

infection control risk assessment (ICRA) an evaluation that anticipates the potential risks of infection transmission associated with construction and renovation projects.

SITE SELECTION

	HEALTHCARE: NC
Credit	SS Credit 1
Points	1 point

Intent

To avoid the development of inappropriate sites and reduce the environmental impact from the location of a building on a site.

Requirements

Do not develop buildings, hardscape, roads or parking areas on portions of sites that meet any of the following criteria:

- Prime farmland as defined by the U.S. Department of Agriculture in the United States Code of Federal Regulations, Title 7, Volume 6, Parts 400 to 699, Section 657.5 (citation 7CFR657.5).
- Previously undeveloped land whose elevation is lower than five feet above the elevation of the 100-year flood as defined by the Federal Emergency Management Agency (FEMA).
- Land specifically identified as habitat for any species on federal or state threatened or endangered lists.
- Land within 100 feet of any wetlands as defined by the U.S. Code of Federal Regulations 40 CFR, Parts 230-233 and Part 22, and isolated wetlands or areas of special concern identified by state or local rule, OR within setback distances from wetlands prescribed in state or local regulations, as defined by local or state rule or law, whichever is more stringent.
- Previously undeveloped land that is within 50 feet of a water body, defined as seas, lakes, rivers, streams and tributaries that support or could support fish, recreation or industrial use, consistent with the terminology of the Clean Water Act.
- Land that prior to acquisition for the project was public parkland, unless land of equal or greater value as parkland is accepted in trade by the public landowner (park authority projects are exempt).

IMPORTANT! This reference guide supplement contains only the reference guide sections that pertain to healthcare projects. Use this supplement alongside the LEED Reference Guide for Green Building Design and Construction for complete credit information. For the omitted sections, refer to the main reference guide.

1. Benefits and Issues to Consider

Environmental Issues

Through their choice of location, project teams have an opportunity to promote sustainable development and create new healthcare facilities that are convenient to the populations they serve. Teams constructing healthcare facilities for suburban, exurban, and rural populations should preserve farmland, environmentally sensitive areas, and other greenfield sites by locating in office parks or retail centers or on previously developed sites. Teams constructing healthcare facilities in urban areas should consider infill sites that have access to transportation and other existing infrastructure. All teams should consider the terrain and community context to ensure that their sites are accessible, particularly for patients who are compromised either physically or mentally.

2. Related Credits

Instead of building on sensitive areas, develop therapeutic gardens, nature trails, and other outdoor amenities to complement clinical care, contributing to the following credits:

- SS Credit 5.1, Site Development—Protect or Restore Habitat
- SS Credit 5.2, Site Development—Maximize Open Space
- SS Credit 9.1, Connection to the Natural World—Places of Respite
- SS Credit 9.2, Connection to the Natural World—Direct Exterior Access for Patients

11. Operations and Maintenance Considerations

If a portion of the site is open to the public as a park or hike-and-bike trail, coordinate protection of environmentally sensitive areas with any community stewardship programs. Many community stewardship programs have a conservation component and draw on local volunteers to restore and maintain environmentally significant areas.

DEVELOPMENT DENSITY AND COMMUNITY CONNECTIVITY

SS CREDIT 2

	HEALTHCARE: NC
Credit	SS Credit 2
Points	1 point

Intent

To channel development to urban areas with existing infrastructure, protect greenfields, and preserve habitat and natural resources. In rural areas, to increase development density on sites with existing or previously developed healthcare facilities rather than on undeveloped rural land.

Requirements

OPTION 1. Development Density

Construct or renovate a building on a previously developed site AND in a community with a minimum density of 60,000 square feet per acre net. The density calculation is based on a typical, two-story downtown development and must include the area of the project being built.

OR

OPTION 2. Community Connectivity

Construct or renovate a building on a site that meets the following criteria:

- Located on a previously developed site,
- Located within 1/2 mile of a residential area or neighborhood with an average density of 10 units per acre net,
- Located within 1/2 mile of at least 10 basic services, and
- Pedestrian access available between the building and the services.

For mixed-use projects, no more than three services within the project boundary may be counted towards the ten basic services, provided it is open to the public. No more than two of the ten services required may be anticipated (i.e., at least eight must be existing and operational). In addition, the anticipated services must demonstrate that they will be operational in the locations indicated within 1 year of occupation of the applicant project.

Examples of basic services include the following:

- Bank
- Place of Worship
- Convenience Grocery
- Day Care Center
- Cleaners
- Fire Station
- Beauty Salon
- Hardware
- Laundry
- Library
- Medical or Dental Office
- Senior Care Facility
- Park
- Pharmacy
- Post Office
- Restaurant
- School
- Supermarket
- Theater
- Community Center
- Fitness Center
- Museum
- Hotel
- Medical Device Supplier
- Home Healthcare Service Provider
- Healthcare Support Agencies
- Family Support Facility
- Rehabilitation Facility

IMPORTANT! This reference guide supplement contains only the reference guide sections that pertain to healthcare projects. Use this supplement alongside the LEED Reference Guide for Green Building Design and Construction for complete credit information. For the omitted sections, refer to the main reference guide.

Proximity is determined by drawing a 1/2-mile radius around a main building entrance on a site map and counting the services within that radius.

OR

OPTION 3. EXISTING RURAL SITES[1]

For previously developed existing rural healthcare campus sites, achieve a minimum development density of 30,000 square feet per acre.

1 For the purposes of this credit, "rural land" is defined in accordance with U.S. Census Bureau definitions: settlements comprising less than 2,500 persons, areas outside incorporated census designated places and the rural portions of extended cities. For additional information, visit http://www.census.gov/population/censusdata/urdef.txt.

SS	
HEALTHCARE: NC	Credit 2

1. Benefits and Issues to Consider

Environmental Issues

Through their choice of location, project teams have an opportunity to promote sustainable development and create new healthcare facilities that are convenient to the populations they serve. Teams constructing healthcare facilities for suburban, exurban, and rural populations should preserve farmland, environmentally sensitive areas, and other greenfield sites by locating in office parks or retail centers or on previously developed sites. Teams constructing healthcare facilities in urban areas should consider infill sites that have access to transportation and other existing infrastructure. All teams should consider the terrain and community context to ensure that their sites are accessible, particularly for patients who are compromised either physically or mentally.

With their large square footage and personnel-intensive operations, healthcare facilities can even discourage sprawl by becoming the centers of new transit-oriented developments.

Economic Issues

New healthcare delivery technologies, such as video links, remote diagnostics, and robotic treatment equipment, can reduce the clinical areas in satellite facilities. Outpatient services can be integrated into schools and community centers, thereby connecting to existing community services and making care convenient and accessible.

As large, personnel-intensive operations, new healthcare facilities can be economic drivers for their immediate surroundings. During the planning phase, an owner should inventory nearby medical-related services so as to complement rather than duplicate existing amenities in the building program.

4. Implementation

During the site selection process, weigh the benefits of locating a new healthcare facility on an existing medical campus versus in a high-growth area outside the urban core. Minimize the building footprint through remote diagnostic and treatment technologies and work with regional planning jurisdictions to identify the project as an anchor for smart growth planning initiatives, such as transit-oriented development.

OPTION 1. Development Density

See the LEED Reference Guide for Green Building Design and Construction for additional information.

OPTION 2. Community Connectivity

In addition to the basic services listed in the LEED Reference Guide for Green Building Design and Construction, the following services can also count toward achievement of this credit: hotels, medical device suppliers, home healthcare service providers, healthcare support agencies or organizations, family support facilities, and rehabilitation facilities.

OPTION 3. Existing Rural Sites

Calculate the density of the existing rural healthcare project campus using Equation 1 of SS Credit 2 in the LEED Reference Guide for Green Building Design and Construction.

Staff working in rural healthcare facilities may drive long distances to and from work each day. Contact regional transit authorities to discuss how increasing the density of patients and staff on a healthcare campus can be leveraged to enhance service. Survey staff to identify which basic services, if provided on campus, would most effectively reduce vehicle mileage associated with personal errands.

7. Documentation Guidance

Refer to LEED Online for the complete descriptions of all required documentation.

- For Options 1 and 2, see the LEED Reference Guide for Green Building Design and Construction.
- For Option 3 (existing rural sites), see the documentation guidance for Option 1, Development Density, in the LEED Reference Guide for Green Building Design and Construction.

9. Exemplary Performance

Based on evidence that higher-density locations can achieve substantially and quantifiably higher environmental benefits, the following threshold requirements can be used to qualify for exemplary performance under the Innovation in Design section. Projects must first meet the requirements of Option 1 under SS Credit 2, Development Density and Community Connectivity. Additionally, the project must meet 1 of the 2 following requirements:

- The project itself must have a density at least double that of the average density within the calculated area (see Equations 1 and 3).

OR

- The average density within an area twice as large as that for the base credit achievement must be at least 120,000 square feet per acre. To double the area, use Equation 2 but double the project site area first.

12. Resources

Websites

Active Design Guidelines: Promoting Physical Activity and Health in Design (2010)
New York City Department of Design and Construction
http://www.nyc.gov/html/ddc/html/design/active_design.shtml
Design guidance at both city and building scales for creating projects that encourage physical activity.

13. Definitions

rural site (1) a settlement with fewer than 2,500 persons, (2) an area outside incorporated and census designated places, or (3) the rural portion of an extended city. See U.S. Census Bureau (http://www.census.gov/population/censusdata/urdef.txt).

BROWNFIELD REDEVELOPMENT

	HEALTHCARE: NC
Credit	SS Credit 3
Points	1 point

Intent

To rehabilitate damaged sites where development is complicated by environmental contamination and to reduce pressure on undeveloped land.

Requirements

Projects can only obtain this point via SS Prerequisite 2, Environmental Site Assessment, by remediating site contamination.

IMPORTANT! This reference guide supplement contains only the reference guide sections that pertain to healthcare projects. Use this supplement alongside the LEED Reference Guide for Green Building Design and Construction for complete credit information. For the omitted sections, refer to the main reference guide.

SS	
HEALTHCARE: NC	Credit 3

1. Benefits and Issues to Consider

Refer to the Benefits and Issues to Consider section in SS Prerequisite 2.

2. Related Credits

Refer to the Related Credits section in SS Prerequisite 2.

11. Operations and Maintenance Considerations

Refer to the Operations and Maintenance Considerations section in SS Prerequisite 2.

12. Resources

Refer to the Resources section in SS Prerequisite 2.

ALTERNATIVE TRANSPORTATION—PUBLIC TRANSPORTATION ACCESS

	HEALTHCARE: NC
Credit	SS Credit 4.1
Points	3 points

Intent

To reduce pollution and land development impacts from automobile use.

Requirements

OPTION 1. Rail Station Proximity

Locate the project within 1/2-mile walking distance (measured from a main building entrance) of an existing or planned and funded commuter rail, light rail or subway station.

For stations located greater than 1/8 mile from building entrance, provide an on-demand shuttle service with a documented service plan.

OR

OPTION 2. Bus Stop Proximity

Locate the project within 1/8-mile walking distance (measured from a main building entrance) of one or more stops for two or more public, campus, or private bus lines usable by building occupants.

IMPORTANT! This reference guide supplement contains only the reference guide sections that pertain to healthcare projects. Use this supplement alongside the LEED Reference Guide for Green Building Design and Construction for complete credit information. For the omitted sections, refer to the main reference guide.

SS	
HEALTHCARE: NC	Credit 4.1

1. Benefits and Issues to Consider

Environmental Issues

Healthcare campuses represent the highest concentration of jobs in many areas of the country. They combine personnel-intensive operations with a high-volume service industry. Ironically, healthcare facilities accessible only by private vehicle can contribute to or exacerbate chronic illnesses, such as asthma and other respiratory conditions, by causing traffic congestion with its emissions and noise pollution. Traffic congestion in and around medical campuses can also contribute to vehicle-related injuries and cause stress in patients, visitors, and staff in an already high-stress environment. Project teams can avoid many of these unintended consequences by providing convenient, low-cost alternatives to single-occupancy vehicle transportation, both on campus and to the surrounding community.

Economic Issues

Many healthcare facilities serve patients with impaired mobility and limited means who may depend on public transportation. Facilities that provide or are near alternative transportation increase the physical and socioeconomic accessibility of their services.

4. Implementation

Consider providing access to shuttle services for all facility users, including visitors and patients. Clearly marked and lighted pedestrian paths from the building entrance to transit and shuttle stops, with signage at crosswalks to alert drivers to the presence of pedestrians, provides safety and promotes using the shuttle service. Provide any necessary protection from the elements along the pathway and at the transit stops. Consider the safety of nighttime staff when designing access pathways.

Program retail space to minimize building occupants' need to travel for basic services.

9. Exemplary Performance

To achieve exemplary performance, meet the following minimum requirements:

- Locate the project within 1/2 mile of at least two existing commuter rail, light rail, or subway lines.
- For stations located more than 1/8 mile from the building entrance, provide an on-demand shuttle service with a documented service plan.

OR

- Locate the project within 1/8 mile of at least two or more stops for four or more public or campus bus lines usable by building occupants.

AND

- Frequency of service must be at least 200 transit rides per day, total, at these stops. A combination of rail and bus lines is allowable. Include a transit schedule and map with the LEED certification submittal.

11. Operations and Maintenance Considerations

On existing healthcare campuses, design access to existing alternative transportation programs. Contact regional transit authorities to discuss how increasing the density of patients and staff on a healthcare campus can be leveraged to enhance existing service. Consider partnering with local public transit authorities to expand service to accommodate nighttime staff.

Coordinate with facilities staff pursuing parallel credits in LEED for Existing Buildings: Operations & Maintenance and/or the Green Guide for Health Care, Operations section.

12. Resources

Websites

Active Design Guidelines: Promoting Physical Activity and Health in Design (2010)
New York City Department of Design and Construction
http://www.nyc.gov/html/ddc/html/design/active_design.shtml
Design guidance at both city and building scales for creating projects that encourage physical activity.

ALTERNATIVE TRANSPORTATION—BICYCLE STORAGE AND CHANGING ROOMS

	HEALTHCARE: NC
Credit	SS Credit 4.2
Points	1 point

Intent

To reduce pollution and land development impacts from automobile use.

Requirements

CASE 1. Commercial or Institutional Projects

Provide secure bicycle racks and/or storage within 200 yards of a building entrance for 5% or more of all Full Time Equivalent (FTE) staff (measured at peak periods)

Provide showers and changing facilities in the building, or within 200 yards of a primary staff building entrance, for 0.5% of FTE staff (measured at peak periods).

CASE 2. Residential Projects

For residential buildings, provide covered storage facilities for securing bicycles for 15% or more of building occupants, in lieu of changing/shower facilities.

IMPORTANT! This reference guide supplement contains only the reference guide sections that pertain to healthcare projects. Use this supplement alongside the LEED Reference Guide for Green Building Design and Construction for complete credit information. For the omitted sections, refer to the main reference guide.

1. Benefits and Issues to Consider

Environmental Issues

Healthcare campuses represent the highest concentration of jobs in many areas of the country. They combine a personnel-intensive operation with a high-volume service industry. Ironically, healthcare facilities accessible only by private vehicle can contribute to or exacerbate chronic illnesses, such as asthma and other respiratory conditions, by causing traffic congestion with its air emissions and noise pollution. Traffic congestion in and around medical campuses can also contribute to vehicle-related injuries and cause stress in patients, visitors, and staff in an already high-stress environment. Project teams can avoid many of these unintended consequences by providing convenient, low-cost alternatives to single-occupancy vehicle transportation, both on campus and to the surrounding community.

Economic Issues

Because showers and changing rooms for staff and residents are often included in the basis of design for most hospitals, the additional cost associated with providing a small number of additional showers for other occupants may be minimal.

4. Implementation

Consider patients' abilities. Some patients treated in medical office buildings, for example, may be able to arrive by bicycle. Encouraging bicycle riding is consistent with health promotion. Owners may wish to make shower and changing facilities available to patients and visitors.

6. Calculations

Determine the required number of secure bicycle storage spaces and changing and showering facilities as follows.

CASE 1. Commercial or Institutional Projects

Calculations for commercial and institutional projects are limited to full-time equivalent (FTE) staff, including clinical, administrative, and on-site outsourced staff. Patients, visitors, and transient occupants, such as visiting physicians and clergy, should be excluded.

STEP 1. Identify the total number of building occupants for each of the following occupancy types:

a. Full-time staff.

b. Part-time staff.

STEP 2. Calculate the total number of FTE staff based on a standard eight-hour occupancy period. For example, an eight-hour occupant has an FTE value of 1.0, a 12-hour occupant has an FTE value of 1.5, and a part-time occupant has an FTE value based on work hours per day divided by 8 (Equation 1).

Equation 1

$$\text{Total FTE Staff} = \frac{\text{Total Staff Occupancy Hours}}{8}$$

STEP 3. Calculate the total number of FTE staff at peak periods.

Project teams may use staffing projections that take into account shift overlap or use a default value of 40% of total FTEs (Equation 2).

SS	
HEALTHCARE: NC	Credit 4.2

Equation 2

Total Peak-Period FTE Staff = Total FTE Staff x 0.4

Project teams not using the default calculation should provide documentation explaining their calculations for peak-period FTE staff.

Peak-period FTE staff calculations must be used consistently for all LEED credits.

STEP 4. Use Equation 3 to calculate the number of secure bicycle spaces to provide.

Equation 3

Staff Bicycle Spaces = Peak-Period FTE Staff x 0.05

STEP 5. Use Equation 4 to calculate the number of showers required for staff.

Equation 4

Staff Showers = Peak-Period FTE Staff x 0.005

CASE 2. Residential Projects

STEP 1. Estimate the number of residents based on the number and size of units. Generally, assume two residents per one-bedroom unit, three residents per two-bedroom unit, etc. If occupancy is not known, see Appendix 1, Default Occupancy Counts, in the LEED Reference Guide for Green Building Design and Construction, for occupancy count requirements and guidance.

STEP 2. Use Equation 5 to determine the number of bicycle spaces for residents.

Equation 5

Resident Bicycle Spaces = Residents x 0.15

8. Examples

EXAMPLE 1. Inpatient Hospital Project

Peak-Period FTE Staff Calculations													
Occupants	Persons		Person-Hours per Day		Total Person-Hours per Day		Hours per Day per FTE		Total FTE Staff		Default Peak-Period Factor (0.4)		Total Peak-Period FTE Staff
Full-time staff													
Administrators	60	x	8	=	480	÷	8	=	60	x	0.4	=	24
Facility operations staff	100	x	8	=	800	÷	8	=	100	x	0.4	=	40
Nurses, nursing aides	50	x	12	=	600	÷	8	=	75	x	0.4	=	30
Staff physicians	15	x	10	=	150	÷	8	=	18.75	x	0.4	=	7.5
Part-time staff													
Medical students	40	x	6	=	240	÷	8	=	30	x	0.4	=	12
Total													**113.5**
Total bicycle storage													6
Total showers													1

In this example, the required number of secure bicycle storage spaces is 6. The required number of changing and showering facilities is 1.

EXAMPLE 2. Residential Healthcare Project

Peak-Period FTE Staff Calculations													
Occupants	Persons		Person-Hours per Day		Total Person-Hours per Day		Hours per Day per FTE		Total FTE Staff		Default Peak-Period Factor (0.4)		Total Peak-Period FTE Staff
Full-time staff													
Administrators	30	x	8	=	240	÷	8	=	30	x	0.4	=	12
Facility operations staff	10	x	8	=	80	÷	8	=	10	x	0.4	=	4
Nurses, nursing aides	8	x	12	=	96	÷	8	=	12	x	0.4	=	4.8
Companions	15	x	12	=	180	÷	8	=	22.5	x	0.4	=	9
Social workers, physical and occupational therapists	5	x	10	=	50	÷	8	=	6.25	x	0.4	=	2.5
Part-time staff													
Staff physicians	3	x	4	=	12	÷	8	=	1.5	x	0.4	=	0.6
Facility operations staff	5	x	4	=	20	÷	8	=	2.5	x	0.4	=	1
Total Peak-Period FTE Staff													**33.9**
Total bicycle storage													17
Total showers, changing rooms													1

Residential Apartment Calculations*					
Unit Type	Units		Bedrooms		Total Residents
Studio, 1-bedroom	100	x	1	=	100
2-bedroom	25	x	2	=	50
Total Residents					**150**
Total bicycle storage					23

*Note: Residents in the licensed nursing home portion of the complex are excluded.

Total Bicycle Storage and Showers	
Bicycle Storage	**Minimum**
Peak-period FTE staff	5
Residential apartments	23
Total	**28**

Showers, changing rooms	Minimum
Peak-period FTE staff	1
Total	**1**

In this example, the required number of secure bicycle storage spaces is 39. The required number of changing and showering facilities is 1.

11. Operations and Maintenance Considerations

Coordinate with facilities staff pursuing parallel credits in LEED for Existing Buildings: Operations & Maintenance and/or the Green Guide for Health Care, Operations section.

12. Resources

Websites

Active Design Guidelines: Promoting Physical Activity and Health in Design (2010)
New York City Department of Design and Construction
http://www.nyc.gov/html/ddc/html/design/active_design.shtml
Design guidance at both city and building scales for creating projects that encourage physical activity.

ALTERNATIVE TRANSPORTATION—LOW-EMITTING AND FUEL-EFFICIENT VEHICLES

	HEALTHCARE: NC
Credit	SS Credit 4.3
Points	1 point

Intent

To reduce pollution and land development impacts from automobile use.

Requireme ts

OPTION 1

Provide preferred parking[1] for low-emitting and fuel-efficient vehicles[2] for 5% of the total vehicle parking capacity of the site. Providing a discounted parking rate is an acceptable substitute for preferred parking for low-emitting/fuel-efficient vehicles. To establish a meaningful incentive in all potential markets, the parking rate must be discounted at least 20%. The discounted rate must be available to all customers (i.e., not limited to the number of customers equal to 5% of the vehicle parking capacity), publicly posted at the entrance of the parking area and available for a minimum of two years.

OR

OPTION 2

Install alternative-fuel fueling stations for 3% of the total vehicle parking capacity of the site. Liquid or gaseous fueling facilities must be separately ventilated or located outdoors.

OR

OPTION 3

Provide low-emitting and fuel-efficient vehicles for 3% of Full Time Equivalent (FTE) staff measured at peak periods.

Provide preferred parking[1] for these vehicles.

OR

OPTION 4

Provide staff access to a low-emitting or fuel-efficient vehicle-sharing program. The following requirements must be met:

- One low-emitting or fuel-efficient vehicle must be provided per 3% of FTE staff measured at peak periods, assuming that one shared vehicle can carry eight persons (i.e., 1 vehicle per 267 FTE occupants). For buildings with fewer than 267 FTE staff, at least one low emitting or fuel-efficient vehicle must be provided.
- A vehicle-sharing contract must be provided that has an agreement of at least two years.

1 "Preferred parking" refers to the parking spots that are closest to the main entrance of the project (exclusive of accessible spaces) or parking passes provided at a discounted price.

2 For the purposes of this credit, "low-emitting/fuel-efficient vehicles" are defined as vehicles that are either classified as Zero Emission Vehicles (ZEV) by the California Air Resources Board or have achieved a minimum green score of 40 on the American Council for an Energy Efficient Economy (ACEEE) annual vehicle rating guide.

IMPORTANT! This reference guide supplement contains only the reference guide sections that pertain to healthcare projects. Use this supplement alongside the LEED Reference Guide for Green Building Design and Construction for complete credit information. For the omitted sections, refer to the main reference guide.

- The estimated number of customers served per vehicle must be supported by documentation.
- A narrative explaining the vehicle-sharing program and its administration must be submitted.
- Parking for low-emitting and fuel-efficient vehicles must be located in the nearest available spaces in the nearest available parking area. Provide a site plan or area map clearly highlighting the walking path from the parking area to the project site and noting the distance.

SS	
HEALTHCARE: NC	Credit 4.3

1. Benefits and Issues to Consider

Environmental Issues

Healthcare ambulances and shuttle buses traditionally run on diesel fuel, which can expose building occupants to air and noise pollution at building entrances. Converting diesel fleets to cleaner vehicles both reduces greenhouse gas emissions and improves the health and well-being of healthcare campus occupants, particularly patients with compromised immune systems.

Economic Issues

Providing a car-share program on-site or participating in a community transportation share program can save time, avoid parking and fuel costs, and reduce emissions, particularly for adjunct staff such as doctors, chaplains, and home caregivers who travel to the healthcare facility on a regular basis.

2. Related Credits

Emissions from fleet parking, pick-up, and drop-off areas may enter the healthcare facility through outdoor air intakes, entryways, and operable windows. See the following credit:

- IEQ Credit 5, Indoor Chemical and Pollutant Source Control

4. Implementation

Alternative-fuel vehicle fleets can provide on-campus and inter-campus transportation and shuttles to remote parking and staff housing. Ambulance and ambulette fleets and carpool or vanpool programs can also used alternative-fuel vehicles.

Additional ventilation or pressurized vestibules may be required to ensure that diesel emissions do not enter the healthcare facility.

6. Calculations

OPTION 1

See the LEED Reference Guide for Green Building Design and Construction, SS Credit 4.3, Calculations section.

OPTION 2

See the LEED Reference Guide for Green Building Design and Construction, SS Credit 4.3, Calculations section.

OPTION 3

Calculations for this credit pathway are limited to full-time equivalent (FTE) staff, including clinical, administrative, and on-site outsourced staff. Patients, visitors, and transient occupants, such as visiting physicians and clergy, should be excluded.

To determine the number of low-emitting and fuel-efficient vehicles required, follow the steps below.

STEP 1. Identify the total number of building occupants for each of the following occupancy types:

a. Full-time staff.

b. Part-time staff.

STEP 2. Calculate the total number of FTE staff based on a standard eight-hour occupancy period. For example, an eight-hour occupant has an FTE value of 1.0, a 12-hour occupant has an FTE value of 1.5, and a part-time occupant has an FTE value based on work hours per day divided by 8 (Equation 1).

Equation 1

$$\text{Total FTE Staff} = \frac{\text{Total Staff Occupancy Hours}}{8}$$

STEP 3. Calculate the total number of FTE staff at peak periods.

Project teams may use staffing projections that take into account shift overlap or use a default value of 40% of total FTEs (Equation 2).

Equation 2

$$\text{Total Peak-Period FTE Staff} = \text{Total FTE Staff} \times 0.4$$

Project teams not using the default calculation should provide documentation explaining their calculations for peak-period FTE staff.

Peak-period FTE staff calculations must be used consistently for all LEED credits.

STEP 4. Use Equation 3 to calculate the required number of vehicles and preferred parking spaces.

Equation 3

$$\text{Vehicles and Preferred Parking Spaces} = \text{Peak-Period FTE Staff} \times 0.03$$

OPTION 4

To determine the required number of low-emitting and fuel-efficient vehicles for a vehicle-sharing program, divide the project's peak-period FTE staff (Equation 2) by 267. That is, one vehicle must be provided for every 267 peak-period FTE staff (Equation 4). If the building has fewer than 267 peak-period FTE staff, provide a least one vehicle.

Equation 4

$$\text{Vehicles in Vehicle-Sharing Program} = \frac{\text{Peak-Period FTE Staff}}{267}$$

8. Examples

Refer to the Examples section under SS Credit 4.2 for guidance on calculating peak-period FTE staff.

11. Operations and Maintenance Considerations

Consider coordinating the parking, pick-up, and drop-off areas for campus fleets with the campus no-idle program, if applicable.

Coordinate with facilities staff pursuing parallel credits in LEED for Existing Buildings: Operations & Maintenance and/or the Green Guide for Health Care, Operations section.

12. Resources

Websites

Active Design Guidelines: Promoting Physical Activity and Health in Design (2010)
New York City Department of Design and Construction
http://www.nyc.gov/html/ddc/html/design/active_design.shtml
Design guidance at both city and building scales for creating projects that encourage physical activity.

ALTERNATIVE TRANSPORTATION—PARKING CAPACITY

	HEALTHCARE: NC
Credit	SS Credit 4.4
Points	1 point

Intent

To reduce pollution and land development impacts from automobile use.

Requirements

CASE 1. Non-Residential Healthcare Projects

OPTION 1

Size parking capacity to meet, but not exceed, minimum local zoning requirements OR health department regulatory authority, whichever is the overriding requirement.

Provide preferred parking[1] for carpools or vanpools for 5% of the total parking spaces.

OR

OPTION 2

For projects that provide parking for less than 5% of full-time equivalent (FTE) staff:

Provide preferred parking for carpools or vanpools, marked as such, for 5% of total parking spaces. Providing a discounted parking rate is an acceptable substitute for preferred parking for carpool or vanpool vehicles. To establish a meaningful incentive in all potential markets, the parking rate must be discounted at least 20%. The discounted rate must be available to all customers (i.e., not limited to the number of customers equal to 5% of the vehicle parking capacity), publicly posted at the entrance of the parking area, and available for a minimum of two years.

OR

OPTION 3

Provide no new parking.

OR

OPTION 4

For projects that have no minimum local zoning requirements, provide 25% fewer parking spaces than the applicable standard listed in the 2003 Institute of Transportation Engineers (ITE) "Parking Generation" study at http://www.ite.org.

CASE 2. Residential Healthcare Licensed Long Term Care Projects

OPTION 1

Size parking capacity to meet, but not exceed, minimum local zoning requirements or health department regulatory authority, whichever is the overriding requirement.

Provide infrastructure and support programs to facilitate shared vehicle use, such as carpool drop-off areas, designated parking for vanpools, car-share services, ride boards and shuttle services to mass transit.

1 For the purposes of this credit "preferred parking" refers to the parking spots that are closest to the main entrance of the project (exclusive of spaces designated for handicapped persons) or parking passes provided at a discounted price.

IMPORTANT! This reference guide supplement contains only the reference guide sections that pertain to healthcare projects. Use this supplement alongside the LEED Reference Guide for Green Building Design and Construction for complete credit information. For the omitted sections, refer to the main reference guide.

SS CREDIT 4.4

Provide preferred parking for carpools or vanpools for 5% of the total parking spaces provided for staff OR, for projects that provide parking for less than 5% FTE staff measured at peak periods, provide preferred parking for carpools or vanpools, marked as such, for 5% of total provided parking spaces. Providing a discounted parking rate is an acceptable substitute for preferred parking for carpool or vanpool vehicles. To establish a meaningful incentive in all potential markets, the parking rate must be discounted at least 20%. The discounted rate must be available to all customers (i.e. not limited to the number of customers equal to 5% of the vehicle parking capacity), publicly posted at the entrance of the parking area and available for a minimum of two years.

OR

OPTION 2

Provide no new parking.

CASE 3. Mixed Use Healthcare Projects (i.e. including residential, retail, and/or medical office components)

OPTION 1

Mixed-use buildings with less than 10% non-residential area must be considered residential and adhere to the residential requirements in Case 2. For mixed-use buildings with more than 10% non-residential area, the non-residential space must adhere to the requirements in Case 1 and the residential component must adhere to residential requirements in Case 2. Note: This option applies only to mixed-use healthcare projects that include residential, retail and/or medical office components.

OR

OPTION 2

Provide no new parking.

SS	
HEALTHCARE: NC	Credit 4.4

1. Benefits and Issues to Consider

Healthcare campuses represent the highest concentration of jobs in many areas of the country. They combine a personnel-intensive operation with a high-volume service industry. Ironically, healthcare facilities accessible only by private vehicle can contribute to or exacerbate chronic illnesses, such as asthma and other respiratory conditions, by causing traffic congestion with its air emissions and noise pollution. Project teams can avoid many of these unintended consequences by providing convenient, low-cost alternatives to single-occupancy vehicle transportation, both on campus and to the surrounding community.

Economic Issues

Because of the high minimum parking requirements for hospitals, many new healthcare buildings are designed as islands in a sea of surface parking. Master planning strategies that create a compact building footprint using strategies such as structured parking can reserve more of the campus for natural habitat. Although structured parking carries an initial cost premium, it can drastically reduce travel distances for outpatients, visitors, and staff.

2. Related Credits

Developing mixed-use healthcare facilities—that is, with residential and retail components—can anchor new smart growth developments by increasing density and establishing a precedent of mixed-use buildings providing multiple basic services. See the following credits:

- SS Credit 2, Development Density and Community Connectivity
- SS Credit 5.2, Site Development—Maximize Open Space

4. Implementation

Design residential and mixed-use healthcare facilities to encourage alternative transportation for residents, visitors, staff, and outside retail customers. Program retail space to minimize building occupants' need to travel for basic services. Institute shuttle bus service for staff members who live in the neighborhood.

6. Calculations

CASE 1

OPTION 1

Multiply the number of parking spaces by 5% to determine the required number of designated carpool or vanpool spaces.

OPTION 2

Calculations for this credit pathway are limited to full-time equivalent (FTE) staff, including clinical, administrative, and on-site outsourced staff. Patients, visitors, and transient occupants, such as visiting physicians and clergy, should be excluded.

STEP 1. Identify the total number of building occupants for each of the following occupancy types:

a. Full-time staff.

b. Part-time staff.

STEP 2. Calculate the total number of FTE staff based on a standard eight-hour occupancy period. For example, an eight-hour occupant has an FTE value of 1.0, a 12-hour occupant has an FTE value of 1.5, and a part-time occupant has an FTE value based on work hours per day divided by 8 (Equation 1).

Equation 1

$$\text{Total FTE Staff} = \frac{\text{Total Staff Occupancy Hours}}{8}$$

STEP 3. Calculate the total number of FTE staff at peak periods.

Project teams may use staffing projections that take into account shift overlap or use a default value of 40% of total FTEs (Equation 2).

Equation 2

$$\text{Total Peak-Period FTE Staff} = \text{Total FTE Staff} \times 0.4$$

Project teams not using the default calculation should provide documentation explaining their calculations for peak-period FTE staff.

Peak-period FTE staff calculations must be used consistently for all LEED credits.

STEP 4. Use Equation 3 to calculate the required number of parking spaces.

Equation 3

$$\text{Parking Spaces} = \text{Peak-Period FTE Staff} \times 0.05$$

CASE 2

OPTION 1

STEP 1. Use Equations 1–3 to calculate 5% of peak-period FTE staff.

STEP 2. If parking is provided for 5% or more of peak-period FTE staff, reserve for carpools or vanpools the number of parking spaces indicated by Equation 3 in staff parking areas.

If parking is provided for less than 5% of peak period FTE staff, reserve for carpools or vanpools the number of parking spaces indicated by Equation 3 in general parking areas.

If discounted parking is provided in lieu of reserved parking spaces, determine the maximum rate to be offered to low-emitting and fuel-efficient vehicle users by multiplying the regular rate by 0.80.

CASE 3: MIXED-USE HEALTHCARE

Verify that the project includes residential, retail, or medical office components.

OPTION 1

Determine the building's gross square footage identified as residential and the gross square footage identified as nonresidential.

Divide the nonresidential area by the total gross square footage of the building.

If the building has less than 10% nonresidential area, apply the residential requirements in Case 2. If the building has 10% or more nonresidential area, apply the nonresidential requirements in Case 1 to nonresidential spaces and the residential requirements in Case 2 to the residential spaces.

8. Examples

Refer to the Examples section under SS Credit 4.2 for guidance on how to calculate peak period FTE staff.

SITE DEVELOPMENT—PROTECT OR RESTORE HABITAT

SS CREDIT 5.1

	HEALTHCARE: NC
Credit	SS Credit 5.1
Points	1 point

Intent

To conserve existing natural areas and restore damaged areas to provide habitat and promote biodiversity.

Requirements

CASE 1. Greenfield Sites[1]

Limit all site disturbance to the following parameters:

- 40 feet beyond the building perimeter;
- 10 feet beyond surface walkways, patios, surface parking and utilities less than 12 inches in diameter;
- 15 feet beyond primary roadway curbs and main utility branch trenches;
- 25 feet beyond constructed areas with permeable surfaces, such as pervious paving areas, stormwater detention facilities and playing fields that require additional staging areas to limit compaction in the constructed area.

CASE 2. Previously Developed[2] Areas or Graded Sites

Restore or protect a minimum of 50% of the site area, excluding the building footprint, or 20% of the total site area, including building footprint, whichever is greater, with native or adapted vegetation[3].

Projects earning SS Credit 2, Development Density and Community Connectivity, may include vegetated roof surface in this calculation if the plants are native or adapted, provide habitat, and promote biodiversity. Projects earning SS Credit 9.1, Connection to the Natural World—Outdoor Places of Respite, may apply the planted areas to this calculation, if the plants are native or adapted, provide habitat and promote biodiversity.

1 Greenfield sites are those that are not previously developed or graded and remain in a natural state.

2 Previously developed areas are those that previously contained buildings, roadways, parking lots or were graded or altered by direct human activities.

3 Native or adapted plants are plants indigenous to a locality or cultivars of native plants that are adapted to the local climate and are not considered invasive species or noxious weeds.

IMPORTANT! This reference guide supplement contains only the reference guide sections that pertain to healthcare projects. Use this supplement alongside the LEED Reference Guide for Green Building Design and Construction for complete credit information. For the omitted sections, refer to the main reference guide.

SS	
HEALTHCARE: NC	Credit 5.1

1. Benefits and Issues to Consider

Environmental Issues

Reducing the construction footprint and integrating native or adapted vegetation into landscaped areas, such as therapeutic gardens and nature trails, can not only protect natural habitat but also enhance clinical practice. Providing patients with access to nature can shorten hospital stays and reduce stress, depression, and the use of pain medication.[4] Native and adapted plants often need no fertilizers, irrigation, or pesticides and thus help reduce a facility's use of resources and sensitive populations' exposure to harmful chemicals.

Economic Issues

Because of the high minimum parking requirements for hospitals, many new healthcare buildings are designed as islands in a sea of surface parking. Master planning strategies that create a compact building footprint using strategies such as structured parking have the added benefit of protecting natural habitat. Although structured parking carries an initial cost premium, it allows for more open space to provide habitat and promote biodiversity.

2. Related Credits

Protected or restored habitat can be integrated into designs for building orientation, open space, and places of respite, contributing to the following credits:

- SS Credit 1, Site Selection
- SS Credit 5.2, Site Development—Maximize Open Space
- SS Credit 9.1, Connection to the Natural World—Places of Respite
- SS Credit 9.2, Connection to the Natural World—Direct Exterior Access for Patients

4. Implementation

Coordinate landscape conservation and restoration with designs for outdoor places of respite. Identify opportunities to connect to regional parks, hike-and-bike trails, and watershed protection projects.

Work with the infection control department to minimize the entry of allergens, mold spores, and other pollutants and irritants through outdoor air intakes, operable windows, and entryways. Ensure that any vegetated roofs are designed to prevent standing water, which can breed microbes and infection vectors, such as mosquitoes.

If a portion of the site is open to the public as a park or hike-and-bike trail, coordinate protection of environmentally sensitive areas with any community stewardship programs. Many community stewardship programs have a conservation component and draw on local volunteers to restore and maintain environmentally significant areas.

9. Exemplary Performance

Projects may earn an Innovation in Design credit for exemplary performance by restoring or protecting a minimum of 75% of the site (excluding the building footprint) or 30% of the total site (including building footprint), whichever is greater, with native or adapted vegetation.

4 Roger Ulrich et al., A Review of the Research Literature on Evidence-Based Healthcare Design, *Health Environments Research and Design Journal* 1(3), 2008 (http://www.herdjournal.com).

11. Operations and Maintenance Considerations

Coordinate operations and maintenance of natural areas that will also be used for clinical or therapeutic purposes with the appropriate clinical departments and landscape facilities staff.

12. Resources

Websites

Active Design Guidelines: Promoting Physical Activity and Health in Design (2010)
New York City Department of Design and Construction
http://www.nyc.gov/html/ddc/html/design/active_design.shtml
Design guidance at both city and building scales for creating projects that encourage physical activity.

Sustainable Sites Initiative (SITES)
http://www.sustainablesites.org/
The Sustainable Sites Initiative has developed a pilot guideline and benchmarking program to inform sustainable design, construction, and maintenance of landscapes, with and without buildings. The program's "Human Health & Well-Being" area of focus provides guidance on ways to maximize the health benefits of landscape design.

13. Definitions

infection control policies and procedures to minimize the risk of spreading infections through cross-contamination.

place of respite an area that connects "healthcare patients, visitors, and staff to health benefits of the natural environment" (Jerry Smith, Green Guide for Health Care Places of Respite Technical Brief, http://www.gghc.org/tools.technical.php).

SITE DEVELOPMENT—MAXIMIZE OPEN SPACE

SS CREDIT 5.2

	HEALTHCARE: NC
Credit	SS Credit 5.2
Points	1 point

Intent

To promote biodiversity by providing a high ratio of open space to development footprint.

Requirements

CASE 1

Reduce the development footprint[1] and/or provide vegetated open space within the project boundary such that the amount of open space exceeds local zoning requirements by 25%.

OR

CASE 2

For areas with no local zoning requirements (e.g. some university campuses, military bases), provide a vegetated open space area adjacent to the building that is equal in area to the building footprint.

OR

CASE 3

Where a zoning ordinance exists, but there is no requirement for open space (zero), provide vegetated open space equal to 20% of the project site area.

ALL CASES

For projects located in urban areas that earn SS Credit 2, Development Density and Community Connectivity, vegetated roof areas can contribute to credit compliance.

For projects located in urban areas that earn SS Credit 2, Development Density and Community Connectivity, pedestrian-oriented hardscape areas can contribute to credit compliance. For such projects, a minimum of 25% of the open space counted must be vegetated.

Wetlands or naturally designed ponds may count as open space if the side slope gradients average 1:4 (vertical: horizontal) or less and are vegetated.

1 Development footprint is defined as the total area of the building footprint, hardscape, access roads and parking.

IMPORTANT! This reference guide supplement contains only the reference guide sections that pertain to healthcare projects. Use this supplement alongside the LEED Reference Guide for Green Building Design and Construction for complete credit information. For the omitted sections, refer to the main reference guide.

1. Benefits and Issues to Consider

Environmental Issues

Reducing the construction footprint and integrating native or adapted vegetation into landscaped areas, such as therapeutic gardens and nature trails, can not only protect natural habitat but also enhance clinical practice. Providing patients with access to nature can shorten hospital stays and reduce stress, depression, and the use of pain medication.[2] Native and adapted plants often need no fertilizers, irrigation, or pesticides and thus reduce a facility's use of resources and sensitive populations' exposure to harmful chemicals.

Economic Issues

Because of the high minimum parking requirements for hospitals, many new healthcare buildings are designed as islands in a sea of surface parking. Master planning strategies that create a compact building footprint using strategies such as structured parking have the added benefit of protecting natural habitat. Although structured parking carries an initial cost premium, it allows for more open space to provide habitat and promote biodiversity.

2. Related Credits

Protected or restored habitat can be integrated into designs for places of respite, contributing to the following credits:

- SS Credit 5.1, Site Selection—Protect or Restore Habitat
- SS Credit 9.1, Connection to the Natural World—Places of Respite
- SS Credit 9.2, Connection to the Natural World—Direct Exterior Access for Patients

4. Implementation

Coordinate landscape restoration with designs for outdoor places of respite. Nature walks and hike-and-bike trails should serve the entire campus and, if possible, extend into the surrounding community. Identify opportunities to connect to regional parks, hike-and-bike trails, and watershed protection projects. Designate greenfields, wetlands, restored areas, and other outdoor areas as places of respite.

Work with the infection control department to minimize the entry of allergens, mold spores, and other pollutants and irritants through outdoor air intakes, operable windows, and entryways. Ensure that any vegetated roofs are designed to prevent standing water, which can breed microbes and infection vectors, such as mosquitoes.

9. Exemplary Performance

Projects may earn an Innovation in Design credit for exemplary performance by demonstrating that they have doubled the amount of open space required for credit achievement. All designated open space must be within the LEED project boundary. For example, projects subject to local zoning requirements must increase the amount of open space provided by 50% instead of by 25%; projects not subject to local zoning requirements must provide open space equal to twice the building footprint; and urban projects where zero open space is required must provide open space equal to 40% of the site area.

2 Roger Ulrich et al., A Review of the Research Literature on Evidence-Based Healthcare Design, Health Environments Research and Design Journal 1(3), 2008 (http://www.herdjournal.com).

11. Operations and Maintenance Considerations

If a portion of the site is open to the public as a park or hike-and-bike trail, coordinate protection of environmentally sensitive areas with any community stewardship programs. Many community stewardship programs have a conservation component and draw on local volunteers to restore and maintain environmentally significant areas. Coordinate operations and maintenance of natural areas that will also be used for clinical or therapeutic purposes with the appropriate clinical departments and landscape facilities staff.

Coordinate with facilities staff pursuing SS Credit 3 in LEED for Existing Buildings: Operations & Maintenance.

12. Resources

Websites

Active Design Guidelines: Promoting Physical Activity and Health in Design (2010)
New York City Department of Design and Construction
http://www.nyc.gov/html/ddc/html/design/active_design.shtml
Design guidance at both city and building scales for creating projects that encourage physical activity.

Sustainable Sites Initiative (SITES)
http://www.sustainablesites.org/
The Sustainable Sites Initiative has developed a pilot guideline and benchmarking program to inform sustainable design, construction, and maintenance of landscapes, with and without buildings. The program's "Human Health & Well-being" area of focus provides guidance on ways to maximize the health benefits of landscape design.

13. Definitions

infection control policies and procedures to minimize the risk of spreading infections through cross-contamination.

place of respite an area that connects "healthcare patients, visitors, and staff to health benefits of the natural environment" (Jerry Smith, Green Guide for Health Care Places of Respite Technical Brief, http://www.gghc.org/tools.technical.php).

STORMWATER DESIGN—QUANTITY CONTROL

	HEALTHCARE: NC
Credit	SS Credit 6.1
Points	1 point

Intent

To limit disruption of natural hydrology by reducing impervious cover, increasing on-site infiltration, reducing or eliminating pollution from stormwater runoff and eliminating contaminants.

Requirements

CASE 1. Sites with Existing Imperviousness 50% or Less

OPTION 1

Implement a stormwater management plan that prevents the post-development peak discharge rate and quantity from exceeding the predevelopment peak discharge rate and quantity for the 1- and 2-year 24-hour design storms.

OR

OPTION 2

Implement a stormwater management plan that protects receiving stream channels from excessive erosion. The stormwater management plan must include stream channel protection and quantity control strategies.

CASE 2. Sites with Existing Imperviousness Greater Than 50%

Implement a stormwater management plan that results in a 25% decrease in the volume of stormwater runoff from the 2-year 24-hour design storm.

IMPORTANT! This reference guide supplement contains only the reference guide sections that pertain to healthcare projects. Use this supplement alongside the LEED Reference Guide for Green Building Design and Construction for complete credit information. For the omitted sections, refer to the main reference guide.

SS	
HEALTHCARE: NC	Credit 6.1

1. Benefits and Issues to Consider

Environmental Issues

Minimizing the site's contribution to nonpoint source water pollution demonstrates community stewardship by asserting healthcare's fundamental role in safeguarding the health of the general public.

Economic Issues

Space is at a premium on healthcare campuses because of the need to reduce travel distances between clinical areas, the spatial requirements of infrastructure, and the large parking lots often required by staff and visitors. The cost of nonstructural stormwater management practices can be offset by integrating stormwater features into the landscape design, particularly areas with clinical benefits, such as places of respite, nature trails, and therapeutic gardens. Project teams can further amortize any cost premiums associated with stormwater management by designing a single system for the entire campus to benefit future construction as well as the LEED project.

2. Related Credits

Stormwater management design can be integrated into designs for places of respite, habitat restoration, and water-efficient landscaping, contributing to the following credits:

- SS Credit 5.1, Site Development—Protect or Restore Natural Habitats
- SS Credit 9.1, Connection to the Natural World—Places of Respite
- SS Credit 9.2, Connection to the Natural World—Direct Exterior Access for Patients
- WE Credit 1, Water-Efficient Landscaping—No Potable Water Use or No Irrigation

4. Implementation

Coordinate stormwater capture and reuse systems with infection control. Consult with the local public health authority, since regulations may not allow graywater to be used for irrigation in areas accessible to patients.

9. Exemplary Performance

No standardized exemplary performance option has been established for this credit. However, project teams may apply for exemplary performance by documenting a comprehensive approach to capture and treat stormwater runoff and demonstrating performance above and beyond the credit requirements. Only 1 exemplary performance credit may be achieved for SS Credit 6.1, Stormwater Design—Quantity Control, and SS Credit 6.2, Stormwater Design—Quality Control.

11. Operations and Maintenance Considerations

For healthcare projects integrating stormwater management into landscape design, work with the infection control department to ensure that water capture, storage, and reuse practices align with infection control policies. Coordinate operations and maintenance of landscaped areas that will also be used for clinical or therapeutic purposes with the appropriate clinical departments and landscape facilities staff.

12. Resources

Websites

Green Guide for Health Care Sustainable Site Design: Stormwater Mitigation Technical Brief, by Teresa Durkin and Marita Roos
http://www.gghc.org/tools.technical.php
Stormwater management best practices for healthcare environments.

Sustainable Sites Initiative (SITES)
http://www.sustainablesites.org/
The Sustainable Sites Initiative has developed a pilot guideline and benchmarking program to inform sustainable design, construction, and maintenance of landscapes, with and without buildings. The program's "Human Health & Well-Being" area of focus provides guidance on ways to maximize the health benefits of landscape design.

13. Definitions

infection control policies and procedures to minimize the risk of spreading infections through cross-contamination.

place of respite an area that connects "healthcare patients, visitors, and staff to health benefits of the natural environment" (Jerry Smith, Green Guide for Health Care Places of Respite Technical Brief, http://www.gghc.org/tools.technical.php).

STORMWATER DESIGN—QUALITY CONTROL

	HEALTHCARE: NC
Credit	SS Credit 6.2
Points	1 point

Intent

To limit disruption and pollution of natural water flows by managing stormwater runoff.

Requirements

Implement a stormwater management plan that reduces impervious cover, promotes infiltration and captures and treats the stormwater runoff from 90% of the average annual rainfall[1] using acceptable best management practices (BMPs).

BMPs used to treat runoff must be capable of removing 80% of the average annual post-development total suspended solids (TSS) load based on existing monitoring reports. BMPs are considered to meet these criteria if:

- They are designed in accordance with standards and specifications from a state or local program that has adopted these performance standards.

OR

- There exists infield performance monitoring data demonstrating compliance with the criteria. Data must conform to accepted protocol [e.g., Technology Acceptance Reciprocity Partnership (TARP), Washington State Department of Ecology] for BMP monitoring.

1 There are 3 distinct climates in the United States that influence the nature and amount of annual rainfall. Humid watersheds are defined as those that receive at least 40 inches of rainfall each year. Semiarid watersheds receive between 20 and 40 inches of rainfall per year, and arid watersheds receive less than 20 inches of rainfall per year. For this credit, 90% of the average annual rainfall is equivalent to treating the runoff from the following (based on climate):
- Humid Watersheds — 1 inch of rainfall
- Semiarid Watersheds — 0.75 inches of rainfall
- Arid Watersheds — 0.5 inches of rainfall

IMPORTANT! This reference guide supplement contains only the reference guide sections that pertain to healthcare projects. Use this supplement alongside the LEED Reference Guide for Green Building Design and Construction for complete credit information. For the omitted sections, refer to the main reference guide.

1. Benefits and Issues to Consider

Refer to the Benefits and Issues to Consider section in SS Credit 6.1.

2. Related Credits

Refer to the Related Credits section in SS Credit 6.1.

9. Exemplary Performance

Refer to the Exemplary Performance section in SS Credit 6.1.

11. Operations and Maintenance Considerations

Refer to the Operations and Maintenance Considerations section in SS Credit 6.1.

12. Resources

Refer to the Resources section in SS Credit 6.1.

13. Definitions

Refer to the Definitions section in SS Credit 6.1.

HEAT ISLAND EFFECT—NONROOF

SS CREDIT 7.1

	HEALTHCARE: NC
Credit	SS Credit 7.1
Points	1 point

Intent

To reduce heat islands[1] to minimize impacts on microclimates and human and wildlife habitats.

Requirements

OPTION 1

Use any combination of the following strategies for 50% of the site hardscape, including roads, sidewalks, courtyards and parking lots:

- Provide shade from the existing tree canopy or within 5 years of landscape installation. Landscaping (trees) must be in place at the time of occupancy.
- Provide shade from structures covered by solar panels that produce energy used to offset some nonrenewable resource use.
- Provide shade from architectural devices or structures that have a solar reflectance index[2] (SRI) of at least 29.
- Use hardscape materials with an SRI of at least 29.
- Use an open-grid pavement system (at least 50% pervious).

OR

OPTION 2

Place a minimum of 50% of parking spaces under cover[3]. Any roof used to shade or cover parking must have an SRI of at least 29, be a vegetated green roof or be covered by solar panels that produce energy used to offset some nonrenewable resource use.

1 Heat islands are defined as thermal gradient differences between developed and undeveloped areas.

2 The solar reflectance index (SRI) is a measure of the constructed surface's ability to reflect solar heat, as shown by a small temperature rise. It is defined so that a standard black surface (reflectance 0.05, emittance 0.90) is 0 and a standard white surface (reflectance 0.80, emittance 0.90) is 100. To calculate the SRI for a given material, obtain the reflectance value and emittance value for the material. SRI is calculated according to ASTM E 1980. Reflectance is measured according to ASTM E 903, ASTM E 1918, or ASTM C 1549. Emittance is measured according to ASTM E 408 or ASTM C 1371.

3 For the purposes of this credit, under cover parking is defined as parking underground, under deck, under roof, or under a building.

IMPORTANT! This reference guide supplement contains only the reference guide sections that pertain to healthcare projects. Use this supplement alongside the LEED Reference Guide for Green Building Design and Construction for complete credit information. For the omitted sections, refer to the main reference guide.

1. Benefits and Issues to Consider

Environmental Issues

Space is at a premium on healthcare campuses because the need to reduce travel distances between clinical areas, the spatial requirements of infrastructure, and the large parking lots often required by staff and visitors. However, programming high-SRI or open-grid paved areas as shaded nature trails or hiking and bicycle trails and integrating therapeutic gardens and nature trails into physical rehabilitation programs can not only mitigate heat island effects but enhance clinical practice as well.

Economic Issues

Because of the high minimum parking requirements for hospitals, many new healthcare buildings are designed as islands in a sea of surface parking. Master planning strategies that create a compact building footprint using strategies such as structured parking can reduce heat islands.

2. Related Credits

Coordinate hardscape design with designs for outdoor places of respite, habitat conservation and restoration, and open space, contributing to the following credits:

- SS Credit 5.1, Site Development—Protect or Restore Habitat
- SS Credit 5.2, Site Development—Maximize Open Space
- SS Credit 9.1, Connection to the Natural World—Places of Respite
- SS Credit 9.2, Connection to the Natural World—Direct Exterior Access for Patients

4. Implementation

Integrate hardscape design into walking paths and other site features encouraging patients, visitors, and staff to engage in physical activity. Consider shading high-SRI surfaces to protect patients with light sensitivities from glare.

If a portion of the site is open to the public as a park or hike-and-bike trail, coordinate protection of environmentally sensitive areas with any community stewardship programs. Many community stewardship programs have a conservation component and draw on local volunteers to restore and maintain environmentally significant areas.

9. Exemplary Performance

Projects may earn an Innovation in Design credit for exemplary performance by demonstrating that either (1) 100% of nonroof impervious surfaces have been constructed with high-albedo or open-grid paving, or will be shaded within 5 years; or (2) 100% of the on-site parking spaces have been located under cover.

11. Operations and Maintenance Considerations

Coordinate operations and maintenance of paths that will also be used for clinical or therapeutic purposes with the appropriate clinical departments and landscape facilities staff.

12. Resources

Websites

Active Design Guidelines: Promoting Physical Activity and Health in Design (2010)
New York City Department of Design and Construction
http://www.nyc.gov/html/ddc/html/design/active_design.shtml
Design guidance at both city and building scales for creating projects that encourage physical activity.

SS	
HEALTHCARE: NC	Credit 7.1

Sustainable Sites Initiative (SITES)

http://www.sustainablesites.org/

The Sustainable Sites Initiative has developed a pilot guideline and benchmarking program to inform sustainable design, construction, and maintenance of landscapes, with and without buildings. The program's "Human Health & Well-Being" area of focus provides guidance on ways to maximize the health benefits of landscape design.

HEAT ISLAND EFFECT—ROOF

SS CREDIT 7.2

	HEALTHCARE: NC
Credit	SS Credit 7.2
Points	1 point

Intent

To reduce heat islands[1] to minimize impacts on microclimates and human and wildlife habitats.

Requirements

OPTION 1

Use roofing materials with a solar reflectance index[2] (SRI) equal to or greater than the values in the table below for a minimum of 75% of the roof surface.

Roofing materials having a lower SRI value than those listed below may be used if the weighted rooftop SRI average meets the following criteria:

$$\frac{\text{Area Roof Meeting Minimum SRI}}{\text{Total Roof Area}} \times \frac{\text{SRI of Installed Roof}}{\text{Required SRI}} \geq 75\%$$

Roof Type	Slope	SRI
Low-sloped roof	≤ 2:12	78
Steep-sloped roof	> 2:12	29

OR

OPTION 2

Install a vegetated roof that covers at least 50% of the roof area.

OR

OPTION 3

Install high-albedo and vegetated roof surfaces that, in combination, meet the following criteria:

$$\frac{\text{Area Roof Meeting Minimum SRI}}{0.75} + \frac{\text{Area of Vegetated Roof}}{0.5} \geq \text{Total Roof Area}$$

Roof Type	Slope	SRI
Low-sloped roof	≤ 2:12	78
Steep-sloped roof	> 2:12	29

1 Heat islands are defined as thermal gradient differences between developed and undeveloped areas.

2 The solar reflectance index (SRI) is a measure of the constructed surface's ability to reflect solar heat, as shown by a small temperature rise. It is defined so that a standard black surface (reflectance 0.05, emittance 0.90) is 0 and a standard white surface (reflectance 0.80, emittance 0.90) is 100. To calculate the SRI for a given material, obtain the reflectance value and emittance value for the material. SRI is calculated according to ASTM E 1980. Reflectance is measured according to ASTM E 903, ASTM E 1918 or ASTM C 1549. Emittance is measured according to ASTM E 408 or ASTM C 1371.

IMPORTANT! This reference guide supplement contains only the reference guide sections that pertain to healthcare projects. Use this supplement alongside the LEED Reference Guide for Green Building Design and Construction for complete credit information. For the omitted sections, refer to the main reference guide.

SS	
HEALTHCARE: NC	Credit 7.2

1. Benefits and Issues to Consider

Environmental Issues

Providing patients with access to nature can shorten hospital stays and reduce stress, depression, and the use of pain medication.[2] Vegetated roofs can provide both views and direct access to nature from patient towers in healthcare facilities. They can also double as therapeutic gardens and places of respite in dense urban areas with zero-lot-line conditions.

Economic Issues

The cost premium associated with vegetated roofs, particularly roof gardens with direct access, can be offset by programming the area to accommodate staff break rooms, family lounges, and rehabilitation gardens.

2. Related Credits

Design vegetated roofs to maximize the viewshed from patient rooms and program them as outdoor places of respite, natural habitat, and open space, contributing to the following credits:

- SS Credit 5.1, Site Development—Protect or Restore Natural Habitat
- SS Credit 5.2, Site Development—Maximize Open Space
- SS Credit 9.1, Connection to the Natural World—Places of Respite
- SS Credit 9.2, Connection to the Natural World—Direct Exterior Access for Patients

4. Implementation

Consider using vegetated roofs as healing gardens. Identify potential sources of funding for vegetated roofs and healing gardens during the initial design phase to ensure that these features remain integral to the design concept throughout the project.

Protect patient towers from the reflection and glare associated with high-SRI roofing materials applied to the lower diagnostic and treatment units.

5. Timeline and Team

Consider potential areas for vegetated roofs early in the design process (i.e., schematic design) so that structural loads can be designed and priced. Introduced later in the project, vegetated roofs are often costly to implement.

9. Exemplary Performance

Projects may earn an Innovation in Design credit for exemplary performance by demonstrating that 100% of the project's roof area (excluding any mechanical equipment, photovoltaic panels, and skylights) consists of a vegetated roof system.

11. Operations and Maintenance Considerations

Work with the infection control and maintenance departments to ensure that any vegetated roofs are properly maintained to prevent standing water and other conditions that could breed microbes and infection vectors, such as mosquitoes.

2 Roger Ulrich et al., A Review of the Research Literature on Evidence-Based Healthcare Design, *Health Environments Research and Design Journal* 1(3), 2008 (http://www.herdjournal.com).

12. Resources

Websites

Active Design Guidelines: Promoting Physical Activity and Health in Design (2010)
New York City Department of Design and Construction
http://www.nyc.gov/html/ddc/html/design/active_design.shtml
Design guidance at both city and building scales for creating projects that encourage physical activity.

Sustainable Sites Initiative (SITES)
http://www.sustainablesites.org/
The Sustainable Sites Initiative has developed a pilot guideline and benchmarking program to inform sustainable design, construction, and maintenance of landscapes, with and without buildings. The program's "Human Health & Well-Being" area of focus provides guidance on ways to maximize the health benefits of landscape design.

13. Definitions

infection control policies and procedures to minimize the risk of spreading infections through cross-contamination.

place of respite an area that connects "healthcare patients, visitors, and staff to health benefits of the natural environment" (Jerry Smith, Green Guide for Health Care Places of Respite Technical Brief, http://www.gghc.org/tools.technical.php).

viewshed an area of land, water, or other environmental element that is visible to the human eye from a fixed vantage point.

LIGHT POLLUTION REDUCTION

	HEALTHCARE: NC
Credit	SS Credit 8
Points	1 point

Intent

To minimize light trespass from the building and site, reduce sky-glow to increase night sky access, improve nighttime visibility through glare reduction and reduce development impact from lighting on nocturnal environments.

Requirements

Project teams must comply with one of the two options for interior lighting AND the requirement for exterior lighting.

For Interior Lighting

OPTION 1

Reduce the input power (by automatic device) of all nonemergency interior luminaires with a direct line of sight to any openings in the envelope (translucent or transparent) by at least 50% between 11 p.m. and 5 a.m. An after-hours override may be provided by a manual or occupant-sensing device provided the override lasts no more than 30 minutes.

OR

OPTION 2

All openings in the envelope (translucent or transparent) with a direct line of sight to any nonemergency luminaires must have shielding (controlled/closed by automatic device for a resultant transmittance of less than 10% between 11 p.m. and 5 a.m.).

For Exterior Lighting

Light areas only as required for safety and comfort. Exterior lighting power densities shall not exceed those specified in ANSI/ASHRAE/IESNA Standard 90.1-2007 with Addenda 1 for the documented lighting zone. Justification shall be provided for the selected lighting zone. Lighting controls for all exterior lighting shall comply with section 9.4.1.3 of ANSI/ASHRAE/IESNA Standard 90.1- 2007, without amendments.

Note: The following areas may be excluded from credit requirements: emergency departments, including helipads, a designated parking area for night staff, a designated parking area for night visitors, pedestrian walkways, service/loading areas and associated circulation routes. Helipad areas shall be illuminated in accordance with applicable transportation requirements.

Classify the project under 1 of the following zones, as defined in IESNA RP-33, and follow all the requirements for that zone:

LZ1: Dark (developed areas within national parks, state parks, forest land and rural areas)
Design exterior lighting so that all site and building-mounted luminaires produce a maximum initial illuminance value no greater than 0.01 horizontal and vertical footcandles at the site boundary and beyond. Document that 0% of the total initial designed fixture lumens (sum total of all fixtures on site) are emitted at an angle of 90 degrees or higher from nadir (straight down).

IMPORTANT! This reference guide supplement contains only the reference guide sections that pertain to healthcare projects. Use this supplement alongside the LEED Reference Guide for Green Building Design and Construction for complete credit information. For the omitted sections, refer to the main reference guide.

LZ2: Low (primarily residential zones, neighborhood business districts, light industrial areas with limited nighttime use and residential mixed-use areas)
Design exterior lighting so that all site and building-mounted luminaires produce a maximum initial illuminance value no greater than 0.10 horizontal and vertical footcandles at the site boundary and no greater than 0.01 horizontal footcandles 10 feet beyond the site boundary. Document that no more than 2% of the total initial designed fixture lumens (sum total of all fixtures on site) are emitted at an angle of 90 degrees or higher from nadir (straight down).

LZ3: Medium (all other areas not included in LZ1, LZ2 or LZ4, such as commercial/ industrial and high-density residential)
Design exterior lighting so that all site and building-mounted luminaires produce a maximum initial illuminance value no greater than 0.20 horizontal and vertical footcandles at the site boundary and no greater than 0.01 horizontal footcandles 15 feet beyond the site. Document that no more than 5% of the total initial designed fixture lumens (sum total of all fixtures on site) are emitted at an angle of 90 degrees or higher from nadir (straight down).

LZ4: High[1] (high-activity commercial districts in major metropolitan areas)
Design exterior lighting so that all site and building-mounted luminaires produce a maximum initial illuminance value no greater than 0.60 horizontal and vertical footcandles at the site boundary and no greater than 0.01 horizontal footcandles 15 feet beyond the site. Document that no more than 10% of the total initial designed fixture lumens (sum total of all fixtures on site) are emitted at an angle of 90 degrees or higher from nadir (straight down).

LZ2, LZ3 and LZ4 - For site boundaries that abut public rights-of-way, light trespass requirements may be met relative to the curb line instead of the site boundary.

For All Zones
Illuminance generated from a single luminaire placed at the intersection of a private vehicular driveway and public roadway accessing the site is allowed to use the centerline of the public roadway as the site boundary for a length of 2 times the driveway width centered at the centerline of the driveway.

1 To be LZ4, the area must be so designated by an organization with local jurisdiction, such as the local zoning authority..

1. Benefits and Issues to Consider

Environmental Issues

Healthcare facilities with 24-7 operations, such as emergency room services, require high external lighting for the safety and security of night staff, patients, and visitors. However, these areas can be located and illuminated such that the lighting scheme does not affect other areas designed with lower lighting levels.

2. Related Credits

Coordinate control of interior perimeter lighting with occupant controllability objectives. In particular, interior light pollution reduction objectives should be balanced with patients' need to control window shades from their beds. See the following credit:

- IEQ Credit 6.1, Controllability of Systems—Lighting

Coordinate schedules for perimeter shading controls with the potential light trespass associated with designs that provide daylight and views to the outdoors from staff areas, such as nursing stations, through patient rooms, as specified in these credits:

- IEQ Credit 8.1, Daylight and Views—Daylight
- IEQ Credit 8.2, Daylight and Views—Views

Design that improves the acoustical environment in areas such as pharmacies and patient rooms can allow nighttime light transmittance through the building envelope. Project teams should therefore coordinate the design for light pollution reduction with this credit:

- IEQ Credit 2, Acoustic Environment

4. Implementation

Interior Lighting

For patient rooms, design lighting schemes that protect privacy, provide individual control over lighting levels, and also reduce light trespass through exterior glazing. Including glazing on interior corridors can allow caregivers to observe a patient without opening the door, thereby limiting noise levels inside, and allow daylight and views of nature to reach staff areas, such as nursing stations. However, unless interior shades are provided, light from staff areas will bleed to patient rooms, disturbing patients' sleeping patterns and canceling the acoustical benefit; light may even exit through the building envelope and contribute to light pollution. Consider installing automated window shades with opaque or semiopaque fabric on both external and applicable internal glazing to prevent light transmission from patient room windows. These systems should be coordinated with patient control systems, as discussed in IEQ Credit 6.1, to protect patients' privacy and sleeping patterns.

Exterior Lighting

Design exterior lighting to protect the safety and security of nighttime staff, patients, and visitors without disturbing the nocturnal habitat surrounding the facility. Consider developing a campus lighting plan to coordinate illumination of areas requiring 24-7 illumination with protecting the nocturnal environment on the remainder of the site.

Limit the size of illuminated parking areas to accommodate only the staff and visitors expected after dark. Lighting for pedestrian walkways between designated nighttime parking areas and the emergency department and staff entrances should be designed to enhance safety without contributing to light pollution.

Clearly illuminate the name of the facility and signage for the emergency department, and provide consistent lighting along driveways to guide patients and visitors.

5. Timeline and Team

Design the light pollution reduction scheme in consultation with emergency department and night-shift staff, as applicable, to ensure that those areas are compact and do not illuminate additional areas. Parking areas and pedestrian paths with necessary high levels of nighttime traffic are excluded from the exterior light pollution calculation.

6. Calculations

Exterior Sky Glow and Light Trespass

Exclude the following areas from the exterior lighting calculation: the emergency department (including helipads), a designated parking area for night staff, a designated parking area for night visitors, pedestrian walkways, service and loading areas, and associated circulation routes. If only a portion of any parking area is designated for nighttime use, only that portion may be excluded from the light pollution reduction calculation.

For additional information, see the LEED Reference Guide for Green Building Design and Construction.

7. Documentation Guidance

As a first step in preparing LEED Online documentation, work through the following measures. Refer to LEED Online for the complete descriptions of all required documentation.

Interior Lighting

- See the LEED Reference Guide for Green Building Design and Construction.

Exterior Lighting

- Develop a photometric site plan showing adherence to allowable light levels. Prepare drawings showing the areas excluded from the calculations.
- See the LEED Reference Guide for Green Building Design and Construction for additional exterior lighting documentation requirements.

12. Resources

Websites

Active Design Guidelines: Promoting Physical Activity and Health in Design (2010)
New York City Department of Design and Construction
http://www.nyc.gov/html/ddc/html/design/active_design.shtml
Design guidance at both city and building scales for creating projects that encourage physical activity.

CONNECTION TO THE NATURAL WORLD—PLACES OF RESPITE

SS CREDIT 9.1

	HEALTHCARE: NC
Credit	SS Credit 9.1
Points	1 point

Intent

To provide outdoor places of respite on the healthcare campus to connect patients, staff and visitors to the health benefits of the natural environment.

Requirements

Provide patient and visitor accessible outdoor places of respite equal to 5% of the net usable program area[1] of the building or project.

Provide additional dedicated outdoor place(s) of respite for staff equal to 2% of the net usable program area of the building or project.

Qualifying areas must meet the following requirements:

- Accessible from within the building or located within 200 feet of a building entrance or access point.
- Located where no medical intervention or direct medical care is delivered.
- Open to fresh air, the sky and the natural elements, including seasonal weather.
- Provide options for shade or indirect sun at a minimum of one seating space per 200 square feet of garden area with one wheelchair space per five seating spaces. Examples of qualifying shade structures include trellises and tree-shaded wheelchair accessible seating areas.
- Non-smoking areas in compliance with IEQ Prerequisite 2, Environmental Tobacco Smoke (ETS) Control.

In addition, qualifying areas must comply with the following:

- Interior atria, greenhouses, solaria or conditioned spaces may be used to meet up to 30% of the required area, if 90% of each qualifying space's square footage achieves a direct line of sight to unobstructed views of nature. If views of nature are exterior to the space, calculate lines of sight between 30 inches and 90 inches above the finish floor.
- Horticulture therapy and other specific clinical or special-use gardens (i.e. a cancer healing garden) unavailable to all building occupants may be used to meet up to 50% of the required area.
- Universal-access natural trails with places to pause that are available to visitors, staff and/or patients may be used to meet up to 30% of the required area, provided trail access is available within 200 feet of a building entrance.
- Provide options for shade or indirect sun at a minimum of one seating space/ 200 square feet of garden area with one wheelchair space per five seating spaces. Examples of qualifying shade structures include trellises and tree-shaded wheelchair accessible seating areas.

1 For the purposes of this credit, "net usable program area" shall be defined as the sum of all interior areas in the project available to house the project's program. Areas housing building equipment, vertical circulation and structure shall be excluded.

IMPORTANT! This reference guide supplement contains only the reference guide sections that pertain to healthcare projects. Use this supplement alongside the LEED Reference Guide for Green Building Design and Construction for complete credit information. For the omitted sections, refer to the main reference guide.

- Exterior places of respite shall comply with the 2010 FGI Guidelines for Design and Construction of Health Care Facilities (Section 1.2-6.3: Design Considerations and Requirements). Existing exterior places of respite on the hospital campus may be used to comply with this credit, provided that the location of the existing spaces meets the credit requirements.

1. Benefits and Issues to Consider

Environmental Issues

Designing healthcare facilities to incorporate nature embraces biophilia, the theory that there is an instinctive bond between human beings and living systems. Providing patients with access to nature may shorten hospital stays and reduce stress, depression, and the use of pain medication. Access to nature can also reduce stress levels in family members and staff. Although outdoor places of respite are not intended to provide direct medical care, they often complement clinical procedures by encouraging physical activity and improving a patient's outlook. Perhaps most importantly, views of and access to nature have been linked to improved patient outcomes.[2]

Most occupants of healthcare facilities are subject to physical and emotional stress. Projects that incorporate places of respite provide access to the calming forces of nature—both visually, from inside the facility, and experientially, through landscaped areas such as healing gardens and nature paths. A garden on the roof of a treatment area, for example, can provide respite for ambulatory patients and their visitors while enhancing the view from patients' rooms. Research increasingly shows that human biological cycles respond to natural cycles. In a stressful, 24-7 environment, it is critical to provide quiet areas that allow users to reconnect to the natural cycles of day and night, seasonal changes, and weather patterns.

Like landscape restoration and stormwater management practices, places of respite have programmatic and clinical justifications.

Economic Issues

Although places of respite may be more expensive to design and install than a conventional lawn, the economic benefits associated with reduced patient length of stay and staff recruitment and retention far outweigh the costs. In particular, staff-only outdoor places of respite can be highly valued by caregivers who work long hours in a fast-paced, stressful, and physically demanding environment. Planning for places of respite may increase the project's marketability to funders, thereby eliminating the cost premium.

2. Related Credits

During the site selection process, consider how a site's natural areas could be preserved or restored as outdoor places of respite, contributing to the following credits:

- SS Credit 1, Site Selection
- SS Credit 5.1, Site Development—Protect or Restore Habitat
- SS Credit 5.2, Site Development—Maximize Open Space

Integrate stormwater management and landscape designs into the design of places of respite, contributing to the following credits:

- SS Credit 6.1, Stormwater Design—Quantity Control
- SS Credit 6.2, Stormwater Design—Quality Control
- WE Credit 1, Water-Efficient Landscaping

Design for places of respite should form part of an integrated approach to designing a healing environment, contributing to the following prerequisite and credits:

- ID Prerequisite 1, Integrative Project Planning and Design
- ID Credit 3, Integrative Project Planning and Design

2 Roger Ulrich et al., A Review of the Research Literature on Evidence-Based Healthcare Design, *Health Environments Research and Design Journal* 1(3), 2008 (http://www.herdjournal.com).

- SS Credit 9.2, Connection to the Natural World—Direct Exterior Access for Patients
- IEQ Credit 2, Acoustic Environment

3. Summary of Referenced Standards

Guidelines for the Design and Construction of Health Care Facilities, 2010 Edition
Facility Guidelines Institute
http://www.fgiguidelines.org/
These guidelines establish the healthcare industry's minimum standard for good practice in design and construction. Extensive appendixes provide information about emerging design and construction trends for HVAC, waste reduction, acoustics, and other sustainability topics. The guidelines are used by 42 states as code or as a reference standard.

4. Implementation

Select appropriate locations for places of respite, taking into account the following:

- Environmental factors (e.g., prevailing winds, building orientation, views, noise).
- Programs of care (e.g., horticultural therapy).
- Needs of specific patient populations (e.g., immunosuppression, sunlight sensitivity, wayfinding and orientation, accessibility, strength and stamina, medical treatments).
- Realistic maintenance levels (e.g., proximity to regularly serviced areas, availability of waste disposal and irrigation infrastructure).
- Potential connections to nature paths or other places of respite.

Separate places of respite that are open to patients and visitors from staff-only areas. Qualifying areas should not be used for regularly scheduled physical rehabilitation.

Integrate gardens and natural environments with the facility's infection control department. This includes addressing concerns about chemical sensitivities and allergens from high-pollen plants.

If interior places of respite are identified, verify that they achieve a direct line of site to views of nature outdoors.

For dedicated protected or preserved natural site areas, see SS Credit 5.1, Site Development—Protect or Restore Habitat.

For projects attempting SS Credit 9.2, Connection to the Natural World—Direct Exterior Access for Patients, ensure that the places of respite meet the requirements for outdoor air quality specified in IEQ Credit 5, Pollutant Source Control, and are more than 100 feet from building exhaust air locations, loading docks, entrances, and roadways subject to idling vehicles.

5. Timeline and Team

Incorporating places of respite into a healthcare facility requires integrated design practices, starting at the project's inception. During visioning and schematic design, project team members, including the architect, civil engineer, landscape architect, and owner groups (particularly patient and staff representatives), should set goals for the extent and programming of places of respite. Address daylight and views in particular. Coordinate access and views to outdoor space with the design for daylit areas.

Include medical planners and architects in planning for building adjacencies and blocking and stacking. Collaborate with the structural engineer to determine the loads for accessible vegetated roofs. Involve clinical staff and infection control if therapeutic gardens are planned for the project, particularly if graywater irrigation systems are under consideration. Involve ecologists and experts in biophilia as necessary.

At the conclusion of each subsequent project phase, evaluate progress toward the team's goals.

During the design development or early construction documents phase, direct the contractor's attention to the ways that landscape protection or restoration and stormwater management practices can support places of respite.

6. Calculations

STEP 1. Calculate the project's net usable program area as outlined in ANSI/BOMA Z65.1–2010, Office Buildings: Standard Methods of Measurement (http://www.boma.org).

STEP 2. Calculate the minimum required square footage of places of respite. Use Equation 1 to calculate the total required square footage for patients' and visitors' areas. Use Equation 2 to calculate the total required square footage for staff areas.

Equation 1

$$\text{Minimum Square Footage for Patients' and Visitors' Areas} = 0.05 \times (\text{Total Net Usable Program Area})$$

Equation 2

$$\text{Minimum Square Footage for Staff Areas} = 0.02 \times (\text{Total Net Usable Program Area})$$

STEP 3. Sum the areas of places of respite for patients and visitors and for staff.

STEP 4. If indoor places of respite have a view of exterior natural areas, determine the area with a direct line of sight by totaling the regularly occupied square footage that meets the following criteria:

- In plan view, the area is within sight lines drawn from perimeter vision glazing.
- In section view, a direct sight line can be drawn from the area to perimeter vision glazing.

The line of sight may be drawn through interior glazing.

Include areas that have a direct line of sight, in plan view, to solaria, greenhouses, and similar indoor places of respite.

STEP 5. If the project includes outdoor places of respite in direct sunlight, ensure that at least one seating space per 200 square feet of respite area has options for shade or indirect sun.

- Identify the square footage of the garden area.
- Sum the number of seating spaces, including wheelchair spaces, within the area.
- Identify the seating spaces in shade or indirect sun.
- Use Equations 3 and 4 to determine compliance.

Equation 3

$$\frac{\text{(Shaded Seating Spaces)}}{\text{(Total Square Footage of Place of Respite)}} \geq 1 / 200$$

Equation 4

$$\frac{\text{(Shaded Wheelchair Seating Spaces)}}{\text{(Total Shaded Seating Spaces)}} \geq 1 / 5$$

7. Documentation Guidance

Refer to LEED Online for the complete descriptions of all required documentation.

- Prepare floor plans that show the total net usable program area of the building or project.
- Prepare site drawings that show all project outdoor places of respite, including existing places of respite, and their distances from building entrances, if applicable. Distinguish between areas accessible to patients and visitors and staff-only areas.
- If the project includes indoor places of respite, prepare floor plans and sections demonstrating that the areas included in the calculation meet the line-of-sight requirements.
- Prepare signage for wayfinding as described in the Facility Guidelines Institute's Guidelines Section 1.2-6, Design Considerations and Requirements.

8. Examples

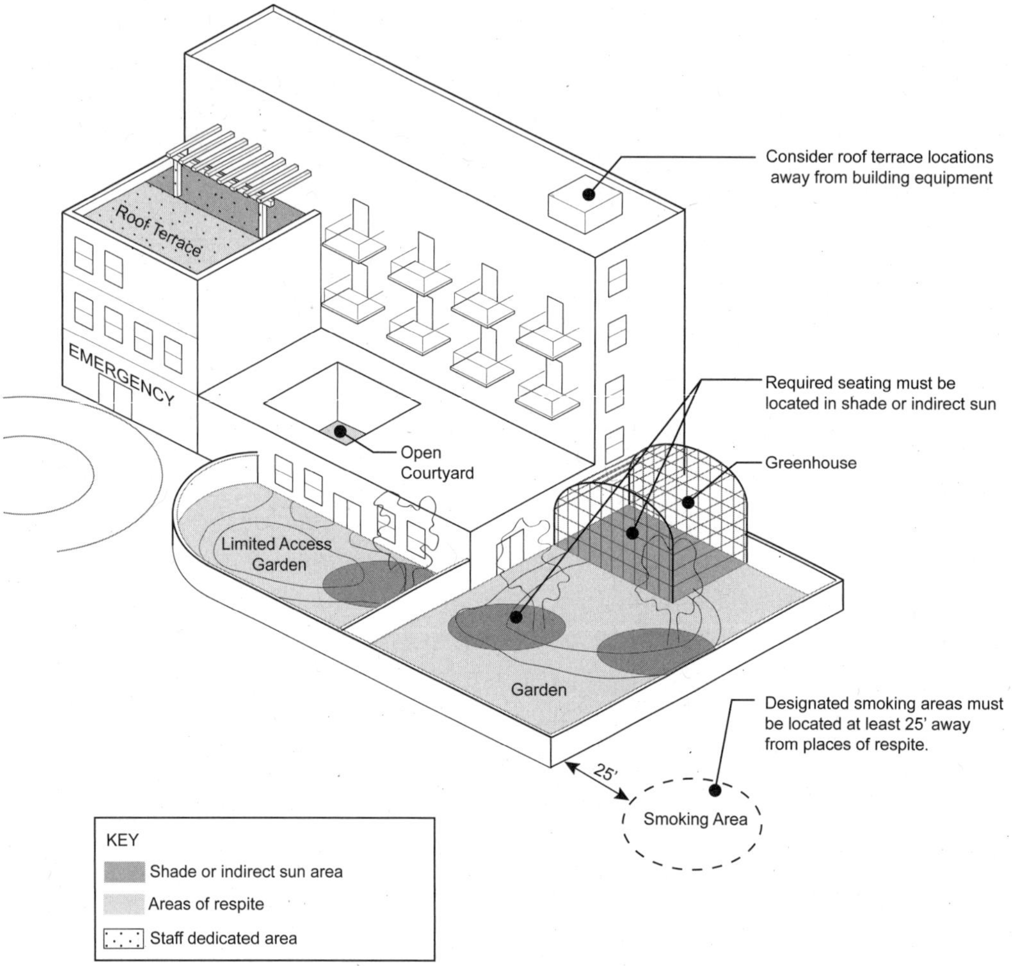

Net Usable Program Area								100,000 sq.ft.
Required Patient and Visitor Area @ 5%								5,000 sq.ft.
Required Staff dedicated Area @ 2%								2,000 sq.ft.
Outdoor Space Type	Accessibility			Shade Optional Seating			Area	
	Staf	Patient	Visitor	Required #	Design #		Allowable sq.ft	Design Area (sq.ft.)
					Regular	Wheelchair		
Garden	X	X	X	17.0	8	2	"no	3,400
Open Courtyard	/	/	/	4.0	2	1		800
Greenhouse	X	X	X	5.3	6	2	< 2,100	1,050
Roof Terrace (Staff access only)	X			12.0	8	2	> 2,000	2,400
Total				38.25	24	7		7,650

Each place of respite has area requirements as well as seating requirements. Seating is to be located in shade or indirect sun. Outdoor spaces meeting the requirements in this example project are a roof terrace accessible by staff only, a greenhouse, and one large garden. The greenhouse is a conditioned space with views to the outdoors from 90% of the space's area. The open courtyard is used for horticulture therapy for specific patients, the total for both spaces cannot exceed 50% of the required square footage. Although there is no requirement for wheelchair seating in the open courtyard, consider the user group when placing wheelchair seating.

9. Exemplary Performance

Projects may earn an Innovation in Design credit for exemplary performance by demonstrating that the project has provided 10% of the net useable program to patient and visitor places of respite AND 4% of the net useable program to staff places of respite.

10. Regional Variations

Specify and install native and adapted plants that meet the credit's sun and shade requirements.

Develop designs that appeal to the social and cultural background of patient populations to ensure that places of respite are inviting. Provide bilingual or trilingual signage as appropriate.

11. Operations and Maintenance Considerations

Work with the infection control department to minimize the entry of allergens, mold spores, and other pollutants and irritants through outdoor air intakes, operable windows, and entryways. Ensure that any vegetated roofs are designed to prevent standing water, which can breed microbes and infection vectors, such as mosquitoes.

If a portion of the site is open to the public as a park or hike-and-bike trail, coordinate protection of environmentally sensitive areas with any community stewardship programs. Many community stewardship programs have a conservation component and draw on local volunteers to restore and maintain environmentally significant areas. Coordinate operations and maintenance of natural areas that will also be used for clinical or therapeutic purposes with the appropriate clinical departments and landscape facilities staff.

12. Resources

Websites

Active Design Guidelines: Promoting Physical Activity and Health in Design (2010)
New York City Department of Design and Construction
http://www.nyc.gov/html/ddc/html/design/active_design.shtml
Design guidance at both city and building scales for creating projects that encourage physical activity.

Green Guide for Health Care Sustainable Site Design: Places of Respite Technical Brief, by Jerry Smith
http://www.gghc.org/tools.technical.php
Best practices for designing outdoor places of respite that provide direct access to nature for patients, visitors, and caregivers in healthcare environments.

Green Guide for Health Care Sustainable Site Design: Stormwater Mitigation Technical Brief, by Teresa Durkin and Marita Roos
http://www.gghc.org/tools.technical.php
Stormwater management best practices for healthcare environments.

Sustainable Sites Initiative (SITES)
http://www.sustainablesites.org/
The Sustainable Sites Initiative has developed a pilot guideline and benchmarking program to inform sustainable design, construction, and maintenance of landscapes, with and without buildings. The program's "Human Health & Well-Being" area of focus provides guidance on ways to maximize the health benefits of landscape design.

13. Definitions

biophilia the hypothesis that humans have an innate need to connect with nature.

infection control policies and procedures to minimize the risk of spreading infections through cross-contamination.

net usable program area the sum of all interior areas available to house a building's functions; areas for building equipment, vertical circulation, and structure are excluded. See ANSI/BOMA Z65.1–2010, Office Buildings: Standard Methods of Measurement (http://www.boma.org).

place of respite an area that connects "healthcare patients, visitors, and staff to health benefits of the natural environment" (Jerry Smith, Green Guide for Health Care Places of Respite Technical Brief, http://www.gghc.org/tools.technical.php).

viewshed an area of land, water, or other environmental element that is visible to the human eye from a fixed vantage point.

CONNECTION TO THE NATURAL WORLD—DIRECT EXTERIOR ACCESS FOR PATIENTS

	HEALTHCARE: NC
Credit	SS Credit 9.2
Points	1 point

Intent

To provide patients and staff with the health benefits associated with direct access to the natural environment.

Requirements

To provide direct access to an exterior courtyard, terrace, garden or balcony with a minimum area of five square feet per patient for 75% of all inpatients AND 75% of qualifying outpatients with clinical Length of Stay (LOS) greater than four hours.

- Qualifying outpatients may include outpatient renal dialysis, infusion therapies, ambulatory surgery intake and stage 2 recovery. Patients with length of stay greater than four hours, whose treatment makes them unable to move, such as emergency, stage 1 surgical recovery, and critical care may be excluded. Places of respite outside the building envelope that meet the requirements of SS Credit 9.1, Connection to the Natural World—Places of Respite, that are immediately adjacent to clinical areas or with direct access from inpatient units may be included in the calculation.
- Qualifying spaces must be designated as non-smoking and meet the requirements of IEQ Prerequisite 2, Environmental Tobacco Smoke (ETS) Control.
- Qualifying spaces must meet the requirement for outdoor air quality enumerated in IEQ Credit 5, Indoor Chemical and Pollutant Source Control, and be located more than 100 feet from building exhaust air locations, loading docks, building entrances and roadways subject to idling vehicles.

IMPORTANT! This reference guide supplement contains only the reference guide sections that pertain to healthcare projects. Use this supplement alongside the LEED Reference Guide for Green Building Design and Construction for complete credit information. For the omitted sections, refer to the main reference guide.

SS	
HEALTHCARE: NC	Credit 9.2

1. Benefits and Issues to Consider

Environmental Issues

Designing healthcare facilities to incorporate nature embraces biophilia, the theory that there is an instinctive bond between human beings and living systems. Providing patients with access to nature may shorten hospital stays and reduce stress, depression, and the use of pain medication. Access to nature can also reduce stress levels in family members and staff. Although outdoor places of respite are not intended to provide direct medical care, they often complement clinical procedures by encouraging physical activity and improving a patient's outlook. Perhaps most importantly, views of and access to nature have been linked to improved patient outcomes.[1]

All occupants of healthcare facilities are subject to physical and emotional stress. Projects that incorporate places of respite provide access to the calming forces of nature—both visually, from inside the facility, and experientially, through landscaped areas such as healing gardens and nature paths. A garden on the roof of a treatment area, for example, can provide respite for ambulatory patients and their visitors while enhancing the view from patients' rooms. Research increasingly shows that human biological cycles respond to natural cycles. In a stressful, 24-7 environment, it is critical to provide quiet areas that allow users to reconnect to the natural cycles of day and night, seasonal changes, and weather patterns.

Like landscape restoration and stormwater management practices, places of respite have programmatic and clinical justifications.

Economic Issues

Although places of respite may be more expensive to design and install than a conventional lawn, the economic benefits associated with reduced patient length of stay and staff recruitment and retention far outweigh the costs. In particular, staff-only outdoor places of respite can be highly valued by caregivers who work long hours in a fast-paced, stressful, and physically demanding environment. Planning for places of respite may increase the project's marketability to funders, thereby eliminating the cost premium.

2. Related Credits

During the site selection process, consider how a site's natural areas could be preserved or restored as outdoor places of respite, contributing to the following credits:

- SS Credit 1, Site Selection
- SS Credit 5.1, Site Development—Protect or Restore Habitat
- SS Credit 5.2, Site Development—Maximize Open Space

Integrate stormwater management and landscape designs into the design of places of respite, contributing to the following credits:

- SS Credit 6.1, Stormwater Design—Quantity Control
- SS Credit 6.2, Stormwater Design—Quality Control
- WE Credit 1, Water-Efficient Landscaping

Design for places of respite should form part of an integrated approach to designing a healing environment, contributing to the following prerequisites and credits:

- ID Prerequisite 1, Integrative Project Planning and Design

1 Roger Ulrich et al., A Review of the Research Literature on Evidence-Based Healthcare Design, Health Environments Research and Design Journal 1(3), 2008 (http://www.herdjournal.com).

- ID Credit 3, Integrative Project Planning and Design
- SS Credit 9.1, Connection to the Natural World—Places of Respite
- IEQ Credit 2, Acoustic Environment

3. Summary of Referenced Standards

There are no referenced standards for this credit.

4. Implementation

This credit encourages exterior or passively conditioned, operable greenhouse or solarium spaces in individual inpatient units, directly adjacent to qualifying outpatient clinical functions. Although circulation corridors and common sitting areas routinely used by patients may provide access, the outdoor spaces are best located adjacent to patient spaces. Access should not include public areas, such as high-traffic lobbies or parking lots.

Locate patient-accessible outdoor spaces so that they are in natural areas or offer pleasant views, preferably of places of respite and other natural site amenities. Outdoor spaces should have a direct line of sight from continually occupied staff workstations. Provide appropriate safety barriers for outdoor spaces that are on upper floors.

Provide plantings where possible. Integrate gardens and natural environments with the facility's infection control department. This includes addressing concerns about chemical sensitivities and allergens from high-pollen plants.

Provide filtered sunlight for the majority of seating and wheelchair space, plus full-sunlight areas as well as full-shade areas where possible.

Qualifying areas should not be used for regularly scheduled physical rehabilitation.

For dedicated protected or preserved natural site areas, see SS Credit 5.1, Site Development—Protect or Restore Habitat.

5. Timeline and Team

Incorporating places of respite into a healthcare facility requires integrated design practices, starting at the project's inception. During visioning and schematic design, project team members, including the architect, civil engineer, landscape architect, and owner groups (particularly patient and staff representatives), should set goals for the extent and programming of places of respite. Address daylight and views in particular. Coordinate access and views to outdoor space with the design for daylit areas.

Include medical planners and architects in planning for building adjacencies and stacking. Collaborate with the structural engineer to determine the loads for accessible vegetated roofs. Involve clinical staff and infection control if therapeutic gardens are planned for the project, particularly if graywater irrigation systems are under consideration. Involve ecologists and experts in biophilia as necessary.

At the conclusion of each subsequent project phase, evaluate progress toward the goals.

During the design development or early construction documents phase, direct the contractor's attention to the ways that landscape protection or restoration and stormwater management practices can support places of respite.

SS	
HEALTHCARE: NC	Credit 9.2

6. Calculations

STEP 1. Calculate the total number of inpatients and qualifying outpatients with clinical length of stay (LOS) greater than four hours.

STEP 2. Use Equation 1 to calculate the minimum required square footage of qualifying places of respite directly accessible to patients.

Equation 1

$$\text{Minimum Area} = \left[0.75 * (\text{Total Number of Inpatients}) + 0.75 * (\text{Total Number of Qualifying Outpatients}) \right] \times 5 \text{ sf}$$

7. Documentation Guidance

As a first step in preparing LEED Online documentation, work through the following measures. Refer to LEED Online for the complete descriptions of all required documentation.

- Prepare site drawings and floor plans that show the qualifying outdoor areas directly accessible to patients that are included in the calculation. Distinguish between inpatient areas and qualifying outpatient areas. Identify any areas that also qualify for SS Credit 9.1.
- Prepare documentation verifying that qualifying spaces meet the requirements of IEQ Prerequisite 2 and IEQ Credit 5 and are more than 100 feet from building exhaust air locations, loading docks, building entrances, and roadways with idling vehicles.

8. Examples

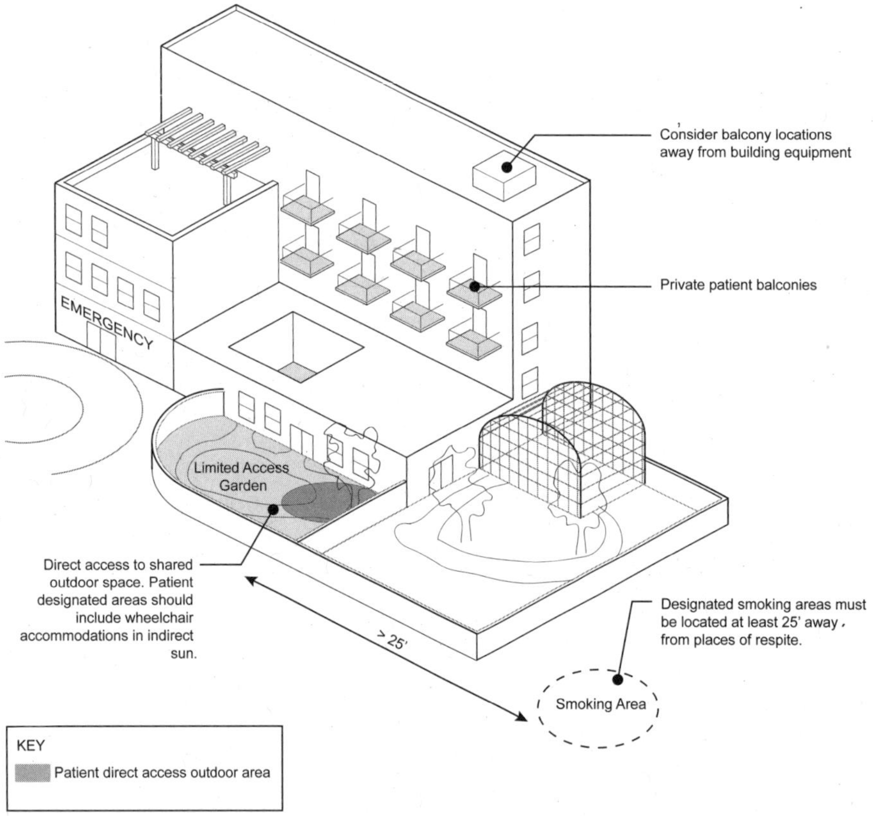

Example project:

Inpatients						
Qualifying Outdoor Space Name	Number of Patients with access		Square Footage		Meets IEQp2?	Meets IEQc5?
	Total Number of Inpatient Beds	Required # of Inpatients with Direct Outdoor Access (75% of total)	Square Footage of Qualifying Outdoor Space Included in Design	Minimum Required square footage (5 sq. ft. X # of patients)		
Private Balconies	10	8	80	50	Yes	Yes
Outpatients						
Outpatients with Length of Stay over 4 hours						
Dialysis						12
Stage 2 Recovery						8
Qualifying Outdoor Space Name	Number of Patients with access		Square Footage		Meets IEQp2?	Meets IEQc5?
	Total Number of Outpatients	Required # of Outpatients with Direct Outdoor Access (75% of total)	Square Footage of Qualifying Outdoor Space Included in Design	Minimum Required square footage (5 sq. ft. X # of patients)		
Limited Access Garden	20	15	200	150	Yes	Yes

The design satisfies the requirement for inpatients by providing balconies for 75% of the inpatients that are larger than 5 sq. ft. each and meet IEQp2 and IEQc5.
The hospital serves two types of outpatients in the rooms directly adjacent to the limited access garden. Outpatients can access this garden without having to pass through the lobby or other public areas of the facility. The garden space is larger than the amount needed to provide each outpatient with at least 5 square feet of space.

9. Exemplary Performance

Projects may earn an Innovation in Design credit for exemplary performance by demonstrating that the project has provided direct access to an exterior courtyard, terrace, garden or balcony with a minimum area of five square feet per patient for 95% of all inpatients AND 95% of qualifying outpatients with clinical Length of Stay (LOS) greater than four hours.

11. Operations and Maintenance Considerations

Coordinate hours of operation for outdoor places of respite with caregivers.

Work with the infection control department to minimize the entry of allergens, mold spores, and other pollutants and irritants through outdoor air intakes, operable windows, and entryways. Ensure that any vegetated roofs are designed to prevent standing water, which can breed microbes and infection vectors, such as mosquitoes.

Coordinate operations and maintenance of natural areas that will also be used for clinical or therapeutic purposes with the appropriate clinical departments and landscape facilities staff.

12. Resources

Websites

Active Design Guidelines: Promoting Physical Activity and Health in Design (2010)
New York City Department of Design and Construction
http://www.nyc.gov/html/ddc/html/design/active_design.shtml
Design guidance at both city and building scales for creating projects that encourage physical activity.

Green Guide for Health Care Sustainable Site Design: Places of Respite Technical Brief, by Jerry Smith
http://www.gghc.org/tools.technical.php
Best practices for designing outdoor places of respite that provide direct access to nature for patients, visitors, and caregivers in healthcare environments.

Green Guide for Health Care Sustainable Site Design: Stormwater Mitigation Technical Brief, by Teresa Durkin and Marita Roos
http://www.gghc.org/tools.technical.php
Stormwater management best practices for healthcare environments.

RIPPLE Database
The Center for Health Design
http://ripple.healthdesign.org
An open source searchable database that provides users with research, design strategies and outcomes from multiple organizations.

Sustainable Sites Initiative (**SITES**)
http://www.sustainablesites.org/
The Sustainable Sites Initiative has developed a pilot guideline and benchmarking program to inform sustainable design, construction, and maintenance of landscapes, with and without buildings. The program's "Human Health & Well-being" area of focus provides guidance on ways to maximize the health benefits of landscape design.

13. Definitions

biophilia the hypothesis that humans have an innate need to connect with nature.

direct access means of entering a space without having to leave the floor or pass through another patient's room, dedicated staff space, service or utility space, or major public space. Patients' and public circulation corridors, common sitting areas, and waiting and day space may be part of a direct access route.

infection control policies and procedures to minimize the risk of spreading infections through cross-contamination.

length of stay (**LOS**) the amount of time a person remains in a healthcare facility as an admitted patient.

place of respite an area that connects "healthcare patients, visitors, and staff to health benefits of the natural environment" (Jerry Smith, Green Guide for Health Care Places of Respite Technical Brief, http://www.gghc.org/tools.technical.php).

viewshed an area of land, water, or other environmental element that is visible to the human eye from a fixed vantage point.

WATER EFFICIENCY

OVERVIEW

Because hospitals are extremely water intensive, often ranking in the top-10 water consumers in their water utility service areas,1,2 the construction of a new hospital or healthcare campus can significantly affect the regional water supply. This is particularly true in water-scarce rural areas. In most healthcare facilities, consumption of process water (used for HVAC systems and medical processes) far exceeds the amount of water used for toilets, lavatories, and showers. One challenge, then, is to conserve water by finding efficiencies in systems as well as fixtures.

Another challenge to water conservation is that a healthcare facility's adherence to infection control guidelines, which aim to minimize the risk of cross-contamination, often involves high-volume water use. Some efficiency technologies, such as using graywater to flush toilets, are not currently allowed inside licensed healthcare facilities.

Process water strategies that have been proven effective in healthcare buildings include closed-loop cooling systems for heat-rejecting equipment, water-efficient food waste disposer systems, and recycling of process water for landscape irrigation or cooling tower blowdown. These strategies can be enhanced by a measurement and verification system that optimizes performance and minimizes the environmental and economic effects associated with water systems.

CREDIT	TITLE	HEALTHCARE
WE Prerequisite 1	Water Use Reduction	Required
WE Prerequisite 2	Minimize Potable Water Use for Medical Equipment Cooling	Required
WE Credit 1	Water Efficient Landscaping—No Potable Water Use or No Irrigation	1
WE Credit 2	Water Use Reduction—Measurement and Verification	1-2
WE Credit 3	Water Use Reduction	1-3
WE Credit 4.1	Water Use Reduction—Building Equipment	1
WE Credit 4.2	Water Use Reduction—Cooling Towers	1
WE Credit 4.3	Water Use Reduction—Food Waste Systems	1

IMPORTANT! This reference guide supplement contains only the reference guide sections that pertain to healthcare projects. Use this supplement alongside the LEED Reference Guide for Green Building Design and Construction for complete credit information. For the omitted sections, refer to the main reference guide.

1 Massachusetts Water Resources Authority, Hospital Information. Available at: http://www.mwra.state.ma.us/04water/html/bullet1.htm. Accessed October 13, 2010.

2 Pacific Institute, Waste Not, Want Not: The Potential for Urban Water Conservation in California. Released November 2003. Available at: http://www.pacinst.org/reports/urban_usage/waste_not_want_not_full_report.pdf

WATER USE REDUCTION

	HEALTHCARE: NC
Prerequisite	WE Prerequisite 1
Points	Required

Intent

To increase water efficiency within buildings to reduce the burden on municipal water supply and wastewater systems.

Requirements

Building Water Use

Employ strategies that in aggregate use 20% less water than the water use baseline calculated for the building (not including irrigation). The baseline shall meet the requirements of the Energy Policy Act (EPAct) of 1992 and subsequent rulings by the Department of Energy, requirements of the EPAct of 2005, and the plumbing code requirements as stated in the 2006 editions of the Uniform Plumbing Code or International Plumbing Code pertaining to fixture performance.[1]

Calculations are based on estimated occupant usage and must include only the following fixtures and fixture fittings (as applicable to the project scope): water closets, urinals, lavatory faucets, and pre-rinse spray valves. Fixtures used for clinical use, such as surgical scrub sinks and exam room sinks are exempt from this calculation.

Table 1: National Efficiency Baselines for Commercial and Residential Water-Using Fixtures, Fittings and Appliances (adapted from information developed and summarized by the U.S. Environmental Protection Agency Office of Water).

Fixtures, Fittings, and Appliances	Current Baseline
Toilets	1.6 gallons per flush (gpf)*
Urinals	1.0 (gpf)
Lavatory (restroom) faucets	2.2 gallons per minute (gpm) at 60 pounds per square inch (psi), private applications only (e.g., hospital patient rooms) 0.5 (gpm) at 60 (psi)** all others except private applications 0.25 gallons per cycle for metering faucets
Pre-rinse spray valves (for food service applications)	Flow rate ≤ 1.6 (gpm)
Showerheads	2.5 gpm at 80 psi per shower stall***

* EPAct 1992 standard for toilets applies to both commercial and residential models.

** In addition to EPAct requirements, the American Society of Mechanical Engineers standard for public lavatory faucets is 0.5 gpm at 60 psi (ASME A112.18.1-2005). This maximum has been incorporated into the national Uniform Plumbing Code and the International Plumbing Code.

*** Residential shower compartment (stall) in dwelling units: The total allowable flow rate from all flowing showerheads at any given time, including rain systems, waterfalls, bodysprays, bodyspas and jets, must be limited to the allowable showerhead flow rate as specified above (2.5 gpm) per shower compartment, where the floor area of the shower compartment is less than 2,500 square inches. For each increment of 2,500 square inches of floor area thereafter or part thereof, an additional showerhead with total allowable flow rate from all flowing devices equal to or less than the allowable flow rate as specified above must be allowed. Exception: Showers that emit recirculated nonpotable water originating from within the shower compartment while operating are allowed to exceed the maximum as long as the total potable water flow does not exceed the flow rate as specified above.

1 Tables adapted from information developed and summarized by the U.S. Environmental Protection Agency (EPA) Office of Water based on requirements of the Energy Policy Act (EPAct) of 1992 and subsequent rulings by the Department of Energy, requirements of the EPAct of 2005, and the plumbing code requirements as stated in the 2006 editions of the Uniform Plumbing Code or International Plumbing Code pertaining to fixture performance.

IMPORTANT! This reference guide supplement contains only the reference guide sections that pertain to healthcare projects. Use this supplement alongside the LEED Reference Guide for Green Building Design and Construction for complete credit information. For the omitted sections, refer to the main reference guide.

AND

Process Water Use

Employ strategies that in aggregate use 20% less water than the process water use baseline calculated for equipment performance requirements as listed in Table 2. Calculations are based on estimated occupant usage and shall include only the following fixtures (as applicable to the project scope): clothes washers, dishwashers, ice machines, food steamers and combination ovens.

Exemptions from calculations:

- Appliances and equipment for which water is used toward human consumption may be excluded. For example, bread misters, soda machines, coffee making machines, misters for produce and fixtures used to fill sinks for washing produce.
- Fixtures whose flow rates are regulated by health codes may be excluded from the calculation. For example, regulated medical equipment is excluded. See WE Prerequisite 2: Minimize Potable Water Use for Medical Equipment Cooling for requirements applicable to heat rejecting medical equipment.

For applicable equipment not addressed in Tables 1 or 2, additional equipment performance baseline requirements may be proposed, provided that documentation supporting the proposed benchmark or industry standard is provided.

Table 2: Equipment Performance Requirements Table

Equipment	Baseline
Commercial Clothes Washer – less than 80 lbs	9 gallon/CF/cycle
Commercial Dishwashers	
Undercounter – high temp	1.98 gallon/rack
Undercounter – low temp	1.95 gallon/rack
Door type – high temp	1.44 gallon/rack
Door type – low temp	1.85 gallon/rack
Single tank rack conveyor – high temp	1.13 gallon/rack
Single tank rack conveyor – low temp	1.23 gallon/rack
Multi-tank rack conveyor – high temp	1.1 gallon/rack
Multi-tank rack conveyor – low temp	0.99 gallon/rack
Flight type	180 gallon/hour
Commercial Ice Machines	
Water-cooled ice machine capacity < 450 lb/day	<25 gal/100 lb ice
Air-cooled ice machine capacity > 450 lb/day	<25 gal/100 lb ice
Air-cooled ice machine with remote condensing unit (w/o remote compressor) capacity < 1000 lb/day	<25 gal/100 lb ice
Air-cooled ice machine with remote condensing unit (w/o remote compressor) capacity > 1000 lb/day	<25 gal/100 lb ice
Air-cooled ice machine with remote condensing unit (with remote compressor) capacity < 934 lb/day	<25 gal/100 lb ice
Air-cooled ice machine with remote condensing unit (with remote compressor) capacity > 934 lb/day	<25 gal/100 lb ice
Air-cooled ice machine Self Contained Unit (SCU)	<25 gal/100 lb ice
Water-cooled ice machines	Must be on closed cooling loop

Equipment	Baseline
Water-cooled ice machines once through cooling	Not allowed
Food Steamers	
Boiler type steam cooker – batch cooking	8 gallon/hour/pan
Boilerless type steam cooker – high production/cook to order	8 gallon/hour/pan
Combination Oven	40 gph
Countertop or stand mounted	40 gph
Roll-in	60 gph
Other equipment	Performance baseline based on industry standards

1. Benefits and Issues to Consider

Environmental Issues

Hospitals are extremely water intensive and often rank among the top-10 water consumers in their water utility service areas.[2,3] The construction of a new hospital or healthcare campus can therefore significantly affect the regional water supply, particularly in water-scarce rural areas.

Economic Issues

In most healthcare facilities, consumption of process water (used for HVAC systems and medical processes) far exceeds the amount of water used for toilets, lavatories, and showers. Plumbing fixtures must meet stringent infection control criteria and withstand high-volume use. For example, aerators are not recommended in hospitals because they can host *Legionella* colonies.[4] As a result, many healthcare projects have not emphasized water use reduction from fixtures. However, as appropriate high-efficiency fixtures become increasingly available, the payback period for investing in domestic water efficiency is shrinking and use of these technologies has increased.

4. Implementation

This credit addresses only inside water consumption; water use for irrigation is addressed by WE Credit 1, Water-Efficient Landscaping—No Potable Water Use or No Irrigation.

Use high-efficiency fixtures (water closets and urinals) to reduce potable water demand. Consider using flow restrictors in faucets (infection control concerns may prevent use of aerators in faucets for staff hand washing). Sensor-operated faucets and flush valves can reduce the volume of water used on a per use basis but are not advisable for faucets used to fill containers, or for flush valves on toilets where bedpan washing is performed.

When selecting equipment, specify efficient fixtures for all water uses. For example, consider prerinse sprayers that reduce duration of use. WaterSense, a partnership program sponsored by EPA, helps consumers identify the most water-efficient products and programs. Some WaterSense-labeled products exceed the requirements of the Uniform Plumbing Code and the International Plumbing Code but can be installed in the same way as conventional EPAct plumbing fixtures and fittings. Consider ENERGY STAR dishwashers, icemakers, and steam cookers, which are, respectively, an average of 25%, 10%, and 90% more water efficient than standard models.

Because of infection control concerns, healthcare facilities may have limited options for using nonpotable water sources (rainwater, stormwater, air-conditioner condensate, or graywater) except as recirculating process water and irrigation. Consider the quality of any alternative source of water for each use and consult the applicable regulatory requirements. Before using nonpotable water with plumbing fixtures and fittings designed for potable water, verify with equipment manufacturers that the supply water quality is acceptable and will not compromise fixture performance or void product warranties.

Industry standards for pipe sizing have not been updated to address new water conservation measures and technologies. Reducing water flows in conventional pipes can change the fluid dynamics in the pipe system, causing less scouring (flushing) of inner pipe surfaces, creating debris deposits, and leading to clogged pipes and the growth of biofilms. Because biofilms are ideal environments for bacteria growth, reduced water flows may raise infection control concerns. Project teams should thus coordinate with the plumbing specialist to ensure that pipes are properly sized to account for water conservation measures.

2 Massachusetts Water Resources Authority, Hospital Information (http://www.mwra.state.ma.us/04water/html/bullet1.htm).
3 *Pacific Institute, Waste Not, Want Not*: The Potential for Urban Water Conservation in California, 2003 (http://www.pacinst.org/reports/urban_usage/waste_not_want_not_full_report.pdf).
4 C.A. Ciesielski et al., Role of Stagnation and Obstruction of Water Flow in Isolation of Legionella pneumophila from Hospital Plumbing, *Applied and Environmental Microbiology* 48(5): 984–87, November 1984 (http://www.ncbi.nlm.nih.gov/pmc/articles/PMC241662/).

6. Calculations

Building Water Use Calculations

For information about how to calculate full-time equivalent occupancy, fixture usage, baseline water consumption, and eligible fixtures, see the Calculations section for WE Prerequisite 1 in the LEED Reference Guide for Green Building Design and Construction.

Process Water Use Calculations

Overall water use reductions must be calculated separately for building water use, equipment regulated by EPAct 1992 (see Table 1), and commercial process water-using equipment (see Table 2). To achieve the prerequisite or earn the related credit, both building water use and commercial process water use must individually meet the credit reduction thresholds.

To determine the commercial process water savings, compare the industry standard baseline, listed in Table 2, with the design case. For equipment not listed in Table 2, teams have the option of developing a baseline using industry benchmarks or other defensible standards; otherwise, the equipment may be omitted from the calculations.

For both the baseline and the design cases, estimate the annual usage of each piece of water-using equipment. Use historical data and/or projections to establish the estimated use.

Next, compute the total annual water use for both the baseline and the design cases. Multiply the number of uses by the amount of water per use (or the duration by the flow rate) for each piece of equipment. Sum the process water use in gallons. Finally, use Equation 1 to determine the overall process water use reduction.

Equation 1

$$\text{Commercial Process Water Use Reduction} = \left[1 - \frac{\text{Annual Design Commercial Process Water Use}}{\text{Annual Baseline Commercial Process Water Use}} \right]$$

7. Documentation Guidance

As a first step in preparing to complete the LEED Online documentation requirements, work through the following measures. Refer to LEED Online for the complete descriptions of all required documentation.

- Determine the type and number of occupants.
- Retain manufacturers' data showing the water consumption rates, manufacturer, and model of each fixture, fitting, and piece of equipment.
- Define any usage groups.
- List plumbing fixtures by usage group, if applicable.
- For commercial water-using equipment not listed in Table 2, maintain documentation of the industry standard baseline water efficiency.
- For each piece of commercial water-using equipment, document assumptions about annual use.
- Complete the water use calculations.

8. Examples

A hospital kitchen has identified its process water–using equipment as follows:

- Ice machine: IMH; 18 gal/100 lbs of ice; annual use, 60,000 lbs of ice.
- Two combination ovens: boilerless; 25 gph; annual use, 2920 hours each.

- Food steamer, 6 gal/hour per pan; 6-pan capacity; annual use, 17,520 pans.
- Dishwasher: high capacity, high temperature; 0.5 gallons per rack; 1,200 racks per day; annual use, 438,000 racks.

The annual water use is determined as follows:

Baseline Case										
Ice machine use	=	default water use per unit of ice	X	annual units of ice	=	25 / 100 lbs of ice	X	60,000lbs of ice	=	15,000 gallons per year
Combination oven use	=	default water use per hour	X	annual hours or operation	=	40 gph	X	5840 hours	=	233,600 gallons per year
Steamer use	=	default water use per pan	X	annual pans	=	8 gph	X	17,520 pans	=	140,160 gallons per year
Dishwasher use	=	default water use per rack	X	annual racks	=	1.1 gal / rack	X	438,000 racks	=	481,800 gallons per year
Total annual design process water use	=	15,000	+	233,600	+	140,160	+	481,800	=	870,560 gallons
Design Case										
Ice machine use	=	default water use per unit of ice	X	annual units of ice	=	13.2 / 100 lbs of ice	X	60,000 lbs of ice	=	7,920 gallons per year
Combination oven use	=	default water use per hour	X	annual hours or operation	=	25 gph	X	5840 hours	=	146,000 gallons per year
Steamer use	=	default water use per pan	X	annual pans	=	6 gph	X	17,520 pans	=	105,120 gallons peryear
Dishwasher use	=	default water use per rack	X	annual racks	=	0.5 gal / rack	X	438,000 racks	=	219,000 gallons per year
Total annual design process water use	=	7,920	+	146,000	=	105,120	+	219,000	=	478,040 gallons

$$1 - \frac{\text{Annual Design Process Water Use}}{\text{Annual Baseline Process Water Use}} = 1 - \frac{478{,}040}{870{,}560} = 45.1\%$$

11. Operations and Maintenance Considerations

Consult with infection control staff regarding all water efficiency strategies under consideration. New fixture technologies are particularly vulnerable to failure in the healthcare setting if they are not properly cleaned and maintained. Consider installing pilot technologies in an existing facility to observe to observe how well the products withstand typical wear and tear and whether they meet infection control requirements. Gather feedback from nurses, doctors, environmental services, building maintenance, and infection control. In addition to training staff on cleaning and maintenance procedures, these demonstrations can help build support for installing water-efficient technologies in the new facility.

Coordinate with facilities staff pursuing parallel credits in LEED for Existing Buildings: Operations & Maintenance and/or the Green Guide for Health Care, Operations section. The Green Guide for Health Care, in particular, addresses the synergies among water efficiency, chemical management, and green cleaning in detail.

12. Resources

Websites

ENERGY STAR Commercial Food Service Products

http://www.energystar.gov/index.cfm?c=commercial_food_service.commercial_food_service

ENERGY STAR is a joint program of the U.S. Environmental Protection Agency and the U.S. Department of Energy that helps Americans save money and protect the environment through energy-efficient products and practices.

WaterSense

http://www.epa.gov/WaterSense/

WaterSense is an EPA-sponsored partnership program that seeks to protect the future of the nation's water supply by promoting water efficiency and enhancing the market for water-efficient products, programs, and practices.

13. Definitions

infection control policies and procedures to minimize the risk of spreading infections through cross-contamination.

process water water used for industrial processes and building systems such as cooling towers, boilers, and chillers. The term can also refer to water used in operational processes, such as dishwashing, clothes washing, and ice making.

MINIMIZE POTABLE WATER USE FOR MEDICAL EQUIPMENT COOLING

WE PREREQUISITE 2

	HEALTHCARE: NC
Prerequisite	WE Prerequisite 2
Points	Required

Intent

To minimize potable water use for medical equipment cooling.

Requirements

For ALL medical equipment in the project, demonstrate that potable water use will be minimized for equipment cooling. Potable water usage is ONLY acceptable in emergency backup systems or where local requirements mandate. The following is required:

- No potable water use for once through cooling for ALL medical equipment that rejects heat. (Note: This credit does not apply to potable water for cooling tower makeup or for other evaporative cooling systems. Refer to WE Credit 4: Process Water Use Reduction for more details.)
- Where local requirements mandate limiting the discharge temperature of fluids into the drainage system, a tempering device must be used that runs water only when the equipment discharges hot water. Alternatively, provide a thermal recovery heat exchanger that allows drained discharge water to be cooled below code-required maximum discharge temperatures while simultaneously preheating inlet makeup water or, if the fluid is steam condensate, return it to the boiler.
- An owner may elect to use potable water in an open-loop (once-through) configuration as the emergency back-up cooling system only, not as the primary cooling system. The primary cooling system in these critical applications MUST be a closed-loop system requiring no potable water usage. Such emergency back-up systems shall only be used in the event that the primary, closed-loop cooling equipment has failed, and such a failure is visually and audibly indicated at the point-of-use and alarmed at a continuously monitored location.

IMPORTANT! This reference guide supplement contains only the reference guide sections that pertain to healthcare projects. Use this supplement alongside the LEED Reference Guide for Green Building Design and Construction for complete credit information. For the omitted sections, refer to the main reference guide.

WE	
HEALTHCARE: NC	Prerequisite 2

1. Benefits and Issues to Consider

Environmental Issues

Several classes of medical equipment—sterilizers, autoclaves, ice machines, x-ray machines, MRI machines, and CT scanners—are required to cool reject water prior to discharge to the sanitary sewer to protect piping connections, but most do not require once-through potable water. Closed-loop heat rejection systems using potable water, nonpotable water, or refrigerants offer the dual benefit of increasing water efficiency and providing an opportunity to capture and reuse the waste heat generated by the medical equipment. As a result of these and other considerations, many local mandates now prohibit the use of once-through cooling, and many hospitals have begun to phase it out.

Economic Issues

First costs for a closed-loop system may be higher, but project teams will realize savings in water. Project teams should consider tying medical equipment cooling systems into the building's mechanical cooling systems to allow for reuse of reject heat.

2. Related Credits

Design choices associated with water efficiency, the capture and reuse of reject heat, the reuse of process water, system functionality, and monitoring of energy and water for medical equipment may support the following credits and prerequisite:

- WE Credit 2, Water Use Reduction—Measurement and Verification
- WE Credit 4.1, Water Use Reduction—Building Equipment
- WE Credit 4.2, Water Use Reduction—Cooling Towers
- EA Prerequisite 1, Fundamental Commissioning of Building Energy Systems
- EA Credit 3, Enhanced Commissioning

4. Implementation

This prerequisite applies to sterilizers, autoclaves, ice machines, x-ray machines, MRI machines, CT scanners, and other medical equipment whose cooling requirements involve large amounts of water and energy. Project teams should design equipment-cooling systems to limit or eliminate potable water use and to capture and reuse the reject heat generated by the equipment.

Install air-cooled or closed-loop cooling instead of open-loop (i.e., once-through) systems for medical equipment. Redundancy for cooling in critical applications may be required; as emergency backups, consider recirculcating systems, draining technology, and holding tanks as well as nonpotable water sources for air-cooled vacuum pumps and once-through cooling systems. Consider designing and installing a dedicated nonpotable water loop to serve multiple pieces of medical equipment. If discharge waste temperature is regulated, consider recovering and reusing the system's waste heat for low-temperature heating (e.g., domestic water preheating).

5. Timeline and Team

Medical equipment is often not specified until late in the design process; however, it can affect HVAC sizing as well as plumbing needs related to reject heat. Coordinate with the facility procurement department and medical planners early in the design phase to estimate medical equipment cooling needs and associated spatial requirements. Design cooling systems that balance environmental, first-cost, and operations and maintenance considerations. Confirm functionality of the systems after installation.

7. Documentation Guidance

As a first step in preparing to complete the LEED Online documentation requirements, work through the following measures. Refer to LEED Online for the complete descriptions of all required documentation.

- Retain manufacturers' data showing the heat gain for medical equipment, cooling load, and cooling system, including tempering device and thermal recovery heat exchanger, if applicable.
- For emergency backup cooling systems, retain manufacturers' data showing the alarm system and provide documentation of the emergency protocol.

9. Exemplary Performance

This prerequisite is not eligible for exemplary performance under the Innovation in Design section.

10. Regional Variations

Local mandates and codes may prohibit the use of once-through cooling for medical equipment because of harmful effects on local ecosystems.

11. Operations and Maintenance Considerations

Additional operations and maintenance may be required to optimize the functioning of closed-loop cooling systems. However, these costs may be partially offset by the water savings. Coordinate water usage and tracking with the facility's measurement and verification protocol, as described in WE Credit 2, Water Use Reduction—Measurement and Verification. Provide facilities staff with manufacturers' operations and maintenance materials.

Coordinate with facilities staff pursuing parallel credits in the Green Guide for Health Care, Operations section, which addresses the synergies between water efficiency and energy efficiency.

12. Resources

Websites

Green Guide for Health Care Reducing Potable Water Use Technical Brief, by Kim Shinn and Walt Vernon
http://www.gghc.org/tools.technical.php
Best practice guidance on potable water efficiency strategies for both domestic and process water applications.

Implementation of Once-Through Cooling Mitigation through Energy Infrastructure Planning and Procurement
California Energy Commission
http://www.energy.ca.gov/2009publications/CEC-200-2009-013/CEC-200-2009-013-SD.PDF
Information on techniques to retrofit existing plants using once-through cooling systems with alternative cooling technologies. See also http://www.energy.ca.gov/siting/once_through_cooling.html.

Top 10 Water Management Techniques
U.S. Environmental Protection Agency
http://www.epa.gov/oaintrnt/water/techniques.htm
Guidance, plus case studies of facilities that have eliminated once-through cooling.

Water and Wastewater Reuse
United Nations Environment Program
http://www.unep.or.jp/ietc/publications/water_sanitation/wastewater_reuse/booklet-wastewater_reuse.pdf
Best practices for wastewater reuse, including cooling of heat-rejecting equipment.

Water Conservation
Whole Building Design Guide
http://www.wbdg.org/resources/water_conservation.php
Best practices for reducing waste from once-through cooling systems.

13. Definitions

closed-loop cooling a system that acts as a heat sink for heat-rejecting building and medical equipment by recirculating water. Because the water is sealed within the system, some closed-loop cooling systems use nonpotable water (such as recycled process water harvested from an air handler's cooling coil condensate).

liquid-ring pump a device that uses centrifugal acceleration to propel water into a rotating ring of liquid that can be cooled via a heat exchanger or cooling tower.

nonpotable water. See **potable water.**

once-through (single-pass) cooling a system in which water from any source is used to transfer heat from equipment or processes and then discharged.

potable water water that meets or exceeds the U.S. Environmental Protection Agency's drinking water quality standards and is approved for human consumption by the state of local authorities having jurisdiction; it may be supplied from wells or municipal water systems.

process water water used for industrial processes and building systems such as cooling towers, boilers, and chillers. The term can also refer to water used in operational processes, such as dishwashing, clothes washing, and ice making.

reject heat a waste byproduct of heat exchangers, which can be found in process-intensive medical equipment.

WATER EFFICIENT LANDSCAPING—NO POTABLE WATER USE OR NO IRRIGATION

	HEALTHCARE: NC
Credit	WE Credit 1
Points	1

Intent

To eliminate the use of potable water, or other natural surface or subsurface water resources available, on or near the project site for landscape irrigation.

Requirements

OPTION 1

Use only captured rainwater, recycled wastewater, recycled graywater or water treated and conveyed by a public agency specifically for nonpotable uses for irrigation.

OR

OPTION 2

Install landscaping that does not require permanent irrigation systems. Temporary irrigation systems used for plant establishment are allowed only if removed within a period not to exceed 18 months of installation.

IMPORTANT! This reference guide supplement contains only the reference guide sections that pertain to healthcare projects. Use this supplement alongside the LEED Reference Guide for Green Building Design and Construction for complete credit information. For the omitted sections, refer to the main reference guide.

WE	
HEALTHCARE: NC	Credit 1

1. Benefits and Issues to Consider

Environmental Issues

Irrigation represents a small percentage of total water use in healthcare facilities.[1,2] In many cases, the graywater produced through building processes such as reverse osmosis and condensate from air-handling units' cooling coils is sufficient to meet the project's irrigation needs. Through an integrative design process, the project team can combine thoughtful planting choices with a process water capture-and-storage system and thereby eliminate the need for potable water for irrigation.

Economic Issues

Using covered or underground cisterns for multiple purposes (such as providing a water source for on-site decorative fountains as well as irrigation) can offset a portion of their cost. Projects on existing campuses may tie into existing irrigation infrastructure if it uses municipally reclaimed nonpotable water (i.e., purple pipe) as its water source.

2. Related Credits

Landscaping with native and adapted plants can be designed as places of respite, contributing to the following credits:

- SS Credit 9.1, Connection to the Natural World— Places of Respite
- SS Credit 9.2, Connection to the Natural World—Direct Exterior Access for Patients

4. Implementation

Healthcare projects should emphasize the creation of outdoor places of respite as a central theme of the landscape design. Prepare long-term development plans with the landscape in mind. For example, nature walks and hike-and-bike trails should serve the entire campus and, potentially, the surrounding community. To facilitate proper maintenance, demarcate greenfields, restored areas, places of respite, and other outdoor areas.

Coordinate systems to capture and reuse stormwater, cooling coil condensate, and other graywater with infection control staff and the local public health authority. Identify whether the project site can connect to a municipally reclaimed water (purple pipe) system. In all cases, coordinate the design of indoor water features with infection control and health code officials. Provide additional filtration and testing of any nonpotable water used for indoor irrigation. Health regulations may not allow graywater use for irrigation in areas that are accessible to patients.

Work with the infection control department to minimize the entry of allergens, mold spores, and other pollutants and irritants through outdoor air intakes, operable windows, and entryways. Ensure that landscaped areas, particularly vegetated roofs, are designed to prevent standing water, which can breed microbes and infection vectors, such as mosquitoes.

5. Timeline and Team

Involve clinical and infection control staff early in the design process if therapeutic gardens are planned for the project, particularly if graywater irrigation systems are under consideration.

7. Documentation Guidance

As a first step in preparing to complete the LEED Online documentation requirements, work through the following measures. Refer to LEED Online for the complete descriptions of all required documentation.

1 Massachusetts Water Resources Authority, Hospital Information (http://www.mwra.state.ma.us/04water/html/bullet1.htm, accessed October 13, 2010).

2 Pacific Institute, *Waste Not, Want Not*: The Potential for Urban Water Conservation in California, 2003 (http://www.pacinst.org/reports/urban_usage/waste_not_want_not_full_report.pdf).

- Perform calculations of the baseline and design case to show the percentage reduction in water demand, and report what portion of irrigation will come from each nonpotable source (if any).
- Prepare a landscape plan showing a planting schedule and irrigation system.
- If health regulations prohibit the use of nonpotable water for irrigation in certain areas of the healthcare campus (such as healing gardens), provide documentation of the requirements.

11. Operations and Maintenance Considerations

When integrating stormwater management into landscape design, work with the infection control department to ensure that water capture, storage, and reuse practices align with infection control policies. Coordinate operations and maintenance of landscaped areas that will also be used for clinical or therapeutic purposes with appropriate clinical departments and landscape facilities staff.

Coordinate with facilities staff pursuing parallel credits in LEED for Existing Buildings: Operations & Maintenance and/or the Green Guide for Health Care, Operations section. The Green Guide for Health Care, in particular, addresses the synergies between water efficiency in irrigation and places of respite.

If a portion of the site is open to the public as a park or hike-and-bike trail, coordinate protection of environmentally sensitive areas with any community stewardship programs. Many community stewardship programs have a conservation component and draw on local volunteers to restore and maintain environmentally significant areas.

12. Resources

Websites

Green Guide for Health Care Sustainable Site Design: Places of Respite Technical Brief, by Jerry Smith
http://www.gghc.org/tools.technical.php
Best practices for designing outdoor places of respite that provide direct access to nature for patients, visitors, and caregivers in healthcare environments.

Green Guide for Health Care Sustainable Site Design: Stormwater Mitigation Technical Brief, by Teresa Durkin and Marita Roos
http://www.gghc.org/tools.technical.php
Stormwater management best practices for healthcare environments.

RIPPLE Database
The Center for Health Design
http://ripple.healthdesign.org
An open-source, searchable database that provides users with research, design strategies, and outcomes from multiple organizations.

Sustainable Sites Initiative (SITES)
http://www.sustainablesites.org/
The Sustainable Sites Initiative has developed a pilot guideline and benchmarking program to inform sustainable design, construction, and maintenance of landscapes, with and without buildings. The program's "Human Health & Well-Being" area of focus provides guidance on ways to maximize the health benefits of landscape design.

WE	
HEALTHCARE: NC	Credit 1

13. Definitions

infection control policies and procedures to minimize the risk of spreading infections through cross-contamination.

place of respite an area that connects "healthcare patients, visitors, and staff to health benefits of the natural environment" (Jerry Smith, Green Guide for Health Care Places of Respite Technical Brief, http://www.gghc.org/tools.technical.php).

process water water used for industrial processes and building systems such as cooling towers, boilers, and chillers. The term can also refer to water used in operational processes, such as dishwashing, clothes washing, and ice making.

WATER USE REDUCTION—MEASUREMENT AND VERIFICATION

WE CREDIT 2

	HEALTHCARE: NC
Credit	WE Credit 2
Points	1-2

Intent

To provide for the ongoing accountability and optimization of building water consumption performance over time.

Requirements

Install meters to track the following water uses (as applicable to the project):

- Cooling tower make-up and blowdown
- Incoming water to the project
- Purified water system (reverse osmosis and/or de-ionized)
- Filter backwash water
- Water use in dietary department
- Water use in laundry
- Outdoor Irrigation systems
- Steam boiler systems make-up water

AND

Install meters to track the water use in any two (for one point) or any three (for two points) of the following:

- Water use in laboratory
- Water use in central sterile and processing department
- Water use in physio- and hydrotherapy treatment areas
- Water use in surgical suite
- Closed-loop hydronic systems make-up water
- Cold-water make-up for domestic hot water systems

AND

The Measurement and Verification (M&V) period shall cover a period of no less than one year of post-construction occupancy.

Use the International Performance Measurement and Verification Protocol (IPMVP) Volume 1, Concepts for Determining Energy and Water Savings, March 2002, to provide for long term continuous measurement of potable cold water uses within the facility. [Option D: Calibrated Simulation (Savings Estimation Method 2 - See Volume III, April 2003, for description of Option D, Savings Estimation Method) – for new construction; or Option B: Retrofit Measure Isolation – for renovation].

IMPORTANT! This reference guide supplement contains only the reference guide sections that pertain to healthcare projects. Use this supplement alongside the LEED Reference Guide for Green Building Design and Construction for complete credit information. For the omitted sections, refer to the main reference guide.

WE	
HEALTHCARE: NC	Credit 2

1. Benefits and Issues to Consider

Environmental Issues

Measurement and verification (M&V) of a building's water use can help optimize performance and minimize the environmental and economic effects associated with water-using systems.

Economic Issues

M&V provides building owners with the tools and data necessary to identify systems that are not functioning as expected, correct problems, tailor water efficiency efforts, and achieve optimum performance. The benefits, both short and long term, are substantial. Given water scarcity in certain areas and the likelihood that water conservation will become a greater necessity, M&V will only become more important.

The cost of continuous monitoring varies with building complexity and, in major renovations, with building system age. First costs involve instrumentation and choice of metering equipment, extent of programming of controls, and labor associated with monitoring and data processing. One cost-effective solution may be to include both water and energy M&V systems in building controls and monitoring plans.

2. Related Credits

Water use reduction, system functionality, and monitoring may support the following prerequisites and credits:

- WE Prerequisite 1, Water Use Reduction
- WE Prerequisite 2, Minimize Potable Water Use for Medical Equipment Cooling
- WE Credit 3, Water Use Reduction
- WE Credit 4.1, Water Use Reduction—Building Equipment
- WE Credit 4.2, Water Use Reduction—Cooling Towers
- EA Prerequisite 1, Fundamental Commissioning of Building Energy Systems
- EA Credit 3, Enhanced Commissioning
- EA Credit 5, Measurement and Verification

3. Summary of Referenced Standards

International Performance Measurement and Verification Protocol (IPMVP), Volume I, EVO, Concepts and Options for Determining Energy and Water Savings (March 2002)
http://www.evo-world.org

The IPMVP document provides guidance on water and energy tracking, measurement, and verification. It addresses measurement issues and factors that affect system performance. The organizational structure is the same as IPMVP Volume III. This document should be used in conjunction with Volume III to develop an M&V plan.

4. Implementation

Implementation of M&V enforces accountability and contributes to optimal performance. Design the building to include equipment to measure water consumption.

The M&V plan should be tailored to the facility, reflect the owner's preferences, and take into account the level of training of facility operators. Option B addresses M&V at the subsystem level and is frequently used in retrofit projects or smaller buildings; Option D focuses on whole-building simulation and calibration. If the team is pursuing EA Credit 5, Measurement and Verification, choose the comparable option for both water and energy. Since anomalies and other valuable findings may be revealed only in detailed information, consider selecting meters that will report frequent, fine-grain data.

Consider installing water meters in conjunction with an irrigation controller using a weather station and water sensors.

5. Timeline and Team

In design development and construction documents, specify the number and types of meters, and review metering placement and trending with the owner and controls contractor. Coordinate with the project's plumbing designer, civil engineer, landscape architect, and others to ensure proper metering types and placement.

During and after construction, set up controls and verify functionality and accuracy of the meters, recalibrating as needed. Record and report water use and identify areas for improvement. Coordinate the design of the M&V plan with the controls contractor.

6. Calculations

Refer to IPMVP Volumes I and III for detailed formulas as well as guidelines on error estimation for the various M&V methods.

Water use savings are calculated according to Equation 1.

Equation 1

$$\text{Savings} = \text{Base Year Usage} - \text{Actual Usage} \pm \text{Adjustments}$$

Adjustments are used to calibrate usage from different time periods. These adjustments often account for changes in factors such as weather, occupancy, and equipment operations.

The baseline for the calculations is based on one year of actual measurements. In the case of a retrofit complying with Option B, the base data and postretrofit data should be based on measurements. The percentage savings can be calculated according to Equation 2.

Equation 2

$$\%\ \text{Savings} = 100\% \times \frac{\text{Base Data} - \text{Postretrofit Data}}{\text{Base Data}}$$

Under Option D, an M&V plan also uses the first year of datato create the baseline. At the end of the first year, determine whether any unusual conditions may have skewed the data.

7. Documentation Guidance

As a first step in completing the LEED Online documentation requirements, work through the following measures. Refer to LEED Online for the complete descriptions of all required documentation.

- Document meter locations and types on plumbing plans and schedules.
- Document the portions of each system being measured and the meter data-recording process (intervals and schedule).
- Develop and retain an IPMVP-compliant water measurement and verification plan.

9. Exemplary Performance

Projects that track water use in more than three of the listed areas are eligible for exemplary performance under the Innovation in Design section.

10. Regional Variations

There are no regional variations for M&V methods. However, water conservation measures may vary depending on the climate.

11. Operations and Maintenance Considerations

Ensure that technical personnel are properly trained in use of M&V systems and in data interpretation especially. Give building operators the information they will need, including the baseline data and the M&V plan.

12. Resources

Websites

Green Guide for Health Care Reducing Potable Water Use Technical Brief, by Kim Shinn and Walt Vernon
http://www.gghc.org/tools.technical.php
Best practice guidance on potable water efficiency strategies for both domestic and process water applications.

National Climatic Data Center
National Oceanic and Atmospheric Administration
http://www.ncdc.noaa.gov
This website is useful for researching local climate information, such as data for energy model calibration calculations. It also includes links to state climate offices.

Top 10 Water Management Techniques
U.S. Environmental Protection Agency
http://www.epa.gov/oaintrnt/water/techniques.htm
Guidance, plus case studies of facilities that have instituted M&V plans.

Water Conservation
Whole Building Design Guide
http://www.wbdg.org/resources/water_conservation.php
Best practices for reducing waste from once-through cooling systems.

Water in a Changing World
United Nations Educational, Scientific, and Cultural Organization
http://unesdoc.unesco.org/images/0018/001808/180850e.pdf
A 2009 assessment of freshwater resources worldwide.

WaterSense
http://www.epa.gov/WaterSense/
WaterSense is an EPA-sponsored partnership program that seeks to protect the future of the nation's water supply by promoting water efficiency and enhancing the market for water-efficient products, programs, and practices.

13. Definitions

backwash water that flows backward through a system. Backwash can be used to unplug filtration media.

closed-loop cooling a system that acts as a heat sink for heat-rejecting building and medical equipment by recirculating water. Because the water is sealed within the system, some closed-loop cooling systems use nonpotable water (such as recycled process water harvested from an air handler's cooling coil condensate).

process water water used for industrial processes and building systems such as cooling towers, boilers, and chillers. The term can also refer to water used in operational processes, such as dishwashing, clothes washing, and ice making.

submeter a device that measures amount or volume (as of water or fuel) for a specific usage rather than the facility's overall usage.

verification checks and tests carried out to determine whether components, subsystems, systems, and interfaces between systems operate in accordance with the contract documents.

WATER USE REDUCTION

	HEALTHCARE: NC
Credit	WE Credit 3
Points	1-3

Intent

To maximize water efficiency within buildings to reduce the burden on municipal water supply and wastewater systems.

Requirements

Project teams earn points by achieving the following percent reductions for both building water use and process water use. The minimum water savings percentage for each point threshold is as follows:

Percentage Reduction	Points
30%	1
35%	2
40%	3

Building Water Use

Employ strategies that in aggregate use less water than the water use baseline calculated for the building (not including irrigation). The baseline shall meet the requirements of the Energy Policy Act (EPAct) of 1992 and subsequent rulings by the Department of Energy, requirements of the EPAct of 2005, and the plumbing code requirements as stated in the 2006 editions of the Uniform Plumbing Code or International Plumbing Code pertaining to fixture performance.[1]

Calculations are based on estimated occupant usage and must include only the following fixtures and fixture fittings (as applicable to the project scope): water closets, urinals, lavatory faucets, and pre-rinse spray valves. Fixtures used for clinical use, such as surgical scrub sinks and exam room sinks are exempt from this calculation.

1 Tables adapted from information developed and summarized by the U.S. Environmental Protection Agency (EPA) Office of Water based on requirements of the Energy Policy Act (EPAct) of 1992 and subsequent rulings by the Department of Energy, requirements of the EPAct of 2005, and the plumbing code requirements as stated in the 2006 editions of the Uniform Plumbing Code or International Plumbing Code pertaining to fixture performance.

IMPORTANT! This reference guide supplement contains only the reference guide sections that pertain to healthcare projects. Use this supplement alongside the LEED Reference Guide for Green Building Design and Construction for complete credit information. For the omitted sections, refer to the main reference guide.

Table 1: National Efficiency Baselines for Commercial and Residential Water-Using Fixtures, Fittings and Appliances

Fixtures, Fittings, and Appliances	Current Baseline
Toilets	1.6 gallons per flush (gpf)*
Urinals	1.0 (gpf)
Lavatory (restroom) faucets	2.2 gallons per minute (gpm) at 60 pounds per square inch (psi), private applications only (e.g., hospital patient rooms) 0.5 (gpm) at 60 (psi)** all others except private applications 0.25 gallons per cycle for metering faucets
Pre-rinse spray valves (for food service applications)	Flow rate ≤ 1.6 (gpm)
Showerheads	2.5 gpm at 80 psi per shower stall****

* EPAct 1992 standard for toilets applies to both commercial and residential models.
** In addition to EPAct requirements, the American Society of Mechanical Engineers standard for public lavatory faucets is 0.5 gpm at 60 psi (ASME A112.18.1-2005). This maximum has been incorporated into the national Uniform Plumbing Code and the International Plumbing Code.
*** EPAct 1992 standard for toilets applies to both commercial and residential models.
**** Residential shower compartment (stall) in dwelling units: The total allowable flow rate from all flowing showerheads at any given time, including rain systems, waterfalls, bodysprays, bodyspas and jets, must be limited to the allowable showerhead flow rate as specified above (2.5 gpm) per shower compartment, where the floor area of the shower compartment is less than 2,500 square inches. For each increment of 2,500 square inches of floor area thereafter or part thereof, an additional showerhead with total allowable flow rate from all flowing devices equal to or less than the allowable flow rate as specified above must be allowed. Exception: Showers that emit recirculated nonpotable water originating from within the shower compartment while operating are allowed to exceed the maximum as long as the total potable water flow does not exceed the flow rate as specified above.

AND

Process Water Use

Employ strategies that in aggregate use less water than the process water use baseline calculated for equipment performance requirements as listed in Table 2. Calculations are based on estimated occupant usage and shall include only the following fixtures (as applicable to the project scope): clothes washers, dishwashers, ice machines, food steamers and combination ovens.

Exemptions from calculations:

- Appliances and equipment for which water is used toward human consumption may be excluded. For example, bread misters, soda machines, coffee making machines, misters for produce and fixtures used to fill sinks for washing produce.
- Fixtures whose flow rates are regulated by health codes may be excluded from the calculation. For example, regulated medical equipment is excluded. See WE Prerequisite 2 for requirements applicable to heat rejecting medical equipment.

For applicable equipment not addressed in Tables 1 or 2, additional equipment performance baseline requirements may be proposed, provided that documentation supporting the proposed benchmark or industry standard is provided.

Table 2: Equipment Performance Requirements Table

Equipment	Baseline
Commercial Clothes Washer – less than 80 lbs	9 gallon/CF/cycle
Commercial Dishwashers	
Undercounter – high temp	1.98 gallon/rack
Undercounter – low temp	1.95 gallon/rack
Door type – high temp	1.44 gallon/rack
Door type – low temp	1.85 gallon/rack
Single tank rack conveyor – high temp	1.13 gallon/rack
Single tank rack conveyor – low temp	1.23 gallon/rack
Multi-tank rack conveyor – high temp	1.1 gallon/rack
Multi-tank rack conveyor – low temp	0.99 gallon/rack
Flight type	180 gallon/hour
Commercial Ice Machines	
Water-cooled ice machine capacity < 450 lb/day	<25 gal/100 lb ice
Air-cooled ice machine capacity > 450 lb/day	<25 gal/100 lb ice
Air-cooled ice machine with remote condensing unit (w/o remote compressor) capacity < 1000 lb/day	<25 gal/100 lb ice
Air-cooled ice machine with remote condensing unit (w/o remote compressor) capacity > 1000 lb/day	<25 gal/100 lb ice
Air-cooled ice machine with remote condensing unit (with remote compressor) capacity < 934 lb/day	<25 gal/100 lb ice
Air-cooled ice machine with remote condensing unit (with remote compressor) capacity > 934 lb/day	<25 gal/100 lb ice
Air-cooled ice machine Self Contained Unit (SCU)	<25 gal/100 lb ice
Water-cooled ice machines	Must be on closed cooling loop
Water-cooled ice machines once through cooling	Not allowed
Food Steamers	
Boiler type steam cooker – batch cooking	8 gallon/hour/pan
Boilerless type steam cooker – high production/cook to order	8 gallon/hour/pan
Combination Oven	40 gph
Countertop or stand mounted	40 gph
Roll-in	60 gph
Other equipment	Performance baseline based on industry standards

WE	
HEALTHCARE: NC	Credit 3

1. Benefits and Issues to Consider
Refer to the Benefits and Issues section in WE Prerequisite 1.

4. Implementation
Refer to the Implementation section in WE Prerequisite 1.

6. Calculations
Refer to the Calculations section in WE Prerequisite 1.

7. Documentation Guidance
Refer to the Documentation Guidance section in WE Prerequisite 1.

8. Examples
Refer to the Examples section in WE Prerequisite 1.

9. Exemplary Performance
Projects may earn an Innovation in Design credit for exemplary performance by demonstrating 45% reduction in projected potable water use.

11. Operations and Maintenance Considerations
Refer to the Operations and Maintenance section in WE Prerequisite 1.

12. Resources
RIPPLE Database
The Center for Health Design
http://ripple.healthdesign.org
An open-source, searchable database that provides users with research, design strategies, and outcomes from multiple organizations.

13. Definitions
process water water used for industrial processes and building systems such as cooling towers, boilers, and chillers. The term can also refer to water used in operational processes, such as dishwashing, clothes washing, and ice making.

WATER USE REDUCTION—BUILDING EQUIPMENT

WE CREDIT 4.1

	HEALTHCARE: NC
Credit	WE Credit 4.1
Points	1

Intent

To reduce or eliminate the use of potable water for non-potable process use in building system equipment.

Requirements

- Install only dry vacuum pumps for central vacuum systems and all other systems except for vacuum systems for sterilizing, which may use oil-lubricated liquid ring pumps.
- Do not install venturi vacuum systems for sterilizers.
- For air compressors, install either air cooling or closed-loop cooling, such as a cooling tower or chilled water system.
- Large frame X-ray processors and/or developers of more than 150 mm (six inches) in length or width shall use film processor water recycling units. Smaller X-ray equipment, such as a dental X-ray film processor, is exempt from this requirement.

IMPORTANT! This reference guide supplement contains only the reference guide sections that pertain to healthcare projects. Use this supplement alongside the LEED Reference Guide for Green Building Design and Construction for complete credit information. For the omitted sections, refer to the main reference guide.

1. Benefits and Issues to Consider

Environmental Issues

Avoiding the use of potable water for process water reduces the total amount withdrawn from rivers, streams, underground aquifers, and other water bodies. It also reduces energy use and chemical inputs at municipal water treatment works, as well as the energy use and greenhouse gas emissions associated with treatment and distribution. According to the U.S. Environmental Protection Agency, U.S. public water supply and treatment facilities consume about 56 billion kilowatt-hours (kWh) per year—enough electricity to power more than 5 million homes for an entire year.[1]

Economic Issues

Reasonably priced, water-efficient equipment and technologies are becoming increasingly available and can lead to substantial energy and water savings. Reductions in water usage may also help stabilize local municipal water rates.

2. Related Credits

Some water-saving technologies affect energy performance and require commissioning. These should be addressed in the measurement and verification plan and may contribute to achievement of the following prerequisites and credits:

- WE Prerequisite 1, Water Use Reduction
- WE Prerequisite 2, Minimize Potable Water Use for Medical Equipment Cooling
- WE Credit 2, Water Use Reduction—Measurement and Verification
- WE Credit 3, Water Use Reduction
- WE Credit 4.2, Water Use Reduction—Cooling Towers
- EA Prerequisite 1, Fundamental Commissioning of Building Energy Systems
- EA Credit 3, Enhanced Commissioning
- EA Credit 5, Measurement and Verification

4. Implementation

Assess the process water equipment needs for the project, based on programmatic considerations and the size of the facility. Specify high-efficiency equipment, appropriately sized, to reduce the potable water demand; consider specifying digital imaging equipment. Whenever possible, use appropriately recycled and treated wastewater for nonpotable applications. Consider onsite treatment and reuse of graywater and work with procurement to specify low- or no-water devices.

5. Timeline and Team

During design development and while preparing construction documents, the architect should coordinate with the MEP engineer, medical equipment planner, and building owner to specify efficient equipment and complete LEED documentation. Coordinate equipment specification with development of the measurement and verification plan (WE Credit 2) and commissioning plan (EA Prerequisite 1 and EA Credit 3).

6. Calculations

There are no calculations required for this credit.

1 U.S. Environmental Protection Agency, WaterSense, Benefits of Water Efficiency (http://www.epa.gov/watersense/water/benefits.htm, accessed November 2008).

7. Documentation Guidance

As a first step in preparing to complete the LEED Online documentation requirements, work through the following measures. Refer to LEED Online for the complete descriptions of all required documentation.

- Retain documents showing the manufacturer, model, and water consumption rates, water recycling rates, or vacuum system for each relevant piece of equipment.

8. Examples

There are no examples for this credit.

9. Exemplary Performance

This credit is not eligible for exemplary performance under the Innovation in Design section.

10. Regional Variations

There are no regional variations for this credit.

11. Operations and Maintenance Considerations

For water-using equipment, ensure that building operators receive any related design documents and manufacturers' specifications. If possible, submeter the water consumption of process uses, particularly for high-volume end uses, to help track water consumption and identify deviations from the specifications or other unexpected patterns that may indicate product failures or occupant misuse.

To ensure continued water savings and satisfaction for the owner and occupants, train maintenance staff in the operations and maintenance of any specialized equipment.

12. Resources

See the LEED Green Building Design and Construction Reference Guide WE Credit 4 for additional resources.

Websites

Green Guide for Health Care Reducing Potable Water Use Technical Brief, by Kim Shinn and Walt Vernon
http://www.gghc.org/tools.technical.php
Best practice guidance on potable water efficiency strategies for both domestic and process water applications.

Water in a Changing World
United Nations Educational, Scientific, and Cultural Organization
http://unesdoc.unesco.org/images/0018/001808/180850e.pdf
A 2009 assessment of freshwater resources worldwide.

13. Definitions

closed-loop cooling a system that acts as a heat sink for heat-rejecting building and medical equipment by recirculating water. Because the water is sealed within the system, some closed-loop cooling systems use nonpotable water (such as recycled process water harvested from an air handler's cooling coil condensate).

graywater untreated wastewater that has not come into contact with toilet waste. Graywater includes used water from bathtubs, showers, and bathroom washbasins, and water from clothes washers and laundry tubs. It does not include wastewater from kitchen sinks or dishwashers, unless a graywater definition established by the authority having jurisdiction in the area has precedence.

WE	
HEALTHCARE: NC	Credit 4.1

nonpotable water. See **potable water**.

potable water water that meets or exceeds EPA's drinking water quality standards and is approved for human consumption by the state of local authorities having jurisdiction; it may be supplied from wells or municipal water systems.

process water water used for industrial processes and building systems such as cooling towers, boilers, and chillers. The term can also refer to water used in operational processes, such as dishwashing, clothes washing, and ice making.

submeter a device that measures amount or volume (as of water or fuel) for a specific usage rather than the facility's overall usage.

WATER USE REDUCTION—COOLING TOWERS

	HEALTHCARE: NC
Credit	WE Credit 4.2
Points	1

Intent

To reduce or eliminate the use of potable water for non-potable process use in building system equipment.

Requirements

- Cooling towers for air conditioning systems, such as chilled water systems, shall achieve a minimum of five cycles of concentration based on a ratio of the conductivity of the water being discharged (blowdown) divided by the conductivity of the feed (makeup) water(s), or four cycles of concentration, if the makeup water hardness exceeds 200 mg/l expressed as calcium carbonate, or shall achieve a minimum discharge (blowdown) concentration of 1500 mg/L (1500 ppm) expressed as calcium carbonate, or 175 mg/L (175 ppm) of silica measured as silicon dioxide, whichever is met first.
- Cooling towers shall be equipped with makeup and blowdown meters, conductivity controllers and overflow alarms and efficient drift eliminators that reduce drift loss to less than, or equal to, 0.001% of recirculating water in a counter-flow tower or 0.005% in a cross-flow tower.
- Use no more potable water than 2.3 gallons per ton hour for cooling tower make-up.
- Projects without cooling towers are ineligible for this credit.

IMPORTANT! This reference guide supplement contains only the reference guide sections that pertain to healthcare projects. Use this supplement alongside the LEED Reference Guide for Green Building Design and Construction for complete credit information. For the omitted sections, refer to the main reference guide.

WE	
HEALTHCARE: NC	Credit 4.2

1. Benefits and Issues to Consider

Environmental Issues

Avoiding the use of potable water for process water reduces the total amount withdrawn from rivers, streams, underground aquifers, and other water bodies. It also reduces energy use and chemical inputs at municipal water treatment works, as well as the energy use and greenhouse gas emissions associated with treatment and distribution. According to the U.S. Environmental Protection Agency, U.S. public water supply and treatment facilities consume about 56 billion kilowatt-hours (kWh) per year—enough electricity to power more than 5 million homes for an entire year.[1]

Economic Issues

Reasonably priced, water-efficient equipment and technologies are becoming increasingly available and can lead to substantial energy and water savings. Reductions in water usage may also help stabilize local municipal water rates. Chemical-free water treatment may provide significant annual savings that can offset first-cost increases.

2. Related Credits

Some water-saving technologies affect energy performance and require commissioning. These should be addressed in the measurement and verification plan and may contribute to achievement of the following prerequisites and credits:

- WE Prerequisite 1, Water Use Reduction
- WE Prerequisite 2, Minimize Potable Water Use for Medical Equipment Cooling
- WE Credit 2, Water Use Reduction—Measurement and Verification
- WE Credit 3, Water Use Reduction
- WE Credit 4.1, Water Use Reduction—Building Equipment
- EA Prerequisite 1, Fundamental Commissioning of Building Energy Systems
- EA Credit 3, Enhanced Commissioning
- EA Credit 5, Measurement and Verification

3. Summary of Referenced Standard

There are no reference standards for this credit.

4. Implementation

Assess the process water equipment needs for the project, based on programmatic considerations and the size of the facility. Install cooling towers with low water needs. Reduce excessive cooling tower blowdown by installing automatic controls and conductivity meters. Consider installing a chemical-free cooling tower system. Reuse process water, such as air-handler condensate, as cooling tower blowdown makeup.

Projects without cooling towers are ineligible for this credit.

5. Timeline and Team

Early in the project, identify potential sources of process water that could be used as cooling tower blowdown makeup water and locate them so that they are convenient to the cooling tower. During design development and while preparing construction documents, the architect and MEP engineer should coordinate cooling tower requirements and water treatment options with the owner.

1 U.S. Environmental Protection Agency, WaterSense, Benefits of Water Efficiency (http://www.epa.gov/watersense/water/benefits.htm, accessed November 2008).

WE	
HEALTHCARE: NC	Credit 4.2

6. Calculations

Use Equation 1 to determine whether the cooling towers meet the credit requirements, based on cooling tower system type. The ratio of conductivity of discharged water to feed water must be at least 4 or 5, depending on the concentration of the feed water, to meet the requirements for this credit.

Equation 1

$$\text{Water Conductivity} = \frac{\text{Discharged Water}}{\text{Feed Water}}$$

7. Documentation Guidance

As a first step in preparing to complete the LEED Online documentation requirements, work through the following measures. Refer to LEED Online for the complete descriptions of all required documentation.

- Perform and retain calculations of the cycles of concentration or chemical concentration criteria per cooling tower specified.
- Retain cutsheets of the cooling tower equipment that show the details of water use and controls.

8. Examples

A closed-loop system in a cooling tower can reduce its need for potable water (Figure 1). The process fluid to be cooled is kept clean in a contaminant-free closed loop. This system uses less potable water than a traditional once-through cooling system.

Figure 1. Water Reuse in Closed-Circuit Cooling Tower

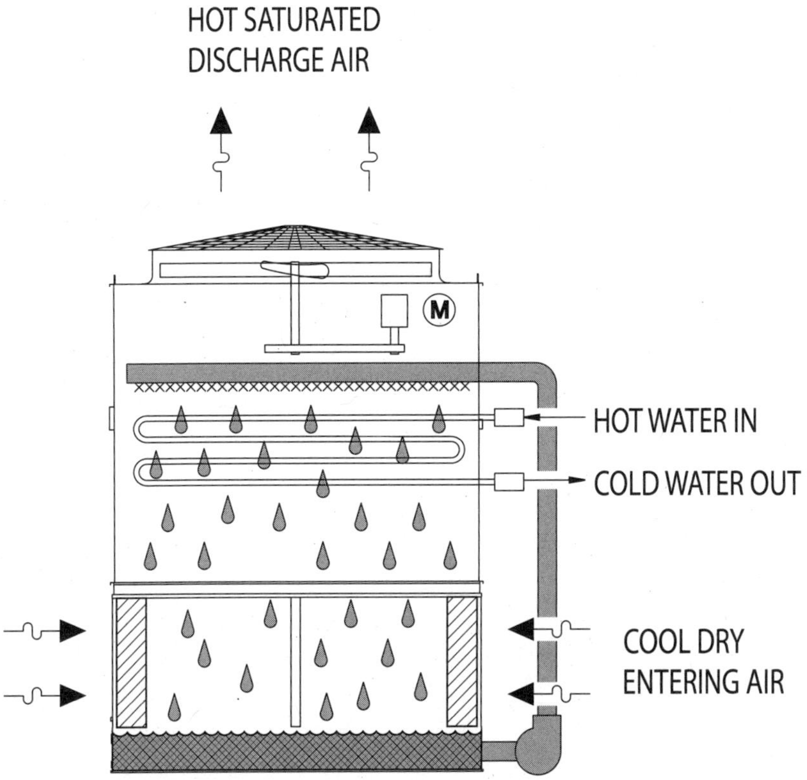

9. Exemplary Performance

This credit is not eligible for exemplary performance under the Innovation in Design section.

10. Regional Variations

There are no regional variations for this credit.

11. Operations and Maintenance Considerations

Ensure cooling towers are appropriately sized and chosen to minimize water usage. Train staff to maintain cycles of concentration and to effectively employ water treatment. Ensure functionality and calibration of automatic controls and conductivity meters.

To ensure continued water savings and satisfaction for owners and occupants, train maintenance staff in the operations and maintenance of any specialized equipment.

12. Resources

Websites

Green Guide for Health Care Reducing Potable Water Use Technical Brief, by Kim Shinn and Walt Vernon
http://www.gghc.org/tools.technical.php
Best practice guidance on potable water efficiency strategies for both domestic and process water applications.

Water in a Changing World
United Nations Educational, Scientific, and Cultural Organization
http://unesdoc.unesco.org/images/0018/001808/180850e.pdf
A 2009 assessment of freshwater resources worldwide.

13. Definitions

closed-loop cooling a system that acts as a heat sink for heat-rejecting building and medical equipment by recirculating water. Because the water is sealed within the system, some closed-loop cooling systems use nonpotable water (such as recycled process water harvested from an air handler's cooling coil condensate).

cycle of concentration the amount of solids in cooling tower recirculation compared with the amount of solids in make-up water. Cycle refers to the number of times dissolved minerals in the water are concentrated compared with makeup water, not to water flow over the tower or to on-off cycles.

nonpotable water. See **potable water**.

potable water water that meets or exceeds EPA's drinking water quality standards and is approved for human consumption by the state of local authorities having jurisdiction; it may be supplied from wells or municipal water systems.

process water water used for industrial processes and building systems such as cooling towers, boilers, and chillers. The term can also refer to water used in operational processes, such as dishwashing, clothes washing, and ice making.

WATER USE REDUCTION—FOOD WASTE SYSTEMS

	HEALTHCARE: NC
Credit	WE Credit 4.3
Points	1

Intent

To reduce or eliminate the use of potable water for non-potable process use in building system equipment.

Requirements

When a food waste disposer system is used, the following requirements must be met:

- Use cold water. (This is a common code requirement.)
- Equip systems with a load sensing device that regulates the water use to 1 gpm in a no-load situation and 3 to 8 gpm in a full-load situation.
- Automatic time shutoff that shall have a ten-minute time-out system with a push button to reactivate.

When pulpers, extractors, scrap basket or strainer-type systems are used, the following requirements must be met:

- Mechanical pulpers/extractors and mechanical scrapper systems shall use no more than 2 gpm of potable water, excluding end-of-day, wash-down cycles.
- Non-mechanical strainer (scrapper) baskets shall not be part of a flowing trough collection system connected to potable water at a rate greater than 2 gpm.
- Automatic time shutoff that shall have a ten-minute time-out system with a push button to reactivate.

IMPORTANT! This reference guide supplement contains only the reference guide sections that pertain to healthcare projects. Use this supplement alongside the LEED Reference Guide for Green Building Design and Construction for complete credit information. For the omitted sections, refer to the main reference guide.

WE	
HEALTHCARE: NC	Credit 4.3

1. Benefits and Issues to Consider

Environmental Issues

Avoiding the use of potable water for process water reduces the total amount withdrawn from rivers, streams, underground aquifers, and other water bodies. Food waste disposer systems can use a lot of potable water and increase the load on the sanitary sewer; the food waste increases the biochemical oxygen demand of the water and places an unnecessary burden on sewage treatment facilities. Water-efficient food waste systems preserve resources because less process-intensive methods can be used to treat wastewater. Food waste can be composted and used in community gardens, providing opportunities for the healthcare facility to demonstrate community stewardship.

Economic Issues

In healthcare facilities, food waste is a significant part of the waste stream. With reduced sewage volumes, water utilities can delay expansion of wastewater treatment facilities and maintain stable water prices.

2. Related Credits

Some water-saving technologies affect energy performance and require commissioning. These should be addressed in the measurement and verification plan and may contribute to achievement of the following prerequisites and credits:

- WE Prerequisite 1, Water Use Reduction
- WE Prerequisite 2, Minimize Potable Water Use for Medical Equipment Cooling
- WE Credit 2, Water Use Reduction—Measurement and Verification
- WE Credit 3, Water Use Reduction
- WE Credit 4.2, Water Use Reduction—Cooling Towers
- EA Prerequisite 1, Fundamental Commissioning of Building Energy Systems
- EA Credit 3, Enhanced Commissioning
- EA Credit 5, Measurement and Verification

4. Implementation

Coordinate with facilities staff to establish programs to compost food waste and divert used fryer oil to local biodiesel manufacturers. Use recycled and treated wastewater for nonpotable applications.

5. Timeline and Team

During design development and while preparing construction documents, the architect should coordinate with the building owner to specify efficient fixtures and appliances (such as load-sensing food disposers) and complete LEED calculations and documentation.

7. Documentation Guidance

As a first step in preparing to complete the LEED Online documentation requirements, work through the following measures. Refer to LEED Online for the complete descriptions of all required documentation.

- Retain documents showing the manufacturer, model, and water consumption rates for food waste systems.

9. Exemplary Performance

This credit is not eligible for exemplary performance under the Innovation in Design section.

10. Regional Variations

Verify food waste requirements with local authorities. Some jurisdictions do not allow the use of food waste disposer systems.

11. Operations and Maintenance Considerations

Coordinate development of food waste systems with facility staff to ensure that it meets all existing protocols. Many healthcare campuses have composting programs and fryer grease collection systems. Some composting vendors accept all food waste; others will not accept meat or dairy.

Coordinate with facilities staff pursuing parallel credits in LEED for Existing Buildings: Operations & Maintenance and/or the Green Guide for Health Care, Operations section. The Green Guide for Health Care, in particular, addresses food service in a comprehensive way, from purchasing and disposal practices to chemical management and green cleaning.

12. Resources

Websites

Food Waste
U.S. Environmental Protection Agency
http://www.epa.gov/osw/conserve/materials/organics/food/
Best practices for reducing food waste.

Waste Management, by Zhang
In B. Metz, O.R. Davidson, P.R. Bosch, R. Dave, and L.A. Meyer (eds.), *Climate Change 2007: Mitigation. Contribution of Working Group III to the Fourth Assessment Report of the Intergovernmental Panel on Climate Change* (Cambridge and New York: Cambridge University Press, 2007)
http://www.ipcc.ch/publications_and_data/publications_ipcc_fourth_assessment_report_wg3_report_mitigation_of_climate_change.htm
How management of waste, including food waste, can help mitigate greenhouse gas emissions.

13. Definitions

nonpotable water. See **potable water**.

potable water water that meets or exceeds EPA's drinking water quality standards and is approved for human consumption by the state of local authorities having jurisdiction; it may be supplied from wells or municipal water systems.

process water water used for industrial processes and building systems such as cooling towers, boilers, and chillers. The term can also refer to water used in operational processes, such as dishwashing, clothes washing, and ice making.

ENERGY AND ATMOSPHERE

OVERVIEW

According to the 2003 Commercial Building Energy Consumption Survey, healthcare facilities have the second-highest average energy usage intensities of any building type, after food service.[1] Healthcare facilities located in energy service areas dependent upon fossil fuel–burning power plants are responsible for a significant percentage of their emissions, including particulates and contaminants linked to chronic respiratory diseases. In addition to these indirect emissions, healthcare facilities can be a major source of airborne contaminants to their immediate surroundings because of their extended operation schedules, backup generators, and process boilers and heaters. Healthcare facilities that work to alleviate these problems by increasing their energy efficiency and developing low-emitting renewable energy sources have the opportunity to stand out as leaders and build public awareness around these issues.

Their consistent energy consumption 24 hours a day, seven days a week, makes many healthcare facilities, particularly inpatient hospitals, the ideal settings for combined heat and power, biomass, and geothermal. The majority of healthcare facilities in the United States are owner-occupied[2] and designed to operate for 50 or more years. As a result, they can consider energy efficiency measures and renewable energy technologies with a longer payback period than properties with a shorter lifespan. On-site renewable power generation is another viable strategy that ensures passive survivability when the electrical grid fails. In this way, hospitals can make sustainable energy strategies fundamental to their mission to protect the health and well-being of patients and staff.

CREDIT	TITLE	HEALTHCARE
EA Prerequisite 1	Fundamental Commissioning of Building Energy Systems	Required
EA Prerequisite 2	Minimum Energy Performance	Required
EA Prerequisite 3	Fundamental Refrigerant Management	Required
EA Credit 1	Optimize Energy Performance	1–24 points
EA Credit 2	On-site Renewable Energy	1–8 points
EA Credit 3	Enhanced Commissioning	1–2 points
EA Credit 4	Enhanced Refrigerant Management	1 point
EA Credit 5	Measurement and Verification	2 points
EA Credit 6	Green Power	1 point
EA Credit 7	Community Contaminant Prevention—Airborne Releases	1 point

IMPORTANT! This reference guide supplement contains only the reference guide sections that pertain to healthcare projects. Use this supplement alongside the LEED Reference Guide for Green Building Design and Construction for complete credit information. For the omitted sections, refer to the main reference guide.

1 U.S. Energy Information Administration. Commercial Buildings Energy Consumption Survey (CBECS) (http://www.eia.doe.gov/emeu/cbecs/contents.html, accessed October 13, 2010).

2 Ibid.

FUNDAMENTAL COMMISSIONING OF BUILDING ENERGY SYSTEMS

	HEALTHCARE
Prerequisite	EA Prerequisite 1
Points	Required

Intent

To verify that the project's energy-related systems are installed and calibrated to perform according to the owner's project requirements, basis of design and construction documents.

Benefits of commissioning include reduced energy use, lower operating costs, fewer contractor callbacks, better building documentation, improved occupant productivity and verification that the systems perform in accordance with the owner's project requirements.

Requirements

The following commissioning process activities must be completed by the project team:

- Designate an individual as the commissioning authority (CxA) to lead, review and oversee the completion of the commissioning process activities.
  - The CxA must have documented commissioning authority experience in at least 2 building projects.
  - The individual serving as the CxA must be independent of the project design and construction management, though the CxA may be an employee of any firm providing those services. The CxA may be a qualified employee or consultant of the owner.
  - The CxA must report results, findings and recommendations directly to the owner.
  - For projects smaller than 50,000 gross square feet, the CxA may be a qualified person on the design or construction team who has the required experience.
- The owner must document the owner's project requirements. The design team must develop the basis of design. The CxA must review these documents for clarity and completeness. The owner and design team must be responsible for updates to their respective documents.
- Develop and incorporate commissioning requirements into the construction documents.
- Develop and implement a commissioning plan.
- Verify the installation and performance of the systems to be commissioned.
- Complete a summary commissioning report.

Commissioned Systems

Commissioning process activities must be completed for the following energy-related systems, at a minimum:

- Heating, ventilating, air conditioning and refrigeration (HVAC&R) systems (mechanical and passive) and associated controls
- Lighting and daylighting controls
- Domestic hot water systems
- Renewable energy systems (e.g., wind, solar)

IMPORTANT! This reference guide supplement contains only the reference guide sections that pertain to healthcare projects. Use this supplement alongside the LEED Reference Guide for Green Building Design and Construction for complete credit information. For the omitted sections, refer to the main reference guide.

EA	
HEALTHCARE: NC	Prerequisite 1

1. Benefits and Issues to Consider

Environmental Issues

Verifying the effectiveness of a healthcare facility's ventilation and other energy-related systems directly relates to infection control effectiveness and is thus a critical component of protecting the health of patients, staff, and other occupants. Implementing a commissioning plan aligns the owner's needs with the design and construction of the facility's systems and will improve indoor environmental quality and energy performance.

Economic Issues

The extended hours of operation of healthcare facilities leaves them particularly susceptible to costs associated with malfunctioning building systems. Testing the building energy systems can help identify and remedy system issues before they create building-level operational problems. Commissioning can also significantly improve energy performance, reduce operating costs, and eliminate inefficiencies by ensuring that systems operate as intended. It has been shown to reduce a healthcare facility's energy consumption by as much as 10%.[1]

4. Implementation

Because of the complexity of most healthcare projects, the commissioning process should be led by a credentialed commissioning specialist, although hospitals and healthcare project teams with competence in design and commissioning may use in-house experts.

Individuals qualified to commission a healthcare facility should possess a high level of experience specific to the healthcare industry in the following areas:

- Energy systems design, installation and operation.
- Commissioning planning and process management.
- Hands-on field experience with energy systems performance, interaction, start-up, balancing, testing, troubleshooting, operation, and maintenance procedures.
- Energy systems automation control knowledge.

Healthcare facility owners are encouraged to consider including water-using systems as well as medical gas, medical vacuum, and sterilization systems in the scope of the commissioning plan, as appropriate. Although not required by this LEED prerequisite, expanding the scope of commissioning can deliver significant financial savings and reduce the risks of faulty infection control or equipment downtime.

13. Definitions

infection control policies and procedures to minimize the risk of spreading infections through cross-contamination.

1 Lawrence Berkeley National Laboratory, Building Commissioning: A Golden Opportunity for Reducing Energy Costs and Greenhouse Gas Emissions, 2009 (http://cx.lbl.gov/documents/2009-assessment/LBNL-Cx-Cost-Benefit.pdf).

MINIMUM ENERGY PERFORMANCE

	HEALTHCARE
Prerequisite	EA Prerequisite 2
Points	Required

Intent

To establish the minimum level of energy efficiency for the proposed building and systems to reduce environmental and economic impacts associated with excessive energy use.

Requirements

OPTION 1. Whole Building Energy Simulation

Demonstrate a 10% improvement in the proposed building performance rating for new buildings, or a 5% improvement in the proposed building performance rating for major renovations to existing buildings, compared with the baseline building performance rating.

Calculate the baseline building performance rating according to the building performance rating method in Appendix G of ANSI/ASHRAE/IESNA Standard 90.1-2007 (with errata but without addenda[1]) using a computer simulation model for the whole building project.

Appendix G of Standard 90.1-2007 requires that the energy analysis done for the building performance rating method include all energy costs associated with the building project. To achieve points using this credit, the proposed design must meet the following criteria:

- Comply with the mandatory provisions (Sections 5.4, 6.4, 7.4, 8.4, 9.4 and 10.4) in Standard 90.1-2007 (with errata but without addenda[1]).
- Include all energy costs associated with the building project.
- Compare against a baseline building that complies with Appendix G of Standard 90.1-2007 (with errata but without addenda[1]). The default process energy cost is 25% of the total energy cost for the baseline building. If the building's process energy cost is less than 25% of the baseline building energy cost, the LEED submittal must include documentation substantiating that process energy inputs are appropriate.
- Obtain an energy performance rating for estimated energy use of both the baseline and proposed design from EPA's ENERGY STAR Target Finder design tool and submit the Statement of Energy Design Intent document, generated by Target Finder, as part of the project's design submittal.

For the purpose of this analysis, process energy is considered to include, but is not limited to, office and general miscellaneous equipment, computers, elevators and escalators, kitchen cooking and refrigeration, laundry washing and drying, lighting exempt from the lighting power allowance (e.g., lighting integral to medical equipment) and other (e.g., waterfall pumps).

Regulated (non-process) energy includes lighting (for the interior, parking garage, surface parking, façade, or building grounds, etc. except as noted above), heating, ventilation and air conditioning (HVAC) (for space heating, space cooling, fans, pumps, toilet exhaust, parking garage ventilation, kitchen hood exhaust, etc.), and service water heating for domestic or space heating purposes.

1 Project teams wishing to use ASHRAE approved addenda for the purposes of this credit may do so at their discretion. Addenda must be applied consistently across all LEED credits.

IMPORTANT! This reference guide supplement contains only the reference guide sections that pertain to healthcare projects. Use this supplement alongside the LEED Reference Guide for Green Building Design and Construction for complete credit information. For the omitted sections, refer to the main reference guide.

EA PREREQUISITE 2

Process loads must be identical for both the baseline building performance rating and the proposed building performance rating. However, project teams may follow the exceptional calculation method (ANSI/ASHRAE/IESNA Standard 90.1-2007 G2.5) to document measures that reduce process loads. Documentation of process load energy savings must include a list of the assumptions made for both the base and the proposed design, and theoretical or empirical information supporting these assumptions.

Projects in California may use Title 24-2005, Part 6 in place of ANSI/ASHRAE/IESNA Standard 90.1-2007 for Option 1.

OR

OPTION 2. Prescriptive Compliance Path: ASHRAE Advanced Energy Design Guide (AEDG) for Small Hospitals and Healthcare Facilities.

Comply with the prescriptive measures of the ASHRAE Advanced Energy Design Guide for Small Hospitals and Healthcare Facilities. The following restrictions apply:

- Buildings must be 90,000 square feet or less.
- Project teams must fully comply with all applicable criteria as established in the AEDG for the climate zone in which the building is located.

OR

OPTION 3. Prescriptive Compliance Path: Prescriptive Path for Energy Improvements in Hospitals

- Buildings must be over 90,000 square feet.

1. Comply with the mandatory provisions (Sections 5.4, 6.4, 7.4, 8.4, 9.4 and 10.4) in ASHRAE Standard 90.1-2007
2. Incorporate all Energy Efficiency Measures (EEMs) listed below:
   - High Performance Windows and Glazing
   - Thermally broken metal window frames
   - U value at the center of glass < 0.29
   - Solar heat gain coefficient at the center of glass < 0.38
   - U value of the window including framing effects < 0.40
3. Lighting Power Density (LPD)
   - Reduce interior LPD a minimum of 10% below IESNA/ASHRAE Standard 90.1 -2007.
   - Reduce exterior lighting power density to 20% below IESNA/ASHRAE 90.1-2007 requirements.
4. Lighting Controls
   - Install occupancy sensor lighting controls, at a minimum, in all offices, storage areas and mechanical spaces to achieve the following lighting energy reduction:
     - Offices: 15% during the day
     - Storage: 60% during the day; 30% at night
     - Mechanical Spaces: 50% for 23 hours/day

5. The HVAC system serving all areas shall include Variable Air Volume (VAV) air handling units supplied by a central chilled water and boiler plant. In addition, provide zoning controls to maintain pressure relationships as specified in the 2010 FGI Guidelines for Design and Construction of Health Care Facilities. Zoning controls shall be used on both supply air and return/exhaust air systems.
6. Reduce fan power a minimum of 10% less than the limit under ASHRAE 90.1-2007.
7. Reduce turndown ratio on VAV boxes in accordance with ASHRAE 90.1-2007 Prescriptive Requirement 6.5.2.1.
8. Design the heating plant, including boilers and auxiliary equipment, to achieve a minimum system efficiency (BTUH output/ BTUH input) of 90%
9. Design hot and chilled water pumps (3 hp or greater) with variable speed drives and a minimum part load ratio of 30%.
10. For fans and pumps, use only motors that meet National Electrical Manufacturers' Association (NEMA) standards for premium efficiency.
11. Chillers shall operate at a maximum of 0.52 kW/ton at full load and an Integrated Part Load Value (IPLV) of 0.399 kW/ton.

1. Benefits and Issues to Consider

Economic Issues

Energy costs make up a significant portion of a facility's operating budget. Healthcare facilities have the second-highest average energy usage intensities (EUI) of any building type, after food service, because of their 24-7 operations and the electrical and space-conditioning loads associated with medical equipment, such as digitalimaging equipment and energy-intensive linear accelerators. In addition, healthcare facilities need high lighting levels for tasks and procedures and have high HVAC loads, particularly for ventilation. As a result, steps that increase the energy efficiency of a healthcare facility can have a high payback over a relatively short period.

3. Summary of Referenced Standards

Advanced Energy Design Guide (AEDG) for Small Hospitals and Healthcare Facilities
http://www.ashrae.org/publications/page/1604
The AEDG provides a simple approach for contractors and designers of small- to medium-sized acute-care, outpatient, and inpatient buildings of 90,000 square feet or less. The guide offers recommendations for achieving a target of 30% energy savings compared with equivalent facilities designed to the minimum requirements of ANSI/ASHRAE/IESNA Standard 90.1–1999.

For additional reference standards, see the LEED Reference Guide for Green Building Design and Construction, LEED for New Construction, EA Prerequisite 2.

4. Implementation

Healthcare projects that are exempted under state energy codes must still meet ANSI/ASHRAE/IESNA Standard 90.1–2007 to comply with the requirements of this prerequisite. Projects in California, although typically exempted from compliance with the state energy code's Title 24–2005, Part 6, may use it in place of ANSI/ASHRAE/IESNA Standard 90.1–2007.

A local code with demonstrated quantitative and textual equivalence to the U.S. Department of Energy standard process for commercial energy code determination may be used to satisfy this prerequisite in lieu of ANSI/ASHRAE/IESNA 90.1–2007. See http://www.energycodes.gov/implement/determinations_com.stm.

OPTION 1. WHOLE-BUILDING ENERGY SIMULATION

Establishing a baseline performance rating is the critical first step in evaluating any proposed building's performance. Healthcare facilities have special characteristics that affect the question of which heating, ventilating, and air-conditioning (HVAC) system type to use for the baseline simulation. ANSI/ASHRAE/IESNA Standard 90.1–2007, Appendix G, Section G3.1.1, reads,

> c. *If the baseline HVAC system type is 5, 6, 7, or 8, use separate single-zone systems conforming with the requirements of System 3 or System 4 (depending on building heat source) for any zones having special pressurization requirements, cross-contamination requirements, or code-required minimum circulation rates.*

In most jurisdictions, a typical hospital will qualify for this exception and thus should use system 3 or 4 (packaged single-zone rooftop systems) for the baseline simulation.

When evaluating a design that involves a district or campus thermal energy plant, see the USGBC reference document Treatment of District or Campus Thermal Energy in LEED v2 and LEED Green Building Design and Construction Reference Guide for guidance on modeling methodology and parameters.

OPTION 2. PRESCRIPTIVE COMPLIANCE PATH: Advanced Energy Design Guide for Small Hospitals and Healthcare Facilities

The Advanced Energy Design Guide for Small Hospitals and Healthcare Facilities (AEDG) represents one method to design and build energy-efficient, small healthcare buildings that use significantly less energy than those built to minimum code requirements. The document supplements existing codes with recommendations; it is not a minimum code or standard.

The healthcare facilities covered by the AEDG are smaller than 90,000 square feet and defined as follows:

- Small acute-care hospitals.
- Small inpatient community hospitals.
- Critical-access hospitals with 25 beds or fewer.
- Outpatient surgical facilities.
- Freestanding birthing centers (similar to outpatient surgical centers).
- Gastrointestinal endoscopy facilities (similar to outpatient surgical centers).
- Renal dialysis centers (similar to medical office buildings).
- Primary-care outpatient centers.
- Small primary (neighborhood) outpatient facilities.
- Freestanding outpatient diagnostic and treatment facilities.
- Freestanding urgent-care facilities.
- Medical office buildings (greater than 20,000 square feet).

The AEDG covers the design of the building envelope; fenestration; lighting systems (including electrical lights and daylighting); heating, ventilating, and air-conditioning (HVAC) systems; building automation and controls; outside air treatment; and service water heating. The recommended measures for those systems must be implemented to achieve Option 2; other measures in the guide can deliver additional savings but are not mandatory.

The AEDG provides prescriptive measures by climate zone. Select the appropriate climate zone and comply with the associated prescriptive measures.

For buildings 90,000 square feet and less in all U.S. climate zones, these measures generally improve energy efficiency by the percentage required under Option 1.

OPTION 3. PRESCRIPTIVE COMPLIANCE PATH: Prescriptive Path for Energy Improvement in Hospitals

In fall 2006 the Green Guide for Health Care began developing an alternative prescriptive path to energy improvements that would meet its requirements for energy performance credits. Through a process that included DOE-2.1E modeling, evaluation of measures for cost effectiveness, climate neutrality, and confidence of energy performance, a prescriptive package was assembled that comprised energy efficiency measures similar to the following list:

- Interior lighting power density 10% less than ASHRAE 90.1–2007.
- High-performance windows and glazing (Uwindow = 0.40; SHGCcog = 0.38).
- Occupancy sensor lighting controls for all applicable areas (including offices and storage areas).

- Central variable air volume (VAV) air-handling units using chilled and heating hot water.
- Fan power reduced 10% less than limit under ASHRAE 90.1–2007, Appendix G.
- Turn-down ratio of 30% on VAV boxes.
- Exterior lighting power density 20% less than ASHRAE 90.1–2007.
- High-efficiency boiler plant (90% thermal operating efficiency).
- Turn-down ratio of 30% for heating hot water and chilled water pumps variable-speed drives.
- High-efficiency variable-speed chillers (0.52 kW/ton at full load, and 0.40 kW/ton IPLV).
- Premium-efficiency motors for fans and pumps.

Teams pursuing the prescriptive compliance path for hospitals larger than 90,000 square feet should use the above energy efficiency measures.

For buildings larger than 90,000 square feet in all U.S. climate zones, these measures generally improve energy efficiency by the percentage required under Option 1.

10. Regional Variations

For small hospitals using Option 2, Prescriptive Compliance Path, comply with the prescriptive measures identified for the project's climate zone in the AEDG, Chapter 3.

11. Operations and Maintenance Considerations

The complexity of healthcare facility building systems, maintenance, inspections, and commissioning makes ongoing procedures essential to ensure that the building operates at the intended efficiency levels.

Hospitals typically have stringent air filtration requirements; regular inspection and replacement of filter media will reduce unnecessary fan power consumption and increase energy efficiency.

12. Resources

Websites

Energy Efficiency Commitment (E2C)
American Society of Healthcare Engineering (ASHE)
http://www.ashe.org/e2c/
A collaboration between ASHE and U.S. EPA to share best practices, cost benefit data, tools, and case studies about energy efficiency in healthcare facilities.

ENERGY STAR for Healthcare
U.S. Environmental Protection Agency
http://www.energystar.gov/index.cfm?c=healthcare.bus_healthcare
Online energy efficiency tools, such as Target Finder and Portfolio Manager, as well as case studies and best practices.

Green Guide for Health Care (GGHC)
http://gghc.org
GGHC provides high-quality resources for designing and operating hospitals and healthcare facilities to be more environmentally friendly, taking into account the design issues unique to healthcare buildings.

Green Guide for Health Care v2.2, Prescriptive Path for Energy Improvement in Hospitals
http://www.gghc.org/resources.greendesign.modelling.php
This prescriptive path, which does not involve detailed calculations or analyses, provides a sensible approach to achieving advanced levels of energy savings for facilities larger than 90,000 square feet.

RIPPLE Database
The Center for Health Design
http://ripple.healthdesign.org
An open-source, searchable database that provides users with research, design strategies, and outcomes from multiple organizations.

FUNDAMENTAL REFRIGERANT MANAGEMENT

	HEALTHCARE
Prerequisite	EA Prerequisite 3
Points	Required

Intent

To reduce stratospheric ozone depletion.

Requirements

Zero use of chlorofluorocarbon (CFC)-based refrigerants in new base building heating, ventilating, air conditioning and refrigeration (HVAC&R) systems. When reusing existing base building HVAC equipment, complete a comprehensive CFC phase-out conversion prior to project completion. Phase-out plans extending beyond the project completion date will be considered on their merits.

IMPORTANT! This reference guide supplement contains only the reference guide sections that pertain to healthcare projects. Use this supplement alongside the LEED Reference Guide for Green Building Design and Construction for complete credit information. For the omitted sections, refer to the main reference guide.

OPTIMIZE ENERGY PERFORMANCE

	HEALTHCARE
Credit	EA Credit 1
Points	1-24 points

Intent

To achieve increasing levels of energy performance beyond the prerequisite standard to reduce environmental and economic impacts associated with excessive energy use.

Requirements

Whole Building Energy Simulation (1–24 points)

Demonstrate a percentage improvement in the proposed building performance rating compared with the baseline building performance rating. Calculate the baseline building performance according to Appendix G of ANSI/ASHRAE/IESNA Standard 90.1-2007 (with errata but without addenda[1]) using a computer simulation model for the whole building project. The minimum energy cost savings percentage for each point threshold is as follows:

New Buildings	Existing Building Renovations	Points
12%	8%	1
14%	10%	2
16%	12%	3
18%	14%	5
20%	16%	7
22%	18%	9
24%	20%	11
26%	22%	13
28%	24%	14
30%	26%	15
32%	28%	16
34%	30%	17
36%	32%	18
38%	34%	19
40%	36%	20
42%	38%	21
44%	40%	22
46%	42%	23
48%	44%	24

Appendix G of Standard 90.1-2007 requires that the energy analysis done for the building performance rating method include all the energy costs associated with the building project. To achieve points under this credit, the proposed design must meet the following criteria:

- Compliance with the mandatory provisions (Sections 5.4, 6.4, 7.4, 8.4, 9.4 and 10.4) in Standard 90.1-2007 (with errata but without addenda[1]).
- Inclusion of all the energy costs within and associated with the building project.

1 Project teams wishing to use ASHRAE approved addenda for the purposes of this credit may do so at their discretion. Addenda must be applied consistently across all LEED credits.

IMPORTANT! This reference guide supplement contains only the reference guide sections that pertain to healthcare projects. Use this supplement alongside the LEED Reference Guide for Green Building Design and Construction for complete credit information. For the omitted sections, refer to the main reference guide.

- Comparison against a baseline building that complies with Appendix G of Standard 90.1-2007 (with errata but without addenda1). The default process energy cost is 25% of the total energy cost for the baseline building. If the building's process energy cost is less than 25% of the baseline building energy cost, the LEED submittal must include documentation substantiating that process energy inputs are appropriate.

For the purpose of this analysis, process energy is considered to include, but is not limited to, office and general miscellaneous equipment, computers, elevators and escalators, kitchen cooking and refrigeration, laundry washing and drying, lighting exempt from the lighting power allowance (e.g., lighting integral to medical equipment) and other (e.g., waterfall pumps).

Regulated (non-process) energy includes lighting (e.g., for the interior, parking garage, surface parking, façade, or building grounds, etc. except as noted above), heating, ventilating, and air conditioning (HVAC) (e.g., for space heating, space cooling, fans, pumps, toilet exhaust, parking garage ventilation, kitchen hood exhaust, etc.), and service water heating for domestic or space heating purposes.

For this credit, process loads must be identical for both the baseline building performance rating and the proposed building performance rating. However, project teams may follow the exceptional calculation method (ANSI/ASHRAE/IESNA Standard 90.1-2007, G2.5) to document measures that reduce process loads. Documentation of process load energy savings must include a list of the assumptions made for both the base and proposed design, and theoretical or empirical information supporting these assumptions.

Projects in California may use Title 24-2005, Part 6, in place of ANSI/ASHRAE/IESNA Standard 90.1-2007 for Option 1.

1. Benefits and Issues to Consider

Refer to the Benefits and Issues section in EA Prerequisite 2.

3. Summary of Referenced Standards

Refer to the Referenced Standards section in EA Prerequisite 2.

4. Implementation

Refer to the Implementation section in EA Prerequisite 2.

9. Exemplary Performance

Projects that demonstrate a percentage improvement in the proposed building performance rating compared with the baseline building performance rating per ASHRAE 90.1-2007 by the following minimum energy cost savings percentages will be considered for 1 additional point under the Innovation in Design category:

- New Building: 50%
- Existing Building Renovation: 46%

10. Regional Variations

Refer to the Regional Variations section in EA Prerequisite 2.

11. Operations and Maintenance Considerations

Refer to the Operations and Maintenance section in EA Prerequisite 2.

12. Resources

Refer to the Resources section in EA Prerequisite 2.

ON-SITE RENEWABLE ENERGY

EA CREDIT 2

	HEALTHCARE
Credit	EA Credit 2
Points	1-8 points

Intent

To encourage and recognize increasing levels of on-site renewable energy self-supply to reduce environmental and economic impacts associated with fossil fuel energy use.

Requirements

Use on-site renewable energy systems to offset building energy costs. Calculate project performance by expressing the energy produced by the renewable systems as a percentage of the building's annual energy cost and use the table below to determine the number of points achieved.

Use the building annual energy cost calculated in EA Credit 1: Optimize Energy Performance or the U.S. Department of Energy's Commercial Buildings Energy Consumption Survey database to determine the estimated electricity use.

The minimum renewable energy percentage for each point threshold is as follows:

Percentage Renewable Energy	Points
1%	1
3%	2
10%	5
20%	6
30%	7
40%	8

IMPORTANT! This reference guide supplement contains only the reference guide sections that pertain to healthcare projects. Use this supplement alongside the LEED Reference Guide for Green Building Design and Construction for complete credit information. For the omitted sections, refer to the main reference guide.

EA	
HEALTHCARE: NC	Credit 2

1. Benefits and Issues to Consider

Environmental Issues

On-site renewable energy generation avoids the health and environmental harms associated with combustion of fossil fuels (whether generated on- or off-site). The use of renewable energy by a healthcare facility reduces air and water pollution, benefiting all community members.

Economic Issues

On-site renewable energy generation reduces a healthcare facility's vulnerability to catastrophic events and loss of external energy sources and increases its resiliency to volatile energy costs.

9. Exemplary Performance

Projects can earn credit for exemplary performance by showing that on-site renewable energy accounts for 50% or more of the annual building energy cost.

ENHANCED COMMISSIONING

	HEALTHCARE
Credit	EA Credit 3
Points	1-2 points

Intent

To begin the commissioning process early in the design process and execute additional activities after systems performance verification is completed.

Requirements

Implement, or have a contract in place to implement, the following additional commissioning process activities in addition to the requirements of EA Prerequisite 1: Fundamental Commissioning of Building Energy Systems and in accordance with the LEED Green Building Design and Construction Reference Guide, 2009 Edition Healthcare Supplement:

OPTION 1 (1 Point)

1. Prior to the start of the construction documents phase, designate an independent commissioning authority (CxA) to lead, review and oversee the completion of all commissioning process activities. The CxA shall, at a minimum, perform Tasks 2, 3, and 6. Other team members may perform Tasks 4 and 5.
   a. The CxA must have documented commissioning authority experience in at least two building projects.
   b. The individual serving as the CxA:
      - Must be independent of the work of design and construction.
      - Must not be an employee of the design firm, though he or she may be contracted through them.
      - Must not be an employee of, or contracted through, a contractor or construction manager holding construction contracts.
      - May be a qualified employee or consultant of the owner.
   c. The CxA must report results, findings and recommendations directly to the owner.
   d. This requirement has no deviation for project size.
2. The CxA must conduct, at a minimum, one commissioning design review of the owner's project requirements, basis of design, and design documents prior to the mid-construction documents phase and back-check the review comments in the subsequent design submission.
3. The CxA must review contractor submittals applicable to systems being commissioned for compliance with the owner's project requirements and basis of design. This review must be concurrent with the review of the architect or engineer of record and submitted to the design team and the owner.
4. Develop a systems manual that provides future operating staff the information needed to understand and optimally operate the commissioned systems.
5. Verify that the requirements for training operating personnel and building occupants have been completed.

IMPORTANT! This reference guide supplement contains only the reference guide sections that pertain to healthcare projects. Use this supplement alongside the LEED Reference Guide for Green Building Design and Construction for complete credit information. For the omitted sections, refer to the main reference guide.

6. The CxA must be involved in reviewing the operation of the building with operations and maintenance (O&M) staff and occupants within 10 months after substantial completion. A plan for resolving outstanding commissioning-related issues must be included.

OPTION 2 (2 points)

Achieve OPTION 1 AND

Commission the building's thermal envelope systems in accordance with the requirements of Option 1. Commissioning of the building envelope shall be in accordance with ASHRAE Guideline 0-2005, the Commissioning Process, and National Institute of Building Sciences (NIBS) Guideline 3-2006, Exterior Enclosure Technical Requirements for the Commissioning Process.

The building thermal envelope entails all exterior wall assemblies separating a building's conditioned spaces from outdoor ambient conditions, including: roof assemblies, vapor barriers, diffusion retarders, air barrier systems, rain-screen layers, flashings, cladding and siding, windows, curtain-wall assemblies, doors, thermal bridges , and utility penetrations, such as piping, electrical conduit, duct-banks and other entry-points made for routing HVAC system components. For major renovations, substantial performance upgrades must be installed on at least 25% of the exterior envelope surface area.

In support of the process requirements in Option 1, the following sequence of steps shall be taken to ensure an effective building thermal envelope commissioning process:

- Convene meeting to review with the entire green building project team the goals and objectives of the process and coordinate/assign the related tasks.
- Conduct building thermal envelope design review.
- Develop thermal envelope commissioning work plan and schedule.
- Develop coordinated documentation plan.
- Ascertain functional performance test and inspection procedures (i.e. determine reference standards).
- Review thermal envelope components and assemblies mock-ups where relevant.
- Conduct scheduled field quality assurance inspections per work plan; document inspections.
- Inspect corrections of defects encountered during inspections.
- Prepare final report.

Note: These are typical steps, but not the only options available.

1. Benefits and Issues to Consider

EA	
HEALTHCARE: NC	Credit 3

Environmental Issues

Envelope commissioning is particularly relevant for healthcare facilities, which are high consumers of energy and place emphasis on indoor environmental quality. Condensation and water infiltration due to faulty envelope systems can lead to mold or mildew growth that can spread quickly, be difficult to remediate, and compromise air quality for occupants. Air leakage and excessive solar heat gain are common problems when envelopes are not commissioned and result in wasted HVAC energy.

A properly designed and installed building envelope with minimal air leakage is crucial to maintaining room pressurization for infection isolation. Aside from wasting energy, a leaky envelope may harm immuno-compromised patients by exposing them to bacteria and viruses from other patients, as well as pollutants and particulates from unfiltered outside air. These conditions can lengthen recovery times and increase infection rates. Envelope commissioning addresses these concerns by identifying and remediating potential problems early in the design and construction process.

Economic Issues

The envelope commissioning process may increase the project cost, and commissioning activities may lengthen construction time. However, the additional cost is generally offset by lower ongoing energy and maintenance costs. The extended operation schedules, high cooling loads, and high ventilation rates of healthcare facilities make them particularly susceptible to energy waste caused by a poorly designed or constructed building envelope. Because of this, the costs of envelope commissioning can have a shorter payback period than commissioning of other building types.

3. Summary of Referenced Standards

ASHRAE Guideline 0-2005, The Commissioning Process

American Society of Heating, Refrigerating and Air-Conditioning Engineers

http://www.ashrae.org/

ASHRAE Guideline 0-2005 provides general instructions for the commissioning of building systems and assemblies to ensure they meet the owner's project requirements. The approach can be applied to systems for new construction projects or existing buildings in need of retrocommissioning. The guideline references supplemental guidelines that provide technical information for commissioning specific systems or assemblies.

National Institute of Building Sciences (NIBS) Guideline 3-2006, Exterior Enclosure Technical Requirements for the Commissioning Process

http://www.nibs.org/

NIBS Guideline 3–2006 was developed as a joint program with ASHRAE and expands on ASHRAE Guideline 0–2005 by describing the technical requirements specific to the commissioning of building envelope systems. It provides step-by-step guidance for every phase of a project to ensure that the envelope systems meet the owner's project requirements.

4. Implementation

OPTION 1

See the LEED Green Building Design and Construction Reference Guide, LEED for New Construction, EA Credit 3.

OPTION 2

Commission the thermal envelope to ensure that it will meet the owner's project requirements.

The envelope commissioning team should review the thermal envelope design and identify elements susceptible to failure before construction begins. Based on this information, the commissioning plan and schedule should include methods for inspection, testing, and documenting results during the construction phase. For major renovation projects, substantial performance upgrades must be installed on at least 25% of the exterior envelope surface area.

Envelope components and system mock-ups to verify their performance. Factory testing of the thermal envelope is not considered sufficient for the purposes of this credit. Schedule inspections throughout construction. All inspections must be documented and any identified defects must be reinspected to verify they were corrected.

After all tests and inspections are complete, prepare a final commissioning report, to be submitted by the commissioning authority. The commissioning team should prepare an operations manual and/or provide training to ensure that building staff are knowledgeable in the operation and maintenance of the envelope systems.

5. Timeline and Team

Involve the commissioning authority in the architectural design early in the process to maximize the benefit of an envelope commissioning design review. Include the envelope commissioning team in predesign meetings so that the commissioning scope and objectives will be clearly defined.

Perform mock-up testing prior to construction to ensure any revisions to the design can be made.

6. Calculations

The envelope commissioning process depends on the systems used and the owner's project requirements. Use NIBS Guideline 3-2006 for any calculations required by the commissioning methods.

7. Documentation Guidance

As a first step in preparing to complete the LEED Online documentation requirements, work through the following measures. Refer to LEED Online for the complete descriptions of all required documentation.

For documentation guidance on Option 1, see the LEED Green Building Design and Construction Reference Guide, LEED for New Construction, EA Credit 3.

For projects pursuing Option 2, incorporate thermal envelope commissioning into the project's commissioning plan and systems list.

9. Exemplary Performance

There is no exemplary performance point available for this credit.

11. Operations and Maintenance Considerations

Coordinate with facilities staff pursuing parallel credits in LEED for Existing Buildings: Operations & Maintenance and the Green Guide for Health Care, Operations Section. The latter explores in great detail the synergies among the building envelope, integrated pest management, moisture control, and green cleaning.

12. Resources

Websites

Commissioning the Building Envelope: Surviving Hurricanes Charley, Frances, and Jeanne, by R. Bruce Parzych and David MacPhaul (National Conference on Building Commissioning, May 4–6, 2005)
http://www.peci.org/ncbc/proceedings/2005/16_Parzych_NCBC2005.pdf
A case study on a successful envelope commissioning process.

Green Guide for Health Care, Operations Section
http://www.gghc.org
Best practices and emerging solutions for healthcare operations, including waste management, environmentally preferable purchasing, integrated pest management, and green cleaning.

Retro-Commissioning & Commissioning Building Envelope Systems to Reduce Health Risks & Improve IAQ: What We Have Learned to Date
Turner Building Science, LLC
http://www.peci.org/ncbc/proceedings/2005/16_Turner_NCBC2005.pdf
Techniques for retrocommissioning and commissioning building envelope systems.

Whole Building Design Guide, HVAC Integration of the Building Envelope
http://www.wbdg.org/resources/env_hvac_integration.php
Best practice guidance on building envelope commissioning.

13. Definitions

envelope commissioning a set of essential best practices used to ensure that the building envelope as installed separates indoors and outdoors as specified in the design documents. Practices include designating an envelope commissioning authority, performing a design review, performing field tests and inspections, and completing a summary commissioning report.

retrocommissioning a set of essential best practices used to ensure that the systems in an existing building perform optimally. Practices include developing a building operating plan that identifies current operating requirements and needs, conducting tests to determine whether systems are performing in accordance with the plan, and making any necessary repairs or changes.

ENHANCED REFRIGERANT MANAGEMENT

	HEALTHCARE
Credit	EA Credit 4
Points	1 point

Intent

To reduce ozone depletion and support early compliance with the Montreal Protocol while minimizing direct contributions to climate change.

Requirements

OPTION 1

Do not use refrigerants.

OR

OPTION 2

Select refrigerants and heating, ventilation, air conditioning and refrigeration (HVAC&R) equipment that minimize or eliminate the emission of compounds that contribute to ozone depletion and climate change. The base building HVAC&R equipment must comply with the following formula, which sets a maximum threshold for the combined contributions to ozone depletion and global warming potential:

$$LCGWP + LCODP \times 10^5 \leq 100$$

Calculation definitions for LCGWP + LCODP x $10^5 \leq 100$
LCODP = [ODPr x (Lr x Life +Mr) x Rc]/Life
LCGWP = [GWPr x (Lr x Life +Mr) x Rc]/Life
LCODP: Lifecycle Ozone Depletion Potential (lb CFC 11/Ton-Year)
LCGWP: Lifecycle Direct Global Warming Potential (lb CO_2/Ton-Year)
GWPr: Global Warming Potential of Refrigerant (0 to 12,000 lb CO_2/lbr)
ODPr: Ozone Depletion Potential of Refrigerant (0 to 0.2 lb CFC 11/lbr)
Lr: Refrigerant Leakage Rate (0.5% to 2.0%; default of 2% unless otherwise demonstrated)
Mr: End-of-life Refrigerant Loss (2% to 10%; default of 10% unless otherwise demonstrated)
Rc: Refrigerant Charge (0.5 to 5.0 lbs of refrigerant per ton of gross ARI rated cooling capacity)
Life: Equipment Life (10 years; default based on equipment type, unless otherwise demonstrated)

For multiple types of equipment, a weighted average of all base building HVAC&R equipment must be calculated using the following formula:

$$\frac{\sum (LCGWP + LCODP \times 10^5) \times Qunit}{Qtotal} \leq 100$$

Calculation definitions for [$\sum$ (LCGWP + LCODP x 10^5) x Qunit] / Qtotal $\leq$ 100
Qunit = Gross ARI rated cooling capacity of an individual HVAC or refrigeration unit (Tons)
Qtotal = Total gross ARI rated cooling capacity of all HVAC or refrigeration

Small HVAC units (defined as containing less than 0.5 pounds of refrigerant) and other equipment, such as standard refrigerators, small water coolers and any other cooling

IMPORTANT! This reference guide supplement contains only the reference guide sections that pertain to healthcare projects. Use this supplement alongside the LEED Reference Guide for Green Building Design and Construction for complete credit information. For the omitted sections, refer to the main reference guide.

equipment that contains less than 0.5 pounds of refrigerant, are not considered part of the base building system and are not subject to the requirements of this credit.

Do not operate or install fire suppression systems that contain ozone-depleting substances such as CFCs, hydrochlorofluorocarbons (HCFCs) or halons.

MEASUREMENT AND VERIFICATION

	HEALTHCARE
Credit	EA Credit 5
Points	2 points

Intent

To provide for the ongoing accountability of building energy consumption over time.

Requirements

Develop and implement a Measurement and Verification (M&V) plan consistent with Option D: Calibrated Simulation (Savings Estimation Method 2) or Option B: Energy Conservation Measure Isolation, as specified in the International Performance Measurement & Verification Protocol (IPMVP) Volume III: Concepts and Options for Determining Energy Savings in New Construction, April 2003.

- The M&V period must cover at least 1 year of post-construction occupancy.
- Provide a process for corrective action if the results of the M&V plan indicate that energy savings are not being achieved.

In addition, provide evidence of the long-term M&V Plan (minimum two years after the M&V period above).

- Develop and implement a long-term M&V Plan consistent with Option B, C, or D of Volume 1 of the IPMVP: Concepts and Options for Determining Energy and Water Savings, March, 2002. The application of Volume I methods is contingent upon establishing a stable base year of operation as a result of the initial Volume III M&V period. If a stable base year cannot be established, the Volume III methods shall be continued into the long-term M&V period.

IMPORTANT! This reference guide supplement contains only the reference guide sections that pertain to healthcare projects. Use this supplement alongside the LEED Reference Guide for Green Building Design and Construction for complete credit information. For the omitted sections, refer to the main reference guide.

1. Benefits and Issues to Consider

Economic Issues

According to the 2003 Commercial Building Energy Consumption Survey, 67% of healthcare facilities in the United States are owner occupied.1 Many of these facilities are also designed to operate 50 or more years. Thus owners have the opportunity to track the performance of the building systems long after construction and ensure a return on costs associated with efficiency measures. Measurement and verification facilitates early identification of problems and promotes optimal operation and energy savings, which can help offset the additional personnel costs for retrocommissioning and monitoring.

2. Related Credits

Consider coordinated M&V plans for water and energy usage:

- WE Credit 2, Water-Use Reduction—Measurement and Verification

3. Summary of Referenced Standards

International Performance Measurement and Verification Protocol, Volume I, DOE/GO-102002-1554, Concepts and Options for Determining Energy and Water Savings, revised March 2002

http://www.evo-world.org

The nonprofit Efficiency Valuation Organization promotes a global marketplace that properly values energy and water efficiency.

Volume I describes best practices for verifying, assessing, and improving energy efficiency, water efficiency, and renewable energy projects. The protocol addresses two dimensions of energy conservation measures: savings determination techniques and disclosure techniques for third-party verification of savings. Chapter 3 describes basic concepts and methodology for determining energy or demand savings over time, including Option B (retrofit isolation), Option C (whole building), and Option D (calibrated simulation).

Volume II addresses indoor environmental quality issues associated with energy efficiency strategies.

Volume III provides guidance on application-specific M&V issues.

4. Implementation

See the LEED Green Building Design and Construction Reference Guide, EA Credit 5, for additional information about establishing an M&V plan under IPMVP, Volume III. Consider developing water and energy M&V plans in concert (see WE Credit 2, Water Use Reduction—Measurement and Verification).

Healthcare-Specific Considerations

For the corrective action process, consider installing diagnostics within the control system to alert staff to problems. Alarms may be set for the following conditions:

- Leaking valves in the cooling and heating coils within air-handling units.
- Missed economizer opportunities (e.g., faulty economizer damper controls).
- Software and manual overrides allowing equipment to operate longer than intended.
- Equipment operation during unusual circumstances (e.g., boiler on when outside air temperature exceeds 65°F).
- Anomalies in energy usage, particularly in critical patient care areas.

1 U.S. Energy Information Administration, Commercial Buildings Energy Consumption Survey (CBECS) (http://www.eia.doe.gov/emeu/cbecs/contents.html, accessed October 13, 2010).

Projects are encouraged to install submeters to monitor healthcare-specific energy loads, such as medical devices and MRIs. Identify circumstances that require data reporting in addition to systems performance monitoring. For example, a facility could establish a regular reporting cycle for critical energy-using systems but review performance trends for smaller systems on an as-needed basis. Train facilities staff on the purpose and necessary content for any regular and customized reports; training will help ensure that the first year of data establish an accurate baseline. In addition to control diagnostics, consider employing retrocommissioning services or dedicating staff to investigate increases or anomalies in energy usage.

Long-Term M&V Plan

Developing a long-term M&V plan involves the following steps:

1. Develop an M&V plan in accordance with credit requirements and establish a credible baseline case. See the LEED Green Building Design and Construction Reference Guide, EA Credit 5, for additional information.
2. Select the applicable IPMVP option (B, C, or D) to develop a long term M&V plan. Options B and D are identical in IPMVP Volume I and Volume III. Option C allows for whole-facility energy monitoring. This approach may save time but does not provide the same level of resolution as Options B and D and therefore may not provide the same cost and energy savings from early detection of problems.

   If a stable baseline case cannot be established under Step 1, continue the Volume III methods developed under the first portion of this credit.

   The long-term M&V plan should include the following elements, some of which may be carried over from the plan developed under the first part of this credit:

   - Description of each energy conservation measure and the intended metric for results.
   - Commissioning procedures for successful implementation of the energy conservation measures.
   - Scope of the plan and estimations of how external factors may affect results.
   - Documentation of the baseline year conditions and actual energy data.
   - Any planned changes, such as new occupancy schedules, as well as methods for making adjustments to the baseline.
   - Postcommissioning or retrofit period.
   - Identification of adjustments needed to establish consistent performance.
   - IPMVP option (B, C, or D) that will be used to calculate savings.
   - Data analysis procedures used in the M&V plan.
   - Metering points and simulation software and characteristics of data collection, stipulated parameters, meter type, and measurement accuracy.
   - Quality assurance procedures.
   - Specifications for data documentation and reporting.
   - Budget required to launch and to administer the M&V plan.

3. Gather energy and operating data for the baseline year, incorporating periodic commissioning activities as applicable to ensure that equipment continues to function as designed.
4. Compute, report, and document energy savings in accordance with the M&V plan. Ensure that measurements are collected on a regular basis and archived for future reference. Consider using a third party to verify the results of the calculated savings.

5. Timeline and Team

This credit extends the M&V period two years beyond the requirements for the corresponding credit in New Construction credit. It is therefore necessary to coordinate development and implementation of the plan with facilities staff, particularly the facility or campus energy manager.

7. Documentation Guidance

As a first step in preparing to complete the LEED Online documentation requirements, work through the following measures. Refer to LEED Online for the complete descriptions of all required documentation.

- Develop an IPMVP-compliant measurement and verification plan.
- Diagram the locations of any meters needed for measurement and update as necessary.

11. Operations and Maintenance Considerations

Coordinate with facilities staff pursuing parallel credits in LEED for Existing Buildings: Operations & Maintenance or the Green Guide for Health Care, Operations section.

13. Definitions

retrocommissioning a set of essential best practices used to ensure that the systems in an existing building perform optimally. Practices include developing a building operating plan that identifies current operating requirements and needs, conducting tests to determine whether systems are performing in accordance with the plan, and making any necessary repairs or changes.

GREEN POWER

	HEALTHCARE
Credit	EA Credit 6
Points	1 point

Intent

To encourage the development and use of grid-source, renewable energy technologies on a net zero pollution basis.

Requirements

Engage in at least a 2-year renewable energy contract to provide at least 35% of the building's electricity from renewable sources, as defined by the Center for Resource Solutions' Green-e Energy product certification requirements.

All purchases of green power shall be based on the quantity of energy consumed, not the cost.

OPTION 1. Determine Baseline Electricity Use

Use the annual electricity consumption from the results of EA Credit 1: Optimize Energy Performance.

OR

OPTION 2. Estimate Baseline Electricity Use

Use the U.S. Department of Energy's Commercial Buildings Energy Consumption Survey database to determine the estimated electricity use.

IMPORTANT! This reference guide supplement contains only the reference guide sections that pertain to healthcare projects. Use this supplement alongside the LEED Reference Guide for Green Building Design and Construction for complete credit information. For the omitted sections, refer to the main reference guide.

COMMUNITY CONTAMINANT PREVENTION—AIRBORNE RELEASES

HEALTHCARE	
Credit	EA Credit 7
Points	1 point

Intent

To prevent contaminant releases to air from products of combustion.

Requirements

Meet California South Coast Air Quality Management District standards for all products of combustion. Do not exceed the emission limits below for products of combustion, as outlined in the following California South Coast Air Quality Management District Rules:

- 1110.2 (Amended February 1, 2008), Emissions from Gaseous- and Liquid-Fueled Internal Combustion Engines
- 1111 (Amended July 8, 1983), NOx Emissions from Natural-Gas-Fired, Fan-Type Central Furnaces
- 1121 (Amended September 3, 2004) Control of Nitrogen Oxides from Residential Type, Natural Gas-Fired Water Heaters
- 1146 (Amended November 17, 2000), Emissions of Oxides of Nitrogen from Industrial, Institutional, and Commercial Boilers, Steam Generators, and Process Heaters
- 1146.1 (Amended May 13, 1994), Emissions of Oxides of Nitrogen from Small Industrial, Institutional, and Commercial Boilers, Steam Generators, and Process Heaters
- 1146.2 (Amended May 5, 2006), Emissions of Oxides of Nitrogen from Large Water Heaters and Small Boilers and Process Heaters

Equipment Types	Oxides of Nitrogen (NO_x)	Volatile Organic Compounds (VOCs)	Carbon Monoxide (CO)
Gaseous and Liquid-Fueled Stationary Engines – Emergency or Standby Power Uses	11[1]ppm	30[1,2]ppm	70[1]ppm
Gaseous and Liquid-Fueled Stationary Engines – Non-Emergency and Non-Standby Power Uses[5]	0.070 lbs/MW-hr[3]	0.10 lbs/MW-hr[4]	0.20 lbs/MW-hr[3]
Landfill and Digestor Gas-Fired Stationary Engines	bhp>500: ppm = 36 x ECF[1,6]	Landfill Gas: 40[1,2] Digestor Gas: 250 x ECF[1,2,6]	2,000 ppm[1]
Natural-Gas-Fired, Fan-Type Central Furnaces (heating only with input rate less than 175,000 BTUH, or heating and cooling with cooling rate of less than 65,000 BTUH)	40 nanograms (calculated as NO_2) per joule of useful heat delivered to the heated space		
Residential Type, Natural Gas-Fired Water Heaters	15 ppm[7] or 10 nanograms (calculated as NO_2) per joule of heat output		

IMPORTANT! This reference guide supplement contains only the reference guide sections that pertain to healthcare projects. Use this supplement alongside the LEED Reference Guide for Green Building Design and Construction for complete credit information. For the omitted sections, refer to the main reference guide.

Equipment Types	Oxides of Nitrogen (NO_x)	Volatile Organic Compounds (VOCs)	Carbon Monoxide (CO)
Boilers, Steam Generators, Water Heaters, and Process Heaters (rated heat input capacity less than or equal to 400,000 BTU per hour)	55 ppm[7] or 40 nanograms (calculated as NO_2) per joule of heat output		
Boilers, Steam Generators, Water Heaters and Process Heaters rated heat input capacity greater than 400,000 BTU per hour and less than or equal to 2,000,000 BTU per hour)	20 ppm[7] or 40 nanograms (calculated as NO_2) per joule of heat output		400 ppm
Boilers, Steam Generators, Water Heaters, and Process Heaters (rated heat input capacity greater than 2,000,000 BTU per hour and less than 5,000,000 BTU per hour)	30 ppm[7] or 0.037 pounds per million BTU of heat input		400 ppm[7]
Boilers, Steam Generators, Water Heaters, and Process Heaters (rated heat input capacity greater than or equal to 5,000,000 BTU per hour)8,9	30 ppm[7] or 0.036 pounds per million BTU of heat input		400 ppm[7]

Notes:
1. Parts per million by volume, corrected to 15% oxygen on a dry basis and averaged over 15 minutes.
2. Measured as carbon.
3. The averaging time of the emission standards is 15 minutes.
4. Mass emissions of VOC shall be calculated using a ratio of 16.04 pounds of VOC per lb-mole of carbon.
5. Emissions limits shall be subject to adjustment for engines that produce combined heat and electrical power (see Rule 1110.2)
6. ECF is the efficiency correction factor.
7. Parts per million by volume, corrected to 3% oxygen on a dry basis.
8. Capacity Factor greater than 25%.
9. Units with a heat input capacity greater than 40 million BTU per hour and an annual heat input greater than 200 x 109 BTU per year shall have a continuous in-stack nitrogen oxides monitor or equivalent verification system in compliance with 40 CFR part 60 Appendix B Specification 2.

For engines of 1,000 bhp and greater, install, operate and maintain in calibration a NOX Continuous Emission Monitoring System (CEMS) with data gathering and retrieval capability.

1. Benefits and Issues to Consider

Environmental Issues

Healthcare facilities can be a major source of airborne contaminants to their immediate surroundings because of their extended operation schedules, backup generators, and process boilers and heaters. The particulates and contaminants released can pose health problems, including respiratory diseases and cardiovascular events. This is particularly important for patients and community members with compromised immune and/or respiratory systems. Reducing on-site airborne releases can help mitigate a portion of a healthcare facility's environmental footprint and publicly demonstrates healthcare's mission to protect human health.

2. Related Credits

Equipment rated to meet the environmental standards required for this credit may still exceed minimum emissions limits if it is not installed and operated correctly. Commissioning this equipment will ensure it operates correctly and cleanly. The commissioning process is addressed by the following credits:

- EA Prerequisite 1, Fundamental Commissioning
- EA Credit 3, Enhanced Commissioning

This credit calls for all stationary products of combustion to meet defined emissions thresholds. Any biomass- or biogas-fueled system used to generate on-site renewable energy must also meet the emissions requirements. On-site renewable energy is addressed by the following credit:

- EA Credit 2, On-Site Renewable Energy

3. Summary of Referenced Standards

California South Coast Air Quality Management District (SCAQMD)

http://www.aqmd.gov

SCAQMD develops regulations to define tolerable levels of contaminants released into the atmosphere. Because of the poor air quality in Southern California, SCAQMD's regulations are among the most stringent in the country. Only the regulations relating to stationary combustion equipment, as described in the Requirements, are applicable to this credit.

4. Implementation

The SCAQMD requirements apply to stationary internal combustion engines with motors greater than 50 brake horsepower and to all stationary gas-fired equipment (although the corresponding rule varies according to equipment size.)

Select combustion equipment and systems that meet the required emissions threshold. Consider including these systems in the commissioning of the facility to ensure they operate at or below their rated emissions levels.

There are two pathways for complying with this credit: either select new equipment that is on SCAQMD's certified equipment list (published for boilers and internal combustion engines), or have the equipment manufacturer comply with certification requirements.

SCAQMD provides guidance on testing protocols for the latter path. For example, the Source Test Protocol for the Measurement of Nitrogen Oxides, Volatile Organic Compounds, Carbon Monoxide, and Oxygen from Stationary Engines Subject to South Coast Air Quality Management District Rule 1110.2 (2008) describes the test conditions, analytical requirements, calculations, QA/QC, and report formats that will demonstrate compliance with the standard. Protocols are outlined for Rules 1111, 1121, 1146, 1146.1, and 1146.2. See http://www.aqmd.gov/tao/methods/stprotocols.html.

As standard best practice toward reducing airborne emissions, provide scrubbers and filters for boilers and diesel generators. Before occupancy, test and certify all filters as installed and placard them for at least annual recertification.

Burn ultra-low-sulfur diesel fuels. Provide air quality abatement equipment for motors that burn fossil fuels.

5. Timeline and Team

During design development, the engineering team should incorporate SCAQMD requirements into the specifications. Include these systems in the commissioning plan to ensure they are operated correctly.

6. Calculations

There are no explicit calculations for this credit; however, assess each type of proposed combustion equipment to ensure compliance with the emissions limits unless it is already on the list of certified equipment.

7. Documentation Guidance

As a first step in preparing to complete the LEED Online documentation requirements, work through the following measures. Refer to LEED Online for the complete descriptions of all required documentation.

- Retain cutsheets and supplemental manufacturer's data showing the emissions, manufacturer, and model for stationary combustion equipment.
- For equipment that is not already certified by SCAQMD, compile testing results consistent with SCAQMD testing protocol.

10. Regional Variations

Project teams in cold regions, where buildings rely more heavily on combustion equipment for boiler systems, should be especially mindful of emissions ratings.

11. Operations and Maintenance Considerations

Ensure that operations and maintenance staff are trained in the proper operation and servicing procedures of combustion equipment, filters, and scrubbers.

12. Resources

Please see USGBC's LEED Registered Project Tools (http://www.usgbc.org/projecttools) for additional resources and technical information.

Websites

Air Resources Board
California Environmental Protection Agency
http://www.arb.ca.gov/homepage.htm
This site provides resources on health effects, emissions reduction strategies, and regulatory development.

Clean Air Act
http://www.epa.gov/air/peg/index.html
The act defines the U.S. Environmental Protection Agency's responsibilities for protecting and improving air quality, and forms the basis for many state-level air quality regulations. The "Plain English Guide" to the act provides background information on air pollution and major provisions.

Health Effects of Diesel Exhaust
Air Resources Board, California Environmental Protection Agency
http://www.arb.ca.gov/research/diesel/diesel-health.htm
A link to numerous research studies documenting the health effects of diesel emissions.

Health Effects Research
Air Resources Board, California Environmental Protection Agency
http://www.arb.ca.gov/research/health/healthres.htm
A summary of studies completed by the Air Resources Board's research program.

South Coast Air Quality Management District
http://www.aqmd.gov/
Detailed information on emissions limits, compliance, and certified equipment, with links to these sites: SCAQM District Rule 1146.2, Emissions of Oxides of Nitrogen from Large Water Heaters and Small Boilers and Process Heaters (http://www.aqmd.gov/rules/doc/r1146/r1146table.html) and SCAQM District, Test Protocols and Technical Guidance Documents (http://www.aqmd.gov/tao/methods/stprotocols.html).

Technical Support Document for Stationary Fuel Combustion Emissions: Proposed Rule for Mandatory Reporting of Greenhouse Gases
U.S. Environmental Protection Agency
http://www.epa.gov/climatechange/emissions/archived/downloads/tsd/TSD%20Stationary%20Combustion%202-02-09.pdf

13. Definitions

product of combustion exhaust gas or flue gas that is emitted as a result of the combustion of natural gas, gasoline, diesel fuel, fuel oil, or coal.

scrubber a device used to trap and remove pollutants from gaseous emissions.

MATERIALS AND RESOURCES

OVERVIEW

A natural priority for the largely nonprofit, mission-driven healthcare industry is sustainable design and operations that improve health and well-being for building occupants and the surrounding community. Prerequisites and credits in the Materials and Resources category encourage this emphasis through practices that prevent pollution, reduce waste, and ensure the selection of sustainably sourced materials.

Pollution prevention is defined under the Pollution Prevention Act of 1990[1] as "source reduction"—that is, reducing or eliminating the sources and proliferation of waste by modifying production and purchasing practices. In the construction industry, perhaps the most effective form of pollution prevention is avoiding construction altogether, whether by renovating existing facilities or by designing new facilities to accommodate future reorganization and expansion.

The clinical procedures and operation of healthcare facilities generate large quantities of waste. Nearly one-quarter of a typical hospital's waste stream is categorized as medical or hazardous waste,[2] the disposal of which may be triple the cost for regular municipal solid waste. Most healthcare facilities must comply with the federal Resource Conservation Recovery Act[3] and the universal waste rule,[4] which require that hazardous waste be either recycled or properly disposed.

Starting with the design of the facility, pollution prevention can reduce both occupants' exposure to harmful chemicals and the costs of regulatory compliance and waste hauling. Project teams for renovations and new construction on existing campuses should perform a hazardous material audit of the site early in design to identify potential sources of contamination and appropriate disposal methods. If hazardous substances, such as mold, mercury, and lead, are discovered, the project's construction waste management program should incorporate safeguards against cross contamination in the solid waste stream. If hazardous substances are mixed with regular waste, it could prevent other recyclable materials from being diverted from landfills and incinerators.

Pollution prevention includes design considerations for handling recyclables and mercury-containing products and devices. Project teams are encouraged to specify building materials, lamps, clinical and building equipment, and furniture that are free of toxic chemicals. By not installing toxic chemicals in the building during initial construction, teams can help reduce the future cost associated with safely collecting and disposing of these materials. Installing low-mercury, long-life fluorescent lamps in conjunction with secure storage for mercury-containing devices will both reduce the total mercury used by the building over its lifespan and help protect occupants from exposure to lamp breakages.

The Materials and Resources section also encourages owners of healthcare facilities to leverage their considerable purchasing power to increase demand for sustainably sourced materials (e.g., materials with recycled content, rapidly renewable materials) and products with low VOC emissions.

IMPORTANT! This reference guide supplement contains only the reference guide sections that pertain to healthcare projects. Use this supplement alongside the LEED Reference Guide for Green Building Design and Construction for complete credit information. For the omitted sections, refer to the main reference guide.

1 Pollution Prevention Act of 1990, U.S. Code Title 42, The Public Health and Welfare, Chapter 133 (http://www.epa.gov/p2/pubs/p2policy/act1990.htm).

2 Tom Badrick, Healthcare Waste Management, *Medical Tourism Magazine*, May 25, 2010 (http://www.medicaltourismmag.com/detail.php?Req=364&issue=17).

3 U.S. EPA, Hazardous Waste Regulations (http://www.epa.gov/osw/laws-regs/regs-haz.htm).

4 U.S. EPA, Universal Waste (http://www.epa.gov/osw/hazard/wastetypes/universal/).

MR OVERVIEW

CREDIT	TITLE	HEALTHCARE
MR Prerequisite 1	Storage and Collection of Recyclables	Required
MR Prerequisite 2	PBT Source Reduction—Mercury	Required
MR Credit 1.1	Building Reuse—Maintain Existing Walls, Floors, and Roof	1–3 points
MR Credit 1.2	Building Reuse—Maintain Existing Interior Nonstructural Elements	1 point
MR Credit 2	Construction Waste Management	1–2 points
MR Credit 3	Sustainably Sourced Materials and Products	1–4 points
MR Credit 4.1	PBT Source Reduction—Mercury in Lamps	1 point
MR Credit 4.2	PBT Source Reduction—Lead, Cadmium, and Copper	2 points
MR Credit 5	Furniture and Medical Furnishings	1–2 points
MR Credit 6	Resource Use—Design for Flexibility	1 point

STORAGE AND COLLECTION OF RECYCLABLES

	HEALTHCARE
Prerequisite	MR Prerequisite 1
Points	Required

Intent

To facilitate the reduction of waste generated by building occupants that is hauled to and disposed of in landfills and incinerators through reduction, reuse, recycling and composting.

Requirements

Provide an easily-accessible area or areas for the collection and storage of materials for recycling for the entire building in accordance with Section 2.1-5.4.1.2 (and Appendix) of the 2010 FGI Guidelines for Design and Construction of Health Care Facilities.

Establish a collection system and controlled areas serving the portion of the building affected by the project dedicated to the separation, storage and collection of materials for recycling including, at a minimum: paper, corrugated cardboard, glass, plastics, metals, batteries and mercury-containing products and devices[1].

1 Applicable mercury-containing products and devices include lamps (such as linear fluorescent, pin-based compact fluorescent, integrally and nonintegrally ballasted compact fluorescent, and high-intensity discharge lamps) and dental wastes (such as scrap amalgam, chair-side traps, and separator wastes).

IMPORTANT! This reference guide supplement contains only the reference guide sections that pertain to healthcare projects. Use this supplement alongside the LEED Reference Guide for Green Building Design and Construction for complete credit information. For the omitted sections, refer to the main reference guide.

MR	
HEALTHCARE: NC	Prerequisite 1

1. Benefits and Issues to Consider[1]

Environmental Issues

Recycling hazardous materials such as mercury and batteries is a priority for healthcare facilities, many of which still rely on incineration as a waste disposal technology. Mercury, a persistent bioaccumulative toxic (PBT) chemical , is a potent neurotoxin and known human carcinogen that has a tendency to persist in the environment and accumulate in organisms high on the food chain. In the United States, women's exposure to mercury and methylmercury (a chemical compound formed when elemental mercury is introduced to water bodies) has reached a level that may damage fetal and infant development.[2]

Although mercury is being phased out of many medical devices, it is still present in many healthcare facilities in fluorescent lamps and devices that measure temperature and pressure. Mercury may be released through breakage during manufacturing, transport, use, maintenance, and disposal. And once released into the environment, it is difficult to contain.

Medical waste may contain up to 50 times more mercury than municipal solid waste.[3] If introduced to the municipal landfill waste stream, mercury can contaminate groundwater or evaporate into the atmosphere. A 1990 study found that medical waste incinerators emitted 50 tons of mercury per year. Following a 1997 report [4] ranking medical waste incinerators as the fourth-largest source of anthropogenic mercury emissions, the healthcare industry committed to virtually eliminate PBTs in their facilities and operations. This commitment is outlined in a 1998 memorandum of understanding [5] between the American Hospital Association and the U.S. Environmental Protection Agency; the goal is the virtual elimination of mercury and mercury-containing devices from hospital waste streams by 2005.

Economic Issues

Mercury-containing waste and some batteries are regulated under the federal Resource Conservation Recovery Act [6] and the universal waste rule, [7] which require that healthcare facilities either recycle or properly dispose of hazardous waste. Environmentally preferable purchasing practices reduce operational costs in two ways. First, source reduction minimizes hazardous waste disposal costs, which may be three times the cost of municipal solid waste disposal. And second, it limits liability by reducing the likelihood of a spill that could expose staff and patients to contamination and entail costly remediation procedures.

2. Related Credits

Two other prerequisites and credits in LEED for Healthcare that target toxic chemical reduction should inform the development of the facility's recycling program:

- MR Prerequisite 2, PBT Source Reduction—Mercury
- MR Credit 4.1, PBT Source Reduction—Mercury in Lamps

2 Reference guide material for this credit draws, with permission, from the following sources: Jamie Harvie, Green Guide for Health Care Mercury Elimination Technical Brief, and Tom Lent, Green Guide for Health Care PBT Elimination from Building Materials Technical Brief (http://www.gghc.org/tools.technical.php).

3 Toxicological Effects of Methylmercury, Committee on the Toxicological Effects of Methylmercury, Board on Environmental Studies and Toxicology, National Research Council, 2000 (http://www.nap.edu/catalog.php?record_id=9899).

4 GGHC technical brief (http://www.gghc.org/documents/TechBriefs/GGHC_TechBrief_Mercury-Elimination.pdf).

5 U.S. EPA, Mercury Study Report to Congress, Volume II: An Inventory of Anthropogenic Mercury Emissions in the United States, Report EPA-452/R-97-004, December 1997 (http://www.epa.gov/ttn/oarpg/t3/reports/volume2.pdf).

6 1998 Memorandum of Understanding between the American Hospital Association and the U.S. Environmental Protection Agency (http://www.h2e-online.org/pubs/Memorandum.pdf).

7 U.S. EPA, Hazardous Waste Regulations (http://www.epa.gov/osw/laws-regs/regs-haz.htm).

3. Summary of Referenced Standards

Guidelines for the Design and Construction of Health Care Facilities, 2010 Edition
Facility Guidelines Institute
http://www.fgiguidelines.org/

These guidelines establish the healthcare industry's minimum standard for good practice in design and construction. Extensive appendixes provide information about emerging design and construction trends for HVAC, waste reduction, acoustics, and other sustainability topics. The guidelines are used by 42 states as code or as a reference standard.

4. Implementation

Healthcare facilities' waste processing must comply with regulations on solid waste, medical waste, hazardous waste, and the Health Insurance Portability and Accountability Act (HIPAA),[8] as well as address infection control concerns connected with recycling and composting storage. This prerequisite addresses recyclable materials generated on-site and hauled away. Although some facilities and campuses include composting in their recycling programs, project teams need address only the materials listed in the requirements to achieve this prerequisite. Healthcare facilities located on campuses with existing recycling programs are encouraged to integrate into any centralized storage facilities or other existing recycling infrastructure.

Building owners and designers should develop a comprehensive program that encourages recycling and makes it easy to collect and transport recyclables through the building. Early in the design process, prepare a waste management plan that covers at least the materials specified in the requirements and identifies collection practices, transfer operations, storage requirements, pick-up frequency, and contamination avoidance for the project building. Address signage in the plan. Coordinate on-site processing of recyclables and haul-away arrangements with storage space and methods of containment to protect health and safety in the facility and in the neighborhood.

Size the collection areas to be used by building occupants and the centralized storage areas accessible to waste haulers based on the projected volume of waste and frequency of pick-up. See Figure 1 for typical hospital waste volumes. When determining the location and size of waste storage areas, allow for compactors, balers, and recycling container staging.

Segregate storage of waste streams to protect building occupants and waste haulers from exposure to hazardous chemicals and biocontamination. Use signage, physical separation, and dedicated waste receptacles to prevent cross-contamination of recyclable materials with medical and/or infectious waste. Design storage for used fluorescent lamps, other mercury-containing devices, and batteries to minimize the possibility of breakage or spills. Plan for all types of mercury-containing devices, including dental wastes, such as scrap amalgam, chair-side traps, and separator wastes. Simplify paper recycling by establishing secure (i.e., HIPAA-compliant) paper-recycling containers for all office paper waste. Glass recycling primarily involves food and beverage containers, not products required to be handled as biohazards. Metal recycling should segregate food and beverage containers from items collected in sharps containers.

5. Timeline and Team

Early in the design phase, seek input from facility staff to determine recycling policies and procedures. Provide a framework for staff input by providing information about recycling procedures, successes, and lessons learned. For healthcare facilities on existing campuses, engage waste management personnel in integrating the new facility's recycling storage, collection, and waste management procedures into campus practices.

8 Health Insurance Portability and Accountability Act (HIPAA) (http://www.hhs.gov/ocr/privacy/).

Innovative operations for hospital kitchens can affect the building design. For example, a food service area designed for fresh food preparation and composting of food waste will be configured differently than a traditional industrial kitchen designed to store, heat, and dispose of prepared food.

11. Operations and Maintenance Considerations[9]

Of the 6,600 tons of waste generated by hospitals every day, 80% to 85% is characterized as nonhazardous solid waste, such as paper, plastic, and glass.[10] Because this waste is not regulated and its improper disposal does not carry heavy fines, it is often downplayed in hospital waste management plans. However, using the results from an audit of an existing facility's waste stream as the foundation for a waste management plan can help operators reduce both the total volume of waste generated by the new facility and its solid waste stream while increasing the volume of recycled products.

Many healthcare institutions now practice environmentally preferable purchasing, pollution prevention, and waste reduction. Consult with waste management and industrial hygiene experts so that the new facility's recycling program follows best practices.

Identify opportunities for waste management standardization among hospitals within the same health system.

Educate all employees about the facility's waste management plan during new employee training and annually.

Coordinate with facilities staff pursuing parallel credits in LEED for Existing Buildings: Operations & Maintenance and/or the Green Guide for Health Care, Operations section. The Green Guide for Health Care, in particular, addresses the synergies between environmentally preferable purchasing, waste reduction, integrated pest management, and green cleaning in great detail.

12. Resources

Websites

Green Guide for Health Care Mercury Elimination Technical Brief, by Jamie Harvie
http://www.gghc.org/tools.technical.php
Best practices for mercury reduction in healthcare facilities, including developing a comprehensive mercury elimination plan and mercury-free construction specifications.

Green Guide for Health Care, Operations Section
http://www.gghc.org
Best practices and emerging solutions for healthcare operations, including waste management, environmentally preferable purchasing, integrated pest management, and green cleaning.

Health Insurance Portability and Accountability Act (HIPAA)
http://www.hhs.gov/ocr/privacy/
HIPAA is the federal regulation that sets the standard for protection of personal health information, whether electronic, written, or oral.

Practice Greenhealth
http://www.practicegreenhealth.org
This website (formerly Hospitals for a Healthy Environment) compiles recycling resources specific to the healthcare environment, from the regulatory considerations unique to healthcare to fluorescent lamp recycling, protecting privacy, electronic waste recycling, composting, and source reduction.

9 O&M Considerations include information from the Green Guide for Health Care, Operations Section
10 Practice Greenhealth, Waste Reduction Fact Sheet (http://cms.h2e-online.org/ee/waste-reduction/).

13. Definitions

	MR
HEALTHCARE: NC	Prerequisite 1

infection control policies and procedures to minimize the risk of spreading infections through cross-contamination.

persistent bioaccumulative toxic (PBT) chemical a substance that poses a long-term risk to both humans and the environment because it persists in the environment for long periods, bioaccumulates up the food chain, and can travel far from the source of contamination. See EPA's website on PBTs (http://www.epa.gov/pbt/).

pollution prevention reducing or eliminating the source and proliferation of waste through modified production and purchasing practices; also called source reduction. See Pollution Prevention Act of 1990 (http://www.epa.gov/p2/pubs/p2policy/act1990.htm).

PBT SOURCE REDUCTION—MERCURY

HEALTHCARE	
Prerequisite	MR Prerequisite 2
Points	Required

Intent

To reduce mercury-containing products and devices and mercury discharge through product substitution, capture and recycling.

Requirements

- As part of the recycling collection system developed in compliance with MR Prerequisite 1: Storage and Collection of Recyclables, identify:
  - types of mercury containing products and devices[1] to be collected,
  - criteria governing how they are to be handled by a recycling program, and
  - disposal methods for captured mercury.
- In facilities delivering dental care, specify and install amalgam separation devices that meet or exceed the standard ISO-11143.
- Comply with the mercury elimination requirement outlined in the 2010 FGI Guidelines for Design and Construction of Health Care Facilities (Section A1.3- 4b: Mercury Elimination).
  - 4.2.1.1 New construction. In new construction, healthcare facilities shall not use mercury-containing equipment, including thermostats, switching devices, and other building system sources. (Lamps are excluded.)
  - 4.2.1.2 Renovation. For renovation, healthcare facilities shall develop a plan to phase out mercury-containing products and upgrade current mercury-containing lamps to high efficiency, low mercury or mercury free lamp technology.
- Do not specify or install preheat, T-9, T-10, or T-12 fluorescents or mercury vapor type high intensity discharge (HID) lamps in the project. Do not specify probe start metal halide HID lamps in interior spaces in the project.
- Only specify and install illuminated exit signs that use Light-Emitting Diode (LED) or Light-Emitting Capacitor (LEC) lamps and use less than 5 watts of electricity.
- Specify and install fluorescent and high-pressure sodium lamps that meet the following criteria:

Fluorescent Lamp	Criteria
T-8 Eight-foot	Maximum 10 mg mercury
T-8 Four-foot or shorter	Maximum 3.5 mg mercury
T-8 U-Bent	Maximum 6 mg mercury
T-5 Linear	Maximum 2.5 mg mercury
T-5 Circular	Maximum 9 mg mercury
Compact fluorescent, non-integral ballast	Maximum 3.5 mg mercury

1 Applicable mercury-containing products and devices include lamps (such as linear and circular fluorescent, integrally and nonintegrally ballasted compact fluorescent, and high-intensity discharge lamps) and dental wastes (such as scrap amalgam, chair-side traps, and separator wastes).

IMPORTANT! This reference guide supplement contains only the reference guide sections that pertain to healthcare projects. Use this supplement alongside the LEED Reference Guide for Green Building Design and Construction for complete credit information. For the omitted sections, refer to the main reference guide.

Fluorescent Lamp	Criteria
Compact fluorescent, integral ballast	Maximum 3.5 mg mercury Energy Star® qualified
High Pressure Sodium Lamp	Criteria
Up to 400-watt	Maximum 10 mg mercury
Above 400-watt	Maximum 32 mg mercury

MR	
HEALTHCARE: NC	Prerequisite 2

1. Benefits and Issues to Consider[2]

Environmental Issues

Recycling hazardous materials such as mercury and batteries is a problem for healthcare facilities, many of which still rely on incineration as a waste disposal technology. Mercury, a persistent bioaccumulative toxic (PBT) chemical, is a potent neurotoxin and known human carcinogen that has a tendency to persist in the environment and accumulate in organisms high on the food chain. In the United States, women's exposure to mercury and methylmercury (a chemical compound formed when elemental mercury is introduced to water bodies) has reached a level that may damage fetal and infant development.[3]

Although mercury is being phased out of many medical devices, it is still present in many healthcare facilities in fluorescent lamps and devices that measure temperature and pressure. Mercury may be released through breakage during manufacturing, transport, use, maintenance, and disposal. And once released into the environment, it is difficult to contain.

Medical waste may contain up to 50 times more mercury than municipal solid waste.[4] If introduced to the municipal landfill waste stream, mercury can contaminate groundwater or evaporate into the atmosphere. A 1990 study found that medical waste incinerators emitted 50 tons of mercury per year. Following a 1997 report[5] ranking medical waste incinerators as the fourth-largest source of anthropogenic mercury emissions, the healthcare industry committed to virtually eliminate PBTs in their facilities and operations. This commitment is outlined in a 1998 memorandum of understanding[6] between the American Hospital Association and the U.S. Environmental Protection Agency; the goal is the virtual elimination of mercury and mercury-containing devices from hospital waste streams by 2005.

Economic Issues

Mercury-containing waste and some batteries are regulated under the federal Resource Conservation Recovery Act[7] and the universal waste rule,[8] which require that healthcare facilities either recycle or properly dispose of hazardous waste. Environmentally preferable purchasing practices reduce operational costs in two ways. First, source reduction minimizes hazardous waste disposal costs, which may be three times the cost of municipal solid waste disposal. And second, it limits liability by reducing the likelihood of a spill that could expose staff and patients to contamination and entail costly remediation procedures.

Alternative building materials and equipment are becoming increasingly available. PBT-free switches and thermostats, for example, are standard. T-8 and T-5 fluorescent lamps offer low mercury content, long life, and high light output and generally cost no more than conventional lamps with higher mercury content; some other mercury-free fluorescent lamps may continue to carry a cost premium. In the long run, purchasing low-mercury lamps with long life and high light output is an economical way to achieve the targeted mercury reduction: such lamps generally cost more up front but have lower maintenance costs and more lumens, so fewer lamps are needed per square foot.

2 Reference guide material for this credit draws, with permission, from the following sources: Jamie Harvie, Green Guide for Health Care Mercury Elimination Technical Brief, and Tom Lent, Green Guide for Health Care PBT Elimination from Building Materials Technical Brief (http://www.gghc.org/tools.technical.php).

3 Toxicological Effects of Methylmercury, Committee on the Toxicological Effects of Methylmercury, Board on Environmental Studies and Toxicology, National Research Council, 2000 (http://www.nap.edu/catalog.php?record_id=9899).

4 GGHC technical brief (http://www.gghc.org/documents/TechBriefs/GGHC_TechBrief_Mercury-Elimination.pdf)

5 U.S. EPA, Mercury Study Report to Congress, Volume II: An Inventory of Anthropogenic Mercury Emissions in the United States, Report EPA-452/R-97-004, December 1997 (http://www.epa.gov/ttn/oarpg/t3/reports/volume2.pdf)..

6 1998 Memorandum of Understanding between the American Hospital Association and the U.S. Environmental Protection Agency (http://www.h2e-online.org/pubs/Memorandum.pdf).

7 U.S. EPA, Hazardous Waste Regulations (http://www.epa.gov/osw/laws-regs/regs-haz.htm).

8 U.S. EPA, Universal Waste (http://www.epa.gov/osw/hazard/wastetypes/universal/).

Healthcare organizations can accelerate demand for nontoxic building materials and products through volume purchasing. As predominantly owner-occupied buildings, healthcare facilities can take advantage of the life-cycle benefits associated with LED lamps and other energy-efficient technologies that contain no or low levels of mercury and boast long life spans.

2. Related Credits

Coordinate specifications for products that may contain mercury with MR Prerequisite 1, Storage and Collection of Recyclables.

Mercury reduction is one piece of a larger strategy to avoid introducing toxic chemicals into the healthcare environment. Coordinate the project's approach to this prerequisite with the following:

- SS Prerequisite 2, Environmental Site Assessment
- SS Credit 3, Brownfield Redevelopment
- MR Credit 3, Sustainably Sourced Materials and Products
- MR Credit 4.1, PBT Source Reduction—Mercury in Lamps
- MR Credit 4.2, PBT Source Reduction—Lead, Cadmium, and Copper
- MR Credit 5, Furniture and Medical Furnishings
- IEQ Prerequisite 3, Hazardous Material Removal or Encapsulation (Renovations Only)
- IEQ Credit 4, Low-Emitting Materials
- IEQ Credit 5, Indoor Chemical and Pollutant Source Control

3. Summary of Referenced Standards

Guidelines for the Design and Construction of Health Care Facilities, 2010 Edition
Facility Guidelines Institute
http://www.fgiguidelines.org/
These guidelines establish the healthcare industry's minimum standard for good practice in design and construction. Extensive appendixes provide information about emerging design and construction trends for HVAC, waste reduction, acoustics, and other sustainability topics. The guidelines are used by 42 states as code or as a reference standard.

ISO-11143, Dentistry, Amalgam Separators
http://www.iso.org/iso/catalogue_detail.htm?csnumber=42288
This standard specifies requirements for the efficacy of amalgam separators. Efficient separator devices reduce the likelihood that unused mercury for dental amalgams will enter municipal wastewater effluent.

U.S. EPA ENERGY STAR
http://www.energystar.gov
ENERGY STAR–qualified compact fluorescent lamps (CFLs) use less energy and produce fewer mercury emissions than incandescent light bulbs. Starting in 2009, CFL product packaging must include the "Hg" [NOTE TO GRAPHIC DESIGNER: PLEASE CREATE A SYMBOL WITH "Hg" INSIDE OF A CIRCLE] symbol and website information to help consumers locate lamp-recycling facilities.

For additional information about ENERGY STAR criteria for fluorescent lamps, see U.S. Department of Energy ENERGY STAR Qualified Light Bulbs: 2009 Partner Resource Guide (http://www.energystar.gov/ia/products/downloads/CFL_PRG.pdf).

For additional information about the relationship between CFLs and mercury, see ENERGY STAR Frequently Asked Questions fact sheet (http://www.energystar.gov/ia/partners/promotions/change_light/downloads/Fact_Sheet_Mercury.pdf).

4. Implementation[9]

Mercury elimination is policy for local, state, federal and international governments as well as major healthcare systems and organizations. Some of the state laws prohibiting some or all uses of mercury-containing building products include the following:

- California State law (SB 633) restricts the use and distribution of mercury fever thermometers and other devices.
- California Health and Safety code (Rule 25214) prohibits the sale of mercury-added thermostats, switches, and relays. It also prohibits the sale of refurbished mercury-added barometers, esophageal dilators, bougie tubes, gastrointestinal tubes, flow meters, hydrometers, psychometers, manometers, pyrometers, sphygmomanometers, and thermometers.
- Connecticut State law (House Bill 5539) bans the sale and distribution of mercury fever thermometers and places restrictions on the sale of other mercury-containing equipment.
- Maine State law (LD 1159) prohibits the sale of mercury in switches, measuring devices (including sphygmomanometers), instruments and thermostats.
- Oregon State law (HB 3007) phases out mercury thermostats and prohibits the sale of fever thermometers and other devices.
- Washington State law (House Bill 1002) requires the labeling of fluorescent lamps that contain mercury and prohibits the sale of mercury-containing items in products such as thermometers and thermostats.

Mercury Collection and Recycling Program

Develop an inventory of all mercury-containing products and equipment in the project. For new construction, include mercury-containing lamps and specialty medical equipment, such as dental amalgam separation devices. For renovation projects, perform an audit of the existing facility to identify all mercury-containing equipment and devices, including dental wastes, such as scrap amalgam, chair-side traps, and separator wastes. At a minimum, the inventory must include the following information:

- Product type.
- Quantity of each product type.
- Criteria for handling and storage after the end of a product's useful life.
- Protocols for spill response.
- Disposal methods for captured mercury.
- Contact information for coordinators of the mercury-recycling program.

Coordinate the development of a recycling program for mercury-containing products with representatives from waste management, purchasing, and industrial hygiene. Avoid bulb crushers, which can expose workers to mercury vapor and generate hazardous waste (crushed bulbs are not classified as universal waste).

9 Information drawn from the Green Guide for Health Care, Operations Section

For additional information about recycling, see MR Prerequisite 1, Storage and Collection of Recyclables.

Dental Amalgam Separators

Specify or confirm existence of amalgam separators that are in compliance with ISO-11143.

Ensure proper disposal of the captured mercury in dental waste (such as scrap amalgam, chair-side traps, and separator wastes) in accordance with MR Prerequisite 1, Storage and Collection of Recyclables.

Elimination of Mercury-Containing Products and Equipment

Establish a project goal for mercury-free products and devices and identify alternative materials and suppliers. Add a LEED general requirements section to Division 01 for LEED performance requirements in overlapping specification sections. Then specify products and materials according to CSI MasterFormat 2004 classifications for Division 01 with mercury elimination requirements for equipment and mercury reduction requirements for lamps. Ensure that mercury limits are clearly specified for any product, piece of equipment, or assembly that might include mercury. Consider digital measurement devices and controls, LED lamps, and very-low-mercury induction lamps. To prevent "hidden" mercury from being installed, incorporate mercury-free requirements into the project's green submittal form.

Teams for renovations and additions should audit existing building products and equipment to identify mercury-containing devices, which may include MRI equipment, wheelchairs, automated beds, cantor tubes, bed warmers, and thermometers. If the total elimination of mercury is not possible, given existing equipment and the project's scope of work, develop a plan to transition to mercury-free devices by project completion.

Virtual Elimination of Mercury in Lamp Specifications

Specify lamps with low mercury content, long life, and high lumen output.

Mercury-containing lamps can expose staff to contamination from breakage during installation and removal. Eight-foot and U-bent lamps may be particularly susceptible to breakage because of their size and configuration. However, very-low-mercury induction lamps, with instant on-off control, have a long life and also use less energy.

LED lamps are a mercury-free alternative to low-wattage fluorescent lamps. They comply with the credit requirements only if they are at least as energy efficient as comparable mercury-containing lamps.

5. Timeline and Team

On existing campuses, determine whether the healthcare organization has contracted with a preferred provider for lighting. Projects that are on existing campuses or part of large health systems should coordinate lamp selection with purchasing protocols to ensure the virtual elimination of mercury throughout the building's life.

During the construction documents phase, project teams should consult with lighting designers, facilities staff, and lighting suppliers, as applicable, to specify a lighting scheme that meets the design needs of the project while minimizing the amount of mercury introduced into the new facility. During construction, project teams should verify that the installed lamps meet the low-mercury specifications.

7. Documentation Guidance

As a first step in preparing to complete the LEED Online documentation requirements, work through the following measures. Refer to LEED Online for the complete descriptions of all required documentation.

- Develop an inventory or lighting schedule of all lighting in the project, including fluorescent and high-pressure sodium lamps. Include lamp type, quantity, and mercury criteria and content. If attempting MR Credit 4, also include start ballast and rated hours information.
- Develop a recycling collection system plan and identify criteria for handling and storage, protocols for spill response, disposal methods for captured mercury, and contact information for staff who coordinate the mercury-recycling program.
- For existing healthcare facilities pursuing the phase-out pathway, develop a phase-out plan and include implementation dates.
- Retain technical specifications for all lamps. Record mercury content and (if pursuing MR Credit 4.1, PBT Source Reduction—Mercury in Lamps) rated hours.
- If the inventory or lighting schedule does not include mercury content, collect documentation from product manufacturers or suppliers that verifies mercury content, lumen output, and lamp life.

Figure 1 is a sample cut sheet showing mercury content and rated hours.

Figure 1. Example Lighting Cut Sheet

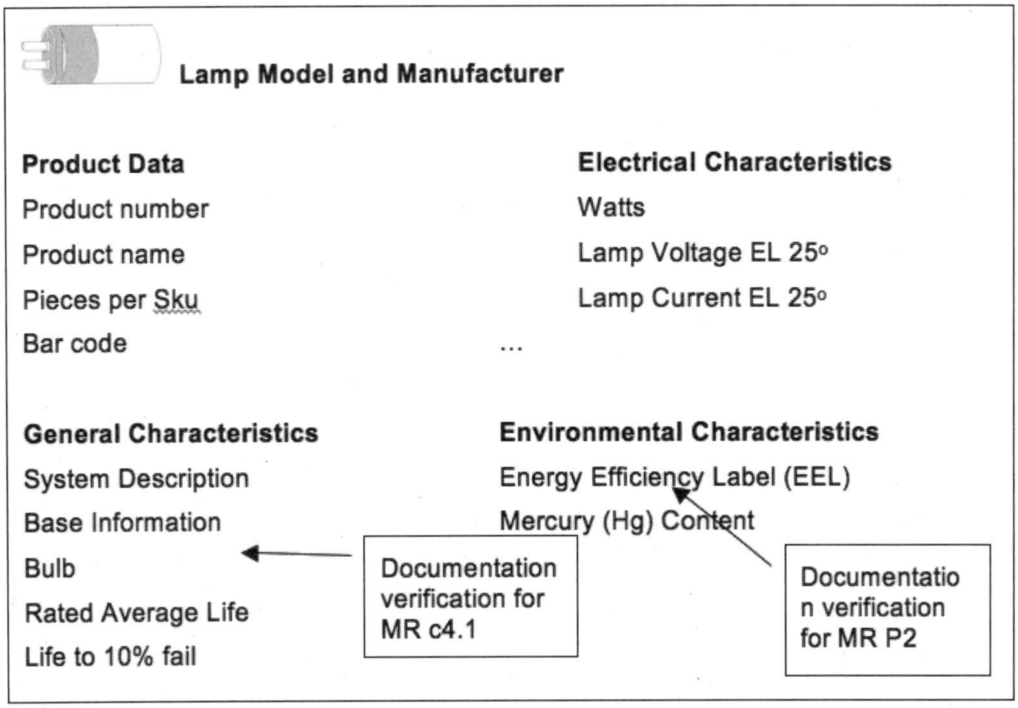

9. Exemplary Performance

This prerequisite is not eligible for exemplary performance under the Innovation in Design section.

10. Regional Variations

There are no regional variations associated with this prerequisite.

11. Operations and Maintenance Considerations

Many healthcare institutions now practice environmentally preferable purchasing, pollution prevention, and waste reduction targeting mercury in particular. Consult with waste management and industrial hygiene experts to ensure that the design considerations for mercury reduction, storage, and recycling are coordinated with mercury spill response policies and enable staff to meet the intent of the Resource Conservation and Recovery Act (RCRA); supplies to clean up spills should be readily available, staffers should be trained in spill response, and hazardous waste haulers should be licensed.

Best practices include training maintenance personnel on how to handle mercury-containing products to avoid breakage or implosion. When a lamp is spent, recycle all mercury-containing lamps at an appropriate facility.

Coordinate with facilities staff pursuing parallel credits in LEED for Existing Buildings: Operations & Maintenance and/or the Green Guide for Health Care, Operations section. The Green Guide for Health Care, in particular, addresses the benefits of coordinating mercury avoidance through environmentally preferable purchasing with waste reduction and recycling practices.

12. Resources

Please see USGBC's LEED Resources & Tools (http://www.usgbc.org/projecttools) for additional resources and other technical information.

Websites

Eliminating Mercury in Hospitals (November 2002)
U.S. Environmental Protection Agency
http://www.epa.gov/region9/waste/p2/projects/hospital/mercury.pdf
An overview of the environmental and health concerns associated with mercury emissions, mercury sources in healthcare facilities, and cost analyses of mercury-free alternatives.

ENERGY STAR® Business Improvement: Purchasing and Procurement
http://www.energystar.gov/index.cfm?c=bulk_purchasing.bus_purchasing
The ENERGY STAR website provides resources to assist procurement officials in making smart purchasing decisions.

Green Guide for Health Care Mercury Elimination Technical Brief, by Jamie Harvie
http://www.gghc.org/tools.technical.php
Best practices for mercury reduction in healthcare facilities, including developing a comprehensive mercury elimination plan and mercury-free construction specifications.

Hazards of Heavy Metal Contamination, by Lars Järup (*British Medical Bulletin* 68: 167–82, 2003)
DOI: 10.1093/bmb/ldg032
http://bmb.oxfordjournals.org/content/68/1/167.full
An overview of the health effects associated with mercury, lead, cadmium, and arsenic; global exposure rates to each substance; and the most prevalent exposure pathways, including via building materials.

Inform Fact Sheet: Mercury-Containing Lamps
http://www.informinc.org/
Information on mercury in fluorescent lamps, purchasing programs for low-mercury-content lamps, specifying and sourcing mercury-free HVAC and building equipment, and related topics.

LampRecycle.org
http://www.nema.org/lamprecycle
This online resource from the National Electric Manufacturers Association provides information on recycling spent mercury-containing lamps, with links to regulations and recycling service providers.

Mercury
U.S. Environmental Protection Agency
http://www.epa.gov/mercury
This comprehensive website offers information about mercury emissions, the use of mercury in manufactured products, human and environmental health effects, and laws and regulations.

Practice Greenhealth
http://www.practicegreenhealth.org
This website (formerly Hospitals for a Healthy Environment) compiles recycling resources specific to the healthcare environment, from the regulatory considerations unique to healthcare to fluorescent lamp recycling, protecting privacy, electronic waste recycling, composting, and source reduction.

RIPPLE Database
The Center for Health Design
http://ripple.healthdesign.org
An open-source, searchable database that provides users with research, design strategies, and outcomes from multiple organizations.

13. Definitions

elemental mercury pure mercury (rather than a mercury-containing compound), the vapor of which is commonly used in fluorescent and other lamp types.

lamp a device that uses electricity to produce light in any of several ways: by heating a wire for incandescence; by exciting a gas that produces ultraviolet light from a luminescent material; by generating an arc that emits visible light and some ultraviolet light; or by inducing excitation of mercury through radio frequencies. Light-emitting diodes packaged as traditional lamps also meet this definition.

lamp life the useful operating life of the sources of artificial light, such as bulbs.

persistent bioaccumulative toxic (PBT) chemical a substance that poses a long-term risk to both humans and the environment because it persists in the environment for long periods, bioaccumulates up the food chain, and can travel far from the source of contamination. See EPA's website on PBTs (http://www.epa.gov/pbt/).

pollution prevention reducing or eliminating the source and proliferation of waste through modified production and purchasing practices; also called source reduction. See Pollution Prevention Act of 1990 (http://www.epa.gov/p2/pubs/p2policy/act1990.htm).

BUILDING REUSE—MAINTAIN EXISTING WALLS, FLOORS, AND ROOF

	HEALTHCARE
Credit	MR Credit 1.1
Points	1–3 points

Intent

To extend the lifecycle of existing building stock, conserve resources, retain cultural resources, reduce waste and reduce environmental impacts of new buildings as they relate to materials manufacturing and transport.

Requirements

Maintain the existing building structure (including structural floor and roof decking) and envelope (the exterior skin and framing, excluding window assemblies and non-structural roofing material). The minimum percentage building reuse for each point threshold is as follows:

Building Reuse	Points
55%	1
75%	2
95%	3

Hazardous materials that are remediated as a part of the project must be excluded from the calculation of the percentage maintained. Calculate the total area of existing exterior envelope and existing building structure to ensure that the credit goals have been met. Building materials demolished to create courtyards to increase daylighting may be counted as retained in calculations for this credit, provided that the new courtyards meet the requirements of IEQ Credit 8.2: Daylight and Views. If the project includes an addition that is more than 2 times the square footage of the existing building, this credit is not applicable.

Use only areas (square footage) to calculate the quantity of preserved materials. The area to be used in the denominator is the sum of all new and reused floor or roof area and the exterior envelope, including the ground floor, to account for slabs-on-grade and footings or the exterior wall area. The area to be used in the numerator is the sum of reused floor, roof or wall area.

IMPORTANT! This reference guide supplement contains only the reference guide sections that pertain to healthcare projects. Use this supplement alongside the LEED Reference Guide for Green Building Design and Construction for complete credit information. For the omitted sections, refer to the main reference guide.

MR	
HEALTHCARE: NC	Credit 1.1

1. Benefits and Issues to Consider

Environmental Issues

The health consequences of hazardous waste make it imperative that project teams protect construction and demolition workers as well as future occupants from potential exposure.

Economic Issues

Because of their lower floor-to-floor heights, inadequate vibration control and ventilation, insufficient structural strength, and other reasons, many older healthcare buildings cannot be renovated for modern clinical use. They can, however, be adapted for administrative offices or other nonregulated healthcare spaces with less stringent requirements. Adaptive use helps preserve the character of a healthcare campus, and reuse of existing building stock can save money and resources.

2. Related Credits

Ensure that the areas contributing to this credit are not double-counted in MR Credit 1.2, Building Reuse—Maintain 50% of Interior Non-Structural Elements.

All healthcare renovation project teams should evaluate the existing site and building for contamination that could expose future occupants to hazardous chemicals, mold, or other risks; see the following prerequisites and credit:

- SS Prerequisite 2, Environmental Site Assessment
- SS Credit 3, Brownfield Redevelopment
- IEQ Prerequisite 3, Hazardous Material Removal or Encapsulation (Renovations Only)

Existing healthcare structures, particularly those built without air-conditioning, are often designed around narrow floor plates with segments that branch off one or several spines. A narrow floor plate provides greater access to daylight and views for all building occupants, including staff working in diagnostic and treatment areas. However, planning critical adjacencies that meet modern standards can present a challenge. Teams renovating existing healthcare buildings should review the following credits early in schematic design to maximize flexibility, particularly in relation to medical space planning and access to views from staff areas:

- MR Credit 6, Resource Use—Design for Flexibility
- IEQ Credit 8.1, Daylight and Views—Daylight
- IEQ Credit 8.2, Daylight and Views—Views

4. Implementation

Incorporate reuse of existing, previously occupied buildings, including structure and envelope elements, into the site master plan. For healthcare organizations in campus settings, consider renovating structures that do not meet modern healthcare construction codes and functional requirements into administrative offices and other nonregulated spaces.

6. Calculations

Refer to the Calculations section in MR Credit 1.1 in the LEED 2009 Reference Guide for Green Building Design and Construction for guidance.

For LEED for Healthcare projects, if structural and envelope elements are demolished to create a courtyard that increases daylighting, the razed material may be counted as retained in the calculations for this credit, provided the new courtyard meets the requirements of IEQ Credit 8.1, Daylight and Views—Daylight.

BUILDING REUSE—MAINTAIN EXISTING INTERIOR NONSTRUCTURAL ELEMENTS

MR CREDIT 1.2

	HEALTHCARE
Credit	MR Credit 1.2
Points	1 point

Intent

To extend the lifecycle of existing building stock, conserve resources, retain cultural resources, reduce waste and reduce environmental impacts of new buildings as they relate to materials manufacturing and transport.

Requirements

Use existing interior nonstructural elements (e.g., interior walls, doors, floor coverings and ceiling systems) in at least 50% (by area) of the completed building, including additions. Hazardous materials that are remediated as a part of the project scope shall be excluded from the calculation of the percentage maintained. If the project includes an addition with square footage more than 2 times the square footage of the existing building, this credit is not applicable.

IMPORTANT! This reference guide supplement contains only the reference guide sections that pertain to healthcare projects. Use this supplement alongside the LEED Reference Guide for Green Building Design and Construction for complete credit information. For the omitted sections, refer to the main reference guide.

MR	
HEALTHCARE: NC	Credit 1.2

1. Benefits and Issues to Consider

Environmental Issues

The health consequences of hazardous waste make it imperative that project teams protect construction and demolition workers as well as future occupants from potential exposure.

Economic Issues

Many older healthcare buildings that cannot be renovated for modern clinical use can be adapted for administrative offices or other nonregulated healthcare spaces with less stringent requirements. Adaptive use helps preserve the character of a healthcare campus and can save money and resources by reusing existing building stock.

Designs meeting modern building and healthcare codes often result in higher floor-to-floor heights and larger total square footage than can be accommodated in much of the healthcare building stock requiring renovation and alteration work today. For example, modern codes require vibration control, minimum air changes that exceed requirements for commercial office buildings, and structural adequacy. HVAC systems require larger, more extensive ductwork. Medical equipment, vertical transportation, and data centers (i.e., IT support) dictate minimum space dimensions for specialized equipment and functions. Additionally, the nature of healthcare planning requires many small, specialized spaces to meet the functional requirements. The flexibility in planning is paramount to achieve efficient, economical layouts.

2. Related Credits

Ensure that the areas contributing to this credit are not double-counted in MR Credit 1.1, Building Reuse—Maintain Existing Walls, Floors, and Roof.

All healthcare renovation project teams should evaluate the site and existing building for contamination that could expose future occupants to hazardous chemicals, mold, or other health concerns, contributing to the following prerequisites and credit:

- SS Prerequisite 2, Environmental Site Assessment
- SS Credit 3, Brownfield Redevelopment
- IEQ Prerequisite 3, Hazardous Material Removal or Encapsulation (Renovations Only)

Existing healthcare structures, particularly those built without air-conditioning, are often designed around narrow floor plates with segments that branch off one or several spines. A narrow floor plate provides greater access to daylight and views for all building occupants, including staff working in diagnostic and treatment areas. However, planning critical adjacencies that meet modern standards can present a challenge. Teams renovating existing healthcare buildings should review the following credits early in schematic design to maximize flexibility, particularly in relation to medical space planning and access to views from staff areas:

- MR Credit 6: Resource Use—Design for Flexibility
- IEQ Credit 8.1: Daylight and Views—Daylight
- IEQ Credit 8.2: Daylight and Views—Views

4. Implementation

Remove elements that pose contamination risks to building occupants. Upgrade components that would improve energy and water efficiency, such as windows, mechanical systems, and plumbing fixtures.

CONSTRUCTION WASTE MANAGEMENT

	HEALTHCARE
Credit	MR Credit 2
Points	1–2 points

Intent

To divert construction and demolition debris from disposal in landfills and incineration facilities. Redirect recyclable recovered resources back to the manufacturing process and reusable materials to appropriate sites.

Requirements

Recycle and/or salvage nonhazardous construction and demolition debris. Develop and implement a construction waste management plan that, at a minimum, identifies the materials to be diverted from disposal and whether the materials will be sorted on-site or comingled. Excavated soil and land-clearing debris do not contribute to this credit. Calculations can be done by weight or volume, but must be consistent throughout. The minimum percentage debris to be recycled or salvaged for each point threshold is as follows:

Recycled or Salvaged	Points
50%	1
75%	2

IMPORTANT! This reference guide supplement contains only the reference guide sections that pertain to healthcare projects. Use this supplement alongside the LEED Reference Guide for Green Building Design and Construction for complete credit information. For the omitted sections, refer to the main reference guide.

2. Related Credits

All healthcare renovation projects should evaluate the existing site and building for contamination that could expose future occupants to hazardous chemicals, mold, or other risks; see the following prerequisites and credit:

- SS Prerequisite 2, Environmental Site Assessment
- SS Credit 3, Brownfield Redevelopment
- IEQ Prerequisite 3, Hazardous Material Removal or Encapsulation (Renovations Only)

Coordinate construction waste recycling efforts, particularly in relation to hazardous waste reduction, storage, and recycling, with the project's overall approach to pollution prevention and recycling. This will contribute to the following prerequisites and credits:

- MR Prerequisite 1, Storage and Collection of Recyclables
- MR Prerequisite 2, PBT Source Reduction—Mercury
- MR Credit 4.1, PBT Source Reduction—Mercury in Lamps
- MR Credit 4.2, PBT Source Reduction—Lead, Cadmium, and Copper

9. Exemplary Performance

Project teams may earn an Innovation in Design credit for exemplary performance by diverting 95% or more of total construction waste.

11. Operations and Maintenance Considerations

Coordinate with facilities staff pursuing parallel credits in LEED for Existing Buildings: Operations & Maintenance and/or the Green Guide for Health Care, Operations section. The Green Guide for Health Care, in particular, addresses the synergies between chemical management and waste reduction.

12. Resources

Green Guide for Health Care Low Impact Construction Practices Technical Brief, by Jim Moler
http://www.gghc.org/tools.technical.php
Construction best practices for a green healthcare facility, including waste reduction and recycling, site and materials management, infection control, and utility and emissions control.

Green Guide for Health Care, Operations Section
http://www.gghc.org
Best practices and emerging solutions for healthcare operations, including waste management, environmentally preferable purchasing, integrated pest management, and green cleaning.

Practice Greenhealth
http://www.practicegreenhealth.org
This website (formerly Hospitals for a Healthy Environment) compiles recycling resources specific to the healthcare environment, from the regulatory considerations unique to healthcare to fluorescent lamp recycling, protecting privacy, electronic waste recycling, composting, and source reduction.

13. Definitions

pollution prevention reducing or eliminating the source and proliferation of waste through modified production and purchasing practices; also called source reduction. See Pollution Prevention Act of 1990 (http://www.epa.gov/p2/pubs/p2policy/act1990.htm).

SUSTAINABLY SOURCED MATERIALS AND PRODUCTS

HEALTHCARE	
Credit	MR Credit 3
Points	1–4 points

Intent

To reduce the environmental burdens of materials and products acquired to construct building and to upgrade building services.

Requirements

One point and up to a maximum of four will be awarded for each 10% of the total value of all building materials and products used in the project (based on cost) that meet the criteria below. If concrete or steel structural elements are applied toward this credit, the project must include at least two other materials or products from CSI MasterFormat Divisions (other than 03 and 05) to attain the first point. Of the total recycled content, no more than 75% may be steel or concrete.

1. The cost of any individual material or product may be added for each of the following sustainability criteria that the material or product meets:

- Salvaged, refurbished or reused materials.

OR

- Recycled content. The recycled content value is determined by multiplying the recycled content fraction of the assembly (based on weight) by the cost of the assembly. The recycled content fraction is the sum of all post-consumer[1] recycled content plus one-half of the pre-consumer[2] content. Note: The same material cannot contribute to both salvaged and recycled content values.

OR

- Regionally sourced/manufactured materials and products that have been extracted, harvested or recovered, as well as manufactured within 500 miles of the project site

OR

- Rapidly renewable materials. The rapidly renewable content value is determined by multiplying the rapidly renewable content fraction of the assembly (based on weight) by the cost of the assembly.

OR

- Wood certified, in accordance with the Forest Stewardship Council's (FSC) Principles and Criteria. The certified wood content value is determined by multiplying the certified wood content fraction of the assembly (based on weight) by the cost of the assembly. Note: Only virgin wood stock shall contribute towards the certified wood criteria. Certified wood shall not contribute to the rapidly renewable criteria.

1 "Post-consumer material" is defined as waste material generated by households or by commercial, industrial and institutional facilities in their role as end-users of the product, which can no longer be used for its intended purpose.

2 "Pre-consumer material" is defined as material diverted from the waste stream during the manufacturing process. Excluded is reutilization of materials, such as rework, regrind or scrap, generated in a process and capable of being reclaimed within the same process that generated it.

IMPORTANT! This reference guide supplement contains only the reference guide sections that pertain to healthcare projects. Use this supplement alongside the LEED Reference Guide for Green Building Design and Construction for complete credit information. For the omitted sections, refer to the main reference guide.

Note: All wood certification requirements will be updated to reflect the new criteria being put forth for member approval across all LEED rating systems.

AND

2. Wall, ceiling and flooring systems and finishes, composite wood, agrifiber and fiberglass products, both exterior and interior adhesives, sealants, coatings, roofing, and waterproofing products must meet the relevant IEQ Credit 4: Low-Emitting Materials requirements to contribute toward the credit.

AND

Mechanical, electrical and plumbing components and specialty items, such as elevators, shall not be included in this calculation. Only include materials permanently installed in the project. Furniture is not included (see Credit 5.1-5.3).

AND

Recycled content shall be defined in accordance with the International Organization of Standards Document ISO 14021-1999—Environmental labels and declarations—Self-declared environmental claims (Type II environmental labeling).

AND

Supplemental cementitious materials derived from coal fired power plant wastes shall not have mercury content >5.5ppb (0.0055 mg/L). Fly ash generated as a by-product of municipal solid waste incinerators does not qualify as a recycled-content material for this credit.

MR	
HEALTHCARE: NC	Credit 3

1. Benefits and Issues to Consider[3]

This credit combines the following credits from the New Construction Rating System:

- MR Credit 3, Materials Reuse
- MR Credit 4: Recycled Content
- MR Credit 5: Regional Materials
- MR Credit 6: Rapidly Renewable Materials
- MR Credit 7: Certified Wood

It also incorporates content from IEQ Credits 4.1–4.4 and 4.6. For additional information about sustainably sourced and low-emitting materials, refer to the Benefits and Issues to Consider sections under these credits in the LEED Reference Guide for Green Building Design and Construction.

Environmental Issues

Healthcare project teams should take care when specifying cementitious materials, including coal combustion residuals (fly ash). Evaluate the trade-off between the beneficial use of recycled content with the human and environmental health consequences of coal-fired energy production. Fly ash contains trace concentrations of heavy metals and other substances that are known to be detrimental to health in sufficient quantities. Potentially toxic trace elements in coal include arsenic, barium, beryllium, cadmium, chromium, copper, lead, mercury, molybdenum, nickel, radium, selenium, thorium, uranium, vanadium, and zinc.[4]

2. Related Credits

This credit combines MR Credits 3, 4, 5, 6, and 7; see the Related Credits sections in these credits for additional information. In particular, coordinate the project's approach to sustainably sourced building materials with the furniture and furnishings specifications in the following credit:

- MR Credit 5, Furniture and Medical Furnishings.

Incorporate the project's approach to specifying sustainably sourced materials into its overall toxic chemical avoidance strategies. See IEQ Credit 4, Low-Emitting Materials, for what products and materials can be included in the credit calculation.

Consider a material's content, whether it can be cleaned with nontoxic products, and its potential to contaminate the construction waste stream. This approach will contribute to achievement of the following prerequisites and credits:

- MR Prerequisite 1, Storage and Collection of Recyclables
- MR Prerequisite 2, PBT Source Reduction—Mercury
- MR Credit 2, Construction Waste Management
- MR Credit 4.1, PBT Source Reduction—Mercury in Lamps
- MR Credit 4.2, PBT Source Reduction—Lead, Cadmium, and Copper

The development of a comprehensive reuse management plan will help determine whether the project meets the requirements of the following credits:

- MR Credit 1, Building Reuse
- MR Credit 2, Construction Waste Management

3 Reference guide material for this credit draws, with permission, from the following sources: Jamie Harvie, Green Guide for Health Care Mercury Elimination Technical Brief, and Tom Lent, Green Guide for Health Care PBT Elimination from Building Materials Technical Brief (http://www.gghc.org/tools.technical.php).

4 U.S. Geological Survey, Radioactive Elements in Coal and Fly Ash: Abundance, Forms, and Environmental Significance, Fact Sheet FS-163-97 (USGS, 1997).

3. Summary of Referenced Standards

Refer to the Referenced Standards sections in MR Credits 3–7 and IEQ Credits 4.1–4.4 and 4.6 in the LEED Reference Guide for Green Building Design and Construction.

4. Implementation

Because of their size, complexity, regulatory constraints, and infection control concerns, healthcare facilities need a flexible and holistic approach to materials specification. A best practice is to establish goals for sustainably sourced materials during the design phase and include them in the project specifications; this is not a LEED requirement, but it can help in achieving the credit. Add a LEED general requirements section to Division 01 to allow for writing LEED performance requirements for overlapping work sections, such as building envelope and structure. Then specify products and materials according to CSI MasterFormat 2004 classifications for Division 01 sustainably sourced material requirements. Ensure that sustainably sourced material criteria are clearly specified. Careful research may be required to determine the material content that can realistically be expected in specific products and materials. Consider including more than one sustainably sourced material option, to provide flexibility.

Ensure that all materials included in the credit calculation must also meet the requirements of IEQ Credit 4, Low-Emitting Materials, to avoid inadvertently exposing immunocompromised occupants to any toxic chemicals in recycled and other sustainably sourced materials.

Include safety (e.g., slip and fall), durability, and cleaning criteria into materials specifications considerations.

Identify opportunities to incorporate salvaged, reused, regional, rapidly renewable, and Forest Stewardship Council–certified wood into the building design, and research potential suppliers. Consider a range of environmental, economic, and performance attributes when selecting products and materials. During construction, ensure that the specified materials are installed and determine their percentage of the total materials installed.

Calculations for this credit apply primarily to CSI MasterFormat™ 2004 Edition Divisions 03-10, 31 (Section 31.60.00 Foundations) and 32 (Sections 32.10.00 Paving, 32.30.00 Site Improvements, and 32.90.00 Planting). Do not include furniture, furnishings, or mechanical, electrical, or plumbing components, appliances, or equipment in the calculations for this credit.

Salvaged, Refurbished, or Reused Materials

Reference the Implementation section in the LEED 2009 Reference Guide for Green Building Design and Construction, MR Credit 3: Materials Reuse.

Recycled Content

Verify that supplemental cementitious materials derived from coal-fired power plant wastes meet credit requirements for mercury content by incorporating mercury threshold requirements into the project's green submittal form and specifications. Prohibit use of fly ash generated as a by-product of municipal solid waste incinerators. Coordinate with the contractor to identify concrete suppliers that do not obtain fly ash from municipal solid waste incinerators.

See the Implementation section under MR Credit 4, Recycled Content, in the LEED Reference Guide for Green Building Design and Construction.

Regionally Sourced or Manufactured Materials and Products

See the Implementation section under MR Credit 5, Regional Materials, in the LEED Reference Guide for Green Building Design and Construction.

Rapidly Renewable Materials

Rapidly renewable materials are defined in LEED as agricultural products, both fiber and animal, that take 10 years or less to grow or raise and can be harvested in a sustainable fashion. Consider specifying materials from producers using low-impact, sustainable agricultural practices that avoid eutrophication, soil depletion, and the use of toxic chemicals.

There are many sustainable agriculture certification programs for rapidly renewable materials; here are three:

- Certified USDA Organic or equivalent state organic standard.
- Grown using environmentally sustainable agricultural methods certified through a program that meets the criteria for full membership in the ISEAL Alliance (e.g., IFOAM organically grown materials). To achieve full membership, a program must demonstrate compliance with ISEAL's codes of good practice and other applicable ISO guides, such as ISO 17011 for Accreditation Bodies. The codes of good practice include Setting Social and Environmental Standards, Assessing the Impacts of Social and Environmental Standards, and Verifying Compliance with Social and Environmental Standards. For additional information, see http://www.isealalliance.org.
- Offset credits for the same crop type grown using environmentally sustainable agricultural methods certified through a program that meets the criteria for full membership in the ISEAL Alliance (e.g., IATP Working Landscape Certificates).

See the Implementation section under MR Credit 6, Rapidly Renewable Materials, in the LEED Reference Guide for Green Building Design and Construction for additional information.

Certified Wood

See the Implementation section under MR Credit 7, Certified Wood, in the LEED Reference Guide for Green Building Design and Construction,.

5. Timeline and Team

Refer to the Timeline and Team sections in MR Credits 3–7 and IEQ Credits 4.1–4.4 and 4.6 in the LEED Reference Guide for Green Building Design and Construction.

6. Calculations

Calculations for this credit are based on the cost of materials purchased for the project that meet at least one of the listed sustainability criteria, compared with the total cost of all materials.

Furniture and furnishings (CSI Division 12 components) are excluded from the calculations for this credit. See MR Credit 5, Furniture and Medical Furnishings.

Do not include mechanical, electrical, and plumbing components or appliances and equipment in the calculations for this credit. Compared with structural and finish materials, mechanical and electrical equipment tends to have a high cost relative to the amount of material it contains, and that high dollar value would skew the results of the calculation, which is based on cost.

Note that built-in casework and built-in millwork items must be included in MR Credit 3.

For all materials that meet at least one of the listed sustainability criteria, record the type of item, cost, and quantity. For each item, also record the sustainability criterion that the item meets. Table 1 shows a sample sustainable materials documentation table. Because some products may meet more than one criterion, LEED for Healthcare supplements the "sustainable value" of such purchases, thereby ensuring that the added environmental benefit or impact reduction caused by products with multiple sustainability elements is reflected in compliance calculations.

For example, if one nonsteel, noncementitious product in the project costs $100 and contains 60% postconsumer recycled content (by weight) and 45% is extracted and manufactured within 500 miles of the project site (by weight), it contributes $105 toward the total sustainable value (60% * $100 + 45% * $100), as long as any applicable materials in that product also meet the requirements in IEQ Credit 4. If this alone were the only sustainable material in the project, and the total amount of materials in the project cost $500, the project would earn two points ($105 / $500 * 100% = 21% sustainable material), since one point is awarded for each 10% of sustainable materials.

If that same project included $190 worth of postindustrial recycled steel in the $500 total, the team would not be able to include the steel as part of the sustainable materials calculations, since that would have exceeded the 75% maximum allowable recycled steel contribution ($190 / [$60 + $190] = 76%).

See Table 1 for an example calculation.

Additional calculation guidance for the sustainability criteria can be found in the LEED Reference Guide for Green Building Design and Construction, under MR Credits 3–7.

7. Documentation Guidance

As a first step in preparing to complete the LEED Online documentation requirements, work through the following measures. Refer to LEED Online for the complete descriptions of all required documentation.

- Record product names, manufacturers' names, costs, and the percentage of sustainably sourced material content. For wall, ceiling, and flooring systems and finishes, exterior and interior adhesives, sealants, coatings, roofing, and waterproofing products, record specific VOC data (g/L, less water) for each product, as well as the corresponding allowable VOC from the referenced standard in IEQ Credit 4. For composite wood, agrifiber, and batt insulation products, confirm that each product does not contain any added urea-formaldehyde.
- Collect cut sheets or manufacturers' letters to document the listed products' relevant sustainable content.
- Track certified wood purchases and retain chain-of-custody documentation. Collect copies of vendor invoices for each certified wood product.
- Maintain a list of actual materials costs, excluding labor and equipment for CSI Division 03–10, 31 (Section 31.60.00 Foundations) and 32 (Sections 32.10.00 Paving, 32.30.00 Site Improvements, and 32.90.00 Planting) only; exclude Division 12.

Table 1. Sustainable Materials Table

Total construction cost for default total materials cost; OR provide total materials cost (exclude labor, equipment):	$100,152,500
Total Sustainably Sourced Content ($):	$10,150,725
Total Percentage Sustainably Sourced Materials:	10.14%
Total Points (1 point for each 10%):	1

Product Information					Sustainably Sourced Criteria								TOTALS
						Recycled Content							
Description of Product	Manufacturer or Vendor name	Material cost per item ($)	# purchased	Total Value as Purchased ($)	% Salvaged Material	% Pre-Consumer Recycled Content * 0.5	% Post-Consumer Recycled Content	Are supplemental cementitious materials derived from coal fired power plant wastes?	% Regional Content	% Rapidly Renewable Content	% FSC Certified Content	Meets IEQ Credit 4 criteria?	
Paint	Acme paint	$0.85/sq. ft.	750,000	$637,500	0%	0%	50%	n/a	0%	0%	0%	Yes	
Linoleum Flooring	Linseed Co.	$5.25/sq. ft.	9,429	$49,500	0%	0%	0%	n/a	0%	5%	0%	Yes	
Ceiling Tiles	Local Ceilings and Floors	$5.25/sq. ft.	300,000	$1,575,000	0%	30%	0%	n/a	12%	5%	0%	No	
				Sub-Total:	$0	$0	$318,750	$0	$0	$2,475	$0	69.63%	$321,225
Concrete & Steel						MAX 75% COMBINED COST							
Cast-in-Place Concrete	AAA Concrete Co.	$3.50/sq. ft.	830,000	$2,905,000	20%	45%	0%	No	95%	0%	0%	Yes	
Structural Steel	STEEL-BILT Fabricators	$2,000/ton	2,155	$4,310,000	0%	10%	75%	n/a	25%	0%	0%		
				Sub-Total:	$581,000	$5,411,250		$0	$3,837,250	$0	$0	100.00%	$9,829,500

8. Examples

Refer to the Examples sections in MR Credits 3–7 and IEQ Credits 4.1–4.4 and 4.6 in the LEED Reference Guide for Green Building Design and Construction.

9. Exemplary Performance

An Innovation in Design credit for exemplary performance is available if the project team documents that the value of sustainably sourced materials used on the project is 50% or more of the total materials cost.

10. Regional Variations

Refer to the Regional Variations sections in MR Credits 3–7 and IEQ Credits 4.1–4.4 and 4.6 in the LEED Reference Guide for Green Building Design and Construction.

11. Operations and Maintenance Considerations

Refer to the Operations and Maintenance Considerations sections in MR Credits 3–7 and IEQ Credits 4.1–4.4 and 4.6 in the LEED Reference Guide for Green Building Design and Construction.

Determine whether the healthcare campus has a green cleaning program. Train environmental services staff in the proper cleaning of unfamiliar finish materials. Consider installing pilot finish materials in an existing hospital to observe wear and tear, slip and fall potential, and cleanability. Gather feedback from nurses, doctors, environmental services, and infection control. In addition to training staff on cleaning and maintenance procedures, these demonstrations can help build support for installing sustainably sourced materials in the new facility.

The duplication, replacement, and repair of regional materials will be easier if information about the installed products has been maintained. Encourage the creation of a sustainable purchasing plan and provide building operators with lists of the installed products and their manufacturers, such as the documentation used in the LEED application.

Coordinate with facilities staff pursuing parallel credits in LEED for Existing Buildings: Operations & Maintenance and/or the Green Guide for Health Care, Operations section. The Green Guide for Health Care, in particular, addresses the synergies among environmentally preferable purchasing, waste reduction, and green cleaning in great detail.

12. Resources

Refer to the Resources sections in MR Credits 3–7 and IEQ Credits 4.1–4.4 and 4.6 in the LEED Reference Guide for Green Building Design and Construction.

Websites

Coal Combustion Residuals

U.S. Environmental Protection Agency

http://epa.gov/epawaste/nonhaz/industrial/special/fossil/coalashletter.htm

Information on coal combustion residuals (fly ash)—the materials that remain after burning coal for electricity—and EPA's proposed rule.

Green Guide for Health Care Low Emitting Materials Technical Brief, by Tom Lent

http://www.gghc.org/tools.technical.php

Best practices for specifying low-emitting adhesives, sealants, paints and coatings, flooring, wall coverings, trim, ceiling materials, composite wood, batt insulation, exterior applied products, and furniture and medical furnishings.

RIPPLE Database
The Center for Health Design
http://ripple.healthdesign.org
An open-source, searchable database that provides users with research, design strategies, and outcomes from multiple organizations.

13. Definitions

Refer to the Definitions sections in MR Credits 3–7 and IEQ Credits 4.1–4.4 and 4.6 in the LEED Reference Guide for Green Building Design and Construction.

PBT SOURCE REDUCTION—MERCURY IN LAMPS

	HEALTHCARE
Credit	MR Credit 4.1
Points	1 point

Intent

To reduce the release of Persistent Bioaccumulative and Toxic (PBTs) chemicals associated with the life cycle of building materials.

Requirements

In addition to the credit goals outlined in MR Prerequisite 2: PBT Source Reduction—Mercury, specify and install long lasting reduced mercury fluorescent lamps consistent with the following minimum criteria:

Fluorescent Lamp	Criteria
T-8 Eight-foot (Standard Output)	24,000 rated hours on instant start ballasts OR program start ballasts (3 hour starts)
T-8 Eight-foot (High Output)	18,000 rated hours on instant start ballasts OR program start ballasts (3 hour starts)
T-8 Four-foot (both Standard and High Output)	30,000 rated hours on instant start ballasts OR 36,000 rated hours on program start ballasts (3 hour starts)
T-8 Two-foot and Three-foot	24,000 rated hours on instant start ballasts OR program start ballasts (3 hour starts)
T-8 U-Bent	18,000 rated hours on instant start ballasts OR 24,000 rated hours on program start ballasts (3 hour starts)
T-5 (both Standard and High Output)	25,000 rated hours on program start ballasts
Compact fluorescent lamps, non-integral ballast	12,000 rated hours
Compact florescent lamps, integral ballast, bare bulb	10,000 rated hours
Compact fluorescent lamps, integral ballast, covered models such as globes, reflectors & A-19s	8,000 rated hours
High Pressure Sodium Lamp	**Criteria**
All HPS	Use non cycling type or replace with LED lamps or induction lamps

Note: Longer lamp life contributes to lower mercury use by reducing the frequency of lamp replacement.
Do not specify or install circular fluorescent lamps on the project.
Do not specify or install probe start metal halide lamps in the project.

IMPORTANT! This reference guide supplement contains only the reference guide sections that pertain to healthcare projects. Use this supplement alongside the LEED Reference Guide for Green Building Design and Construction for complete credit information. For the omitted sections, refer to the main reference guide.

MR	
HEALTHCARE: NC	Credit 4.1

1. Benefits and Issues to Consider

Refer to the Benefits and Issues to Consider section in MR Prerequisite 2.

2. Related Credits

Refer to the Related Credits section in MR Prerequisite 2.

3. Summary of Referenced Standards

Refer to the Referenced Standards section in MR Prerequisite 2.

4. Implementation

Refer to the Implementation section in MR Prerequisite 2.

5. Timeline and Team

Refer to the Timeline and Team section in MR Prerequisite 2.

6. Calculations

Refer to the Calculations section in MR Prerequisite 2.

7. Documentation Guidance

Refer to the Documentation Guidance section in MR Prerequisite 2.

8. Examples

Refer to the Examples section in MR Prerequisite 2.

9. Exemplary Performance

This credit is not eligible for exemplary performance under the Innovation in Design section.

10. Regional Variations

There are no regional variations associated with this credit.

11. Operations and Maintenance Considerations

Refer to the Operations and Maintenance section in MR Prerequisite 2.

12. Resources

Refer to the Resources section in MR Prerequisite 2.

13. Definitions

Refer to the Definitions section in MR Prerequisite 2.

PBT SOURCE REDUCTION—LEAD, CADMIUM, AND COPPER

	HEALTHCARE
Credit	MR Credit 4.2
Points	2 points

Intent

To reduce the release of Persistent Bioaccumulative and Toxic (PBTs) chemicals associated with the life cycle of building materials.

Requirements

Specify substitutes for materials manufactured with lead and cadmium, as follow:

- Specify and use 100% lead-free solder and flux used to connect plumbing pipe on-site for water intended for human consumption that meets the California AB1953 standard that solder must not contain more than 0.2% lead, and flux not more than a weighted average of 0.25% for wetted surfaces.
- Specify and use pipes, pipe fittings, plumbing fittings and faucets for water intended for human consumption that meets the California AB1953 standard of a weighted average lead content of the wetted surface area of not more than 0.25% lead.
- Specify and use lead-free roofing and flashing.
- Specify and use electrical wire and cable with lead content <300ppm.
- Specify no use of interior or exterior paints containing cadmium or lead. Green Seal certified paints or paints meeting Green Seal criteria exclude metals including cadmium, lead, mercury, antimony, and hexavalent chromium.

For copper pipe applications, reduce or eliminate joint-related sources of copper corrosion:

- use mechanically crimped copper joint system, or
- specify that all solder joints are compliant with ASTM B828 and specify and use ASTM B813 flux.

For renovation projects, ensure the removal and appropriate disposal of disconnected wires with lead stabilizers, consistent with the 2002 National Electric Code requirements.

Note: To comply with the intent of this credit, specify "100% lead free" products. The "lead free" label as defined by the EPA's Safe Drinking Water Act (SDWA) (http://www.epa.gov/safewater/sdwa/index.html) does not provide adequate screening for the purposes of this credit because these products may still contain lead.

The SDWA defines "lead free" as:

- Solders and flux containing 0.2% lead or less.
- Pipes, pipe fittings, and well pumps containing 8% lead or less.
- Lead used for radiation shielding and copper used for MRI shielding are exempt from the requirements of this credit.

IMPORTANT! This reference guide supplement contains only the reference guide sections that pertain to healthcare projects. Use this supplement alongside the LEED Reference Guide for Green Building Design and Construction for complete credit information. For the omitted sections, refer to the main reference guide.

1. Benefits and Issues to Consider[1]

Environmental Issues

Avoiding hazardous materials, such as lead and cadmium, is particularly important for healthcare facilities. Both lead and cadmium are persistent bioaccumulative toxic chemicals (PBT); they have a tendency to persist in the environment, accumulate in organisms high on the food chain, and can cause harm even in very small doses. PBTs released during the manufacture, use, or disposal of a product can threaten the health of plants and animals many miles away. It is therefore critical to eliminate emissions at their source through purchasing practices.

Economic Issues

Alternative building materials and equipment are becoming increasingly available. PBT-free paints and coatings, for example, are standard. For other products, such as lead radiation barriers, PBT-free alternatives continue to carry a significant cost premium. Healthcare organizations can accelerate demand for nontoxic products through volume purchasing.

2. Related Credits

PBT reduction is one piece of a larger strategy to avoid introducing toxic chemicals into the healthcare environment. Coordinate the project's approach to this credit with the following:

- SS Prerequisite 2, Environmental Site Assessment
- SS Credit 3, Brownfield Redevelopment
- MR Prerequisite 2, PBT Source Reduction—Mercury
- MR Credit 4.1, PBT Source Reduction—Mercury in Lamps
- MR Credit 5, Furniture and Medical Furnishings
- IEQ Credit 4, Low-Emitting Materials
- IEQ Credit 5, Indoor Chemical and Pollutant Source Control

For renovation projects, incorporate the removal and appropriate disposal of disconnected wires with lead stabilizers into demolition specifications, in compliance with the following prerequisite:

- IEQ Prerequisite 3, Hazardous Material Removal or Encapsulation (Renovations Only)

3. Summary of Referenced Standards

ASTM B813

http://www.astm.org/Standards/B813.htm

This standard addresses liquid and past fluxes for joining by soldering of copper and copper alloy pieces.

ASTM B828, Standard Practice for Making Capillary Joints by Soldering of Copper and Copper Alloy Tube and Fittings

http://www.astm.org/Standards/B828.htm

This standard addresses the techniques required to produce leak-tight soldered joints between copper and copper alloy pieces using exclusively lead-free solders.

California AB1953

http://info.sen.ca.gov/pub/05-06/bill/asm/ab_1951-2000/ab_1953_bill_20060930_chaptered.html

This standard prohibits the use of pipe, pipe or plumbing fitting or fixture, solder, or flux that is not lead free in plumbing fixtures. "Lead free" is defined as containing ffi 0.25% lead.

1 Reference guide material for this credit draws, with permission, from the following source: Tom Lent, Green Guide for Health Care PBT Elimination from Building Materials Technical Brief (http://www.gghc.org/tools.technical.php).

Green Seal certified paints
http://www.greenseal.org
Paints meeting Green Seal requirements do not contain cadmium or lead. They are also low emitting and therefore meet the requirements of EA Credit 4, Low-Emitting Materials.

2002 National Electric Code
http://www.nfpa.org
This regulation outlines the national standard for installing electrical wiring and cables, including proper procedures for the removal and appropriate disposal of disconnected wires with lead stabilizers.

4. Implementation

Establish a project goal for lead- and cadmium-free products and identify alternative products and suppliers. Add a LEED general requirements section to Division 01 to allow for writing LEED performance requirements for overlapping work sections, such as building envelope and structure. Then specify products and materials according to CSI MasterFormat 2004 classifications for Division 01. Ensure that PBT avoidance criteria are clearly specified. Careful research may be required to determine the material content that can realistically be expected in specific products and materials. Consider silver and other lead-free solder, solderless copper connectors and polyethylene piping, aluminum flashing and Green Seal–compliant paints. Some equipment, such as relay contacts, may have minute amounts of hidden cadmium; these uses are allowed.

For renovation projects, existing solder, flux, pipes, pipe fittings, faucets, roofing, flashing, electrical cable, cable, paints, and mechanical pipe connections that are not included in the scope of work may be excluded when determining compliance for this credit.

Although lead used for radiation shielding and copper used for MRI shielding are exempt from credit requirements, consider alternative shielding materials.

Plumbing

Incorporate requirements for 100% lead-free solder and flux into project specifications. Specify no- or low-lead faucets, valves, and appurtenances. Emphasize correct use of ASTM B813 fluxes, since using excess flux or a corrosive flux can cause early pipe failures.

Include safeguards against copper corrosion in piping in the project specifications. Consider noncopper tubing where its use is permitted. When installing copper pipes, minimize copper leaching rates by using the following best practices[2]:

- Use large-diameter piping to keep velocities low: cold line < 8 ft/s; hot line < 4–5 ft/s.
- Ensure that return lines in a circulating hot water system have the same diameter as the supply lines.
- Avoid stagnant sections by minimizing direction and size changes.
- Use compatible materials. When multiple materials do need to be joined, specify insulating unions.
- Specify copper or brass straps for supporting copper pipe.
- Prevent electrical currents by grounding directly to a copper rod driven into the ground. Do not attach a grounding wire to water pipes. Route wires away from water pipes and do not use galvanized nails that touch copper piping.
- Avoid induced stresses. Provide enough pipe support and allow for thermal expansion.

2 Preventing Corrosion Protects San Francisco Bay: A Fact Sheet for Designers (http://www.sanjoseca.gov/esd/PDFs/cu_designers_05_03.pdf).

- Emphasize careful reaming of cut ends in order to reduce turbulence. Unreamed tubing corrodes and fails more quickly than tubing that is properly reamed.[3]
- Use stainless steel piping and components for industrial process water supplies, heat exchangers, chillers, and condensers when operating temperatures exceed 140°F.
- Incorporate coupons or easy-access inspection points into long stretches of pipe to simplify corrosion monitoring.
- Provide flanged fittings or unions for pumps and other devices that must be removed for maintenance. This reduces soldering to aged pipe.

5. Timeline and Team

Establish PBT avoidance goals early in the project. Many product substitutions do not require major modifications to a project's design, but some may increase the construction budget. The owner, architect, civil engineer, MEP engineers, and other relevant project team members should evaluate the design and specifications at each project milestone to identify opportunities to minimize or eliminate materials and products containing PBTs without compromising building performance or the construction budget.

7. Documentation Guidance

As a first step in preparing to complete the LEED Online documentation requirements, work through the following measures. Refer to LEED Online for the complete descriptions of all required documentation.

- Track specified and installed materials by preparing a table of relevant standards for each product. Check product MSDS and manufacturers' documentation to ensure credit compliance.
- Prepare roofing, electrical wiring and painting schedules noting the "100% lead"- and cadmium-free specifications.
- Specify 100% lead-free and cadmium-free roofing, electrical wiring, and paints; advise contractors that material content will be a criterion in all substitution reviews.
- If the project is a major renovation, identify any materials outside the scope of work that do not meet the credit requirements.

9. Exemplary Performance

This credit is not eligible for exemplary performance under the Innovation in Design section.

11. Operations and Maintenance Considerations

Many healthcare institutions now practiced environmentally preferable purchasing, pollution prevention, and waste reduction. Consult with waste management and industrial hygiene experts to align lead, cadmium, and copper corrosion avoidance with best practices and protocols.

Coordinate with facilities staff pursuing parallel credits in the Green Guide for Health Care, Operations section. The Green Guide for Health Care addresses ways to avoid PBTs through environmentally preferable purchasing, waste reduction, and recycling practices.

3 Copper Development Association.

12. Resources

Websites

Copper Aquatic Life Criteria, Ambient Water Quality Criteria for Copper (2007)
U.S. Environmental Protection Agency
http://water.epa.gov/scitech/swguidance/waterquality/standards/criteria/aqlife/pollutants/copper/
A scientific assessment of copper's level of toxicity in various aquatic environments.

Green Guide for Health Care PBT Elimination from Building Materials Technical Brief, by Tom Lent
http://www.gghc.org/tools.technical.php
Best practices for specifying building materials, furniture, and medical furnishings with low levels or no persistent bioaccumulative toxics.

Hazards of Heavy Metal Contamination, by Lars Järup (*British Medical Bulletin* 68: 167–82, 2003)
DOI: 10.1093/bmb/ldg032
http://bmb.oxfordjournals.org/content/68/1/167.full
An overview of the health effects associated with mercury, lead, cadmium, and arsenic; global exposure rates to each substance; and the most prevalent exposure pathways, including via building materials.

Introduction to Indoor Air Quality, Lead
U.S. Environmental Protection Agency
http://www.epa.gov/iaq/lead.html
Information about the health effects associated with lead, its most prevalent exposure pathways to adults and children, and best practices and resources for reducing potential exposure in the indoor environment.

Preventing Corrosion Protects San Francisco Bay, a Fact Sheet for Designers
Bay Area Clean Water Agencies and Bay Area Pollution Prevention Group
http://www.sanjoseca.gov/esd/PDFs/cu_designers_05_03.pdf
An overview of the environmental benefits associated with reducing copper corrosion, as well as design best practices that can help reduce or prevent it from occurring.

Safe Drinking Water Act
U.S. Environmental Protection Agency
http://water.epa.gov/lawsregs/rulesregs/sdwa/index.cfm
The act, passed in 1974, is the federal law that sets quality standards for drinking water. It protects both the drinking water system and its sources, such as rivers, lakes, wells, and reservoirs.

13. Definitions

lead-free as defined by EPA regulations under the Safe Drinking Water Act, a label that allows small amounts of lead in solders, flux, pipes, pipe fittings, and well pumps, as opposed to 100% lead-free (ANSI–NSF Standard 61).

persistent bioaccumulative toxic (PBT) chemical a substance that poses a long-term risk to both humans and the environment because it persists in the environment for long periods, bioaccumulates up the food chain, and can travel far from the source of contamination. See EPA's website on PBTs (http://www.epa.gov/pbt/).

pollution prevention reducing or eliminating the source and proliferation of waste through modified production and purchasing practices; also called source reduction. See Pollution Prevention Act of 1990 (http://www.epa.gov/p2/pubs/p2policy/act1990.htm).

FURNITURE AND MEDICAL FURNISHINGS

	HEALTHCARE
Credit	MR Credit 5
Points	1–2 points

Intent

To enhance the environmental and human health performance attributes associated with freestanding furniture[1] and medical furnishings products.

Requirements

A percentage of the total value of all freestanding furniture and medical furnishings, including mattresses, foams, panel fabrics, cubicle curtains, window coverings, and other textiles, used in the project (based on cost) must meet the criteria in one of the three options below. The minimum percentage for each point is as follows:

% of Total Material	Points
30%	1
40%	2

Built-in casework and built-in millwork items must be included in the base building calculations, even if manufactured offsite. The dollar value of any individual product may be included in the total qualifying value if the product meets the criteria of any of the three options.

OPTION 1

All components of a furniture or medical furnishing assembly, including textiles, finishes and dyes, must contain less than 100 parts per million (ppm) of at least four of the five following chemical groups:

- Urea formaldehyde.
- Heavy metals including mercury, cadmium, lead, antimony.
- Hexavalent chromium in plated finishes consistent with the Restriction of the Use of Certain Hazardous Substances of the European Union Directive (EU RoHS).
- Stain and non-stick treatments derived from Perfluorinated Compounds (PFCs), including Perfluorooctanoic Acid (PFOA).
- Added antimicrobial treatments.

If the total weight is more than five percent of the product by weight, furniture components must be included.

OPTION 2

All components of a furniture or medical furnishing assembly,(including textiles, finishes and dyes, must contain less than 100 parts per million (ppm) of at least two of the five chemicals of materials listed in Option 1 AND the product must meet or exceed the indoor air quality requirements of California's Special Environmental Requirements, Specifications Section 01350, updated with California Department of Public Health Standard Method for the Testing and Evaluation of Volatile Organic Chemical Emissions from Indoor Sources Using Environmental Chambers version 1.1 (CDPH/EHLB Standard

1 Furniture is defined as any fixtures, such as shelving, tables, storage units, chairs, desks or cabinets, purchased as a free standing or modular unit, regardless of where the assembly takes place.

IMPORTANT! This reference guide supplement contains only the reference guide sections that pertain to healthcare projects. Use this supplement alongside the LEED Reference Guide for Green Building Design and Construction for complete credit information. For the omitted sections, refer to the main reference guide.

Method v1.1) as determined by independent laboratory testing and using the standard office building furniture protocol parameters.

The following programs currently utilize 01350 requirements for compliance for furniture:

- Scientific Certification Systems (SCS) Indoor Advantage Gold Environmental Certification Program
- Greenguard Product Emission Standard for Children & Schools

OPTION 3

All components of a furniture or medical furnishing assembly, including textiles, finishes and dyes, must meet the sustainably sourced materials criteria (salvaged, recycled, rapidly renewable, FSC-certified wood, local manufactured) of the MR Credit 3: Sustainably Sourced Materials and Products. Note: Furniture and medical furnishings do not contribute to MR Credit 3.

MR	
HEALTHCARE: NC	Credit 5

1. Benefits and Issues to Consider[2]

Environmental Issues

Sustainably sourced furniture and furnishings can reduce a healthcare facility's ecological footprint while improving its indoor environmental quality.

Avoiding hazardous substances such as mercury, cadmium, lead, antimony, hexavalent chromium, and perfluorinated compounds (PFCs) is particularly important for healthcare facilities. These persistent bioaccumulative toxic (PBT) chemical have a tendency to persist in the environment, accumulate in organisms high on the food chain, and can cause harm even in very small doses, contributing to cancer, endocrine disruption, brain and nervous system damage, birth defects, and impaired childhood development. PBTs released during the manufacture, use, or disposal of a product can threaten the health of plants and animals many miles away. It is therefore critical to eliminate emissions at their source through purchasing practices. PBT avoidance is also consistent with a European Union directive, Restriction of the Use of Certain Hazardous Substances.[3] Since 2006, when this regulation came into force in the European Union, access to low- and nontoxic products has greatly increased.

Nanotechnology can benefit society, but it also poses risks because of nanoscale materials' ability to cross biological barriers that protect human organs and tissues. Preliminary studies have reported toxic effects of nanomaterials on the lungs, heart, reproductive system, kidneys, and skin. Given uncertainty about the toxic effects of nanomaterials, such as added antimicrobial treatments, a precautionary approach regarding their use is appropriate.[4]

Healthcare project teams should minimize emissions of volatile organic compounds (VOCs) from furniture and furnishings to minimize the risk of exposure to sensitive populations, such as immuno-compromised patients. VOCs can compromise air quality that has been otherwise protected through building material specifications and construction practices.

Economic Issues

Healthcare furniture and furnishings are designed for clinical use and meet high standards of durability and cleanability. Over the past decade, product lines specific to healthcare applications have lagged behind other sectors (such as office furniture) in integrating sustainable material choices, such as nontoxic and low-emitting cores, fabrics, and foams. However, manufacturers have recently begun to respond to demand in the healthcare market, increasing availability and selection of more healthful product lines.

Although sustainably sourced furniture and furnishings can carry a first-cost premium, healthcare organizations can accelerate demand for these products through volume purchasing. As a predominantly owner-occupied building sector, healthcare can take advantage of the life-cycle benefits associated with sustainably sourced products that are durable and easily reconfigured or moved to accommodate changes in interior remodeling.

Materials with high VOC emissions can exacerbate illnesses and allergies; these products may lengthen hospital stays for patients and contribute to illness-related absences and lower productivity for staff. Repercussions include increased expenses and liability for building owners, operators, and insurance companies. The construction and operations markets are driving product manufacturers to offer low-VOC alternatives to conventional building products, and the cost of these products is generally competitive.

2 Reference guide material for this credit draws, with permission, from the following sources: Tom Lent, Green Guide for Health Care Low Emitting Materials Technical Brief; Tom Lent, Green Guide for Health Care PBT Elimination from Building Materials Technical Brief; and Lorissa MacAllister, Green Guide for Health Care Furniture and Medical Furnishings Technical Brief (http://www.gghc.org/tools.technical.php).

3 RoHS (Restriction of the Use of Certain Hazardous Substances of the European Union) Directive (http://www.rohs.eu/english/index.html).

4 Green Guide for Health Care Version 2.2, Operations, December 2008 (http://www.gghc.org/tools.2.2overview.php).

MR	
HEALTHCARE: NC	Credit 5

2. Related Credits

Coordinate the project's approach to furniture and furnishings with the approach to sustainably sourced building materials specifications, contributing to the following credit:

- MR Credit 3, Sustainably Sourced Materials and Products

Because the intent of this credit is to reduce odorous, irritating, or harmful indoor air contaminants, coordinate furniture and furnishings specifications with the following credit:

- IEQ Credit 4, Low-Emitting Materials

Incorporate the project's approach to specifying sustainably sourced materials into its overall toxic chemical avoidance strategies. See IEQ Credit 4, Low-Emitting Materials, for what products and materials can be included in the credit calculation.

Consider a material's content, whether it can be cleaned with nontoxic products, and its potential to contaminate the construction waste stream. This approach will contribute to achievement of the following prerequisites and credits:

- MR Prerequisite 1, Storage and Collection of Recyclables
- MR Prerequisite 2, PBT Source Reduction—Mercury
- MR Credit 2, Construction Waste Management
- MR Credit 4.1, PBT Source Reduction—Mercury in Lamps
- MR Credit 4.2, PBT Source Reduction—Lead, Cadmium and Copper

Address scheduling strategies and the use and tracking of furniture and furnishings in the contractors' orientation training, covered under these two credits:

- IEQ Credit 3.1, Construction Indoor Air Quality Management Plan—During Construction
- IEQ Credit 3.2, Construction Indoor Air Quality Management Plan—Before Occupancy

Indoor air quality is affected by sources generated within the building itself and introduced into its spaces. Both sources are addressed in the following prerequisite and credit:

- IEQ Prerequisite 2, Environmental Tobacco Smoke (ETS) Control
- IEQ Credit 5, Indoor Chemical and Pollutant Source Control

3. Summary of Referenced Standards

Refer to the Referenced Standards section in MR Credit 3, Sustainably Sourced Materials and Products.

California Department of Public Health, Standard Method for the Testing and Evaluation of Volatile Organic Chemical Emissions from Indoor Sources Using Environmental Chambers, Version 1.1, February 2010 (CDPH/EHLB Standard Method v1.1)
California Department of Public Health, Indoor Air Quality Section, Environmental Health Laboratory Branch, Division of Environmental and Occupational Disease Control
http://www.cal-iaq.org/vocs/voc-publications

This standard is the emissions-testing method for California Specification 01350. Version 1.1 was released in February 2010 and supersedes the previous version, Standard Practice for the Testing of Volatile Organic Emissions from Various Sources Using Small-Scale Environmental Chambers (2004).

The method applies to any product generally used in an enclosed indoor environment. It establishes the procedures for product sample collection, emissions testing, indoor concentration modeling, and documentation requirements associated with quantifying the emissions of volatile organic chemicals from various sources using environmental chambers. It also establishes performance criteria for specific chemicals of interest. These criteria are specifically for evaluating potential chronic health risks from inhalation exposures of vapor-phase organic chemicals.

Restriction of the Use of Certain Hazardous Substances of the European Union Directive (EU RoHS)
http://www.rohs.eu/english/index.html
RoHS is a regulation in the European Union that sets limits on the levels of lead, cadmium, mercury, hexavalent chromium, polybrominated biphenyl (PBB), and polybrominated diphenyl ether (PBDE) flame retardants in new electrical and electronic equipment.

4. Implementation

Establish goals for sustainably sourced furniture and medical furnishings during the design phase and include them in the project specifications. Decide which credit option is most advantageous for the project.

Incorporating sustainability criteria into furniture schedules and specifications is not a LEED requirement, but it can help in achieving the credit. Add a LEED general requirements section to Division 01 to allow for writing LEED performance requirements for overlapping work sections. Then specify furniture and furnishings in Division 12 according to CSI MasterFormat 2004 classifications for Division 01 sustainably sourced material requirements. Careful research may be required to determine the material content that can realistically be expected in specific products.

Identify opportunities to incorporate salvaged, reused, regional, rapidly renewable, and Forest Stewardship Council–certified wood into furniture, including case pieces, seating, and filing systems, and medical furnishings, such as exam tables, stools, and carts. Consider a range of environmental, economic, and performance attributes when selecting products.

Under Option 1 and Option 2, used furniture is not exempt and must meet the content and emissions requirements of the credit. Projects that install large quantities of used furniture may find Option 3 advantageous.

During construction, ensure that the specified products are installed and determine their percentage of the total products installed.

To reduce construction waste (see MR Credit 2), consider requiring the product manufacturer to follow an integrated sustainable packaging and shipping plan. Coordinate with the furniture supplier to minimize fuel waste and packaging by using full truckloads and dedicated trucks whenever possible. Through scheduling, routing, and coordination of deliveries, encourage full truckloads and minimized travel. Minimize double handling to reduce loss and damage. Require that easily damaged products (such as glazing) have transparent packaging to allow visual assessment of damaged products. Request that orders ship complete (no backorders) to minimize the number of shipments. Incorporate packaging requirements into the plan, including a requirement that the supplier use specialized furniture carriers and trucks to minimize packaging needs. Further minimize packaging by palletizing and packing products in bulk. Require the manufacturer to ship products in reusable packaging (such as blanket wrapping) and retrieve the packaging after delivery.

5. Timeline and Team

A goal of incorporating sustainably sourced furniture and furnishings can affect costs, the demolition phase (if furniture will be salvaged from an existing facility), and the ultimate design of the project. Coordination among the owner, architect or design team, and contractor should begin early, in the predesign phase of interior design, and continue through design development so that sustainably sourced choices can be creatively and efficiently worked into the basis of design. Documentation should likewise begin early.

During predesign, the project team should assess opportunities for reusing furniture and furnishings and set goals accordingly. If existing furnishings are on-site at the beginning of the construction process, the contractor should plan to store and conserve them. This is an opportunity in the project timeline for any necessary repair and refurbishment. Inventory furnishings in the existing facility, identify likely items for reuse, determine storage areas, and tally the potential savings. The ideal time for this is during the design development phase of work, when the projected cost benefits of reuse can have the greatest impact on the project's finances.

If new furniture will be purchased, the architect should incorporate sustainably sourced furniture and furnishings into the design and then, during the construction documents and specifications development phase, identify potential suppliers. Run preliminary calculations as soon as a project budget is available, to set appropriate targets.

All project team members, including the general contractor and subcontractors, should consult with suppliers before the buyout phase to determine the availability of products and the specific amount of sustainably sourced content within each product type. Careful planning before construction can minimize capital expenses and enable the project team to verify whether the procured products meet project targets. During construction, the contractor should document and track the cost and quantity of the products. This recordkeeping will aid the project team in the credit submittal process.

6. Calculations

Calculations for this credit are based on the material cost of furniture and furnishings purchased for the project, including all freestanding furniture. Generally, this credit includes products specified in CSI 2004 Division 12, Furniture. Note that built-in millwork and casework must be included in MR Credit 3 under the base building calculations; it is excluded from MR Credit 5. The value of a piece of furniture that meets criteria under more than one option can be counted more than once (see Examples, below).

Materials costs include all taxes, transportation, and other expenses to deliver the material to the project site; exclude any cost for labor and equipment once the material has been delivered to the site.

Track the cost of all furniture and furnishings purchased for the project. For salvaged furniture, this cost will be the replacement value. The replacement value can be determined by pricing a comparable piece of furniture or furnishing in the local market, excluding labor and shipping. If a project team receives a discount from a vendor, the replacement value should reflect the discounted price as opposed to the list value. If the actual cost paid for the reused or salvaged product is below the cost of an equivalent new item, use the higher value (actual cost) in the calculations. If the cost to reclaim an item found on-site is less than the cost of an equivalent new item, use the cost of the new item (i.e., replacement cost).

Material Assemblies

Assemblies are products made of multiple materials, either in their formulation (e.g., particle board) or in their manufacture (e.g., workstation components). For assembly content, the fraction of the assembly that is considered sustainably sourced is determined by weight. Multiply the sustainable content fraction of the assembly by the cost of assembly to determine the sustainable content cost value.

No consideration is given to relative costs of the materials or the subcomponents when calculating these percentages of recycled content. For example, a pound of steel in a window assembly is of equal significance in determining recycled content as a pound of fabric on a movable wall panel.

Refer to the Calculations section under MR Credit 3, Sustainably Sourced Materials, and also see MR Credits 3–7 in the LEED Reference Guide for Green Building Design and Construction for information on how to calculate Option 3.

7. Documentation Guidance

As a first step in preparing to complete the LEED Online documentation requirements, work through the following measures. Refer to LEED Online for the complete descriptions of all required documentation.

- Incorporate the credit requirements into the project's green submittal form and appropriate specifications sections.
- Record product names, manufacturers' names, costs, and the percentage of sustainably sourced material content.
- Collect cutsheets or manufacturers' letters to document the listed products' content.
- For projects pursuing Option 3, track certified wood purchases and retain chain-of-custody documentation. Collect copies of vendor invoices for each certified wood product.
- Maintain a list of actual materials costs, excluding labor and equipment for CSI Division 12.

8. Examples

See Table 1 for an example demonstrating the weighted calculation for sustainably sourced furniture and furnishings.

Furniture that meets the criteria for more than one option can be counted twice. For example, if a purchased unit costs $100 and 95% of the product by weight meets Option 1 and 100% meets Option 2, that purchase would contribute $200 toward the sustainable purchases total.

In Option 3, the combined value of the sustainable content in furniture and furnishings must be at least 10% of the total furniture and furnishings value. For example, if the furniture and furnishing stock in the project contains 4% postconsumer content, 4% rapidly renewable materials, and 2% local materials, the total sustainable value is 10%, and the project would qualify.

9. Exemplary Performance

An Innovation in Design credit for exemplary performance is available for projects achieving a 50% threshold of achievement.

10. Regional Variations

The availability of locally manufactured furniture and medical furnishings varies. A project team in a manufacturing region will have more choices, as well as more opportunities for the reclamation rather than disposal of materials at the end of their useful lives, and can specify particular regional sources.

When considering sustainable furniture and furnishings, give attention to the entire life cycle of the product within the region and how it will affect the local environment.

11. Operations and Maintenance Considerations

Include durability and cleaning criteria in specifications for furniture and medical furnishings. Determine whether the healthcare campus has instituted a green cleaning program. Consider installing pilot furniture and medical furnishings in an existing hospital to observe how well the products withstand typical wear and tear and whether they meet infection control requirements. Gather feedback from nurses, doctors, environmental services, and infection control. In addition to training staff on cleaning and maintenance procedures, these demonstrations can help build support for installing sustainably sourced products in the new facility.

Table 1. Sustainable Materials Table: Furniture and Furnishings

Total Furniture Material Cost (excluding labor):	**$200,000**
Total Sustainably Sourced Furniture & Medical Furnishings (OPTION 1 + OPTION 2 + OPTION 3):	**$70,500**
Percentage Sustainably Sourced Furniture & Medical Furnishings:	**35.25%**
Total Points (30%: 1 point; 40%: 2 points):	**1**

Product Information					CHEMICAL GROUPS (OPTION 1 = 4 minimum, OPTION 2 = 2 minimum)					
Description of Product	**Manufacturer or Vendor name**	**Material cost per item ($)**	**# purchased**	**Total Value as Purchased ($)**	Contains less than 100 parts per million (ppm) of urea-formaldehyde resin?	Contains less than 100 parts per million (ppm) of heavy metals including mercury, cadmium, lead, antimony?	Contains less than 100 parts per million (ppm) of hexavalent chromium in plated finishes (per RoHS)?	Contains less than 100 parts per million (ppm) of stain and non-stick treatments derived from Perfluorinated Compounds (PFCs), including Perfluorooctanoic Acid (PFOA)?	Contains less than 100 parts per million (ppm) of added antimicrobial treatments?	Total # Compliant Chemical Groups
Workstation Chairs	Sit-EZ Distributors	$200.00	100	$20,000	Yes	Yes	Yes	Yes	No	4
Waiting Room Chairs	Sit-EZ Distributors	$150.00	25	$3,750	Yes	Yes	Yes	No	No	3
Modular Workstations	NU Modular, Inc.	$1,000.00	100	$100,000	n/a	n/a	n/a	n/a	n/a	0

Table 1. Sustainable Materials Table: Furniture and Furnishings (continued)

OPTION 2	OPTION 1 & 2 TOTALS		OPTION 3							OPTION 3 TOTAL
Product meets or exceeds IAQ requirements of CDPH/EHLB Standard Method 1.1?	Total product value of products compliant with Option 1	Total product value of products compliant with Option 2	% Salvaged Material	% Pre-Consumer Recycled Content * 0.5	% Post-Consumer Recycled Content	% Regional Content	% Rapidly Renewable Content	% FSC Certified Content	Meets IEQ Credit 4 criteria?	Total product value of products compliant with Option 3
No	$20,000		0%	0%	10%	0%	0%	0%	Yes	
Yes		$3,750	0%	10%	5%	0%	0%	25%	Yes	
No			0%	30%	0%	12%	5%	0%	Yes	
	Sub-Total OPTION 3:		$0	$30,375	$2,188	$12,000	$5,000	$938	100%	$50,500

MR	
HEALTHCARE: NC	Credit 5

Implement a sustainable purchasing, maintenance, and waste management policy for furniture and medical furnishings during the building's operation. In many cases, the furniture package is separate from the capital budget and adheres to a later schedule than the remainder of the project budget. Coordinating with the purchasing department campuses and with large healthcare organizations, because a furniture and furnishings policy may be already in operation. Help building operators find low-emitting furniture systems for future installations by providing them with the list of compliant products used on the new construction or renovation project.

Ensure that furniture and furnishings have an "end of life" reclamation destination. Prioritize products that are designed for disassembly, recyclability, biodegradability, or are part of a "take back" program.

Coordinate with facilities staff pursuing parallel credits in LEED for Existing Buildings: Operations & Maintenance and/or the *Green Guide for Health Care, Operations* section. *The Green Guide for Health Care*, in particular, addresses the benefits of coordinating PBT avoidance through environmentally preferable purchasing with waste reduction and recycling practices.

12. Resources

Please see USGBC's LEED Registered Project Tools (http://www.usgbc.org/projecttools) for additional resources and technical information.

Websites

Consumer Products Treated with Pesticides
U.S. Environmental Protection Agency
EPA 735-F-03-006, http://www.epa.gov/pesticides/factsheets/treatart.htm
Regulations on consumer products (including building materials) treated with antimicrobial agents. These treatments are identified by EPA as treatments that protect the product itself; they are not proven to protect users from exposure to microorganisms.

Definition of Standard Office Environments for Evaluating the Impact of Office Furniture Emissions on Indoor VOC Concentrations, by R.D. Carter and J.S. Zhang (ASHRAE *Transactions* 113(2): 466–77, 2007)
An overview of a study to define a representative "worst-case" office space that could be used to estimate the effects of furniture VOC emissions on indoor air quality.

Evaluation of Antimicrobial Property Claims in Finishes and Fabrics, by Erica Stewart (Kaiser Permanente, 2006)
http://www.healthybuilding.net/healthcare/KP_Antimicrobial_Position_Paper.pdf
A literature review on the effectiveness of antimicrobial treatments added to finishes and fabrics to improve infection control in the healthcare environment. The author concludes that insufficient evidence exists to warrant specifying building materials with added antimicrobial agents.

Furniture Sustainability Standard and level™ Certification Program
Business and Institutional Furniture Manufacturers Association (BIFMA) e3-2008
http://www.levelcertified.org
This third-party sustainability certification program was developed by BIFMA for the furniture industry. The system assesses products based on the following criteria: materials, energy and atmosphere, human and ecosystem health, and social responsibility.

The Future of Fabric: Health Care, by Julie Silas, Jean Hansen, and Tom Lent
http://www.healthybuilding.net/healthcare/FutureOfFabric.pdf
An overview of fabrics used in the healthcare environment, with information on chemicals that should be avoided and emerging alternatives that are safer and more environmentally friendly than conventional options.

Get a Whiff of This: The Lowdown on Product Emissions Testing, by Nadav Malin (*Environmental Building News*, September 2006)
Posted with permission at http://www.bifma.org/standards/FES/FES%20Cont%20Ed%20Materials/EBN_Product_Emissions.pdf
An overview of VOC emissions testing and compares testing programs. It also addresses emerging topics, such as semivolatile organic compounds.

Green Guide for Health Care Furniture and Medical Furnishings Technical Brief, by Lorissa MacAllister
http://www.gghc.org/tools.technical.php
Best practices for specifying nontoxic, sustainably sourced furniture and furnishings in the healthcare environment.

Green Guide for Health Care Low Emitting Materials Technical Brief, by Tom Lent
http://www.gghc.org/tools.technical.php
Best practices for specifying low-emitting adhesives, sealants, paints and coatings, flooring, wall coverings, trim, ceiling materials, composite wood, batt insulation, exterior applied products, and furniture and medical furnishings.

Green Guide for Health Care PBT Elimination from Building Materials Technical Brief, by Tom Lent
http://www.gghc.org/tools.technical.php
Best practices for specifying building materials, furniture, and medical furnishings with low levels or no persistent bioaccumulative toxics.

Greenguard Children & Schools Certification
http://www.greenguard.org/en/manufacturers/manufacturer_childrenSchools.aspx
This third-party certification program for indoor environmental quality applies to furniture and other materials and products used in an indoor environment. Children & Schools, targeted to the educational and healthcare environment, is more stringent than Greenguard certification, setting emissions control criteria with a body burden correction factor, chronic reference VOC exposure levels, and limits on phthalate emissions.

Scientific Certification Systems (SCS) Indoor Advantage Gold Certification
http://www.scscertified.com/gbc/indoor_air_quality.php
This third-party certification program for indoor environmental quality applies to furniture and other materials and products used in an indoor environment.

13. Definitions

added antimicrobial agent a substance added to a product (such as paint or flooring) that kills or inhibits growth of microorganisms. Some products, such as linoleum, exhibit natural antimicrobial properties. However, adding antimicrobial agents to building finishes has not been scientifically proven to reduce infection transfer more effectively than standard cleaning procedures. See U.S. EPA factsheet, Consumer Products Treated with Pesticides (http://www.epa.gov/pesticides/factsheets/treatart.htm).

chain-of-custody a tracking procedure for a product from the point of harvest or extraction to its end use, including all successive stages of processing, transformation, manufacturing, and distribution.

component an item that, when assembled with other elements, makes up modular furniture. Modular furniture components include panels (walls, partitions, dividers), work surfaces, storage elements, electrical and data cables, connectors, and supports.

engineered nanomaterial a substance designed at the molecular (nanometer) level to take advantage of its small size and novel properties that are generally not seen in its conventional bulk counterpart. See http://www.nicnas.gov.au/publications/information_sheets/general_information_sheets/nis_nanomaterials_pdf.pdf.

freestanding furniture movable furnishings. Freestanding furniture may be anchored to a wall for seismic or stability requirements.

infection control policies and procedures to minimize the risk of spreading infections through cross-contamination.

market value the amount that either was paid or would have been paid for a product; it is presumed to be less than replacement value.

persistent bioaccumulative toxic (PBT) chemical a substance that poses a long-term risk to both humans and the environment because it persists in the environment for long periods, bioaccumulates up the food chain, and can travel far from the source of contamination. See EPA's website on PBTs (http://www.epa.gov/pbt/).

pollution prevention reducing or eliminating the source and proliferation of waste through modified production and purchasing practices; also called source reduction. See Pollution Prevention Act of 1990 (http://www.epa.gov/p2/pubs/p2policy/act1990.htm).

refurbished material an item that has completed its life cycle and is refurbished for reuse without substantial alteration of its form. Refurbishing involves renovating, repairing, restoring, or generally improving the appearance, performance, quality, functionality, or value of a product.

remanufactured material an item that is made into another product. One example is concrete that is crushed and used as subbase.

replacement value the estimated cost of replacing a used product. This value may be equal to the cost of a similar new product or based on a new product with comparable features.

salvaged material an item recovered from an existing building or construction site and reused. Common salvaged materials include structural beams and posts, flooring, doors, cabinetry, brick, and decorative items.

RESOURCE USE—DESIGN FOR FLEXIBILITY

	HEALTHCARE
Credit	MR Credit 6
Points	1 point

Intent

To conserve resources associated with the construction and management of buildings by designing for flexibility and ease of future adaptation, and service life of constituent components and assemblies.

Requirements

Increase building flexibility and ease of adaptive reuse over the life of the structure by employing a minimum of three of the following design and/or space planning strategies:

- Use of interstitial space[1] serving for a minimum 20% of project diagnostic and treatment or other clinical floor area [calculation based on Departmental Gross Square Foot (DGSF)]. Design distribution systems for electrical, information technology, communication, medical gases, and sprinklers with the capability to control multiple zones in clinical spaces. (Inpatient units are included in this calculation.)
- Provide programmed soft space[2], such as administration/storage, equal to a minimum of 5% of total clinical space. Locate soft space adjacent to clinical departments that anticipate growth. Determine strategy for future accommodation of displaced soft space (calculation based on project DGSF).
- Provide shelled space[3] equal to a minimum of 5% of total project departmental clinical space; locate where it can be occupied without displacing occupied space (calculation based on project DGSF).
- Identify horizontal expansion capacity for diagnostic and treatment or other clinical space equal to a minimum of 30% of existing gross square footage (excluding inpatient units) without demolition of occupied space (other than at the connection point of future expansion). Reconfiguration of additional existing occupied space that has been constructed with demountable partition systems is permitted. Or design for future vertical expansion on a minimum of 75% of the roof, ensuring that existing operations and service systems will be able to operate at or near capacity during the expansion.
- Designate location(s) for future above-grade parking structure(s) equal to 50% of existing on-grade parking capacity, with direct access to the main hospital lobby/circulation/vertical transportation pathways.
- Use of demountable partitions for 50% of applicable areas as a strategy for future flexibility.
- Use movable/modular casework for a minimum of 50% of casework and custom millwork. (Calculation is based upon the combined value of the twoelements, as determined by the cost estimator or contractor).

1 "Interstitial space" is an n intermediate space located between floors, often used to run mechanical equipment, wiring, and other support services to the occupied floors above and/or below.

2 "Soft space" is a lightly programmed area that can be easily displaced to allow a neighboring area, such as a clinical department, opportunity to expand.

3 "Shell space" is an area designed to be fitted out for future expansion. Shell spaces are enclosed by the exterior building shell, but otherwise left unfinished.

IMPORTANT! This reference guide supplement contains only the reference guide sections that pertain to healthcare projects. Use this supplement alongside the LEED Reference Guide for Green Building Design and Construction for complete credit information. For the omitted sections, refer to the main reference guide.

1. Benefits and Issues to Consider[4]

Environmental Issues

Healthcare practices and technologies are rapidly evolving, often requiring changes in the physical layout of the facility. In 2005, renovations accounted for fully one-third of the total cost of acute-care hospital construction in the United States.[5] The amount of construction waste associated just with churn often dwarfs the environmental consequences of initial construction. Buildings designed for adaptive use, in contrast, are more easily renovated and expanded. Reusing movable wall partitions, for example, reduces the solid waste generated by demolition of the old walls and avoids raw material extraction for new walls. A building with durable, flexible, adaptive, generic spaces can be more easily altered for new equipment and infrastructure requirements, with a consequent reduction in waste.

Economic Issues

The financial burden of churn is considerable. Healthcare project teams can minimize the time, money, and waste associated with churn over a building's lifetime by incorporating integrated building systems that support a changing care delivery system and minimize the effect of change on operations. Facilities designed to accommodate adaptive use also allow for more efficient planning and greatly reduce the time and cost attributed to full-blown renovation projects.

2. Related Credits

A healthcare design that allows for flexibility requires that the entire project team commit to the integrated design process starting during the predesign phase, contributing to the following prerequisite and credit:

- ID Prerequisite 1, Integrative Project Planning and Design
- ID Credit 3, Integrative Project Planning and Design

Making flexibility a goal can influence the design in a number of ways—for example, by standardizing construction material sizes to reduce waste during new construction. It can also help the project team think creatively about how to make best use of an existing building or how to provide daylight and views to staff areas. These strategies contribute to the following credits:

- MR Credit 1, Building Reuse
- MR Credit 2, Construction Waste Management
- IEQ Credit 8, Daylight and Views

Flexibility is also related to LEED prerequisites and credits for reducing exposure to toxic chemicals and improving indoor environmental quality, because it may limit the materials selection to modular systems. Consider components that can be removed and reused in future reconfigurations or salvaged during future renovations. See the following credits:

- MR Credit 3, Sustainably Sourced Materials and Products
- MR Credit 5, Furniture and Medical Furnishings
- IEQ Credit 2, Acoustic Environment
- IEQ Credit 4, Low-Emitting Materials

4 Reference guide material for this credit drawn, with permission, from the following source: Green Guide for Health Care unpublished working technical brief. http://www.gghc.org

5 Dave Carpenter, The Boom Goes On, *Hospitals & Health Networks*, March 2006 (http://www.hhnmag.com/hhnmag_app/jsp/articledisplay.jsp?dcrpath=HHNMAG/PubsNewsArticle/data/2006March/0603HHN_FEA_Construction&domain=HHNMAG).

MR	
HEALTHCARE: NC	Credit 6

4. Implementation

At the beginning of design, flexibility is often listed as a priority because project teams know that it increases a building's longevity and allows adaptation for advances in healthcare practices and technology. During the programming stage, however, it is often pushed aside because of the complexity of establishing critical adjacencies in clinical areas and settling departmental turf battles. In addition, many flexibility strategies that are effective for commercial office buildings, such as underfloor air distribution and movable wall systems, are either not allowed by regulations or are functionally inappropriate for healthcare structures. These strategies complicate compliance with several requirements particular to the healthcare environment, such as the sound transmission ratings required by the Health Insurance Portability and Accountability Act (HIPAA) of 1996.[6]

- Strategies that allow flexibility to accommodate future modifications include the following: Modular, generic spaces and repetitive design elements. Optimize space by planning multiple uses for individual spaces, alternative officing (whereby unassigned, flexible workstations are shared by multiple users), and universal sizing (e.g., standardized rooms and workstations).
- Use of standard material sizes. Perform dimensional planning for standard material sizes, using 2-foot incremental dimensions. For example, an 8-by-12-foot room generally creates less waste than one measuring 7 1/2 by 11 1/3 feet.
- Repetitive design elements. Using repetitive dimensions throughout the design of the project facilitates cutting in large batches in a single location, which in turn facilitates recycling and efficient disposal of cutoffs.
- Acuity-adaptable and universal patient rooms. Adopt acuity-adaptable and universal design concepts both to enhance the quality of patient care and to minimize future changes to patient rooms.
- Design for future adaptability. Ample floor-to-floor heights and raised floor distribution systems or interstitial space will simplify future modifications. Install undifferentiated "technology floors" that can accommodate surgery, cardiology, and radiology programs in equally sized, adaptable modules.
- Shell or "soft" space located adjacent to major clinical areas. Determine which clinical programs are likely to grow and locate shell or soft space to permit their expansion without major disruption or reconfiguration.
- Corridors and stairways that support future additions without demolition of occupied space. Locate stairs to provide an alternative to elevator use while simultaneously avoiding exit tunnels. This will cause less disruption during future construction as well as reduce waste from demolition.
- Building systems and components that are easy to disassemble and reconfigure. Install interior partitions and modular, demountable building systems that can be relocated, reused, or salvaged in the future. Reduce future renovation costs by including detailing for screws and bolts in place of nails and adhesives. Install systems that enable lighting and controls to be moved throughout an interior space without the need to rewire or reconfigure.

6 Health Insurance Portability and Accountability Act (HIPAA) (http://www.hhs.gov/ocr/privacy/).

5. Timeline and Team

The challenge of designing and constructing a healthcare facility with a high degree of flexibility requires early commitment from the owner, architect, medical planner, MEP engineers, structural engineer, and contractor, among others. The project team should develop measurable goals at the integrated design charrette during the predesign or schematic design phase and assess progress at each project milestone.

During design development or, at the latest, early in the construction document phase, coordinate construction details and construction material dimensions with the contractor, and coordinate changes that affect mechanical, electrical, and plumbing systems with the MEP engineer and commissioning agent.

Inspect the site during construction to verify that the universal design criteria and other standardizations have been carried out.

6. Calculations

Interstitial Space, Soft Space, and Shell Space

- Step 1. Calculate the project's departmental gross square footage by adding the area of all departments in the building program, starting from the centerline of the walls separating a department from adjacent spaces. Include walls and corridors interior to the department in the calculation.
- Step 2. Use Equation 1 to calculate the total required square footage for interstitial space and use Equation 2 to calculate the total required square footage for soft space and shell space.

Equation 1

Minimum Interstitial Area (sf) = 0.2 X (Departmental Gross Square Footage, including Inpatient Units)

Equation 2

Minimum Soft and Shell Area (sf) = 0.05 X (Departmental Gross Square Footage for Clinical Spaces)

Horizontal Expansion

Step 1. Calculate the project's gross square footage by summing the square footage of the entire building, including exterior walls, mechanical spaces, and covered areas. Exclude inpatient areas from the calculation.

Step 2. Use Equation 3 to calculate the total required square footage for horizontal expansion.

Equation 3

Minimum Horizontal Expansion Area (sf) = 0.3 X (Existing Gross Square footage, excluding Inpatient Units)

Vertical Expansion

Identify 75% of the roof square footage that could accommodate vertical expansion without critically disrupting existing operations and service systems.

Future Parking Structure

Calculate the square footage required to accommodate 50% of existing on-grade parking in an above-grade parking structure, and identify an eligible location on-site for this expansion.

Demountable Partitions

Identify the spaces in the building that could use demountable partitions. Areas where demountable partitions are inapplicable include inpatient nursing units (such as ICU), surgery, postanesthesia care units, emergency department treatment areas, and acute trauma. If other areas should be excluded as well, provide the rationale.

Calculate the area of the spaces actually enclosed by demountable partitions; it should be at least 50% of the total square footage of the spaces that could use demountable partitions.

Casework and Custom Millwork

Calculate the value of casework and custom millwork that is movable or modular; it should be at least 50% of the combined value of all casework and millwork in the project.

7. Documentation Guidance

As a first step in preparing to complete the LEED Online documentation requirements, work through the following measures. Refer to LEED Online for the complete descriptions of all required documentation.

- Prepare site drawings, floor plans, and sections, as applicable, showing compliance with the flexibility strategies pursued by the project.

9. Exemplary Performance

This credit is not eligible for exemplary performance under the Innovation in Design section.

10. Regional Variations

Building codes and construction best practices, as well as healthcare regulations, vary by region and will influence which flexibility design practices are most appropriate for the project.

11. Operations and Maintenance Considerations

Gather feedback from healthcare executives, nurses, doctors, and facilities staff to identify which flexibility strategies are most likely to anticipate the organization's future needs. For healthcare projects on existing campuses, a master plan may provide valuable information about the organization's vision for the future.

Coordinate with facilities staff pursuing parallel credits in LEED for Existing Buildings: Operations & Maintenance and/or the Green Guide for Health Care, Operations section. The Green Guide for Health Care, in particular, addresses how flexible design can minimize construction waste and exposure of building occupants to dust and debris from renovations and expansions.

12. Resources

Design for Disassembly in the Built Environment
King County, WA
http://www.lifecyclebuilding.org/files/DfDseattle.pdf
Guidelines for integrating the concept of disassembly (of both building materials and systems) into the design process.

Designing with Vision: A Technical Manual for Material Choices in Sustainable Construction (2000)
California Integrated Waste Management Board
http://www.ciwmb.ca.gov/ConDemo/Pubs.htm
Chapter 8 offers best practice guidance on how to optimize use of building materials in sustainable construction, including strategies to reuse materials and reduce overall material use in construction.

Dimensional Coordination of Rectilinear Building Parts
American Society for Testing and Materials (ASTM) E577–85:2002
http://www.astm.org/Standards/E577.htm
Information on using modular coordination of standard materials sizes to achieve economies in design, detailing, production, and construction.

Guideline for Design for Disassembly and Adaptability in Buildings
Canadian Standards Association (CSA) Z782-06
http://www.csa.ca/cm/ca/en/guideline-for-design-for-disassembly-in-buildings
Guidelines for designing nonresidential structures with disassembly and adaptability in mind.

Health Insurance Portability and Accountability Act (HIPAA)
http://www.hhs.gov/ocr/privacy/
HIPAA is the federal regulation that sets the standard for protection of personal health information, whether electronic, written, or oral.

High Performance Building Guidelines (1999)
New York City Department of Design and Construction
http://www.nyc.gov/html/ddc/downloads/pdf/guidelines.pdf
Comprehensive best practices for sustainable design, including consideration for future flexibility.

13. Definitions

churn the movement of workstations and people within a space.

demountable partition a temporary interior wall that can be easily reconfigured. In a healthcare facility, acoustical concerns and embedded equipment, as in a surgery suite, may prevent demountable partitions from being used.

departmental gross square footage (DGSF) the square footage of a diagnostic and treatment or clinical department, calculated from the centerline of the walls separating the department from adjacent spaces. Walls and circulation space within the department are included in the calculation.

interstitial space the area between occupied floors, often used to run mechanical equipment, wiring, and other support services to the adjacent occupied floors.

modular (movable) casework shelving and cabinetry designed to be easily installed and moved or reconfigured.

shell space an area designed to be fitted out for future expansion. A shell space is enclosed by the building envelope but otherwise left unfinished.

soft space an area whose functions can be easily changed. Examples include administrative offices or conference rooms adjacent to a lab with specialized equipment and infrastructure that are difficult to relocate; if the lab needs to expand, the offices or conference rooms can be moved.

INDOOR ENVIRONMENTAL QUALITY

OVERVIEW

Healthcare facilities house several types of occupants who may have compromised immune systems: patients suffering from a variety of health complaints, caregivers who work long hours in stressful circumstances, and visiting family members under severe emotional and sometimes physical strain.

Recent emphasis on minimizing the transmission of infections within the healthcare environment has led to more stringent ventilation and infection control standards. Project teams can take advantage of these requirements to establish comprehensive strategies for enhancing indoor air quality at the outset of project development rather than addressing air quality exclusively as a ventilation issue.

The priority of healthcare projects should be source reduction, since heliports, ambulances, sterilization procedures, and other healthcare activities generate emissions. Exterior source reduction includes discouraging smoking, moving delivery trucks and generators away from air intakes and major entrances, pressurizing vestibules (particularly at emergency department entrances), and minimizing exterior noise. Inside source reduction can include using less toxic sterilants, low-emitting materials, and nontoxic cleaners. These changes can have additional benefits, if sterilization rooms do not have to be isolated or if cleaning can take place less frequently or during daytime (saving money on overtime).

Other indoor environmental quality criteria can also affect the building design. Acoustical control, if integrated into the design, can influence everything from building orientation and massing to floor layouts for patient rooms and nurse stations. Daylight and views can have a similarly radical effect, particularly in diagnostic and treatment spaces.

Many healthcare projects embrace indoor environmental quality strategies as a public manifestation of their mission and find that the benefits are measurable in staff retention as well as increased satisfaction, reduced length of stay, and improved outcomes for patients.

CREDIT	TITLE	HEALTHCARE
IEQ Prerequisite 1	Minimum Indoor Air Quality Performance	Required
IEQ Prerequisite 2	Environmental Tobacco Smoke (ETS) Control	Required
IEQ Prerequisite 3	Hazardous Material Removal or Encapsulation (Renovations Only)	Required
IEQ Credit 1	Outdoor Air Delivery Monitoring	1 Point
IEQ Credit 2	Acoustic Environment	1 Point
IEQ Credit 3.1	Construction Indoor Air Quality Management Plan—During Construction	1 Point
IEQ Credit 3.2	Construction Indoor Air Quality Management Plan—Before Occupancy	1 Point
IEQ Credit 4	Low-Emitting Materials	1–4 Points
IEQ Credit 5	Indoor Chemical and Pollutant Source Control	1 Point
IEQ Credit 6.1	Controllability of Systems—Lighting	1 Point
IEQ Credit 6.2	Controllability of Systems—Thermal Comfort	1 Point
IEQ Credit 7	Thermal Comfort—Design and Verification	1 Point
IEQ Credit 8.1	Daylight and Views—Daylight	2 Points
IEQ Credit 8.2	Daylight and Views—Views	1–3 Points

IMPORTANT! This reference guide supplement contains only the reference guide sections that pertain to healthcare projects. Use this supplement alongside the LEED Reference Guide for Green Building Design and Construction for complete credit information. For the omitted sections, refer to the main reference guide.

MINIMUM INDOOR AIR QUALITY PERFORMANCE

	HEALTHCARE
Prerequisite	IEQ Prerequisite 1
Points	Required

Intent

To establish minimum indoor air quality (IAQ) performance to enhance indoor air quality in buildings, thus contributing to the comfort and well-being of the occupants.

Requirements

Meet the minimum requirements of Sections 6 through 6 of ASHRAE Standard 170-2008, Ventilation of Health Care Facilities (with errata but without addenda[1]).

AND

CASE 1. Mechanically Ventilated Spaces

Mechanical ventilation systems must be designed using the ventilation rates in Section 7 of the standard, the requirements of the 2010 FGI Guidelines for Design and Construction of Health Care Facilities (Table 2.1-2) or the applicable local code, whichever is more stringent.

CASE 2. Naturally Ventilated Spaces

Naturally ventilated buildings or portions of the buildings must comply with ASHRAE Standard 62.1-2007, Ventilation for Acceptable Indoor Air Quality, Paragraph 5.1 (with errata but without addenda[1]).

1 Project teams wishing to use ASHRAE-approved addenda for the purposes of this prerequisite may do so at their discretion. Addenda must be applied consistently across all LEED credits.

IMPORTANT! This reference guide supplement contains only the reference guide sections that pertain to healthcare projects. Use this supplement alongside the LEED Reference Guide for Green Building Design and Construction for complete credit information. For the omitted sections, refer to the main reference guide.

IEQ	
HEALTHCARE: NC	Prerequisite 1

1. Benefits and Issues to Consider

Environmental Issues

Ventilation is particularly important in healthcare facilities because inadequate dilution of recirculated air with outdoor air can expose vulnerable occupants to harmful levels of indoor pollutants. Children, pregnant women, the elderly, and those with allergies, asthma, or chemical sensitivities are especially at risk from poor indoor air quality. Studies have shown that medical staff, who work long hours in a highly stressful environment, are also vulnerable because of the effect of stress and lack of sleep on the immune system.[2]

2. Related Credits

Dense neighborhoods and heavy traffic as well as on-site emissions and existing site contamination can degrade the quality of outside air for ventilation. See the following prerequisites and credits:

- SS Prerequisite 2, Environmental Site Assessment
- SS Credit 4, Alternative Transportation
- SS Credit 3, Brownfield Redevelopment
- EA Credit 7, Community Contaminant Prevention—Airborne Releases
- IEQ Prerequisite 3, Hazardous Material Removal or Encapsulation (Renovations Only)

3. Summary of Referenced Standards

Guidelines for the Design and Construction of Health Care Facilities (2010)
Facility Guidelines Institute
http://www.fgiguidelines.org/
These guidelines establish the healthcare industry's minimum standard for good practice in design and construction. Extensive appendixes provide information about emerging design and construction trends for HVAC, waste reduction, acoustics, and other sustainability topics. Forty-two U.S. states use the guidelines as code or as a reference standard.

ASHRAE 170–2008, Ventilation of Health Care Facilities
This standard defines ventilation system design requirements for environmental comfort, infection control, and odor control. The standard is incorporated into the Guidelines for the Design and Construction of Health Care Facilities, referenced above.

6. Calculations

Design criteria for mechanically ventilated spaces are detailed in ASHRAE 170–2008, Section 7. For spaces not covered there, follow the ASHRAE 62.1–2007 methodology.

Requirements by space types are given in ASHRAE 170–2008, Table 7-1. Minimum outside air requirements are given in units of air changes per hour (ACH). Outside air requirements in ACH can be converted to cubic feet per minute (cfm) using Equation 1.

Equation 1.

$$OA_{cfm} = V_{BZ} = OA_{ACH} \times \frac{V}{60}$$

Where:

OA_{cfm} is the outside air requirement in cfm and is equivalent to V_{BZ} from the ASHRAE 62.1–2007 calculations.

2 World Health Organization, Technical Meeting on Sleep and Health, January 2004 (http://www.euro.who.int/__data/assets/pdf_file/0008/114101/E84683.pdf).

OA_{ACH} is the outside air requirement in air changes per hour from Table 7-1.

V is the volume of the space in cubic feet.

60 is the conversion factor from rate per hour to rate per minute.

Once the breathing zone outdoor airflow requirements are determined from ASHRAE 170–2008 or ASHRAE 62.1–2007, as appropriate, see the LEED Reference Guide for Green Building Design and Construction, IEQ Prerequisite 1, to calculate the zone and system outdoor airflow rates.

7. Documentation Guidance

As a first step in preparing to complete the LEED Online documentation requirements, work through the following measures. Refer to LEED Online for the complete descriptions of all required documentation.

- Demonstrate compliance with the applicable sections of ASHRAE 170–2008 or local licensing requirements, whichever is more stringent; see Calculations.
- For additional documentation guidance, see the LEED Reference Guide for Green Building Design and Construction, IEQ Prerequisite 1.

12. Resources

Guidelines for Environmental Infection Control in Health-Care Facilities: Recommendations of Centers for Disease Control (CDC) and the Health Care Infection Control Practices Advisory Committee (HICPAC)
U.S. Department of Health and Human Services, Centers for Disease Control and Prevention, Morbidity and Mortality Weekly Report, Recommendations and Reports June 6, 2003 / Vol. 52 / No. RR-10, http://www.cdc.gov/mmwr/preview/mmwrhtml/rr5210a1.htm
Outlines environmental infection control guidelines and strategies aimed at reducing risk of exposure to infection in the healthcare setting.

I-Beam: The Future of IAQ in Buildings, United States Environmental Protection Agency
EPA 402-C-01-001, December 2002, IAQ Building Education and Assessment Model (I-Beam), http://www.epa.gov/iaq/largebldgs
Indoor air quality toolkit for large buildings. Includes guidelines and best strategies, assessment tools, and template action plans.

Natural Ventilation for Infection Control in Health Settings
World Health Organization, 2009
http://www.who.int/water_sanitation_health/publications/natural_ventilation.pdf
A literature review and guidelines on the links between natural ventilation and infection control in hospitals

13. Definitions

infection control policies and procedures to minimize the risk of spreading infections through cross-contamination.

ENVIRONMENTAL TOBACCO SMOKE (ETS) CONTROL

	HEALTHCARE
Prerequisite	IEQ Prerequisite 2
Points	Required

Intent

To prevent or minimize exposure of building occupants, indoor surfaces and ventilation air distribution systems to environmental tobacco smoke (ETS).

Requirements

OPTION 1

Prohibit smoking in the building.

Prohibit on-property smoking within 50 feet of entries, outdoor air intakes, bus stops, qualifying places of respite, operable windows, and other locations where occupants could inadvertently come in contact with ETS when occupying, entering or leaving the building. Provide signage to allow smoking in designated areas, prohibit smoking in designated areas or prohibit smoking on the entire property.

Designated smoking areas may not be located in or proximate to places of respite used to meet the requirements of SS Credit 9.1: Connection to the Natural World—Places of Respite or SS Credit 9.2: Connection to the Natural World--Direct Exterior Access for Patients.

OR

OPTION 2

For residential healthcare occupancies only where accommodation for resident smoking is programmatically mandated:

Prohibit smoking in resident rooms and all common areas of the building.

Locate any exterior designated smoking areas including balconies where smoking is permitted, at least 50 feet from entries, outdoor air intakes, bus stops, operable windows and other locations where occupants could inadvertently come in contact with ETS when occupying, entering or leaving the building. Provide signage to allow smoking in designated areas, prohibit smoking in designated areas, or prohibit smoking on the entire property.

All exterior doors and operable windows in the residential units shall be gasketed to minimize leakage from outdoors.

Provide designated smoking rooms as mandated by the functional program designed to effectively contain, capture and remove ETS from the building. At a minimum, the smoking room must be directly exhausted to the outdoors, away from air intakes and building entry paths, with no re-circulation of ETS-containing air to non-smoking areas, and enclosed with sealed deck-to-deck partitions. Operate exhaust sufficient to create a negative pressure differential with respect to the surrounding spaces of at least an average of 5 Pascals (Pa) (0.02 inches of water gauge) and a minimum of 1 Pa (0.004 inches of water gauge) when the door(s) to the smoking room are closed.

Verify performance of the smoking room's differential air pressures by conducting 15 minutes of measurement, with a minimum of one measurement every ten seconds, of

IMPORTANT! This reference guide supplement contains only the reference guide sections that pertain to healthcare projects. Use this supplement alongside the LEED Reference Guide for Green Building Design and Construction for complete credit information. For the omitted sections, refer to the main reference guide.

the differential pressure in the smoking room with respect to each adjacent area and in each adjacent vertical chase with the doors to the smoking room closed. Conduct the testing with each space configured for worst case conditions of transport of air from the smoking room's (with closed doors) to adjacent spaces.

IEQ	
HEALTHCARE: NC	Prerequisite 2

1. Benefits and Issues to Consider

Environmental tobacco smoke poses health risks, particularly to immunocompromised patients, and therefore smoking should be excluded from indoor areas. Although many healthcare campuses have prohibited smoking to protect patient health, some medical treatments, such as substance abuse and psychiatric programs, allow smoking for clinical reasons.

2. Related Credits

ETS is a source of on-site emissions, similar to products of combustion and idling ambulances. Smoking areas should be located away from entrances, air intakes, operable windows, and outdoor places of respite to avoid exposing patients either inside or outside the building. The following credits are relevant:

- SS Credit 4.1, Alternative Transportation—Public Transportation Access
- SS Credit 9.1, Connection to the Natural World—Places of Respite
- SS Credit 9.2, Connection to the Natural World—Direct Exterior Access for Patients
- EA Credit 7, Community Contaminant Prevention—Airborne Releases
- IEQ Credit 3.1, Construction Indoor Air Quality Management Plan—During Construction
- IEQ Credit 5, Indoor Chemical and Pollutant Source Control

3. Summary of Referenced Standards

There are no referenced standards for this prerequisite.

4. Implementation

Consider prohibiting smoking on the entire site. If that strategy is not possible, designate a smoking area at least 50 feet away from entries, outdoor air intakes, bus stops, qualifying places of respite, operable windows, and other locations where occupants and visitors could inadvertently come in contact with ETS.

Locate healing gardens, exterior therapeutic areas, and other places of respite at a distance and upwind from smoking areas.

See the LEED Reference Guide for Green Building Design and Construction for additional information on designated smoking rooms.

11. Operations and Maintenance Considerations

Align the project's no-smoking policy with existing campus or organization policies if they meet or exceed prerequisite requirements. Coordinate education and signage about the no-smoking policy with smoking prevention programs.

12. Resources

Respiratory Health Effects of Passive Smoking: Lung Cancer and Other Disorders

U.S. Environmental Protection Agency

http://cfpub1.epa.gov/ncea/cfm/recordisplay.cfm?deid=2835

The results of an EPA risk assessment on the public health effects of secondhand smoke.

HAZARDOUS MATERIAL REMOVAL OR ENCAPSULATION (RENOVATIONS ONLY)

	HEALTHCARE
Prerequisite	IEQ Prerequisite 3
Points	Required

Intent

To reduce building occupants' potential exposure to hazardous materials, such as asbestos, mercury, lead, PCBs, and mold, in existing buildings undergoing renovation.

Requirements

Develop and implement a hazardous material management program for the construction and pre-occupancy phases of the building.

Identify the applicable local, state and federal regulatory requirements.

Obtain survey records that identify where hazardous materials are located in the building and on the site so that the material(s) present can be addressed appropriately in the ongoing hazardous material management program. If the existing survey records do not cover all areas of the building, conduct a survey to identify where hazardous materials are present in the remaining areas of the building. Include a plan for capture of historical mercury sources in demolition plans, including, but not limited to, piping infrastructure. Collection of any mercury devices shall be designated for recycling and preclude overseas donation/disposal.

Contract must include requirements for reporting and investigating suspect mold encountered in demolition. Identify and remedy the source of water and/or moisture to prevent future mold development.

Remediate contaminated materials with recognized procedures performed by licensed abatement contractors to protect workers, building occupants and the public.

Use lead containment methodologies to prevent release into the air to protect people and prevent soil contamination.

Ensure the removal and appropriate disposal of disconnected wires with lead stabilizers.

Obtain a letter from the licensed abatement contractor stating that all hazardous materials within the affected demolition or renovation areas have been removed or encapsulated, and that all sources of mold/mildew have been identified and remedied. Provide a certified letter of destruction to the owner for record.

IMPORTANT! This reference guide supplement contains only the reference guide sections that pertain to healthcare projects. Use this supplement alongside the LEED Reference Guide for Green Building Design and Construction for complete credit information. For the omitted sections, refer to the main reference guide.

IEQ	
HEALTHCARE: NC	Prerequisite 3

1. Benefits and Issues to Consider[1]

Environmental Issues

Asbestos, mercury, and lead—all hazardous substances—are commonly found in healthcare facilities. Asbestos exposure has been linked to lung cancers, such as mesothelioma, and chronic lung diseases, such as asbestiosis. If asbestos is present in buildings slated to be renovated or demolished, federal regulations require that it be remediated, through either encapsulation or removal.[2]

Mercury, lead, and polychlorinated biphenyls (PCBs) are persistent bioaccumulative toxicants (PBTs), substances that have a tendency to persist in the environment and accumulate in organisms high on the food chain. Many PBTs can cause harm even in minute doses, through cancer, endocrine disruption, brain and nervous system damage, birth defects, and impaired childhood development. PBTs released during the manufacture, use, or disposal of a product can threaten the health of plants and animals many miles away. It is therefore critical to eliminate emissions at their source.

Following a 1997 report[3] ranking medical waste incinerators as the fourth-largest source of anthropogenic mercury emissions, the healthcare industry committed to virtually eliminate PBTs in its facilities and operations. This commitment is outlined in a 1998 memorandum of understanding[4] between the American Hospital Association and the U.S. Environmental Protection Agency, which targets PBTs through pollution prevention and waste reduction. Many healthcare institutions that began PBT elimination projects in their facilities operations are now extending these efforts to construction projects. Because the healthcare industry has historically used significant amounts of mercury that may be difficult to isolate in existing buildings, extra diligence is required to capture or recover mercury and isolate it from waste streams that may enter the environment.

Lead is a potent neurotoxin with particularly deleterious effects on the developing brains of fetuses, infants, and children. Exposure to even minuscule amounts of lead can cause harm[5]. Ensuring that lead-based paint and wires and cables with lead stabilizers are properly removed and disposed of is thus imperative.

Economic Issues

Although hazardous material encapsulation and remediation can be expensive, it is required in many jurisdictions because of the consequences for human health. Proper hazardous material removal reduces liability and can increase occupants' productivity by removing sources of potential irritants, such as mold, from the indoor environment. Particular care should be taken to avoid exposing construction workers and occupants in nearby areas.

2. Related Credits

Coordinate hazardous material capture and proper disposal with the following prerequisite and credits for existing building reuse, environmentally preferable purchasing, and identifying, handling, and disposing of hazardous substances:

- SS Prerequisite 2, Environmental Site Assessment
- SS Credit 3, Brownfield Redevelopment
- MR Prerequisite 1, Storage and Collection of Recyclables

1 Background information on hazardous removal and encapsulation draws, with permission, from Green Guide for Health Care PBT Elimination from Building Materials Technical Brief, by Tom Lent; Green Guide for Health Care Mercury Elimination Technical Brief, by Jamie Harvie; and Green Guide for Health Care Furniture and Medical Furnishings Technical Brief, by Lorissa MacAllister (http://www.gghc.org/tools.technical.php).

2 http://www.epa.gov/asbestos/pubs/help.html#health.

3 U.S. Environmental Protection Agency, Mercury Study Report to Congress, Volume II: An Inventory of Anthropogenic Mercury Emissions I the United States, Report EPA-452/R-97-004, December 1997 (http://www.epa.gov/ttn/oarpg/t3/reports/volume2.pdf).

4 1998 MOU between U.S. Environmental Protection Agency and American Hospital Association (http://cms.h2e-online.org/about/mou).

5 U.S. Environmental Protection Agency, An Introduction to Indoor Air Quality: Lead (http://www.epa.gov/iaq/lead.html).

- MR Prerequisite 2, PBT Source Reduction—Mercury
- MR Credit 1.1, Building Reuse—Maintain Existing Walls, Floors, and Roof
- MR Credit 1.2, Building Reuse—Maintain Existing Interior Nonstructural Elements
- MR Credit 4.1, PBT Source Reduction—Mercury in Lamps
- MR Credit 4.2, PBT Source Reduction—Lead, Cadmium, and Copper
- MR Credit 5, Furniture and Medical Furnishings
- IEQ Credit 4, Low-Emitting Materials
- IEQ Credit 5, Indoor Chemical and Pollutant Source Control

3. Summary of Referenced Standards

There are no referenced standards for this prerequisite.

4. Implementation

Using the results from the environmental site assessment performed under SS Prerequisite 2, develop a hazardous material management program to identify hazardous materials, including mold, mercury, lead, and asbestos, in the existing building or on the site. Use this program as a baseline for surveying and assessing hazardous materials in compliance with local, state, and federal regulatory requirements. This plan may outline the following:

- Mercury elimination and recovery (see MR Prerequisite 1, Storage and Collection of Recyclables, and MR Prerequisite 2, PBT Source Reduction—Mercury).
- Capture of mercury from pipes and other sources during demolition.
- Lead containment, removal, and disposal, with particular attention to construction and demolition debris, which may include lead-containing radiation protection systems.
- Separation of sheet lead, lead-lined gypsum board products, and lead-lined doors, frames, and glazing products for salvage or reprocessing.
- An explanation of how the hazardous material management program will address hazardous materials remaining in the building on an ongoing basis.

Teams may elect to decontaminate biological pathogens, if applicable.

Review hazardous material removal work done in the building and on the building site and use this information to prepare the history-based component of the hazardous material survey. Determine where hazardous material has been removed and where it remains, and describe how the remaining material is being addressed.

Sample likely locations in the building and on the site to see whether hazardous material is present. If the survey identifies additional hazardous materials, include their removal or encapsulation in the hazardous material management program.

Engage an environmental testing agency and licensed abatement professional to audit building systems and materials and determine protocols and procedures to encapsulate or remove materials, as appropriate.

Mercury may require special remediation attention in the renovation or demolition of an existing healthcare facility because it may be present in traps, light fixtures, interfloor spaces, and places where medical equipment has broken over the years, providing an unanticipated but significant hazard to construction and demolition crews.

In renovations, old wires and cable that contain lead stabilizer should be removed, per the 2002 National Electric Code. Follow safety precautions when removing old cable and ensure that workers wear proper respiratory protection; seal removed cables in plastic bags. Old cable can be recycled at certain facilities.

Even common renovation activities can involve the risk of lead contamination, if particles of lead-based paint are not contained. The U.S. Environmental Protection Agency recommends the following methods of lead containment in renovation projects where lead contamination is a risk:

- Contain the work area, including covering doors and furniture that cannot be moved, and seal off vents.
- Avoid practices that generate large amounts of lead-contaminated dust. Prohibit open-flame burning or torching and heat guns operating at temperatures above 1100°F. Sanders, grinders, needle guns, and other power tools should be equipped with shrouds and HEPA vacuum attachments.
- Use water to mist areas before sanding or scraping. Score paint before removing components. Pry or pull apart components instead of breaking them.
- Clean up thoroughly and regularly. Use a HEPA vacuum and wet wiping and mopping with plenty of rinse water before the space is unsealed[6].

Specify and install materials that are inherently mold and mildew resistant to minimize the possibility of future problems.

5. Timeline and Team

Early in the design phase, ask facilities staff whether hazardous material policies and procedures are already in place. For healthcare facilities on existing campuses, integrate remediation procedures into campus industrial hygiene practices.

This prerequisite should be implemented together with the prerequisites and credits listed in the Related Credits section.

6. Calculations

There are no calculations required for this prerequisite.

7. Documentation Guidance

As a first step in preparing to complete the LEED Online documentation requirements, work through the following measures. efer to LEED Online for the complete descriptions of all required documentation.

- Develop a hazardous material management program for the construction and preoccupancy phases of the building, including, at a minimum, applicable regulatory requirements, survey records identifying the locations of hazardous materials, and remediation procedures.
- Retain contracts for all remediation activities.
- Obtain a letter from the licensed abatement contractor stating that all hazardous materials within the affected demolition or renovation areas have been removed or encapsulated, all sources of mold and mildew have been identified and remedied, and approved lead containment methodologies have been employed.

8. Examples

Figure 1 illustrates a sample hazardous material management program.

6 U.S. Environmental Protection Agency, Renovate Right: Important Lead Hazard Information for Families, Child Care Providers, and Schools, April 2010 (http://www.epa.gov/lead/pubs/brochure.htm).

Figure 1.

Sample Outline of Hazardous Material Management Program

1. Policy/Purpose
    a. It is the policy of XYZ HOSPITAL that all renovation and demolition projects shall identify and remediate all Hazardous Materials, as defined by ABC REGULATIONS, in a manner posing no substantial hazard to human health or the environment and in accordance with local, state, and federal regulations.
2. Regulatory Classification
    a. ABC REGULATIONS define XYZ HOSPITAL as a "SMALL/MEDIUM/LARGE quantity generator," which is a facility that generates ... and is therefore required to ...
3. Survey Records of Hazardous Material Locations in the Existing Building

Survey Date	Hazardous Material	Location	Suggested Method of Remediation

4. Roles and Responsibilities
5. Hazardous Material Handling
    a. Assessment Procedures
    b. Transportation Procedures
    c. Hazardous Material Storage
    d. Hazardous Material Classifications
    e. Preparedness and Prevention Procedures
    f. Worker Protection

9. Exemplary Performance

This prerequisite is not eligible for exemplary performance under the Innovation in Design section.

10. Regional Variations

Hazardous materials regulations vary by region. Differences in construction practices can also result in higher concentrations of some types of hazardous materials in certain regions. Contact the regional EPA office or registry of toxic substances for information on which hazardous materials may be present in existing healthcare buildings.

11. Operations and Maintenance Considerations

A healthcare institution's hazardous material management program may not refer specifically to construction materials. Consult with waste management and industrial hygiene experts to ensure that the construction and preoccupancy hazardous material management program aligns with existing policies.

Coordinate with facilities staff pursuing parallel credits in LEED for Existing Buildings: Operations & Maintenance and/or the Green Guide for Health Care, Operations section. The Green Guide for Health Care, in particular, addresses the synergies between environmentally preferable purchasing, waste reduction, and chemical management in great detail.

12. Resources

Guidelines for the Design and Construction of Health Care Facilities (2010)
Facility Guidelines Institute
http://www.fgiguidelines.org/
The healthcare industry's minimum standards for good practice in design and construction. Extensive appendices provide information about emerging design and construction trends for HVAC, waste reduction, acoustics, and other sustainability topics. Forty-two states use these guidelines as code or as a reference standard.

Guidelines on Assessment and Remediation of Fungi in Indoor Environments (2008)
New York City Department of Health and Mental Hygiene
http://www.nyc.gov/html/doh/html/epi/moldrpt1.shtml
Best practices for building owners and managers, environmental contractors, and environmental consultants. **Note:** The guidance is not meant for use in critical-care facilities, such as intensive-care units.

National Electric Code (2002)
National Fire Protection Association
http://www.nfpa.org
The national standard for installing electrical wiring and cables, including proper procedures for the removal and appropriate disposal of disconnected wires with lead stabilizers.

U.S. Code of Federal Regulations (**CFR**)
http://www.gpoaccess.gov/cfr/
29 CFR 1910.1000, Air Contaminants.
40 CFR 273, Standards for Universal Waste Management.
40 CFR 761, Polychlorinated Biphenyls (PCBs) Manufacturing, Processing, Distribution in Commerce, and Use Prohibitions.
40 CFR Part 61, Subpart M, National Emission Standard for Asbestos.

U.S. Environmental Protection Agency
Identification of Dangerous Levels for Lead; Final Rule, http://www.epa.gov/fedrgstr/EPATOX/2001/January/Day-05/t84.pdf.

Lead in dust, soil and paint, http://www.epa.gov/opptintr/lead/pubs/regulation.htm.

Mold, http://www.epa.gov/mold/mold_remediation.html.

National Emission Standards for Hazardous Air Pollutants (NESHAP) 40 CFR 61, http://www.epa.gov/enviro/html/rad/rad_cfr_part61.html.

RCRA in Focus: Construction, Demolition, and Renovation, EPA-530-K-04-005, http://www.epa.gov/wastes/inforesources/pubs/infocus/rif-c&d.pdf.

U.S. Toxic Substances Control Act (TSCA), http://www.epa.gov/regulations/laws/tsca.html.
15 USC s/s 2601 et seq. (1976), http://www.eh.doe.gov/oepa/laws/tsca.html.

13. Definitions

certified letter of destruction a written statement provided by a vendor (such as a licensed abatement contractor) to an owner acknowledging receipt of specified material, outlining how it will be protected prior to destruction, and verifying that it will be appropriately destroyed or abated.

hazardous material management program a set of procedures for assessing, managing, and disposing of dangerous substances.

OUTDOOR AIR DELIVERY MONITORING

	HEALTHCARE
Credit	IEQ Credit 1
Points	1 point

Intent

To provide capacity for ventilation system monitoring to help sustain occupant comfort and well-being.

Requirements

Install permanent monitoring systems that provide feedback on ventilation system performance to ensure that ventilation systems maintain design minimum ventilation requirements. Configure all monitoring equipment to generate an alarm when airflow values or carbon dioxide (CO_2) levels vary by 10% or more from the design values via either a building automation system alarm to the building operator or a visual or audible alert to the building occupants.

AND

CASE 1. Mechanically Ventilated Spaces

Monitor CO_2 concentrations within all densely occupied spaces (those with a design occupant density of 25 people or more per 1,000 square feet). CO_2 monitors must be between 3 and 6 feet above the floor.

Provide a direct outdoor airflow measurement device capable of measuring the minimum outdoor air intake flow with an accuracy of plus or minus 5% of the design minimum outdoor air rate, as defined by ASHRAE Standard 170-2008 (with errata but without addenda[1]) for mechanical ventilation systems where 20% or more of the design supply airflow serves non-densely occupied spaces[2].

CASE 2. Naturally Ventilated Spaces

Monitor CO_2 concentrations within all naturally ventilated spaces. CO_2 monitors must be between 3 and 6 feet above the floor. One CO_2 sensor may be used to monitor multiple non-densely occupied spaces if the natural ventilation design uses passive stack(s) or other means to induce airflow through those spaces equally and simultaneously without intervention by building occupants.

1 Project teams wishing to use ASHRAE-approved addenda for the purposes of this credit may do so at their discretion. Addenda must be applied consistently across all LEED credits.

2 CO_2 monitoring is required in densely occupied spaces, in addition to outdoor air intake flow measurement.

IMPORTANT! This reference guide supplement contains only the reference guide sections that pertain to healthcare projects. Use this supplement alongside the LEED Reference Guide for Green Building Design and Construction for complete credit information. For the omitted sections, refer to the main reference guide.

IEQ	
HEALTHCARE: NC	Credit 1

1. Benefits and Issues to Consider

Environmental Issues

Ventilation is particularly important in healthcare facilities because inadequate dilution of recirculated air with outdoor air can expose vulnerable occupants to harmful levels of indoor pollutants. Children, pregnant women, the elderly, and those with allergies, asthma, or chemical sensitivities are especially at risk from poor indoor air quality. Studies have shown that medical staff, who work long hours in a highly stressful environment, are also vulnerable because of the effect of stress and lack of sleep on the immune system.[3]

Economic Issues

Hospitals are mandated by code to provide higher rates of outdoor air ventilation than other occupancy types. The tolerances proposed for this credit will ensure that outdoor airflow rates are within +/- 10% of design flow rates. This level of accuracy is warranted for hospitals, and airflow sensors with +/-5% accuracy are commonly available at minimal cost.

2. Related Credits

Dense neighborhoods and heavy traffic as well as on-site emissions and existing site contamination can degrade the quality of outside air for ventilation. See the following prerequisites and credits:

- SS Prerequisite 2, Environmental Site Assessment
- SS Credit 4: Alternative Transportation,
- SS Credit 3, Brownfield Redevelopment
- EA Credit 7, Community Contaminant Prevention—Airborne Releases
- IEQ Prerequisite 3, Hazardous Material Removal or Encapsulation (Renovations Only)

3. Summary of Referenced Standards

ASHRAE 170-2008, Ventilation of Health Care Facilities

http://www.fgiguidelines.org/

This standard defines ventilation system design requirements for environmental comfort, infection, and odor control. The standard is incorporated into the Guidelines for the Design and Construction of Health Care Facilities, 2010 Edition, published by the Facility Guidelines Institute.

7. Documentation Guidance

As a first step in preparing to complete the LEED Online documentation requirements, work through the following measures. Refer to LEED Online for the complete descriptions of all required documentation.

- Document that settings on alarms for mechanical ventilation systems comply with ASHRAE 170–2008.
- For additional documentation guidance, see the LEED Reference Guide for Green Building Design and Construction, IEQ Credit 1.

3 World Health Organization, Technical Meeting on Sleep and Health, January 2004 (http://www.euro.who.int/__data/assets/pdf_file/0008/114101/E84683.pdf).

ACOUSTIC ENVIRONMENT

	HEALTHCARE
Credit	IEQ Credit 2
Points	1-2 points

Intent

To provide building occupants with an indoor healing environment free of intrusive or disruptive levels of sound.

Requirements

Design the facility to meet or exceed the sound and vibration criteria outlined in the *2010 FGI Guidelines for Design and Construction of Health Care Facilities* (aka *2010 FGI Guidelines*) and the reference document on which it is based, Sound and Vibration Design Guidelines for Health Care Facilities (aka *2010 SV Guidelines*).

OPTION 1 (1 Point)

Sound Isolation

Design sound isolation to achieve speech privacy, acoustical comfort and minimal annoyance from noise-producing sources. Consider sound levels at both the source and receiver locations, the background sound at the receiver locations, and the occupant's acoustical privacy and acoustical comfort needs. Speech privacy is defined as "Techniques... to render speech unintelligible to casual listeners" by ANSI T1.523-2001, Telecom Glossary 2007.

Design the facility to meet the criteria outlined in the sections of the *2010 FGI Guidelines* Table 1.2-3: Design Criteria for Minimum Sound Isolation Performance between Enclosed Rooms and Table 1.2-4 Speech Privacy for Enclosed Room and Open-Plan Spaces (*2010 FGI Guidelines* and *2010 SV Guidelines*).

Calculate or measure sound isolation and speech privacy descriptors achieved for representative adjacencies as necessary to confirm compliance with criteria as identified in Sections1.2-6.1.5 and 1.2-6.1.6 (including associated sections of the Appendix) of the *2010 FGI Guidelines* and the reference standard on which it is based: the *SV Guidelines*.

Room Noise

Consider background sound levels generated by all building mechanical-electrical-plumbing systems, air distribution systems and other facility noise sources under the purview of the project building design-construction team.

Design the facility to meet the *2010 FGI Guidelines* Table 1.2-2 Minimum-Maximum Design Criteria for Noise in representative interior rooms and spaces.

Calculate or measure sound levels in representative rooms and spaces of each type as necessary to confirm compliance with criteria in the above referenced table using a sound level meter that conforms to ANSI S1.4 for type 1 (precision) or type 2 (general purpose) sound measurement instrumentation. For spaces not listed in Table 1.2-2, refer to the *ASHRAE 2007 Handbook*, Chapter 47, Sound and Vibration Control, Table 42.

IMPORTANT! This reference guide supplement contains only the reference guide sections that pertain to healthcare projects. Use this supplement alongside the LEED Reference Guide for Green Building Design and Construction for complete credit information. For the omitted sections, refer to the main reference guide.

OPTION 2 (2 Points)

Achieve OPTION 1 AND

Acoustical Finishes

Specify materials, products systems installation details, and other design features to meet the *2010 FGI Guidelines* Table 1.2-1 Design Room Sound Absorption Coefficients. (including associated sections of the Appendix) and its reference the *2010 SV Guidelines*.

Calculate or measure the room average sound absorption coefficients for representative unoccupied rooms of each type in the building, as necessary, to confirm conformance with requirements for this credit.

Site Exterior Noise

Minimize the impact of site exterior noise on building facility occupants produced by all exterior noise sources—road traffic, aircraft flyovers, railroads, on-site heliports, emergency power generators during maintenance testing, outdoor facility MEP and building services equipment. Also minimize impacts on the surrounding community produced by all facility MEP equipment and activities as required to meet the lower of the local applicable codes or Table 1.2-1 of the *2010 FGI Guidelines* and the supporting Table 1.3-1 of the *2010 SV Guidelines*.

Comply with the appropriate sections of the *2010 FGI Guidelines* for each category:

- Heliports - A1.3-3.6.2.2
- Generators - 2.1-8.3.3.1
- Mechanical Equipment - 2.1-8.2.1.1
- Building Services - A2.2-5.3

Measure and analyze data to determine the Exterior Noise Classification (A, B, C, or D) of the facility site. See Table A1.2a: Categorization of Health Care Facility Sites by Exterior Ambient Sound in the *2010 FGI Guidelines* and Table 1.3-1 in its reference standard, the *2010 SV Guidelines*.

Design the building envelope composite STC rating based on the *2010 FGI Guidelines* for the Categorization of Health Care Facility Sites by Exterior Ambient Sound and analyze contract documents to show conformance with requirements for this credit.

For Exterior Site Exposure Categories B, C or D calculate or measure the sound isolation performance of representative elements of the exterior building envelope to determine the composite sound transmission class (STC_c) rating for representative façade sections as necessary. Measurements shall generally conform to the current edition of ASTM E966 Standard Guide for Field Measurements of Airborne Sound Insulation of Building Façades and Façade Elements.

1. Benefits and Issues to Consider

Environmental Issues[4]

Levels of noise (defined as unwanted sound) in healthcare facilities of all types have risen steadily for four decades and often significantly exceed recommended levels by as much as 20 to 40 dBA. As a result, it is a leading source of dissatisfaction in patient and staff surveys. Noise is an environmental pollutant that can compromise patient outcomes, interfere with communication and cause medical errors, damage the hearing of newborns, elevate stress among patients and staff, and reduce satisfaction levels for all building occupants. Noise can also reduce privacy—a right protected by law and expected by patients, families, and healthcare professionals. Research shows that patients in healthcare facilities with reduced noise levels are more satisfied, have more privacy, sleep better, have lower blood pressure, and better understand staff instructions. Staff in less noisy healthcare environments report increased job satisfaction and improved sleep.

Acoustical design is therefore an essential component of an optimum healing environment. Some operational realities—equipment noise, alarms, human behavior—are outside the purview of the design team alone. This credit addresses acoustic criteria falling within the design team's scope of influence and encompasses noise, sound, privacy, and vibration.

Economic Issues

Noise reduction and privacy improvement are significant aspects of environmental quality that yield clear economic benefits: shorter patient stays, fewer readmissions, improved patient outcomes, fewer medical errors, reduced use of pain medication, improved patient satisfaction, improved staff satisfaction, and less employee burnout. Costs associated with reducing noise and improving privacy should be weighed against these eight potential benefits.

2. Related Credits

A comprehensive green building design process integrates consideration of acoustics and speech privacy into the design program along with the following related credits and prerequisites:

- MR Credit 3, Sustainably Sourced Materials and Products
- MR Credit 4.1, PBT Source Reduction—Mercury
- MR Credit 4.2, PBT Source Reduction—Lead, Cadmium, and Copper
- MR Credit 5, Furniture and Medical Furnishings
- MR Credit 6, Resource Use—Design for Flexibility
- IEQ Credit 4, Low-Emitting Materials
- IEQ Credit 8.1, Daylight and Views—Daylight
- IEQ Credit 8.2, Daylight and Views—Views
- ID Prerequisite 1, Integrated Project Planning and Design
- ID Credit 3, Integrated Project Planning and Design
- SS Credit 9.1, Connection to the Natural World—Places of Respite
- SS Credit 9.2, Connection to the Natural World—Direct Exterior Access for Patients

Noise-producing vehicles and pieces of equipment may also generate on-site particulate and gaseous emissions. Acoustical treatment for exterior noise should therefore be coordinated with

4 This section is based on published research findings in peer-reviewed medical journals; see the Resources section, below, in particular, Patients First: Ensuring Quieter Hospital Environments, by Montague et al.

the following credits:

- EA Credit 7, Community Contaminant Prevention—Airborne Releases
- IEQ Credit 5, Indoor Chemical and Pollutant Source Control

3. Summary of Referenced Standards

FGI Guidelines for the Design and Construction of Health Care Facilities (2010)
Facility Guidelines Institute
http://www.fgiguidelines.org/
These guidelines and the reference standard on which they are based (see below) establish the healthcare industry's minimum standard for good practice in design and construction, with information about emerging design and construction trends for HVAC, waste reduction, acoustics, and other sustainability topics. Forty-two U.S. states use these guidelines as code or a reference standard.

Sound and Vibration Design Guidelines for Hospital and Healthcare Facilities, V2.0 (January 2010)
http://www.fgiguidelines.org/
This is the sole source for the acoustic and speech privacy provisions in the 2010 FGI Guidelines. The document includes design guidance and is available from FGI.

Telecom Glossary (2007)
American National Standard T1.523-2001
http://www.its.bldrdoc.gov/projects/devglossary/
This glossary offers a concise definition of speech privacy. Definitions of speech privacy in the ANSI, ASTM, and ISO standards are consistent with this definition.

ANSI S1.4: American National Standard Specification for Sound Level Meters
American National Standards Institute (ANSI)
http://www.ansi.org
This standard provides specifications relating to acoustic measurement devices and how to measure certain sound characteristics.

ASHRAE Handbook, Chapter 47, Sound and Vibration Control, 2007 HVAC Applications
American Society of Heating, Refrigerating, and Air-Conditioning Engineers
http://www.ashrae.org
Mechanical, electrical, and plumbing (MEP) equipment is a major source of sound and vibration in buildings, and its effects on the overall acoustic environment must be considered. Chapter 47 of the ASHRAE Handbook provides an integrated approach to the design of sound and vibration controls.

ASTM E966 Standard Guide for Field Measurements of Airborne Sound Insulation of Building Façades and Façade Elements
ASTM International
http://www.astm.org
This standard provides procedures for measuring sound-level reduction or sound transmission loss through a building façade.

4. Implementation

Healthcare facilities face three major acoustic challenges:

- Achieving adequate speech privacy to comply with HIPAA and other privacy protection statutes.

- Controlling background noise produced by building systems, medical equipment, paging systems, clinical alarms, conversation, rolling carts, cleaning equipment, and other sources.
- Minimizing sound, whether produced inside a room or transmitted from nearby exterior or interior spaces, that reflects from hard surfaces and contributes to sound reverberation.

To help achieve speech privacy, consider using partial-height barriers in open-plan areas and isolating partitions in closed-plan areas. Sound-absorptive finish materials can help absorb speech, and electronic sound masking can provide privacy.

Locate activities and sources of excessive noise away from patient rooms and other noise-sensitive areas, such as intensive-care units and neonatal and pediatric intensive-care units (ICUs, NICUs, PICUs). Where necessary, use buffer spaces and treat sound-reflective room surfaces with sound-absorptive materials to minimize unwanted speech sound and reverberation.

Locate patient rooms and other noise-sensitive areas away from sources of exterior and interior noise. Locate general-use televisions and other media in public and staff areas so that their sound does not interfere with communication in patient and staff areas. In patient rooms, provide headsets or pillow speakers for televisions and radios to avoid transmitting unwanted sound to nearby areas.

Instead of installing speakers for area-wide paging, consider the use of wireless intercom and nurse call systems that silently alert individual staffers. Where area-wide paging is required, consider installing multiple low-level loudspeakers.

Consider specifying and installing noise-level sensor systems, which provide visual feedback to staff when designated acoustic thresholds are exceeded.

Consider the concerns of infection control committees when recommending materials that are sound absorbing. The U.S. Centers for Disease Control addresses only surfaces that routinely touch patients (e.g., bed rails, light switches, door handles, call buttons); there are no special requirements for acoustic materials. Review manufacturers' product data sheets for information on cleaning protocols for acoustic materials.

Applicable Spaces

Acoustic guidelines should be followed for healthcare spaces as indicated in the *FGI 2010 Guidelines*. NICUs, for example, have special needs because of the effects of noise on newborns; see the *FGI 2010 Guidelines* and its supporting reference, the *SV Guidelines*, for further information on these spaces. For spaces not listed by FGI, use the criteria for spaces with similar functions, or consult the current edition of the *ASHRAE Handbook*.

Measurement

Project teams can either calculate (model) or measure compliance with requirements for both the sound isolation and the acoustic finishes options. Although teams are encouraged to pursue either calculation or measurement consistently in each credit option, a combined approach may be appropriate for areas that are difficult to model accurately.

For projects pursuing the measurement compliance path, prepare a testing plan that addresses all applicable requirements before construction is completed. Acoustic testing is extremely difficult to schedule in occupied, fully functioning healthcare facilities. Accordingly, tests should be scheduled during facility commissioning, before occupancy.

The following sections correspond to chapters in the *2010 SV Guidelines*.

Speech Privacy and Sound Isolation (see the *SV Guidelines*, Chapter 4, Sound Isolation Performance of Constructions)

Sound isolation measures address speech privacy. HIPAA regulations require that staff exercise discretion when discussing health concerns. Sound isolation measures should therefore be incorporated into all spaces where personal health information may be discussed.

Two approaches to providing adequate speech privacy are common. The first is to reduce sound transmission between spaces by installing improved partition assemblies (for enclosed rooms) and partial-height partitions and sound-absorptive room finishes (for open-plan spaces). The second is to provide an adequate level of continuous background sound.

A building's MEP sounds generally do not provide the continuous, innocuous background sound required to achieve speech privacy because they are too variable and too difficult to control within useful limits. Electronic masking systems are a more reliable approach. These systems can be used in nearly all types of healthcare settings and are often essential in open-plan areas, such as waiting rooms, patient admission counters and carrels, outpatient clinics, administrative offices, and even some clinical treatment spaces.

Speech privacy in open-plan spaces is a special challenge but can be achieved through the following measures:

- Highly sound-absorptive acoustic ceilings and wall treatments.
- Relatively tall partial-height partitions that break the line of sight between talkers and potential listeners.
- Distance between talkers and potential listeners.
- Low-level, continuous background sound(electronic sound masking).

Although most rooms and open spaces in healthcare facilities require "normal" speech privacy, some areas need a higher, "confidential" level. Confidential speech privacy is generally required in admitting areas, doctor-patient consultation rooms, psychiatric and psychological interviewing and testing rooms, hematology labs, clinical areas, and patient exam rooms, among other areas.

"Secure" speech privacy, the highest level, is generally defined as the total inaudibility of speech in adjacent spaces. This level of privacy may be required in special clinical areas, such as hearing test booths, speech therapy rooms, and special psychiatric suites. Required sound isolation performance for these areas is covered by other standards.

Room Noise (see the *SV Guidelines*, Chapter 3, Room Noise Levels)

Control ambient noise, including mechanical systems noise, by selecting quiet fans that rotate at slow speeds, changing filters on a regular basis, locating sound attenuators at variable air volume terminal boxes where needed, installing vibration isolators on rotating and vibrating equipment, providing duct attenuation, designing ductwork to minimize "cross-talk" from one room to another, and controlling airflow velocity within the ductwork to minimize turbulence noise.

Coordinate measures to improve sound isolation between patient rooms and circulation areas or corridors where such measures do not interfere with patient care operations or other clinical considerations. Vision panels in doors and large windows into rooms enable staff to supervise patients from outside, without opening their doors to noise. Provide doors with gaskets, or install close-fitting doors to minimize sound leakage. Where appropriate, install electronic sound masking to maintain continuous background sound levels at or slightly above the lower limit of the criteria range for a particular room type in the *2010 FGI Guidelines* and *2010 SV Guidelines*.

Acoustic Finishes (see the *SV Guidelines*, Chapter 2, Acoustical Finishes and Details)

Coordinate finish selections with sustainable sourcing and low-emissions criteria to achieve the required room average sound absorption coefficients. In addition, consider incorporating the following into the materials selection process:

- Sound-absorptive wall coverings, panels, window coverings, ceiling materials, flooring materials (such as carpeting, where appropriate), and upholstered furnishings.
- Ceiling materials with ceiling attenuation class (CAC) ratings of 35 or greater for spaces with noisy plenum equipment, walls that do not extend up to the deck, or rooms with sound transmission paths through the ceiling plenum.
- Cushion-backed flooring products that reduce footfall and cart rolling noise.
- Sound-absorbing finish materials in patient and visitor waiting areas and circulation spaces.
- Additional acoustic treatments on walls, floors, and ceilings in and around open nursing stations and open staff consulting areas in inpatient units.

Site Exterior Noise (see the SV Guidelines, Chapter 1, Site Exterior Noise)

Measure the site's existing day-night level (DNL) average sound at building façades. Using the methods of the 2010 FGI Guidelines and SV Guidelines, determine the corresponding minimum composite sound transmission class (STC_c) rating. Design the overall building envelope, including roofs, accordingly.

Implement controls on exterior MEP equipment and systems to reduce sound levels at building façades to 65 dBA or less, and 70 dBA for emergency power equipment. Implement controls on building equipment and systems, including fresh air and exhaust air grilles, to reduce sound levels at neighboring residential properties to either the sound level permitted by applicable local codes and ordinances or the level indicated in the *2010 FGI Guidelines* and *2010 SV Guidelines* based on the existing DNL, whichever is less.

In addition, provide both patients and staff with individual acoustic control. The ability to minimize an unwanted noise by closing a door or window or by changing the volume of a TV, radio, or white noise machine can alleviate the stress associated with noisy environments.

5. Timeline and Team

Address acoustics and privacy issues as early as possible in the design process. Since architectural proportions and finish materials, structural, mechanical, electrical, and other considerations affect sound isolation, room noise, and overall acoustical performance, the project design construction team should consider acoustics in the early schematic design phase of planning. During this phase, the architect, healthcare facility planner, and MEP engineers should identify potentially noisy equipment and high-activity areas and locate them away from patient rooms and other spaces where quiet is required. The design team should consult with staff and patient advocates. Often, acoustic problems identified early can be solved by simply rearranging spaces or selecting more acoustically effective design options. Architects, designers, and specifiers must understand the acoustic needs of diagnostic and treatment areas, inpatient units, public areas, and other special requirements of the particular healthcare facility.

Also early in the design process (and no later than the design development phase), the architect, mechanical engineer, electrical engineer, and contractor should jointly specify methods to achieve acoustic performance goals.

The architect, MEP engineers, and heliport consultant should work closely with the civil engineer and landscape architect to ensure that the site layout (including heliport location), circulation routes, and idling zones minimize noise for patient areas and the surrounding neighborhoods.

6. Calculations

Follow the measurement or calculation guidelines in the referenced standards (the *FGI 2010 Guidelines* and *the SV Guidelines*).

7. Documentation Guidance

As a first step in preparing to complete the LEED Online documentation requirements, work through the following measures. Refer to LEED Online for the complete descriptions of all required documentation.

- Maintain documentation demonstrating compliance with the performance criteria outlined in referenced standards.
- Maintain manufacturers' documentation for the acoustic characteristics of noise-producing equipment and all acoustic finish materials.
- Maintain laboratory test data for sound-isolating assemblies.
- Document the installed surface areas of sound-absorptive materials on interior elevations and reflected ceiling plans.

8. Examples

Refer to the 2010 Sound and Vibration Design Guidelines for Health Care Facilities and the research literature cited in the Resources section, below.

9. Exemplary Performance

This credit is not eligible for exemplary performance under the Innovation in Design section.

10. Regional Variations

Local factors can affect the ambient noise around healthcare facilities. For example, local noise codes may affect the allowable noise emissions from exterior hospital equipment.

11. Operations and Maintenance Considerations

To ensure that the design strategies to reduce the sources of ambient noise are not negated by occupants' behavior, consider instituting a "quiet environment" program to promote a healing environment through reducing noise, particularly for NICUs and other critical care areas. The program might include policies on speaker phones, televisions in open areas, and talking in hallways.

Provide signage and educational materials that explain the quiet policy to visitors and encourage their participation.

Help building operators find acoustically appropriate products and materials for repairs or alterations by providing them with a list of compliant products. Consider equipping operations staff with sound-level meters so that they can perform periodic acoustic assessments and correct any deficiencies.

12. Resources

Please see USGBC's LEED Registered Project Tools (http://www.usgbc.org/projecttools) for additional resources and technical information.

Acoustical Society of America
www.acousticalsociety.org

Institute of Noise Control Engineering
www.inceusa.org

National Council of Acoustical Consultants
www.ncac.com
The following websites, peer-reviewed articles, and other primary sources substantiate the statements in this Reference Guide. For further information, search PubMed, which lists more than 5,000 citations related to noise in healthcare facilities and many more on privacy.

Sound and Vibration: Design Guidelines for Health Care Facilities, January 1, 2010, Public Draft 2.0, including guidelines for NICUs (SV Guidelines)
http://www.fgiguidelines.org/interim_pubs.html
These guidelines, the reference standard for all acoustics issues in the 2010 FGI Guidelines, contain design suggestions and background information regarding acoustic and privacy design for all types of healthcare facilities. The guidelines were commissioned by FGI and prepared by the ad hoc Joint Subcommittee on Speech Privacy and Healthcare Acoustics TC-AA.NS.SC, a technical subcommittee of the Acoustical Society of America, the Institute of Noise Control Engineers, and the National Council of Acoustical Consultants.

International Commission on the Biological Effects of Noise (ICBEN)
www.icben.org
The commission, founded in 1972, has the largest collection of international research on the effects of noise on humans. Research conferences are held every four years.

Guideline for Disinfection and Sterilization in Healthcare Facilities, by W.A. Rutala, D.J. Weber, and HICPAC (Chapel Hill, NC: Centers for Disease Control, 2008)

Updating the Guideline Methodology of the Healthcare Infection Control Practices Advisory Committee (HICPAC), by C.A. Umpsheid, R.K. Agarwal, and P.J. Brennan (2009)
http://www.cdc.gov/hicpac/Disinfection_Sterilization/toc.html
These reports delineate specific requirements from the Centers for Disease Control for the cleanability of all materials used in a healthcare facility.

Validating Acoustic Guidelines for Healthcare Facilities, by J.M. Solet, O.M. Buxton, J.M. Ellenbogen, W. Wang, and A. Carballeira (2010)
http://www.healthdesign.org/chd/research
This five-year-long clinical study, known as the Harvard Sound Sleep Study, was organized by the SV Guidelines drafting committee at Harvard Medical School to validate the FGI 2010 Guidelines, and funded by the Facility Guidelines Institute Foundation, the American Architects for Health Foundation, and the Center for Health Design Research Coalition.

Noise Levels in Johns Hopkins Hospital, by I.J. Busch-Vishniac, J.E. West, C. Barnhill, T. Hunter, D. Orellana, and R. Chivukula (*Journal of the Acoustical Society of America* 118: 3629, 2005)

Noise in the Adult Emergency Department of Johns Hopkins Hospital, by D. Orellana, I.J. Busch-Vishniac, and J.E. West (*Journal of the Acoustical Society of America* 121: 1996, 2007)

Further Studies of Hospital Noise Control at the Johns Hopkins Hospital: Part 2(A), by T.Y. Hsu, E.E. Ryherd, J.E. West, C.L. Barnhill, M. Swisher, and N. Levit (*Journal of the Acoustical Society of America* 127: 1805, 2010)

Architectural Acoustics Principles and Practice, 2nd edition, by W. Cavanaugh, G. Tocci, and J. Wilkes (New York: John Wiley, 2009)
Chapters 2, 3, and 6 of this book, by two of the lead authors of the *FGI Guidelines* and *SV Guidelines*, address acoustic design considerations and materials selection for meeting LEED for Healthcare requirements.

Patients First: Ensuring Quieter Hospital Environments, by K.M. Montague, C.M. Blietz, and M. Kachur (*American Journal of Nursing, 2009*)
www.nursingcenter.com/library/JournalArticle.asp?Article_ID=931031
One of a series of four papers from the Planetree Alliance, the pioneers of the patient-centered care and evidence-based design movements. This paper outlines the health effects of noise and cites medical literature to support specific strategies for incorporating noise control and speech privacy into healthcare facilities.

Recommended Standards for Newborn ICU Design, by R.D. White (*Journal of Perinatology* 26, S2-S18, Doi:10.1038/sj-jp 7211587, 2006)
This article summarizes a 15-year project to develop and test evidence-based acoustic guidelines for the design and construction of NICUs. In 2010, these NICU guidelines were accepted into the SV Guidelines and FGI 2010 Guidelines.

Noise Pollution, a Modern Plague, by L. Hagler and L. Goines (*Southern Medical Journal*, 2007)
http://www.ncbi.nim.nih.gov/pubmed/17396733

Effects of Noise Contribute to Physicians' Challenges, by L. Hagler and L. Goines (*Southern Medical Journal*, 2007)
http://www.ncbi.nlm.nih.gov/pubmed/17396723

Influence of Intensive Coronary Care Acoustics on the Quality of Care and Physiological State of Patients, by I. Hagerman, G. Rasmanis, V. Blomkvist, R. Ulrich, and T. Theorell (*International Journal of Cardiology* 98: 267–70, 2005)

Sound Control for Improved Outcomes in Health Care Settings (2007)
Center for Health Design
http://www.healthdesign.org/chd/research/sound-cotrol-improved-outcomes-healthcare-setttings?page=10
A short bibliography.

Green Guide for Health Care Acoustic Environment Technical Brief, by B. Davenny, W.J. Cavanaugh, and D.M. Sykes (2007)
http://www.gghc.org/tools.technical.php
Best practices for designing a healthcare facility's acoustical performance. Some of the strategies presented in this 2007 publication have been updated in the *2010 FGI Guidelines* and *the SV Guidelines*.

13. Definitions

A complete list of definitions of acoustics terms relevant to healthcare facility design can be found in the FGI 2010 Guidelines and its supporting reference, the *SV Guidelines*.

A-weighted decibel (dBA) sound pressure level measured with a conventional frequency weighting that roughly approximates how the human ear hears different frequency components of sounds at typical listening levels for speech. (ANSI S12.60–2002)

composite sound transmission class (STC_c) the STC rating of any assembly comprising two or more subassemblies.

dBA See **A-weighted decibel.**

hertz (Hz) the unit of frequency of sound and vibration. One Hz equals 1 cycle per second.

HVAC system equipment, distribution systems, and terminals that provide the processes of heating, ventilating, or air-conditioning to a building or portion of a building. (ASHRAE 90.1–2007)

reverberation the repeated reflection or scattering of sound on the surfaces within an enclosed space. (ANSI S12.60–2002)

room sound absorption coefficient the sum of the room surface areas times their sound absorption coefficients divided by the room surface area. It is a dimensionless quantity that characterizes the reverberant character of the room and is related to the surface treatments and areas of those treatments in a room.

sound absorption coefficient (α) the ability of a material to absorb sound, calculated as the ratio of sound energy absorbed by a material to the amount of sound energy incident on the material. It is frequency dependent and ranges from 0.00 (completely sound-reflecting) to 1.00 (completely sound-absorptive).

sound transmission class (**STC**) the ability of a material to prevent the transmission of sound between two spaces, expressed as a single number and determined by sound transmission loss measured in a laboratory (ASTM E90) using a method defined by standards (ASTM E413). The higher the STC rating the greater the ability of a material or system of materials in an assembly to reduce the transmission of sound between two spaces.

speech transmission index (**STI**) a measure of the extent to which speech is intelligible in the presence of ambient sound and other acoustic effects, such as reverberation. STI varies from 0 (totally unintelligible) to 1.0 (perfectly intelligible). STI is most often used to evaluate the performance of electronic sound reinforcement and paging systems. (IEC 60268-16)

STC_c See **composite sound transmission class.**

CONSTRUCTION INDOOR AIR QUALITY MANAGEMENT PLAN—DURING CONSTRUCTION

	HEALTHCARE
Credit	IEQ Credit 3.1
Points	1 point

Intent

To reduce indoor air quality (IAQ) problems and noise and vibration resulting from construction and/or renovation process in order to help sustain the comfort and well-being of construction workers and building occupants.

Requirements

Develop and implement an Environmental Quality Management Plan (EQMP) for the construction and preoccupancy phases of the building. Minimize air and noise pollution during the construction process as prescribed below.

For renovations, additions adjacent to occupied facilities or phased occupancy in new construction:

- Follow the *2010 FGI Guidelines* for Design and Construction of Health Care Facilities and the Joint Commission on standards to establish an integrated infection control team comprised of the owner, designer and contractor to evaluate infection control risk and document the required precautions in a project-specific plan.
- Use the Infection Control Risk Assessment (ICRA) standard published by the American Society of Healthcare Engineering (ASHE) and the U.S. Centers for Disease Control and Prevention (CDC), as a guideline for construction activities to assess risk and to select mitigation procedures.

For all projects:

- Develop and implement a moisture control plan to address measures that will maintain dry conditions to protect stored on-site and installed absorptive materials from moisture damage. Immediately remove from site and properly dispose of any materials susceptible to microbial growth and replace with new, undamaged materials. Also include strategies for protecting the building from moisture intrusion and occupant exposures to dangerous mold spores.
- If permanently installed air handlers are used during construction:
  - Filtration media with a minimum efficiency reporting value (MERV) of 8 must be used at each return air grille, as determined by ASHRAE Standard 52.2-1999 (with errata but without addenda[1]).
  - Protect active outdoor air intakes and return air grilles with filtration media.
  - Temporary filter media must be evaluated and replaced as necessary.
  - Replace all filtration media immediately prior to occupancy.

1 Project teams wishing to use ASHRAE-approved addenda for the purposes of this credit may do so at their discretion. Addenda must be applied consistently across all LEED credits.

IMPORTANT! This reference guide supplement contains only the reference guide sections that pertain to healthcare projects. Use this supplement alongside the LEED Reference Guide for Green Building Design and Construction for complete credit information. For the omitted sections, refer to the main reference guide.

- Volatile Organic Compound (VOC) Absorption – Schedule construction procedures to minimize exposure of absorbent materials to VOC emissions. Complete "wet" construction procedures such as painting and sealing before storing or installing "dry" absorbent materials such as carpet or ceiling tiles. These materials accumulate pollutants and release them over time. Store fuels, solvents and other sources of VOCs separately from absorbent materials.
- Tobacco Products – Prohibit the use of tobacco products inside the building and within 50 feet (or greater, if local jurisdiction requires) of the building entrance during construction.
- Noise and Vibration Exposure to Occupants and Construction Crews – Develop a plan based upon the British Standard (BS 5228) to reduce noise emissions and vibrations from construction equipment and other non-road engines by specifying low-noise emission design or the lowest decibel level available that meets performance requirements in the British Standard to insure it is within acceptable limits to the occupants. Construction crews must wear ear protection in areas where sounds levels exceed 85 dB for extended period of times.

	IEQ
HEALTHCARE: NC	Credit 3.1

1. Benefits and Issues to Consider

Environmental Issues

Health impacts associated with construction practices in healthcare settings are regulated through infection control risk assessment (ICRA) policies and procedures in the FGI Guidelines for Construction of Health Care Facilities, which have been adopted by many U.S. states. The ICRA and FGI guidelines require minimizing effects on building occupants in adjacent occupied areas. This credit calls for even more stringent requirements to ensure healthful conditions both indoors and outdoors and protect the health of patients, staff, visitors, and construction workers.

3. Summary of Referenced Standards

Guidelines for the Design and Construction of Health Care Facilities (2010)
Facility Guidelines Institute
http://www.fgiguidelines.org/
The healthcare industry's minimum standards for good practice in design and construction. Extensive appendices provide information about emerging design and construction trends for HVAC, waste reduction, acoustics, and other sustainability topics. Forty-two U.S. states use these guidelines as code or as a reference standard.

Joint Commission
http://www.jointcommission.org/
Guidance on establishing an integrated infection control team comprising the owner, designer, and contractor, to evaluate infection control risk and document the required precautions in a project-specific plan.

Infection Control Risk Assessment (ICRA) Standard
American Society of Healthcare Engineering (ASHE) and the U.S. Centers for Disease Control and Prevention (CDC)
http://www.ashe.org/advocacy/organizations/CDC/pdfs/assessment_icra.pdf
Guidelines for assessing risk and selecting mitigation procedures in construction activities.

British Standard BS 5228
http://shop.bsigroup.com
A standard for noise emissions and vibrations from construction equipment and other nonroad engines.

4. Implementation

Adopt an environmental quality management plan based on an infection control risk assessment standard to protect the HVAC system, control pollutant sources, and interrupt contamination pathways during construction. The plan should address moisture control, HVAC protection, VOC source control, protection from environmental tobacco smoke, noise and vibration protection for occupants and construction crews, and for renovations and additions, an infection control risk assessment.

Moisture Control

Prepare a written program to guide actions to prevent mold and mildew growth. Best practices include the following:

- Maintaining a relative humidity level of 60% or less once absorptive finish materials have been installed.
- Protecting stored on-site or installed absorptive materials from moisture damage.
- Immediately removing and properly disposing of any materials with stains, mold, mildew, or other evidence of water damage and replacing them with new, undamaged materials.

A complete guide to preventing mold and reducing the probability of recurrence can be found in the U.S. Environmental Protection Agency's Mold Remediation in Schools and Commercial Buildings (EPA 402-K- 01-001; http://www.epa.gov/mold/mold_remediation.html). The ANSI/GREENGUARD Environmental Institute Mold and Moisture Management Standard for New Construction (ANSI/GEI-MMS 1001; http://greenguard.org/technicalCenter/tech_standards.aspx#1) contains a comprehensive overview of the principles and practices associated with moisture control and serves as a resource in developing commissioning plans and operations and maintenance guides.

HVAC Protection

See the LEED Reference Guide for Green Building Design and Construction, IEQ Credit 3.1, Implementation section, for information about HVAC protection.

VOC Source Control

See the LEED Reference Guide for Green Building Design and Construction, IEQ Credit 3.1, Implementation section, for information about VOC source reduction practices.

Tobacco Products

Develop a no-smoking policy, post signs, and educate construction staff on the importance of protecting the project from tobacco smoke contamination.

Noise and Vibration

Develop a plan to reduce noise and vibration emissions on and around the construction site. At a minimum, the plan should address the following issues.

Surrounding community. The site determines the necessary level and type of noise and vibration controls. To prevent construction on existing healthcare campuses from disturbing sensitive patients, for example, apply noise insulation to the glazing on patient rooms. Also protect surrounding residential neighborhoods. When scheduling construction activities, take into consideration ambient noise, the level of continuous construction noise, and short-term noise and vibration (as from a wrecking ball or jackhammer). Vibration can damage buildings adjacent to the construction site. If any historic or otherwise sensitive buildings are nearby, consider performing an assessment and tailoring allowable levels of construction vibration to minimize the project's impact on its neighbors. For example, demolition may require a staged approach rather than a single, coordinated blast of explosives.

Construction worker training and protective equipment. In addition to providing ear protection, train construction staff in the proper use and maintenance of noise- and vibration-producing equipment to protect nearby workers, staff, and patients. Ensure that workers know how to verify that they are meeting the noise and vibration requirements established for the project. Determine which areas of the site will require special protection from noise; protective gear may be necessary for workers in these areas even if they are not operating the equipment themselves. The contractor should post readily visible signage in these areas indicating that the use of protective gear is required. The contractor should also maintain a log or other monitoring system for worker training, proper operation of construction equipment, and wearing of protective gear.

Source reduction. General measures for source reduction include no-idling requirements, properly graded and maintained circulation paths, and sequential equipment start-up policies. To reduce site construction noise, use rubber chutes for disposal of construction waste. Include noise and vibration as criteria when selecting equipment, or retrofit existing equipment with noise and vibration attenuators. Some retrofit strategies can greatly reduce total dBA (A-weighted decibels) and the vibrations generated by the equipment. For example, the noise from diesel engines can be attenuated by installing an exhaust silencer system or by encapsulating the engine inside an acoustic barrier. Replacing a diesel piece of equipment with an electric counterpart eliminates on-site emissions in addition to reducing noise and vibration pollution.

Major sources of noise and vibrations should be housed in acoustical and vibration enclosures, as outlined in Annex B of British Standard BS 5228. Temporary buildings, such as the construction site office, can be placed strategically to buffer neighbors from construction noise and vibration. Temporary berms resulting from earth-moving activities can also serve this purpose.

Infection Control Risk Assessment (ICRA)

For renovations, additions adjacent to occupied facilities, and phased-occupancy new construction, the plan should include an infection control risk assessment, performed by an infection control team. The CDC-ASHE document outlines a process to address the potential risks of infection transmission associated with construction and renovation projects. Construction activity levels, ranging from noninvasive activities to major demolition and construction projects, are rated for patient risk, ranging from low to high. The resulting classification of infection control precautions can help project teams reduce the risk of infection transmission during construction.

5. Timeline and Team

On existing healthcare campuses, engage infection control staff early in the design process, to ensure that the construction indoor air quality management plan aligns with infection control policies. Coordinate the construction no-smoking policy with campus smoking policies.

7. Documentation Guidance

As a first step in preparing to complete the LEED Online documentation requirements, work through the following measures. Refer to LEED Online for the complete descriptions of all required documentation.

- Write a construction indoor air quality management plan for use during demolition and construction; it should include infection control risk assessment requirements, the moisture control plan, HVAC protection, VOC source control, the no-smoking policy, and noise and vibration control measures.
- Maintain a detailed photo log of the indoor air quality management practices followed during construction.

8. Examples

See the ASHE/CDC ICRA Matrix of Precautions for Construction & Renovations for an example of an infection control construction permit, which can be used to verify compliance with the project's risk assessment.

11. Operations and Maintenance Considerations

Develop the construction environmental quality management plan with the help of the infection control department and other relevant facilities staff. For renovations and additions, ensure that the plan complies with campus protocols governing infection control, particularly in adjacent operational areas.

12. Resources

Websites

Control of Drywall Sanding Dust Exposures
National Institute for Occupational Safety and Health (NIOSH)
http://www.cdc.gov/niosh/, NIOSH Publication No. 99-113
Best practice guidance on minimizing the dust generated by drywall sanding.

Green Guide for Health Care Low Impact Construction Practices Technical Brief,
by Jim Moler
http://www.gghc.org/tools.technical.php
Construction best practices for a green healthcare facility, including waste reduction and recycling, site and materials management, infection control, and utility and emissions control.

Guidelines for Environmental Infection Control in Health-Care Facilities: Recommendations of Centers for Disease Control and the Health Care Infection Control Practices Advisory Committee
U.S. Department of Health and Human Services, Centers for Disease Control and Prevention, *Morbidity and Mortality Weekly Report* 52(RR-10): 1–42 (June 6, 2003)
http://www.cdc.gov/mmwr/preview/mmwrhtml/rr5210a1.htm
Environmental infection control guidelines and strategies aimed at reducing risk of exposure to infection in the healthcare setting.

Mold and Moisture Management Standard for New Construction
American National Standards Institute, GREENGUARD Environmental Institute
ANSI/GEI-MMS 1001, http://greenguard.org/technicalCenter/tech_standards.aspx#1
A comprehensive overview of the principles and practices associated with moisture control.

Mold Remediation in Schools and Commercial Buildings
U.S. Environmental Protection Agency
EPA 402-K-01-001, http://www.epa.gov/mold/mold_remediation.html
A complete guide to preventing mold and reducing the probability of its recurring.

13. Definitions

A-weighted decibel (dBA) sound pressure level measured with a conventional frequency weighting that roughly approximates how the human ear hears different frequency components of sounds at typical listening levels for speech. (ANSI S12.60–2002)

environmental quality management plan a set of measures to minimize contamination and protect human health, often applied to construction activities.

infection control policies and procedures to minimize the risk of spreading infections through cross-contamination.

infection control risk assessment (ICRA) an evaluation that anticipates the potential risks of infection transmission associated with construction and renovation projects.

vibration dose value (VDV) a measure of continuous, rapid to-and-fro movement, derived from the number and duration of vibration events over a period of time.

CONSTRUCTION INDOOR AIR QUALITY MANAGEMENT PLAN—BEFORE OCCUPANCY

	HEALTHCARE: NC
Credit	IEQ Credit 3.2
Points	1 point

Intent

To reduce indoor air quality (IAQ) problems resulting from construction or renovation to help sustain the comfort and well-being of construction workers and building occupants.

Requirements

Develop an IAQ management plan and implement it after all finishes and furnishings have been installed and the building has been completely cleaned before occupancy.

OPTION 1. Flush-Out[1]

PATH 1

After construction ends, prior to occupancy and with all interior finishes installed, install new filtration media and, perform a building flush-out by supplying a total air volume of 14,000 cubic feet of outdoor air per square foot of floor area while maintaining an internal temperature of at least 60° F and relative humidity no higher than 60%.

OR

PATH 2

If occupancy is desired prior to completion of the flush-out, the space may be occupied following delivery of a minimum of 3,500 cubic feet of outdoor air per square foot of floor area. Once the space is occupied, it must be ventilated at a minimum rate of 0.30 cubic feet per minute (cfm) per square foot of outside air or the design minimum outside air rate determined in IEQ Prerequisite 1: Minimum Indoor Air Quality Performance, whichever is greater. During each day of the flush-out period, ventilation must begin a minimum of 3 hours prior to occupancy and continue during occupancy. These conditions must be maintained until a total of 14,000 cubic feet per square foot of outside air has been delivered to the space. Note: All finishes and furnishings must be installed prior to flush out.

OR

OPTION 2. Air Testing

Conduct baseline IAQ testing after construction ends and prior to occupancy using testing protocols consistent with the EPA Compendium of Methods for the Determination of Air Pollutants in Indoor Air and as additionally detailed in the LEED Reference Guide for Green Building Design and Construction, 2009 Edition Healthcare Supplement.

1 All finishes must be installed prior to flush-out.

IMPORTANT! This reference guide supplement contains only the reference guide sections that pertain to healthcare projects. Use this supplement alongside the LEED Reference Guide for Green Building Design and Construction for complete credit information. For the omitted sections, refer to the main reference guide.

IEQ CREDIT 3.2

Demonstrate that the contaminant maximum concentration levels listed below are not exceeded:

Contaminant	Maximum Concentration
Formaldehyde	20 micrograms per cubic meter
Particulates (PM10)	20 micrograms per cubic meter
Total volatile organic compounds (TVOCs)	200 micrograms per cubic meter
4-Phenylcyclohexene (4-PCH)*	3 micrograms per cubic meter
Carbon monoxide (CO)	9 part per million and no greater than 2 parts per million above outdoor levels

* This test is only required if carpets and fabrics with styrene butadiene rubber (SBR) latex backing are installed as part of the base building systems.

For each sampling point where the maximum concentration limits are exceeded, conduct an additional flush-out with outside air and retest the noncompliant concentrations. Repeat until all requirements are met. When retesting noncompliant building areas, take samples from the same locations as in the first test, although it is not required.

Conduct the air sample testing as follows:

- All measurements must be conducted prior to occupancy, but during normal occupied hours with the building ventilation system started at the normal daily start time and operated at the minimum outside air flow rate for the occupied mode throughout the test.
- All interior finishes must be installed, including but not limited to millwork, doors, paint, carpet and acoustic tiles. Movable furnishings such as workstations and partitions should be in place for the testing, although it is not required.
- The number of sampling locations will depend on the size of the building and number of ventilation systems. For each portion of the building served by a separate ventilation system, the number of sampling points must not be less than 1 per 25,000 square feet or for each contiguous floor area, whichever is larger. Include areas with the least ventilation and greatest presumed source strength.
- Air samples must be collected between 3 and 6 feet from the floor to represent the breathing zone of occupants, and over a minimum 4-hour period.

IEQ	
HEALTHCARE: NC	Credit 3.2

1. Benefits and Issues to Consider

Environmental Issues

High-quality indoor air, free from harmful levels of contaminants, is an imperative for healthcare facilities to avoid exacerbating patients' chronic conditions.

4. Implementation

See the LEED Reference Guide for Green Building Design and Construction, IEQ Credit 3.2, Implementation section, for guidance on flush-out and air quality testing procedures.

Project teams that conduct additional chemical testing not required by this credit can consult the California Office of Environmental Health Hazard Assessment's chronic reference exposure levels, the Occupational Safety and Health Administration's permissible exposure limits, and the American Conference of Governmental Industrial Hygienists' threshold limit values.

12. Resources

Websites

Chronic Reference Exposure Levels
California Office of Environmental Health Hazard Assessment
http://www.oehha.ca.gov/air/chronic_rels/AllChrels.html
A table of acute, eight-hour, and chronic reference exposure limits to hazardous substances.

Green Guide for Health Care Low Impact Construction Practices Technical Brief,
by Jim Moler
http://www.gghc.org/tools.technical.php
Construction best practices for a green healthcare facility, including waste reduction and recycling, site and materials management, infection control, and utility and emissions control.

Permissible Exposure Limits (**PELs**)
Occupational Safety & Health Administration
http://www.osha.gov/SLTC/pel/
OSHA sets standards to protect workers from exposure to hazardous substances.

Threshold Limit Values (**TLVs**)
American Conference of Governmental Industrial Hygienists)
http://www.acgih.org
Guidelines to assist industrial hygienists in the control of health hazards associated with exposure to chemical substances.

LOW-EMITTING MATERIALS

	HEALTHCARE
Credit	IEQ Credit 4.1
Points	1-4 points

Intent

To reduce the quantity of indoor air contaminants that are odorous, irritating and/or harmful to the comfort and well-being of installers and occupants.

Requirements

One point (maximum four) can be achieved for each group of materials that comply with the requirements.

GROUP 1: Interior Adhesives and Sealants

All adhesives and sealants used on the interior of the building (i.e., inside of the weatherproofing system and applied on-site) must comply with the following requirements as applicable to the project scope[1]:

- Adhesives, Sealants and Sealant Primers must comply with South Coast Air Quality Management District (SCAQMD) Rule #1168. Volatile organic compound (VOC) limits listed in the table below correspond to an effective date of July 1, 2005 and rule amendment date of January 7, 2005.
- Aerosol Adhesives must comply with Green Seal Standard for Commercial Adhesives GS-36 requirements in effect on October 19, 2000.

Adhesives and sealants shall contain no carcinogen or reproductive toxicant components present at more than 1% of total mass of the product as defined in the California Office of Environmental Health Hazard Assessment's (OEHHA) list entitled "Chemicals Known to the State to Cause Cancer" or the Reproductive Toxicity, Safe Drinking Water and Toxic Enforcement Act of 1986 (Proposition 65).

GROUP 2: Wall and Ceiling Finishes

Paints and coatings used on the interior of the building—defined as inside of the weatherproofing system and applied on-site—shall not exceed the VOC content limits established in South Coast Air Quality Management District (SCAQMD) Rule 1113, Architectural Coatings. (Rules in effect on July 1, 2008.)

Ceiling tiles, including suspended acoustical tiles, and wall coverings shall comply with the testing and product requirements of the California Department of Public Health Standard Method for the Testing and Evaluation of Volatile Organic Chemical Emissions from Indoor Sources Using Environmental Chambers version 1.1 (CDPH/EHLB Standard Method v1.1) modeled using the standard office building protocol parameters and certified as compliant by an independent third party.

GROUP 3: Flooring

Carpet and all hard surface flooring installed in the building interior shall comply with the testing and product requirements of the California Department of Public Health

1 The use of a VOC budget is permissible for compliance with this credit.

IMPORTANT! This reference guide supplement contains only the reference guide sections that pertain to healthcare projects. Use this supplement alongside the LEED Reference Guide for Green Building Design and Construction for complete credit information. For the omitted sections, refer to the main reference guide.

Standard Method for the Testing and Evaluation of Volatile Organic Chemical Emissions From Indoor Sources Using Environmental Chambers version 1.1 (CDPH/EHLB Standard Method v1.1), modeled using the standard office building protocol parameters and certified as compliant by an independent third party. Mineral-based finish flooring products, such as tile, masonry, terrazzo, and cut stone without integral organic-based coatings and sealants and unfinished/untreated solid wood flooring, qualify for credit without any IAQ testing requirements. However, associated, site-applied adhesives, grouts, finishes and sealers must be compliant for a mineral-based or unfinished/untreated solid wood flooring system to qualify for credit.

All carpet cushion installed in the building interior shall comply with the requirements of the Carpet and Rug Institute Green Label program.

All flooring related adhesives shall comply with the requirements of Group 1. Grout shall comply with requirements for ceramic tile adhesive.

Concrete, wood, bamboo, cork and other floor finishes, such as sealer, stain and finish, shall not exceed the VOC limits established in South Coast Air Quality Management District (SCAQMD) Rule 1113, Architectural Coatings, rules in effect on July 1, 2008.

GROUP 4: Composite Wood, Agrifiber Products and Batt Insulation Products

Composite wood and agrifiber products used on the interior of the building—defined as inside of the weatherproofing system—shall contain no added urea-formaldehyde resins. Laminating adhesives used to fabricate on-site and shop-applied composite wood and agrifiber assemblies shall contain no added urea-formaldehyde resins.

Composite wood and agrifiber products are defined as particleboard, medium density fiberboard (MDF), plywood, wheat board, strawboard, panel substrates and door cores. Materials considered furniture, fixtures, and equipment (FF&E) are not considered base building elements and are not included.

Batt insulation products shall contain no added formaldehyde, including urea formaldehyde, phenol formaldehyde, and urea-extended phenol formaldehyde.

GROUP 5: Exterior Applied Products

Adhesives, sealants, coatings, roofing and waterproofing materials—defined as from the weatherproofing system out and applied on-site—shall comply with the VOC limits of California Air Resources Board (ARB) 2007 Suggested Control Measure (SCM) for Architectural Coatings and South Coast Air Quality Management District (SCAQMD) Rule 1168 effective July 1, 2005.

Roofing installations shall not use hot-mopped asphalt installation techniques.

Parking lots and other paved surfaces shall not use coal tar sealants.

For any waterproofing, asphalt roofing needing repair, parking lot sealing or other high VOC emissions outdoor construction process, create a plan to manage fumes and avoid infiltration to occupied spaces. Comply with procedures established by NIOSH's Asphalt Fume Exposures During the Application of Hot Asphalt to Roofs (Publication No. 2003-112).

Reference Table for all IEQ Credit 4 Groups			
Architectural Adhesives (SCAQMD 1168)	VOC Limit [g/L less water]	Specialty Adhesives (SCAQMD 1168)	VOC Limit [g/L less water]
Indoor Carpet Adhesives	50	PVC Welding	510
Carpet Pad Adhesives	50	CPVC Welding	490
Wood Flooring Adhesives	100	ABS Welding	325
Rubber Floor Adhesives	60	Plastic Cement Welding	250
Subfloor Adhesives	50	Adhesive Primer for Plastic	550
Ceramic Tile Adhesives	65	Contact Adhesive	80
VCT & Asphalt Adhesives	50	Special Purpose Contact Adhesive	250
Drywall & Panel Adhesives	50	Structural Wood Member Adhesive	140
Cove Base Adhesives	50	Sheet Applied Rubber Lining Operations	850
Multipurpose Construction Adhesives	70	Top & Trim Adhesive	250
Structural Glazing Adhesives	100		
Interior Sealants (SCAQMD 1168)		Sealant Primers (SCAQMD 1168)	250
Architectural	250	Architectural Non Porous	775
Other	420	Architectural Porous	750
		Other	750
Exterior Coatings (CARB SCM)		Substrate Specific Applications (SCAQMD 1168)	
Aluminum Roof Coatings	400	Metal to Metal	30
Basement Specialty Coatings	400	Plastic Foams	50
Concrete Curing Compounds	350	Porous Material (except wood)	50
Concrete/Masonry Sealers	100	Wood	30
Driveway Sealers	50	Fiberglass	80
Driveway Sealers	50	Interior Coatings (SCAQMD 1113)	
Floor Coatings	100	Paints (flat & non-flat, except anti-rust)	50
Industrial Maintenance Coatings	250	Clear wood finishes (varnish, lacquer or sanding sealers)	275
Non flat coatings	100	Floor coatings	50
Non flat high gloss	150	Primers and undercoaters	100
Primers, Sealants, and Undercoaters	100	Swimming pool coatings	340
Quick Dry Enamels	150	Sealers: Waterproofing & all others	100
Reactive Penetrating Sealer	350	Shellacs: Clear	730
Rust Preventative Coatings	250	Shellacs: Pigmented	550
Stains	250	Stains	100
Stone Consolidant	450	Aerosol Adhesives (GS-36)	
Traffic Coatings	100	General purpose mist spray	65% VOCs by weight
Waterproofing Membranes	250	General purpose web spray	55% VOCs by weight
Wood Coatings	275	Special purpose aerosol adhesives (all types)	70% VOCs by weight

1. Benefits and Issues to Consider

Environmental Issues

Address VOC emissions from both interior and exterior products to minimize the risk of exposure for construction workers, staff, patients, and the surrounding community. Because healthcare construction projects often involve expansions of existing, occupied buildings or new construction adjacent to operating buildings, potential contamination of indoor air is a common problem.

For additional information on Benefits and Issues to Consider, see the LEED Reference Guide for Green Building Design and Construction, IEQ Credits 4.1–4.4 and 4.6.

2. Related Credits

Review product emissions data in concert with sustainability and toxic chemical criteria, contributing to the following prerequisite and credits:

- MR Prerequisite 2, PBT Source Reduction—Mercury
- MR Credit 3, Sustainably Sourced Materials and Products
- MR Credit 4.1, PBT Source Reduction—Mercury in Lamps
- MR Credit 4.2, PBT Source Reduction—Lead, Cadmium, and Copper

Because the intent of this credit is to reduce odorous, irritating, and harmful indoor air contaminants throughout the facility, project teams should consider low-emitting materials alongside compliant purchases for the following credit:

- MR Credit 5, Furniture and Medical Furnishings

Acoustic elements within the building may require special materials and installation considerations; see the following credit:

- IEQ Credit 2, Acoustic Environment

For additional information on related credits, see the LEED Reference Guide for Green Building Design and Construction IEQ, Credits 4.1–4.4 and 4.6.

3. Summary of Referenced Standards

Suggested Control Measure for Architectural Coatings (2007)
California Air Resources Board
http://www.arb.ca.gov/coatings/arch/Approved_2007_SCM.pdf
Guidance for local air quality management districts in California on VOC limits for architectural coatings, including roof coatings, traffic marking coatings, driveway sealers, and other exterior products.

California Department of Public Health Standard Method for the Testing and Evaluation of Volatile Organic Chemical Emissions from Indoor Sources Using Environmental Chambers Version 1.1 (February 2010)
California Department of Public Health, Indoor Air Quality Section, Environmental Health Laboratory Branch, Division of Environmental and Occupational Disease Control
http://www.cal-iaq.org/vocs/voc-publications
CDPH/EHLB Standard Method v1.1 is the emissions testing method for California Specification 01350. Version 1.1, released in February 2010, supersedes the 2004 version, Standard Practice for the Testing of Volatile Organic Emissions from Various Sources Using Small-Scale Environmental Chambers.

From the scope of the CDPH Standard Method v1.1: "This method applies to any product category generally used within the envelope of an enclosed indoor environment. The method is applicable to products that can be tested whole or by representative sample in environmental chambers. This includes, as examples, paints, other architectural coatings and finishes, sealants, adhesives, wallcoverings, floor coverings, acoustical ceilings, wood paneling, wall and ceiling insulation used in public and commercial office buildings, schools, residences and other building types.

"This method establishes performance criteria for specific chemicals of interest. These criteria are specifically for evaluating potential chronic health risks from inhalation exposures of vapor phase organic chemicals emitted by the products covered within the scope."

California Proposition 65 List of Chemicals Known to the State to Cause Cancer or Reproductive Toxicity
California Environmental Protection Agency, Office of Environmental Health Hazard Assessment (OEHHA)
Safe Drinking Water and Toxic Enforcement Act of 1986 (Proposition 65)
http://www.oehha.ca.gov/prop65.html
Proposition 65 is intended to protect drinking water sources in California from contaminants that could cause reproductive harm and cancer. This list, published annually, helps fulfill the regulation's additional mandate to inform the public about potential exposure to these chemicals.

Green Label Testing Program
Carpet and Rug Institute
http://www.carpet-rug.com
Green Label Plus is an independent, ISO Guide 65–accredited certification and testing program that identifies carpets and carpet cushions with very low VOC emissions. The criteria were developed by the Carpet and Rug Institute (CRI), a trade organization, in coordination with California's Sustainable Building Task Force and the California Department of Health Services (now Department of Public Health). The CRI website describes the program, explains the VOC emissions criteria, and lists certified products with their certification numbers. Products certified in the Green Label program undergo annual emissions tests.

Green Seal Standard 36 (GS-36)
http://www.greenseal.org/certification/standards/commercial_adhesives_GS_36.cfm
Green Seal is an independent, nonprofit organization that strives to achieve a healthier and cleaner environment by identifying and promoting products and services that cause less toxic pollution and waste, conserve resources and habitats, and minimize global warming and ozone depletion. GS-36 sets VOC limits for commercial adhesives. The standard took effect in 2000.

Asphalt Fume Exposures during the Application of Hot Asphalt to Roofs
National Institute for Occupational Safety and Health (NIOSH)
http://www.cdc.gov/niosh/docs/2003-112/
NIOSH, an agency within the U.S. Department of Health and Human Services, provides research, information, education, and training related to practices that ensure safe and healthful working environments. This publication (No. 2003-112) provides guidance on how to reduce workers' exposure to asphalt fumes during the application of hot asphalt to roofs.

Rule 1113, Architectural Coatings
South Coast Air Quality Management District (SCAQMD)
http://www.aqmd.gov/rules/reg/reg11/r1113.pdf
The mission of the South Coast Air Quality Management District, a governmental organization in southern California, is to maintain healthful air quality for residents. The organization has established source-specific standards to reduce harmful emissions.

Rule 1168, VOC Limits (January 7, 2005)
South Coast Air Quality Management District (SCAQMD)
http://www.aqmd.gov/rules/reg/reg11/r1168.pdf
The mission of the South Coast Air Quality Management District, a governmental organization in southern California, is to maintain healthful air quality for residents. The organization has established source-specific standards to reduce harmful emissions. Adhesives, sealants, and sealant primers must comply with Rule 1168. The VOC limits listed in the IEQ Credit 4 Requirements table below correspond to an effective date of July 1, 2005, and a rule amendment date of January 7, 2005. Aerosol adhesives must comply with Green Seal Standard for Commercial Adhesives GS-36 requirements that went in effect on October 19, 2000.

4. Implementation

IEQ Credit 4, Low-Emitting Materials, applies to products and installation processes that can adversely affect the air quality of a project and expose occupants to the off-gassing of contaminants.

The size, complexity, regulatory constraints, and infection control concerns of healthcare facilities require a more flexible and holistic approach to specifying sustainable building materials. Establish goals for low-emitting materials during the design phase and specify no- and low-VOC materials in construction documents. To establish low-emitting material goals into project specifications, first add a LEED general requirements section to Division 01 to allow for writing LEED performance requirements for overlapping work sections. Then, specify products and materials according to CSI MasterFormat 2004 classifications for Division 01 low-emitting material requirements. Ensure that VOC limits are clearly stated in each section of the specifications where paints, coatings, adhesives and sealants, roofing, and waterproofing materials are addressed. Careful research may be required to determine the VOC emissions that can realistically be expected in specific products and materials. Track procurement during construction. See MR Credit 5, Furniture and Medical Furnishings, for additional information on VOC emissions requirements for furniture and furnishings.

For products complying with CDPH/EHLB Standard Method v1.1, look for ISO Guide 65–accredited third-party certification programs using laboratories that are ISO 17025 accredited to the CDPH Standard Method v1.1. Ask about the specifics of each product claim. Verify that the exposure scenario was in accordance with the CDPH Standard Method v1.1. Some manufacturers use their own "branded" test methodology—an approach that can stifle competition among laboratories and promote products or materials that would not be certified under a third-party program. The CDPH standard method v1.1 is available for use by any qualified laboratory. Programs that follow it can identify products that are compliant with the requirements of this credit. Note that CDPH Standard Method v1.1/Section 01350 is considered a minimum standard; it does not cover all VOCs and chemicals that can affect indoor environmental quality.

Composition Limits

This testing approach sets limits on the amount of some chemical substances, such as VOCs, per volume of product material. The threshold limits and content within a particular product are generally expressed in grams per liter (g/L). Four groups in this credit use this approach: interior adhesives and sealants, wall and ceiling finishes, flooring, and exterior applied products. The fifth group—composite wood, agrifiber products, and batt insulation products—also disallows any added urea-formaldehyde resins. Composition limits are beneficial but they do not always correlate well with emitted quantities of VOCs or off-gassing.

Emissions Limits

This testing approach sets limits on the amount of off-gassing that can occur over a period of time. This approach is used in two groups, wall and ceiling finishes, and flooring. It is also used in MR Credit 5, Furniture and Medical Furnishings.

GROUP 1: Interior adhesives and sealants. Common adhesive and sealant products to evaluate include general construction adhesives, flooring adhesives, plumbing adhesives, cove base adhesives, fire-stopping sealants, caulking, and duct sealants.

GROUP 2: Wall and ceiling finishes. Note that paint tints can add substantially to VOC levels. Use only low- or zero-VOC tints, particularly for richer tints. Avoid paints with added antimicrobials. Avoid field-applied painting entirely by using prefinished metals.

GROUP 3: Flooring. Consider installing modular flooring materials that are easily replaced, thereby reducing the emissions associated with renovations. Select flooring that can be maintained using nontoxic cleaning products and practices.

GROUP 4: Composite wood, agrifiber products, and batt insulation products. Consider composite wood, agrifiber, and fiberglass products that are free of all formaldehyde chemicals, including phenol formaldehyde. Many manufacturers are shifting to methylene diphenyl diisocyanate (MDI) and soy-based binders as safer alternatives to formaldehyde-based binder. Specify laminating adhesives for field- and shop-applied assemblies that contain no added urea-formaldehyde resins.

GROUP 5: Exterior applied products. Specify self-adhering, cold adhesive, torch-applied, or heat-weldable membranes and installation techniques for membrane roofing installations instead of hot asphalt. Use of prefinished metal panels and products can reduce field-applied painting.

For additional information on implementation, see the LEED Reference Guide for Green Building Design and Construction, IEQ Credits 4.1–4.4 and 4.6.

5. Timeline and Team

Refer to the Timeline and Team sections in the LEED Reference Guide for Green Building Design and Construction, IEQ Credits 4.1–4.4 and 4.6.

6. Calculations

Refer to the Calculations sections in the LEED Reference Guide for Green Building Design and Construction, IEQ Credits 4.1–4.4 and 4.6.

7. Documentation Guidance

As a first step in preparing to complete the LEED Online documentation requirements, work through the following measures. Refer to LEED Online for the complete descriptions of all required documentation.

- Maintain a list of the qualifying products used on the project. For each, include the manufacturer's name, product name, and specific VOC data (g/L, less water), as well as the corresponding allowable VOC from the referenced standard. For composite wood, agrifiber, and batt insulation, confirm that the products contain no added urea-formaldehyde.
- If using the VOC budget approach, track the amount of product used.

11. Operations and Maintenance Considerations

Include safety (e.g., slip and fall), durability, and cleaning criteria in materials specifications considerations. Determine whether the healthcare campus has instituted a green cleaning program. Train environmental services staff in the proper cleaning of unfamiliar finish materials. Consider installing pilot finish materials in an existing hospital to observe wear and tear, slip and fall potential, and cleanability. Gather feedback from nurses, doctors, environmental services, and infection control. In addition to training staff on cleaning and maintenance procedures, these demonstrations can help build support for installing sustainably sourced materials in the new facility.

Coordinate with facilities staff pursuing parallel credits in LEED for Existing Buildings: Operations & Maintenance and/or the Green Guide for Health Care, Operations section. The Green Guide for Health Care, in particular, addresses the synergies among environmentally preferable purchasing, green cleaning, and healthy environmental quality in great detail.

For additional information on Operations and Maintenance Considerations, see the LEED Reference Guide for Green Building Design and Construction, IEQ Credits 4.1–4.4 and 4.6.

12. Resources

Websites

Evaluation of Antimicrobial Property Claims in Finishes and Fabrics, by Erica Stewart (Kaiser Permanente, 2006)
http://www.healthybuilding.net/healthcare/KP_Antimicrobial_Position_Paper.pdf
A literature review on the effectiveness of antimicrobial treatments added to finishes and fabrics to improve infection control in the healthcare environment. The author concludes that insufficient evidence exists to warrant specifying building materials with added antimicrobial agents.

Get a Whiff of This: The Lowdown on Product Emissions Testing, by Nadav Malin (*Environmental Building News*, September 2006)
Posted with permission at http://www.bifma.org/standards/FES/FES%20Cont%20Ed%20Materials/EBN_Product_Emissions.pdf
An overview of VOC emissions testing and compares testing programs. It also addresses emerging topics, such as semivolatile organic compounds.

Green Guide for Health Care Low Emitting Materials Technical Brief, by Tom Lent
http://www.gghc.org/tools.technical.php
Best practices for specifying low-emitting adhesives, sealants, paints and coatings, flooring, wall coverings, trim, ceiling materials, composite wood, batt insulation, exterior applied products, and furniture and medical furnishings.

ISO/IEC 17025
International Organization for Standardization
http://www.iso.org
This standard outlines the general requirements for laboratories and other organizations that conduct testing, calibration, and sampling. It can be used to establish a laboratory's level of competency.

ISO/IEC Guide 65
International Organization for Standardization
http://www.iso.org
Organizations operating third-party certification programs are accredited in accordance with this standard.

For additional Resources, see the LEED Reference Guide for Green Building Design and Construction, IEQ Credits 4.1–4.4 and 4.6.

13. Definitions

coal tar sealant an emulsion containing a by-product of coal, used to seal parking lots and driveways. Coal tar sealants typically have a 5% concentration of polycyclic aromatic hydrocarbons (PAHs), a known carcinogen that can contaminate water bodies.

hot-mopped asphalt a multilayer roof consisting of asphalt, applied with a mop, between roofing membranes. Installation of this type of roofing can expose workers to asphalt fumes.

infection control policies and procedures to minimize the risk of spreading infections through cross-contamination.

semivolatile organic compound (**SVOC**) a pollutant that vaporizes only at high temperatures and is found mainly in dust and on indoor surfaces (such as furniture and finishes) rather than in the air. Examples include plasticizers (such as phthalates), halogenated flame retardants, and pesticides.

For additional definitions, see the LEED Reference Guide for Green Building Design and Construction, IEQ Credits 4.1–4.4 and 4.6.

INDOOR CHEMICAL AND POLLUTANT SOURCE CONTROL

	HEALTHCARE
Credit	IEQ Credit 5
Points	1 point

Intent

To minimize building occupant exposure to potentially hazardous particulates and chemical pollutants.

Requirements

Design to minimize and control the entry of pollutants into buildings and later cross-contamination of regularly occupied areas through the following strategies:

- Employ permanent entryway systems at least 10 feet long in the primary direction of travel to capture dirt and particulates entering the building at regularly used exterior entrances. Acceptable entryway systems include permanently installed grates, grills and slotted systems that allow for cleaning underneath. Roll-out mats are acceptable only when maintained on a weekly basis by a contracted service organization.

AND

- Minimize the entry of contaminants into the building from vehicles, pesticides, herbicides, helipads, diesel generators, designated smoking areas, sources of exhaust air, and other sources of potential contaminant as follows:

  Provide pressurized entryway vestibules at high-volume building entrances:

  Ensure, through the results of mathematical modeling [e.g. Computational Fluid Dynamics (CFD), Gaussian Dispersion Analyses] and/or physical modeling (e.g. wind tunnel, tracer gas) that the air contaminant concentrations at outdoor air intakes are less than the thresholds established for the project under worst case meteorological conditions.

  Demonstrate that outside air intake concentrations pollutants meet the limits in the following table OR demonstrate by calculations that indoor concentrations shall not exceed 2.5% of the exposure limits listed in the table.

Pollutants	Maximum Outside Air Intake Concentrations	Standard
Regulated by National Ambient Air Quality Standard (NAAQS)	Allowable Annual average OR 8-hour or 24-hour average where an annual standard does not exist OR Rolling 3 month average	National Ambient Air Quality Standard (NAAQS)
Other air contaminants	2.5% of 8-hour and short term/ceiling limits	Most stringent of the following: Occupational Safety and Health Administration (OSHA) – Permissible Exposure Limits (PELs) American Council of Governmental Industrial Hygienists (ACGIH) – Threshold Limit Values (TLVs) National Institute of Occupational Health and Safety (NIOSH) – Recommended Exposure Limits (RELs)

IMPORTANT! This reference guide supplement contains only the reference guide sections that pertain to healthcare projects. Use this supplement alongside the LEED Reference Guide for Green Building Design and Construction for complete credit information. For the omitted sections, refer to the main reference guide.

AND

Design to minimize and control cross-contamination of regularly occupied areas:

- Where hazardous gases or chemicals may be present or used—garages, soiled utility areas, sterilization and disinfection areas, housekeeping/laundry areas and copying/printing rooms—exhaust each space sufficiently to create negative pressure with respect to adjacent spaces with the doors to the room closed. For each of these spaces, provide self-closing doors and deck-to-deck partitions or a hard-lid ceiling. The exhaust rate shall be at least six air changes per hour with no air re-circulation. (For rooms containing disinfectant and sterilant applications, provide a minimum of 12 air changes per hour.) The pressure differential with the surrounding spaces shall be at least 5 Pa (0.02 inches of water gauge) on average and 1 Pa (0.004 inches of water) at a minimum, when the doors to the rooms are closed.

1. Benefits and Issues to Consider[1]

Environmental Issues

Outdoor pollutants can enter a healthcare facility through receiving bays, doorways, windows, and air intakes and then mix with indoor air contaminants from building finishes, upholstery, operations (e.g., sterilization and laundry), and clinical activities (e.g., laboratory work and anesthesia). The resulting poor air quality can affect the health of patients, staff, and visitors, causing skin, ear, nose, and throat irritation and exacerbating asthma.[2] Compromised air quality may lengthen hospital stays for patients and cause sick days and lower productivity for staff. Prolonged chemical exposure may increase chemical sensitivities and require medication. Although the full range of health effects associated with airborne contaminants is uncertain, the precautionary principle calls for reducing exposure.

The sources of airborne contaminants are often not easily relocated or eliminated, however, because of clinical needs and critical adjacencies in diagnostic and treatment areas. For example, the need to sterilize medical equipment quickly and efficiently may outweigh concerns about occupants' exposure to toxic sterilants, such as gluteraldehyde and ethylene oxide. Likewise, the need to provide immediate access to medical care in the emergency department may preclude locating the ambulance idling zone away from building entrances and outdoor air intakes. A comprehensive approach to minimizing sources of contamination is required to overcome these programmatic and operational challenges.

Economic Issues

To minimize contaminant concentrations at outdoor air intakes and outdoor seating areas through building design, many healthcare projects engage a modeling specialist during the design phase. This can add first costs to the project, but the results may reduce liability and safeguard the health of both building occupants and the surrounding community.

2. Related Credits

The following credits complement the chemical source reduction and management practices outlined in this credit:

- EA Credit 7, Community Contaminant Prevention—Airborne Releases
- IEQ Credit 4, Low-Emitting Materials

3. Summary of Referenced Standards

National Ambient Air Quality Standards (NAAQS)

http://www.epa.gov/ttn/naaqs/

The NAAQS, developed by the U.S. Environmental Protection Agency (EPA) to comply with the Clean Air Act Amendments of 1990, address six principal pollutants and provide implementation strategies to meet the standards.

1. Carbon monoxide (CO) forms when fossil fuels are not fully combusted. The highest levels of CO in outside air typically occur during colder months, when temperature inversions trap air pollution below a layer of warm air. The most common sources include motor vehicle exhaust, nontransportation fuel combustion, and cigarette smoke.

   Design strategies: Locate outdoor air intakes away from vehicle pathways. See also EA Credit 7, Community Contaminant Prevention—Airborne Releases.

1 Reference guide material for this credit draws, with permission, from Green Guide for Health Care Indoor/Outdoor Chemical & Pollutant Source Control Technical Brief, by Lorissa MacAllister (http://www.gghc.org/tools.technical.php).

2 For more information on the relationship between the healthcare environment and asthma, see Risks to Asthma Posed by Indoor Health Care Environments: A Guide to Identifying and Reducing Problematic Exposures, Health Care without Harm, 2006 (http://www.noharm.org).

2. Lead (Pb) is found both naturally in the environment and in manufactured products. In the United States, automobile emissions are no longer a source of atmospheric lead because leaded gasoline has been phased out; current sources include leaded aviation gasoline, waste incinerators, and utilities. Lead is also present in dust from pre-1970s paint and other lead-based products.

   Design strategies: Avoid use of products containing lead and specify "100% lead free" products. See Credit 4.2, PBT Source Reduction—Lead, Cadmium, and Copper, for more details. If the facility has an incineration plant, verify that lead is removed from its emissions.

3. Nitrogen dioxide (NO2) emissions come from fossil fuel combustion (for transportation and electricity generation) and solvents.

   Design strategies: Locate outdoor air intakes away from vehicle areas. See also EA Credit 7, Community Contaminant Prevention Airborne Releases.

4. Ground-level ozone (O3), the primary constituent of smog, is created through a chemical reaction between nitrogen oxides and volatile organic compounds (VOCs) in the presence of sunlight. Sources include motor vehicle exhaust, gasoline vapors, and chemical solvents. Ozone typically reaches harmful concentrations in urban areas, particularly during warm summer months.

   Design strategies: Locate outdoor air intakes away from vehicle areas. Provide containment and appropriate storage for solvents to minimize leakage. Avoid materials containing VOCs (e.g., certain paints and adhesives). See also IEQ Credit 4, Low-Emitting Materials.

5. Particulate matter (PM) is "a complex mixture of extremely small particles and liquid droplets. Particle pollution is made up of a number of components, including acids (such as nitrates and sulfates), organic chemicals, metals, and soil or dust particles."[3] PM includes dust, dirt, soot, and smoke generated from construction sites and smokestacks, as well as chemical combinations from reactions of sulfur dioxide and nitrogen oxides with the atmosphere. Both PM10 (coarse particles, with diameters of 2.5 to 10 micrometers) and PM2.5 (fine particles, with diameters less than 2.5 micrometers) can be inhaled and affect respiratory health.

   Design strategies: Locate outdoor air intakes away from vehicle areas. Eliminate ambulance idling or move idling zones away from building entrances and outdoor air intakes. Locate heliports downwind from outdoor air intakes. Develop and implement an environmental quality management plan during construction and before occupancy. See also IEQ Credits 3.1 and 3.2, Construction Indoor Air Quality Management Plan.

6. Sulfur dioxide (SO2), a major component of acid precipitation, is formed by the combustion of sulfur-containing fuels (e.g., coal and oil). Common sources are power plants and industrial boilers.

   Design strategies: Locate outdoor air intakes away from vehicle areas. Avoid on-site use of sulfur-containing fuels.

Permissible Exposure Limits (PELs)
Occupational Safety and Health Administration (OSHA)
http://www.osha.gov/SLTC/pel/
Set with workers' health in mind, the permissible exposure limits are based on an eight-hour weighted average exposure. The enforceable standards include limits for approximately 500

3 U.S. Environmental Protection Agency, Particulate Matter website (http://www.epa.gov/air/particlepollution/).

substances, including formalde yde, asbestos, and mercury. See the website for a complete list of contaminants covered by this standard. Many states have adopted standards and designed enforcement based on these federal standards.

Threshold Limit Values (TLVs)
American Council of Governmental Industrial Hygienists
http://www.acgih.org/
These guidelines (they are not standards) help industrial hygienists assess safe levels of exposure to chemical substances commonly found in the workplace.

Recommended Exposure Limits (RELs)
National Institute for Occupational Safety and Health (NIOSH)
http://www.cdc.gov/niosh/npg/pgintrod.html
The NIOSH Pocket Guide to Chemical Hazards (NIOSH Publication 2005-149) lists exposure limits for 677 chemicals or substance groupings found in the workplace and includes recommendations on measures to prevent or reduce exposure. The guide also includes the permissible exposure limits developed by OSHA (see above).

4. Implementation

Identify potential sources of pollutants, both indoor and outdoor, and design to minimize exposure, with a goal of source elimination and reduction. Designers should use their best judgment when determining the sources to include. Consider which sources could affect indoor air quality and identify possible entry points. Some affected areas, such as pedestrian walkways and places of respite, may be outside the building.

Outdoor Pollutants

The quality of air entering a healthcare facility through outdoor air intakes, windows, and entryways establishes the baseline air quality for its indoor environment. Identify any on-site emissions sources and address potential indoor contamination through a combination of measures:

- Locate outdoor air intakes away from on-site emissions sources.
- Move pollutant sources away from entryways, operable windows, and outdoor air intakes.
- Reduce emissions at the source (e.g., by filtering air contaminants entering or leaving exhaust systems).
- Increase the height of exhaust stacks or use exhaust systems that dilute emissions and increase dispersion, such as strobic fans.

Common contaminant sources for healthcare facilities may include the following:

- Emergency diesel generators.
- Idling vehicles, including ambulances and helicopters.
- Bio-safety hood exhausts.
- Food service exhausts.
- Boiler and other gas-fired equipment.
- Sterilizer exhausts.
- Housekeeping area exhausts.
- Smoking areas.

See the 2007 ASHRAE HVAC Applications Handbook, Chapter 44, for information on designing exhaust stacks and placing outdoor air intakes. Chapter 45 of the handbook provides guidance on improving indoor air quality if the ambient outdoor air has high concentrations of contaminants. Employing some of these strategies may result in energy efficiency trade-offs.

Permanent Entryway Systems

See the LEED Reference Guide for Green Building Design and Construction, IEQ Credit 5, Implementation section, for information about permanent entryway systems.

Pressurized Entryway Vestibules

Locating pressurized vestibules at high-volume building entrances minimizes the opportunity for particulate matter and other contaminants to enter the healthcare facility.

Outdoor Air Intakes

Calculate the pollution concentration expected at the facility's outdoor air intakes by running a dispersion model (using either mathematical modeling or a physical model). Full-scale field-testing is not an acceptable compliance path for this credit, since it is nearly impossible to change air intake locations once the building is constructed.

Mathematical modeling simulates the meteorological conditions, the contaminant plumes from on-site emissions sources, and the contaminant concentrations at outdoor air intakes. Examples of mathematical modeling include analytical models and computational fluid dynamics.

Physical modeling involves placing a small-scale model of the facility and its surroundings into a wind tunnel or similar evaluation chamber. Concentrations of tracer gas released from exhaust sources are measured at outdoor air intakes and converted to full-scale concentration values. Physical modeling is best for simple terrain and massing, since accuracy can be difficult to achieve.

Conduct the following modeling tests:

Level 1. Screening under worst-case meteorological conditions. Base the worst-case conditions on the location's meteorological record (typically 20 to 40 years of data) for wind speed and direction. Determine which is worse, strong wind or low wind, with a direct line of sight from each source to the project building. Determine whether air contaminant concentrations at outdoor air intakes are less than allowable limits. The emissions contributions of some sources may be insufficient to merit the next level of modeling. For emissions sources that either exceed or only meet the applicable NAAQS, PEL, TLV, and/or REL standards, conduct Level 2 tests.

Level 2. Testing for barely compliant and noncompliant concentrations. Using more detailed inputs for the atmospheric processes, building geometry, and emissions concentration estimates, verify either of the following:

- Outside air intake concentrations meet the requirements listed in the referenced standards. If the precise composition of chemical exhaust is unpublished, document how the team arrived at its components and concentrations. This model can be a more refined version of the model developed for the Level 1 screening.

OR

- Indoor concentrations do not exceed 2.5% of the exposure limits listed in the referenced standards. This model may require a different methodology from the dispersion model, such as the RISK Indoor Air Quality computer model developed by EPA (http://www.epa.gov/appcdwww/iemb/model.htm).

For additional information about air quality modeling, visit EPA's Support Center for Regulatory Atmospheric Modeling (SCRAM) website (http://www.epa.gov/scram001) and identify the EPA regional modeling contact (http://www.epa.gov/scram001/guidance_regions.htm). The sample air quality analysis checklist (http://www.epa.gov/scram001/guidance/guide/checklist.pdf) provides detailed guidance on how to develop a successful model.

Indoor Pollutants

Segregate and ventilate indoor pollutant sources. Isolate areas for chemical use, sterilants, and cleaning product storage and provide them with direct exhaust and drainage systems for contaminants. Anticipate the potential for such uses in the future and design to accommodate further zoning after initial building occupancy.

In diagnostic and treatment areas, provide utility rooms with negative pressure and direct exhaust to accommodate sterilization systems and other medical equipment that requires chemical use. Consider centralized high-level disinfection and/or sterilization practices to reduce the number of satellite locations and increase quality control. Consider automatic washers and less toxic methods of sterilization and high-level disinfection of instruments. Create a committee to standardize best management practices for high-level disinfection to increase safety and reduce workers' exposure.

Use alternative equipment or laboratory methods that reduce use of hazardous materials. Use automated laboratory equipment that maximizes sample throughput while minimizing sample size, reagent quantity, and waste streams. Develop decanting procedures that eliminate waste or allow for recycling of waste streams. Minimize the volume of hazardous materials maintained in laboratories by developing a just-in-time inventory and delivery system. Provide dedicated, centralized areas for receiving, returning, and safely disposing of hazardous materials. Include an area for reporting all hazardous material transactions to a central inventory system.

For additional information about negative pressurization and air change rates, see the LEED Reference Guide for Green Building Design and Construction, IEQ Credit 5.

5. Timeline and Team

Identify sources of pollutants in schematic design narratives. Develop air quality dispersion models once the initial programming has been completed, early in the project design, to ensure that emissions sources are well removed from major entryways, outdoor air intakes, and exterior places of respite.

Many of the topics addressed by this credit affect operational activities (such as sterilization and cleaning) as well as lab research and other clinical activities. Coordinate development of an indoor pollutant source control plan with facility staff as early in the design phase as possible. At a minimum, include laboratory staff, central sterilization, environmental services, infection control, and energy management in the development process.

6. Calculations

There are no calculations for this credit.

7. Documentation Guidance

As a first step in preparing to complete the LEED Online documentation requirements, work through the following measures. Refer to LEED Online for the complete descriptions of all required documentation.

- Retain documentation, such as floor plans, showing the location of entryway systems, the location of pressurized vestibules, and all rooms for chemical mixing, sterilization, or high-level disinfection of instruments.

- Compile documentation demonstrating that all pressurized vestibules, chemical use areas, and copy rooms have been designed to comply with the credit goals.
- Compile documentation demonstrating that the pollutant levels at outside air intakes meet the credit requirements. Explain the assumptions made about sources of pollutants, including their distance from the building. If using a mathematical model, record the type of software used.

8. Examples

The EPA air quality analysis checklist (http://www.epa.gov/scram001/guidance/guide/checklist.pdf) provides a format for the data required to assess compliance with the NAAQS.

11. Operations and Maintenance Considerations

Include infection control and environmental services in materials selection to address cleaning protocols and reduce the toxicity of waxers, strippers, and other agents required to clean and disinfect interior finishes, furniture, and furnishings. Develop materials handling and processing guidelines as a part of initial building design, and monitor implementation of the guidelines as a part of final building commissioning. The guidelines should reduce consumption of hazardous materials and prevent contamination of the surrounding environment.

Work with environmental, health, and safety personnel and local code officials in developing an action plan to control sources of indoor pollutants.

Coordinate with facilities staff pursuing parallel credits in LEED for Existing Buildings: Operations & Maintenance and/or the Green Guide for Health Care, Operations section. The Green Guide for Health Care, in particular, addresses infection control and chemical management in great detail.

12. Resources

Websites

ASHRAE HVAC Applications Handbook (2007)
American Society of Heating, Refrigerating, and Air-Conditioning Engineers
http://www.ashrae.org/
Chapter 44 provides information about the proper design of exhaust stacks and the placement of outdoor air intakes to avoid adverse air quality impacts.

Chapter 45 provides information about how to improve indoor air quality if available outdoor air contains undesirable gaseous contaminants at unacceptable concentrations.

Best Practices, Modeling Exhaust Dispersion for Specifying Acceptable Exhaust/Intake Designs
Laboratories for the 21st Century
http://www.labs21century.gov/pdf/bp_modeling_508.pdf
Best practice guidance on the benefits of analyzing outdoor air pollutant dispersion as well as modeling to determine the expected concentration of pollution at outdoor air intakes.

Green Guide for Health Care Indoor/Outdoor Chemical & Pollutant Source Control Technical Brief, by Lorissa MacAllister
http://www.gghc.org/tools.technical.php
Best practices for controlling potential sources of on-site contamination through source reduction, appropriate ventilation, and pollution source isolation and containment.

Indoor Air Quality Modeling
U.S. Environmental Protection Agency
http://www.epa.gov/appcdwww/iemb/model.htm
Guidance and technical resources, including the RISK indoor air quality computer model, for modeling pollutant concentrations in indoor air.

NIOSH Pocket Guide to Chemical Hazards
National Institute for Occupational Safety and Health
http://www.cdc.gov/niosh/docs/2003-154/method-c.html
User-friendly guidance on testing and calculations of hazardous chemicals, searchable by chemical.

Support Center for Regulatory Atmospheric Modeling (SCRAM)
U.S. Environmental Protection Agency, Technology Transfer Network
http://www.epa.gov/scram001/
Technical support on dispersion, photochemical, and receptor models of the six principal pollutants regulated by NAAQS. EPA regional modeling contact:
http://www.epa.gov/scram001/guidance_regions.htm
Sample air quality analysis checklist:
http://www.epa.gov/scram001/guidance/guide/checklist.pdf

40 CFR Part 51, Revision to the Guideline on Air Quality Models: Adoption of a Preferred General Purpose (Flat and Complex Terrain) Dispersion Model and Other Revisions; Final Rule
U.S. Environmental Protection Agency
http://www.epa.gov/scram001/guidance/guide/appw_05.pdf
Regulatory guidelines for assessing criteria air pollutants under the Clean Air Act, including how to calculate design concentrations under worst-case meteorological conditions.

CONTROLLABILITY OF SYSTEMS—LIGHTING

	HEALTHCARE
Credit	IEQ Credit 6.1
Points	1 point

Intent

To provide a high level of lighting system control by individual occupants or specific groups in multi-occupant spaces (e.g., conference areas, critical care areas, emergency room areas) and promote their productivity, comfort and well-being.

Requirements

For All Occupants

Provide lighting system controls for all shared multi-occupant spaces to enable adjustments that meet group needs and preferences.

AND

For Staff Areas

Provide individual lighting controls for 90% (minimum) of the FTE staff (measured at peak periods) to enable adjustments to suit individual task needs and preferences.

AND

For Patient Areas

Provide individual lighting controls for 90% (minimum) of patients to enable adjustments to suit individual task needs and preferences.

Install lighting controls that are readily accessible from the patient bed. In multi-occupant patient spaces, such as recovery rooms, emergency departments, infusion areas, and similar open areas, provide individual lighting controls.

In private rooms, provide occupant controls that are readily accessible from the patient bed for exterior window shades, blinds, and/or curtains. Exempted areas include in-patient critical care, pediatric and psychiatric patient rooms.

IMPORTANT! This reference guide supplement contains only the reference guide sections that pertain to healthcare projects. Use this supplement alongside the LEED Reference Guide for Green Building Design and Construction for complete credit information. For the omitted sections, refer to the main reference guide.

IEQ	
HEALTHCARE: NC	Credit 6.1

1. Benefits and Issues to Consider

Environmental Issues

Reduced control over one's environment can lead to emotional distress. Because of the great variety of occupants and activities in a healthcare facility, individual control cannot be extended to all elements of the indoor environment. However, designing lighting and thermal controls to maximize responsiveness to individual needs can markedly improve both patients' and staff members' experience.

Economic Issues

Initial costs for mechanisms that allow patients to control shading from their beds are offset by increased patient comfort and reduced staff time spent raising and lowering shades for patients instead of delivering medical care.

4. Implementation

Coordinate the medical equipment and lighting designs early in the design process to minimize the costs associated with handheld devices for patients or nurse call systems and changes to headwall layouts. Document anticipated space uses to identify the level and type of controllability best suited to the application and identify spaces that will not include patient-controlled lighting.

6. Calculations

Shared Multioccupant Spaces

See the LEED Reference Guide for Green Building Design and Construction, IEQ Credit 6.1, Calculations section.

Adjustable Task Lighting

Identify workstation locations intended for individual use by peak-period staff, including all nursing stations, private offices, open-plan workstations, and reception stations. Confirm that at least 90% of these spaces have task lighting that enables adjustment to suit individual needs. At a minimum, the occupant must be able to turn the fixture on and off. Ideally, the occupant can easily reposition the fixture and have multiple light levels. The fixture should be appropriate for the task.

See the LEED Reference Guide for Green Building Design and Construction, IEQ Credit 6.1, Calculations section, for additional information on lighting control in offices and other regularly occupied spaces.

Patient Areas

Calculate the percentage of individual lighting controls in patient areas as follows.

STEP 1. Determine the total number of inpatient and outpatient positions in the project by counting patient beds, infusion chairs, exam rooms, recovery room bays, and other locations where patients receive clinical care.

STEP 2. Use Equation 1 to calculate the number percentage of individual lighting controls provided. At least 90% of patient positions must have individual controls.

Equation 1.

$$\text{\% Patients with Lighting Controls} = \frac{\text{Inpatient and Outpatient Positions with Lighting Controls}}{\text{Inpatient and Outpatient Positions}}$$

7. Documentation Guidance

As a first step in preparing to complete the LEED Online documentation requirements, work through the following measures. Refer to LEED Online for the complete descriptions of all required documentation.

- Retain design information on mechanical shade controls for patient rooms.
- For additional documentation guidance, see the LEED Reference Guide for Green Building Design and Construction, IEQ Credit 6.1.

11. Operations and Maintenance Considerations

Seek input from nursing staff on the advantages and disadvantages of providing mechanical shading devices in patient rooms.

For mechanical shade controls, include maintenance schedules in the facility's building operation plan. Ensure that building staff know the level of lighting controllability of each room so that they can assign patients and residents to spaces with the appropriate level of controllability.

CONTROLLABILITY OF SYSTEMS—THERMAL COMFORT

	HEALTHCARE
Credit	IEQ Credit 6.2
Points	1 point

Intent

To provide a high level of thermal comfort system control[1] by individual occupants or specific groups in multi-occupant spaces and promote their productivity, comfort and well-being.

Requirements

Provide individual thermal comfort controls for every single occupant patient room.

AND

Provide individual thermal comfort controls for 50% (minimum) of the remaining building occupants to enable adjustments to meet individual needs and preferences. Operable windows may be used in lieu of controls for occupants located 20 feet inside and 10 feet to either side of the operable part of a window. The areas of operable window must meet the requirements of ASHRAE Standard 62.1-2007 paragraph 5.1 Natural Ventilation (with errata but without addenda[2]).

AND

Provide comfort system controls for all shared multi-occupant spaces to enable adjustments that meet group needs and preferences.

Conditions for thermal comfort are described in ASHRAE Standard 55-2004 (with errata but without addenda[2]) and include the primary factors of air temperature, radiant temperature, air speed and humidity. Comfort system control for the purposes of this credit is defined as the provision of control over at least one of these primary factors in the occupant's local environment.

1 For the purposes of this credit, comfort system control is defined as control over at least 1 of the following primary factors in the occupant's vicinity: air temperature, radiant temperature, air speed and humidity.

2 Project teams wishing to use ASHRAE-approved addenda for the purposes of this credit may do so at their discretion. Addenda must be applied consistently across all LEED credits.

IMPORTANT! This reference guide supplement contains only the reference guide sections that pertain to healthcare projects. Use this supplement alongside the LEED Reference Guide for Green Building Design and Construction for complete credit information. For the omitted sections, refer to the main reference guide.

IEQ	
HEALTHCARE: NC	Credit 6.2

1. Benefits and Issues to Consider

Environmental Issues

Reduced control over one's environment can lead to emotional distress. Because of the great variety of occupants and activities in a healthcare building, individual control cannot be extended to all elements of the indoor environment. However, designing lighting and thermal controls to maximize responsiveness to individual needs can markedly improve both patients' and staff members' experience.

4. Implementation

Installing thermal controls is common practice for inpatient rooms but rare elsewhere in healthcare facilities. Provide individual thermal controls for each single-occupant inpatient room. Zone multioccupant patient areas, such as infusion bays, using the same approach as for other multioccupant spaces.

Occupant control of ventilation or airflow may conflict with regulatory requirements for ventilation rates and pressurization in healthcare facilities. Designs should therefore provide sufficient control to moderate temperature and airflow within code limits.

6. Calculations

Individual Thermal Comfort

Determine that individual thermal comfort controls are installed in all inpatient rooms.

Identify all other spaces in the project intended for individual use, such as nurse workstations, private offices, open-plan workstations, and reception stations. Confirm that 50% or more of individuals occupying these locations have at least one means of individual control over thermal comfort.

Operable windows may be used in lieu of individual controls for occupants located within 20 feet of the exterior wall and within 10 feet of either side of the operable part of the window. The operable portion of the window must comply with the free-opening size criterion of ANSI/ASHRAE 62.1–2007, Section 5.1; the minimum area of the window that opens is 4% of the net floor area. For example, for an area 20 feet by 20 feet per window, the opening size should be 16 square feet.

Shared Multioccupant Spaces

See the LEED Reference Guide for Green Building Design and Construction, IEQ Credit 6.2, Calculations section.

THERMAL COMFORT—DESIGN AND VERIFICATION

	HEALTHCARE: NC
Credit	IEQ Credit 7
Points	1 point

Intent

To provide a comfortable thermal environment that supports and promotes occupant productivity and well-being and provide for the assessment of building occupant's thermal comfort over time.

Requirements

Design heating, ventilating and air conditioning (HVAC) systems and the building envelope to meet the requirements of ASHRAE Standard 55-2004, Thermal Comfort Conditions for Human Occupancy (with errata but without addenda[1]), and local codes or current 2010 FGI Guidelines for Design and Construction of Health Care Facilities (Table 2.1-2: Ventilation Requirements for Areas Affecting Patient Care in Hospitals and Outpatient Facilities), where local codes do not apply. Demonstrate design compliance in accordance with the Section 6.1.1 documentation.

Provide a permanent monitoring system to ensure that the building performs to the desired comfort criteria as determined above.

Agree to implement a thermal comfort survey of building occupants[2] within a period of six to 18 months after occupancy. The survey shall collect anonymous responses about thermal comfort in the building, including an assessment of overall satisfaction with thermal performance and identification of thermal comfort-related problems. Agree to develop a plan for corrective action if the survey results indicate that more than 20% of occupants are dissatisfied with thermal comfort in the building. The plan shall include measurement of relevant environmental variables in problem areas in accordance with ASHRAE Standard 55-2004 (with errata but without addenda[1]) and 2010 FGI Guidelines for Design and Construction of Health Care Facilities.

1 Project teams wishing to use ASHRAE-approved addenda for the purposes of this credit may do so at their discretion. Addenda must be applied consistently across all LEED credits.

2 In acute care hospitals and outpatient healthcare projects, occupants are defined as full-time staff. For residential health care occupancies, such as long term care or rehabilitation facilities, occupants include both full-time staff and residents.

IMPORTANT! This reference guide supplement contains only the reference guide sections that pertain to healthcare projects. Use this supplement alongside the LEED Reference Guide for Green Building Design and Construction for complete credit information. For the omitted sections, refer to the main reference guide.

3. Summary of Referenced Standards

Guidelines for the Design and Construction of Health Care Facilities (2010)
Facility Guidelines Institute
http://www.fgiguidelines.org/
These guidelines establish the healthcare industry's minimum standard for good practice in design and construction. Extensive appendixes provide information about emerging design and construction trends for HVAC, waste reduction, acoustics, and other sustainability topics. Forty-two U.S. states use the guidelines as code or as a reference standard.

4. Implementation

This credit combines two credits from LEED 2009 for New Construction: IEQ Credit 7.1, Thermal Comfort—Design, and IEQ Credit 7.2, Thermal Comfort—Verification. See the Implementation sections for those credits in the LEED Reference Guide for Green Building Design and Construction.

The following building occupants are eligible to complete the thermal comfort survey:

- For acute-care hospitals and outpatient healthcare projects, full-time staff only.
- For residential healthcare occupancies, such as long-term care or rehabilitation facilities, full-time staff and residents.

5. Timeline and Team

Refer to the Timeline and Team sections for IEQ Credit 7.1, Thermal Comfort—Design, and IEQ Credit 7.2, Thermal Comfort—Verification, in the LEED Reference Guide for Green Building Design and Construction.

6. Calculations

Refer to the Calculations sections for IEQ Credit 7.1, Thermal Comfort—Design, and IEQ Credit 7.2, Thermal Comfort—Verification, in the LEED Reference Guide for Green Building Design and Construction.

7. Documentation Guidance

Refer to the Documentation Guidance section for IEQ Credit 7.1, Thermal Comfort—Design, and IEQ Credit 7.2, Thermal Comfort—Verification, in the LEED Reference Guide for Green Building Design and Construction.

8. Examples

Refer to the Examples section for IEQ Credit 7.1, Thermal Comfort—Design, and IEQ Credit 7.2, Thermal Comfort—Verification, in the LEED Reference Guide for Green Building Design and Construction.

9. Exemplary Performance

This credit is not eligible for exemplary performance under the Innovation in Design section.

10. Regional Variations

Refer to the Regional Variations section for IEQ Credit 7.1, Thermal Comfort—Design, and IEQ Credit 7.2, Thermal Comfort—Verification, in the LEED Reference Guide for Green Building Design and Construction.

11. Operations and Maintenance Considerations

Refer to the Operations and Maintenance section for IEQ Credit 7.1, Thermal Comfort—Design, and IEQ Credit 7.2, Thermal Comfort—Verification, in the LEED Reference Guide for Green Building Design and Construction.

Coordinate with facilities staff pursuing parallel credits in LEED for Existing Buildings: Operations & Maintenance and/or the *Green Guide for Health Care, Operations* section. The *Green Guide for Health Care*, in particular, emphasizes the importance of providing a healing environment for patients, visitors, and staff.

13. Definitions

Occupants: In acute care hospitals and outpatient healthcare projects, occupants are defined as full-time staff. For residential health care occupancies, such as long term care or rehabilitation facilities, occupants include both full-time staff and residents.

DAYLIGHT AND VIEWS—DAYLIGHT

	HEALTHCARE
Credit	IEQ Credit 8.1
Points	2 points

Intent

To provide building occupants with a connection between indoor spaces and the outdoors through the introduction of daylight and views into the regularly occupied areas of the building.

Requirements

Achieve a minimum of two points under IEQ Credit 8.2: Daylight and Views—Views.

AND

Install daylight responsive controls in 100% of the area that meets the daylight quantity thresholds below. Daylight controls must switch or dim electric lights in response to the presence or absence of daylight illumination in the space.

AND

For a minimum of 75% of more of the perimeter area used to qualify under IEQ Credit 8.2, achieve daylighting in at least the following spaces, through 1 of the 4 options:

OPTION 1. Simulation

Demonstrate through computer simulations that 75% or more of perimeter area used to qualify under IEQ Credit 8.2 achieve daylight illuminance levels of a minimum of 25 footcandles (fc) and a maximum of 500 fc in a clear sky condition on September 21 at 9 a.m. and 3 p.m. Areas with illuminance levels below or above the range do not comply. However, designs that incorporate view-preserving automated shades for glare control may demonstrate compliance for only the minimum 25 fc illuminance level.

OR

OPTION 2. Prescriptive

Use a combination of side-lighting and/or top-lighting to achieve a total daylighting zone (the floor area meeting the following requirements) that is at least 75% of the perimeter area used to qualify under IEQ Credit 8.2:

For the Side-lighting Daylight Zone (see diagram on the next page):

- Achieve a value, calculated as the product of the visible light transmittance (VLT) and window-to-floor area ratio (WFR) of daylight zone between 0.150 and 0.180. The window area included in the calculation must be at least 30 inches above the floor.

$$0.150 < VLT \times WFR < 0.180$$

- The ceiling must not obstruct a line in section that joins the window-head to a line on the floor that is parallel to the plane of the window; Is twice the height of the window-head above the floor in, distance from the plane of the glass as measured perpendicular to the plane of the glass.
- Provide sunlight redirection and/or glare control devices to ensure daylight effectiveness.

IMPORTANT! This reference guide supplement contains only the reference guide sections that pertain to healthcare projects. Use this supplement alongside the LEED Reference Guide for Green Building Design and Construction for complete credit information. For the omitted sections, refer to the main reference guide.

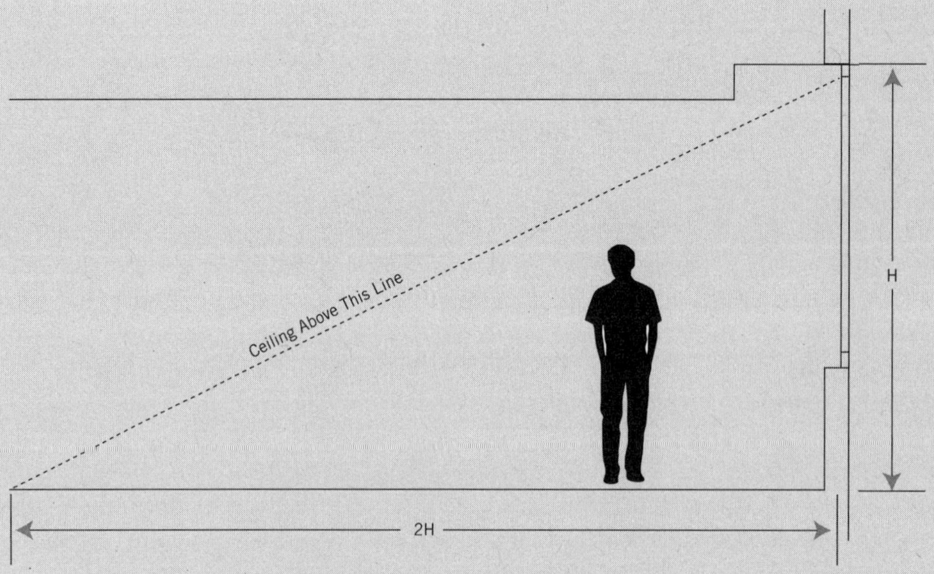

For Top-lighting Daylight Zone (see diagram on the next page):

- The daylight zone under a skylight is the outline of the opening beneath the skylight, plus in each direction the lesser of:
  - 70% of the ceiling height,

  OR

  - 1/2 the distance to the edge of the nearest skylight,

  OR

  - The distance to any permanent opaque partition (if transparent show VLT) farther than 70% of the distance between the top of the partition and the ceiling.
- Achieve skylight roof coverage between 3% and 6% of the roof area with a minimum 0.5 VLT.
- The distance between the skylights must not be more than 1.4 times the ceiling height.
- A skylight diffuser, if used, must have a measured haze value of greater than 90% when tested according to ASTM D1003. Avoid direct line of sight to the skylight diffuser.

Exceptions for areas where tasks would be hindered by the use of daylight will be considered on their merits.

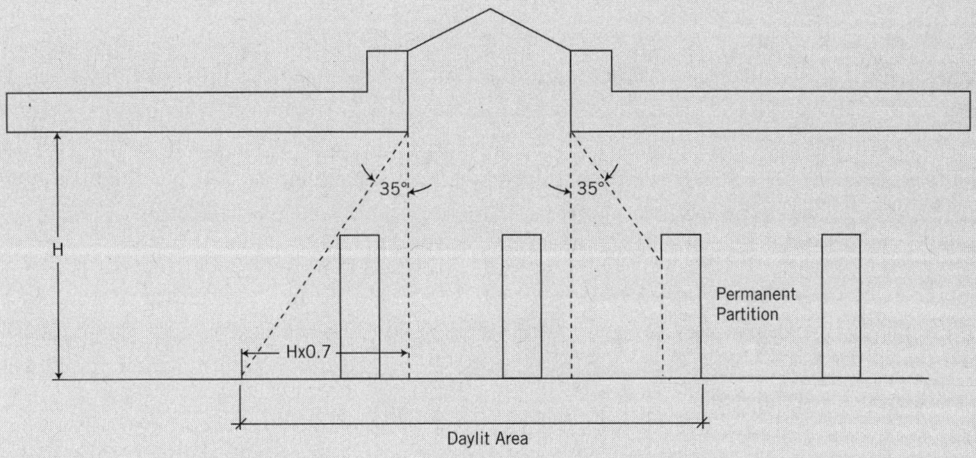

OR

OPTION 3. Measurement

Demonstrate through records of indoor light measurements that a minimum daylight illumination level of 25 fc has been achieved in at least 75% of the perimeter area used to qualify under IEQ Credit 8.2. Measurements must be taken on a 10-foot grid for all occupied spaces and recorded on building floor plans.

Only the square footage associated with the portions of rooms or spaces meeting the minimum illumination requirements may be counted in the calculations.

For all projects pursuing this option, provide daylight redirection and/or glare control devices to avoid high-contrast situations that could impede visual tasks. Exceptions for areas where tasks would be hindered by daylight will be considered on their merits.

OR

OPTION 4. Combination

Any of the above calculation methods may be combined to document the minimum daylight illumination in at least 75% of the perimeter area used to qualify under IEQ Credit 8.2. The different methods used in each space must be clearly recorded on all building plans.

In all cases, only the square footage associated with the portions of rooms or spaces meeting the requirements may be applied toward the total area calculation required to qualify for this credit.

In all cases, provide glare control devices to avoid high-contrast situations that could impede visual tasks. Exceptions for areas where tasks would be hindered by the use of daylight will be considered on their merits.

IEQ	
HEALTHCARE: NC	Credit 8.1

1. Benefits and Issues to Consider

Environmental Issues

Designing healthcare facilities with access to daylight and views of the outdoors embraces the concept of biophilia, the hypothesis that human beings need to connect with nature. Research shows that humans respond to natural cycles. In a stressful, 24-7 environment that houses both patients and staff at all hours, it is critical to provide quiet areas that support healing by allowing users to reconnect to the natural cycles of day and night, seasonal changes, and weather patterns.

Hospitals' high energy intensity (with its associated carbon emissions) is due to many factors, but deep, windowless floor plates dependent on electric lighting and mechanical ventilation are more energy intensive than narrow, daylit floor plates of equivalent area. Designing hospitals that incorporate daylight and views can improve energy performance and help occupants function when electrical service is disrupted.

Economic Issues

U.S. hospitals typically have a "plinth-tower" arrangement, with inpatient towers sitting on top of a diagnostic and treatment (D&T) block. In each tower, most of the perimeter is occupied by inpatient bed spaces, with windows; nursing stations and other staff areas inside, without direct access to daylight or views. In the D&T block, the perimeter is usually programmed for public spaces and circulation; the clinical areas, support spaces, and administrative offices are inside leaving staff with limited access to daylight. In order to ensure that both staff and patient areas provide access to daylight, the daylight and views credits deal with inpatient areas and other areas separately.

In current hospital design, there are many reasons why the D&T block is designed without access to daylight. The deep floor plate design of the D&T block has the benefit of reducing distance to critical adjacencies and provides uniform grids and bays for flexibility in future layout and servicing. Equipment lines all four walls and often is embedded into the ceiling and floor, eliminating opportunities for both windows and skylights. Fire code and privacy requirements also reduce opportunities and increase the initial cost associated with glazing in these areas. There are options to meet the code and design requirements of modern North American hospitals and provide both staff and patients with access to daylight and views.

Courtyards and articulated designs[1] (i.e., C, F, E, or comb shapes) provide access to daylight and views by narrowing the floor plate. Designing a hospital to provide adequate daylight and views for all building occupants often involves rethinking the fundamental building typology. These designs can increase the initial cost because of the additional perimeter wall and additional glazing. However, reason to do so comes from the growing body of evidence linking access to daylight and views of nature with improved health outcomes. Daylight can reduce depression in patients and reduce agitation among elderly patients with dementia.[2] Providing patients with views and access to nature can shorten hospital stays and reduce stress, depression, and the use of pain medication.[3] The increased satisfaction for patients, staff, and visitors can translate into economic benefits.

2. Related Credits

The calculations for this credit use the qualifying spaces from IEQ Credit 8.2, Daylight and Views—Views, as the baseline. Project teams calculate the percentage of space within a specified distance

1 *Sustainable Healthcare Architecture*, Guenther and Vittori (John Wiley & Sons, 2008)

2 R. Ulrich and C. Zimring, "The Role of the Physical Environment in the Hospital of the 21st Century: A Once in a Lifetime Opportunity," report to the Center for Health Design for the Designing the 21st Century Hospital Project, 2004 (http://www.rwjf.org/files/publications/other/RoleofthePhysicalEnvironment.pdf).

3 Roger Ulrich et al., A Review of the Research Literature on Evidence-Based Healthcare Design, Health Environments Research and Design Journal 1(3), 2008 (http://www.herdjournal.com).

of the perimeter wall; to achieve this daylighting credit, 75% of this qualifying space must meet the daylight quantity minimums.

Window shading in patient rooms should be controllable from the patient's bed, as required by IEQ Credit 6.1, Controllability of Systems—Lighting.

Design for daylight and views should form part of an integrated approach to designing a healing environment, contributing to the following prerequisites and credits:

- ID Prerequisite 1, Integrative Project Planning and Design
- ID Credit 3, Integrative Project Planning and Design
- SS Credit 9.1, Connection to the Natural World: Places of Respite
- SS Credit 9.2, Connection to the Natural World: Direct Exterior Access for Patients
- IEQ Credit 2, Acoustic Environment

3. Summary of Referenced Standards

There are no referenced standards for this credit.

4. Implementation

Meet the requirements of IEQ Credit 8.2, Daylight and Views—Views, for noninpatient areas prior to pursuing this credit.

5. Timeline and Team

Educate physicians, nurses, medical staff, administrators, and medical planners about the benefits of providing daylight and views to back-of-house and clinical areas in addition to public areas and patients' rooms. Provide case studies, peer-reviewed literature, and tours of other healthcare facilities that have implemented these strategies to demonstrate the benefits and lessons learned. Gather feedback from project stakeholders and team members early in the design process regarding any concerns associated with providing daylight and views. Engage the facility's green team, if applicable. An interdepartmental dialogue about daylight and views can help build support for the idea and tailor the design approach to complement the healthcare organization's mission and services.

If operable windows are under consideration, coordinate with infection control, facilities managers, MEP engineers, and landscape architects to ensure that sources of emissions, pollutants, and irritants are not located near these openings.

Because of possible site constraints, begin pursuing the goal early in the design process, at the programming stage, when block planning is tested and initial design parameters are established. Collaborate with medical planners to develop a design that maximizes critical adjacencies, interior design flexibility, and access to daylight and views.

During schematic design and design development, locate glazing to maximize daylight and views while protecting patients' privacy.

Coordinate lighting controls with the lighting designer or electrical engineer early in construction documents development.

6. Calculations

Identify which spaces qualify under IEQ Credit 8.2. Use those spaces as the basis for all IEQ Credit 8.1 calculations.

See the LEED Reference Guide for Green Building Design and Construction, IEQ Credit 8.1, Daylight and Views—Daylight, for guidance on calculations.

7. Documentation Guidance

As a first step in preparing to complete the LEED Online documentation requirements, work through the following measures. Refer to LEED Online for the complete descriptions of all required documentation.

- Develop documentation—such as floor plans, sections, and lighting control schedules—showing the daylight control methods used on the project.
- See the LEED Reference Guide for Green Building Design and Construction for additional guidance on documentation.

8. Examples

See the Examples section in the LEED Reference Guide for Green Building Design and Construction, IEQ Credit 8.2.

9. Exemplary Performance

Projects that achieve 90% daylighting based on the credit requirements and guidelines are eligible for exemplary performance under the Innovation in Design section.

11. Operations and Maintenance Considerations

Calibrate automated daylight sensors and controls on an ongoing basis, per the manufacturer's recommendations.

Coordinate with facilities staff pursuing parallel credits in LEED for Existing Buildings: Operations & Maintenance and/or the Green Guide for Health Care, Operations section. The Green Guide for Health Care, in particular, emphasizes the importance of providing a healing environment for patients, visitors, and staff.

12. Resources

Websites

The Impact of Light on Outcomes in Healthcare Settings, by Anjali Joseph (Center for Health Design, Issue Paper 2, 2006)
http://www.rwjf.org/files/publications/other/CHD_Issue_Paper2.pdf
A literature review of evidence-based research on the clinical outcomes associated with daylight in the healthcare setting.

Incentivizing the Daylit Hospital: The Green Guide for Health Care Approach, by Ray Pradinuk (*Health Environmental Research and Design Journal*, Sustainable Design Issue, Summer 2009)
http://www.herdjournal.com
Details on the methodology behind the Green Guide for Health Care and LEED for Healthcare Daylight and Views credits.

Integrated Lighting Tools and Resources
Betterbricks
http://www.betterbricks.com/detailPage.aspx?ID=706
This web page includes links to daylighting tools and resources, including the factsheet "Daylighting Hospital Patient Rooms," which provides findings from a joint study by the Energy Studies in Buildings Laboratory (Department of Architecture, University of Oregon) and Zimmer Gunsul Frasca Architects.

Targeting 100! Envisioning the High Performance Hospital, Implications for a New, Low Energy, High Performance Prototype, by Heather Burpee and Joel Loveland (University of Washington, 2010).
http://www.integrateddesignlab.com/Seattle/Resources/HD_Research.html
This report, from the University of Washington's Integrated Design Lab, explores the energy and cost implications of designing a hospital in compliance with Architecture 2030. It compares two building types—a typical postwar plan and an articulated layout that allows extensive access to daylight—in energy usage, construction costs, and lifecycle costs, among other design elements.

13. Definitions

biophilia the hypothesis that humans have an innate need to connect with nature.

infection control policies and procedures to minimize the risk of spreading infections through cross-contamination.

DAYLIGHT AND VIEWS—VIEWS

IEQ CREDIT 8.2

	HEALTHCARE: NC
Credit	IEQ Credit 8.2
Points	1-3 points

Intent

To provide building occupants a connection to the outdoors through the introduction of daylight and views into the regularly occupied areas of the building.

Requirements

Provide access to views that meet the following criteria below.

INPATIENT UNITS (1 point)

A minimum of 90% of the inpatient staff and public areas shall be within 20 feet—or twice the window head height, whichever is smaller—of the perimeter. All such perimeter areas must have windows that provide at least an 11° angle of unobstructed view in the vertical and horizontal direction.

NON-INPATIENT AREAS (1-2 points)

In the block planning stage, configure the building floor plates such that the area within 15 feet of the perimeter exceeds the perimeter area requirement as determined by the table outlined below.

Confirm at the conclusion of detailed planning that 90% of the perimeter rooms have windows that provide at least an 11° angle of unobstructed view in the vertical and horizontal direction.

Perimeter Non-IPU Area with Window Access Required		
Floor plate area (bgsf)	**Threshold A: 1 point**	**Threshold B: 2 points**
Up to 15,000	7348	8248
20,000	8785	9985
25,000	10087	11587
30,000	11292	13092
35,000	12425	14525
40,000	13500	15900
45,000	14528	17228
50,000 and larger	15516	18516

For both in-patient and non-inpatient areas, portions of side lit areas beyond the 15' view area boundary that meet the requirements of IEQ Credit 8.1: Daylight and Views—Daylight may be included in the qualifying areas of this credit.

For calculation methodology for floor plates that vary in size and configuration, see the LEED Reference Guide for Green Building Design & Construction, 2009 Edition Healthcare Supplement.

IMPORTANT! This reference guide supplement contains only the reference guide sections that pertain to healthcare projects. Use this supplement alongside the LEED Reference Guide for Green Building Design and Construction for complete credit information. For the omitted sections, refer to the main reference guide.

IEQ	
HEALTHCARE: NC	Credit 8.2

1. Benefits and Issues to Consider

Environmental Issues

Designing healthcare facilities with access to daylight and views of the outdoors embraces the concept of biophilia, the hypothesis that human beings need to connect with nature. Research shows that humans respond to natural cycles. In a stressful, 24-7 environment that houses both patients and staff at all hours, it is critical to provide quiet areas that support healing by allowing users to reconnect to the natural cycles of day and night, seasonal changes, and weather patterns.

Hospitals' high energy intensity (with its associated carbon emissions) is due to many factors, but deep, windowless floor plates dependent on electric lighting and mechanical ventilation are more energy intensive than narrow, daylit floor plates of equivalent area. Designing hospitals that incorporate daylight and views can improve energy performance and help occupants function when electrical service is disrupted.

Economic Issues

U.S. hospitals typically have a "plinth-tower" arrangement, with inpatient towers sitting on top of a diagnostic and treatment (D&T) block. In each tower, most of the perimeter is occupied by inpatient bed spaces, with windows; nursing stations and other staff areas inside, without direct access to daylight or views. In the D&T block, the perimeter is usually programmed for public spaces and circulation; the clinical areas, support spaces, and administrative offices are inside leaving staff with limited access to daylight. In order to ensure that both staff and patient areas provide access to daylight, the daylight and views credits deal with inpatient areas and other areas separately. The Daylight and Views credits deal with inpatient areas and other areas separately.

In current hospital design, there are many reasons why the D&T block is designed without access to daylight. The deep floor plate design of the D&T block has the benefit of reducing distance to critical adjacencies and provides uniform grids and bays for flexibility in future layout and servicing. Equipment lines all four walls and often is embedded into the ceiling and floor, eliminating opportunities for both windows and skylights. Fire code and privacy requirements also reduce opportunities and increase the initial cost associated with glazing in these areas.

Courtyards and articulated designs[1] (i.e., C, F, E, or comb shapes) provide access to daylight and views by narrowing the floor plate. Designing a hospital to provide adequate daylight and views for all building occupants often involves rethinking the fundamental building typology. These designs can increase the initial cost because of the additional perimeter wall and additional glazing. However, reason to do so comes from the growing body of evidence linking access to daylight and views of nature with improved health outcomes. Daylight can reduce depression in patients and reduce agitation among elderly patients with dementia.[2] Providing patients with views and access to nature can shorten hospital stays and reduce stress, depression, and the use of pain medication.[3] The increased satisfaction for patients, staff, and visitors can translate into economic benefits.

2. Related Credits

The calculation for IEQ Credit 8.1, Daylight and Views—Daylight, uses this credit as its baseline.

Window shading devices in patient rooms should be controllable from the patient's bed, as required by IEQ Credit 6.1, Controllability of Systems—Lighting.

1 *Sustainable Healthcare Architecture*, Guenther and Vittori (John Wiley & Sons, 2008)

2 R. Ulrich and C. Zimring, "The Role of the Physical Environment in the Hospital of the 21st Century: A Once in a Lifetime Opportunity," report to the Center for Health Design for the Designing the 21st Century Hospital Project, 2004 (http://www.rwjf.org/files/publications/other/RoleofthePhysicalEnvironment.pdf).

3 Roger Ulrich et al., A Review of the Research Literature on Evidence-Based Healthcare Design, Health Environments Research and Design Journal 1(3), 2008 (http://www.herdjournal.com).

Design for daylight and views should form part of an integrated approach to designing a healing environment, contributing to the following prerequisites and credits:

- ID Prerequisite 1, Integrative Project Planning and Design
- ID Credit 3, Integrative Project Planning and Design
- SS Credit 9.1, Connection to the Natural World: Places of Respite
- SS Credit 9.2, Connection to the Natural World: Direct Exterior Access for Patients
- IEQ Credit 2, Acoustic Environment

3. Summary of Referenced Standards

There are no referenced standards for this credit.

4. Implementation[4]

Design to maximize the square footage of the healthcare facility with access to views, defined as a direct line of sight to the outdoors via vision glazing within an 11-degree angle of an occupant's typical location in a space. This credit requires project teams to assess the views for inpatient units separately from other areas.

Lobbies, public areas, and patient rooms are usually daylit. D&T areas, ambulatory areas, support departments (such as kitchens, central sterile supply, pharmacies, and laboratories) are rarely daylit, even if they are located near the building perimeter. This credit encourages project teams to design the building to maximize interior daylighting for both patients and staff.

Inpatient Units

Inpatient units are defined as all medical, surgical, maternity, specialty, and intensive-care units where the patient's length of stay exceeds 23 hours. Many inpatient units are designed in a "racetrack" configuration, with a ring of patient rooms surrounding staff areas and family support areas. The staff spaces are thus in the core of the building, limiting staff access to daylight and views. Creative planning that retains the operational benefits of easy access to patients' rooms while placing staff and public spaces on the perimeter is required for credit achievement.

Articulated floor plans with double-loaded corridors, which place patient rooms on either side of a hallway, improve access to both daylight and views. The articulated floor plate reduces the overall depth and, compared with a block floor plate, allows daylight to illuminate a greater proportion of the building. This creates opportunities to provide daylight for nursing stations and other work areas. In T-shaped configurations with perimeter rooms, the windowless inside corner rooms can be used for storage, equipment, and vertical transportation. Nursing stations can be located closer to patient rooms, and wayfinding for visitors is easier.

Noninpatient Buildings and Areas

Noninpatient spaces include public spaces, diagnostic and treatment areas, ambulatory units, and all areas of the facility other than the inpatient units. They can be daylit either through an articulated plan or by inserting courtyards or light wells into a large block; see Examples. Although the articulated plan is more widely used, the courtyard option both increases overall access to daylight and reduces travel time between departments. It also gives the facility flexibility to expand and contract department size when clinical practices shift and technology drives changes in spatial configurations. Credit 8.2 requirements are based on achieving increased floor area within 15 feet of perimeter walls.

4 Content for the Implementation section used with permission from Ray Pradinuk, Doubling *Daylight in Sustainable Healthcare Architecture*, Guenther and Vittori (John Wiley & Sons, 2008)

5. Timeline and Team

Educate physicians, nurses, medical staff, administrators, and medical planners about the benefits of providing daylight and views to back-of-house and clinical areas in addition to public areas and patients' rooms. Provide case studies, peer-reviewed literature, and tours of other healthcare facilities that have implemented these strategies to demonstrate the benefits and lessons learned. Gather feedback from project stakeholders and team members early in the design process regarding any concerns associated with providing daylight and views. Engage the facility's green team, if applicable. An interdepartmental dialogue about daylight and views can help build support for the idea and tailor the design approach to complement the healthcare organization's mission and services.

Because of possible site constraints, begin pursuing the goal early in the design process, at the programming stage, when block planning is tested and initial design parameters are established. Collaborate with medical planners to develop a design that maximizes critical adjacencies, interior design flexibility, and access to daylight and views.

During schematic design and design development, locate glazing to maximize daylight and views while protecting patients' privacy.

6. Calculations

Inpatient Areas

STEP 1. Calculate the qualifying floor area. Using the building program and floor plans, determine the usable square footage of regularly occupied staff and public areas that are within 20 feet of the perimeter or twice the window head height, whichever is less. If 90% or more of the net area of a room or space is within the distance requirement, the entire area of the space qualifies. If less than 90% of the net area of the room is within the distance requirement, use only the qualifying area in the calculation.

The following service spaces may be excluded from the calculations: soiled and clean utility rooms, equipment and general storage, toilets, staff lockers, nourishment rooms, medication areas, environmental services rooms, and information technology spaces.

Include in the calculations any break rooms, team rooms, conference rooms, offices (shared or private), on-call spaces, and staff charting stations, whether centrally located or distributed in the corridors (one per patient room). Centrally located charting stations are compliant if they meet the distance requirements from the perimeter. Distributed charting stations qualify if they have a direct line of sight to perimeter glazing regardless of their distance from the perimeter.

If the project has multiple floors, calculate the cumulative area of all staff and public spaces for all inpatient unit floors and determine whether the total qualifying area meets the 90% requirement.

STEP 2. Verify the line of sight. Each space included in the qualifying square footage must have at least an 11-degree angle of unobstructed view in both the vertical and the horizontal direction from a typical location in the room.

- Using a floor plan, determine the line of sight to the outdoors for each window. Open doorways do not count. See Figure 1.
- Using representative building sections, draw a line at the eye level of a typical occupant across the section to establish eye height and any obstruction to the perimeter glazing. Eye level for a patient in a bed may be 60 inches, and for a seated person, 42 inches. Draw one or more representative sight lines from a point at eye height in the regularly occupied space to the perimeter vision glazing. The view must fall within that angle (Figure 2, level 2).

- Total the floor area of all spaces that meet all the above criteria and divide the sum by the total nursing unit usable floor area (with service spaces excluded) to determine whether the inpatient unit meets the 90% access-to-views requirement.

IEQ	
HEALTHCARE: NC	Credit 8.2

Figure 1. Floor Plan Showing Compliant Area

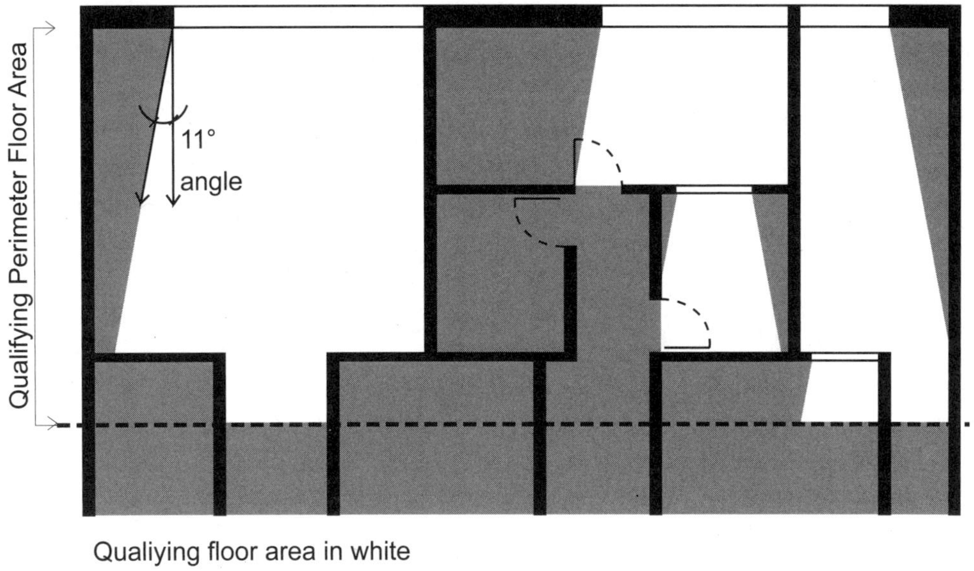

Figure 2. Section Showing Areas with Views

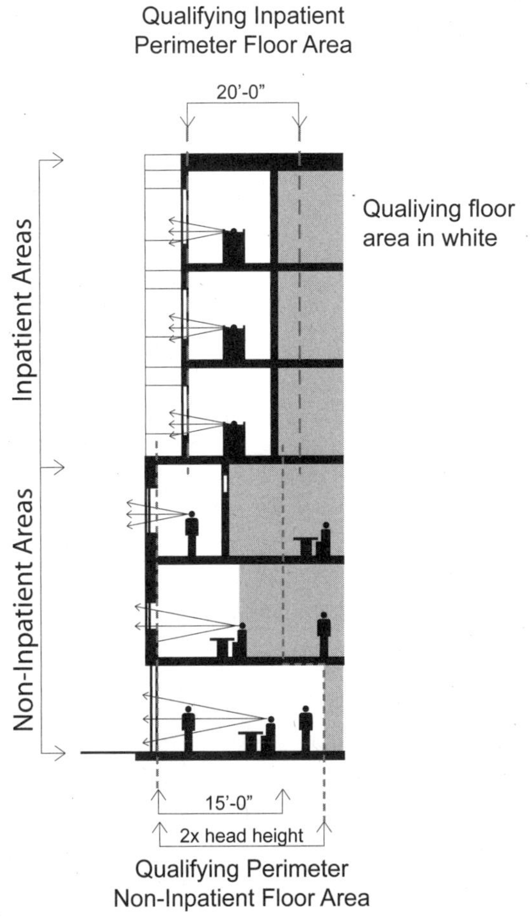

Noninpatient Buildings and Areas

This portion of the credit should be used for all areas other than inpatient units. Because noninpatient areas are often highly variable, each floor must be calculated separately; create a table summarizing the total floor area and qualifying area for each floor.

The initial component of the Credit 8.2 calculation (Steps 1 and 2) can be completed in the early stages of design, at block planning. At this point, project teams can determine whether massing decisions are likely to achieve the credit intent and adjust accordingly. Step 3, calculating whether the resultant perimeter has incorporated glazing for views, may be determined at a later point in the design phase. For Credit 8.1, Daylighting, at least 75% of the qualifying area must have the required daylighting illuminance levels..

STEP 1. Calculate the total floor area. Using the floor plans, determine the usable square footage of each floor plate. Refer to the Requirements table for the total floor area, by floor plate size, that must be within 15 feet of a qualifying perimeter wall.

STEP 2. Calculate the qualifying floor area. Determine the area of each floor plate that is within 15 feet of a qualifying perimeter wall, defined as a perimeter wall that is capable of providing a view. Below-grade walls with areaways and walls that abut adjacent buildings do not qualify.

Refer to Table 1. If the total qualifying area equals or exceeds Threshold A, the building may be eligible for one point. If it equals or exceeds Threshold B, the building may be eligible for two points.

For portions of the perimeter wall with full-height glazing, the qualifying area may be extended beyond the 15-foot limit to twice the head height of the windows; both single-story and multistory spaces are eligible.

STEP 3. Confirm the perimeter glazing provisions: 90% of areas must have windows that provide an unobstructed view at an 11-degree angle in the horizontal and vertical directions from a typical location in the room. Corner rooms are included if they have at least one wall with glazing.

7. Documentation Guidance

As a first step in preparing to complete the LEED Online documentation requirements, work through the following measures. Refer to LEED Online for the complete descriptions of all required documentation.

- Maintain documentation—such as floor plans, sections, and elevations—showing the location of qualifying perimeter spaces with views that meet the credit requirements. If there are no programmatic or architectural differences among inpatient unit floors (i.e., all are identical), only one floor calculation is required.

8. Examples

The larger the floor plate, the less the percentage of perimeter area with daylight (Figure 3).

Figure 3. Effect of Floor Plate Size on Daylighting

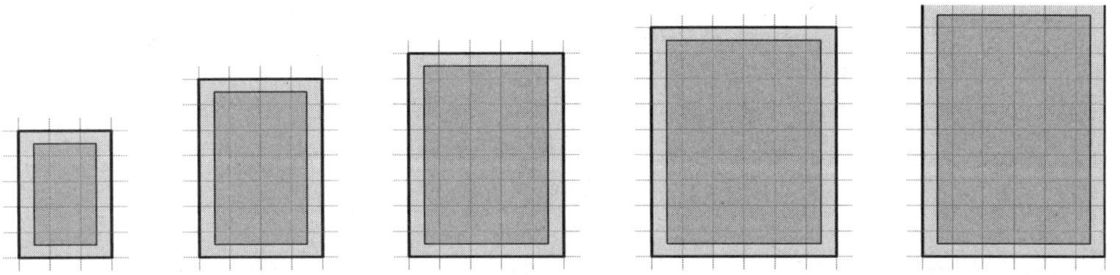

Area (square feet)				
13,500	25,200	36,000	48,600	54,000
Daylit Floor Area (percentage of Area)				
46.7	35.7	30.0	25.9	25.0

The floor plates in Figure 4 have the same square footage. When the floor plate is broken up with three small courtyards as opposed to one large one, more areas of the building can have access to daylight.

Figure 4. Daylighting with One Large Courtyard versus Three Small Courtyards

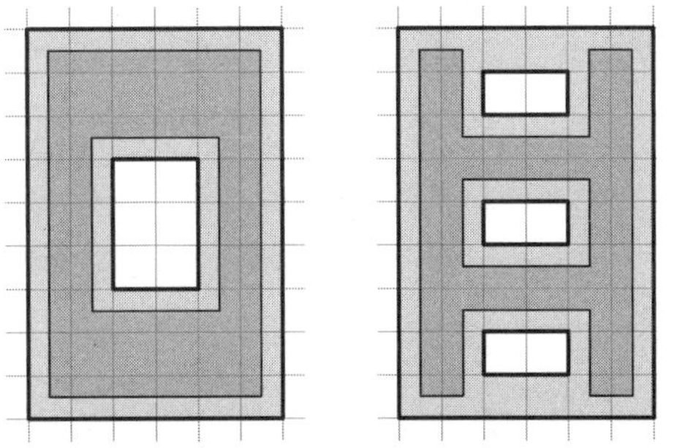

Area (square feet)	
43,200	43,200
Daylit Floor Area (percentage of Area)	
41.7	50.0
Daylit Floor Area added by Courtyard(s) (square feet)	
5,400	10,800

The three floor plates in Figure 5 have the same square footage, but the articulated plans receive considerably more daylight.

Figure 5. Effect of Articulated Floor Plan on Daylighting

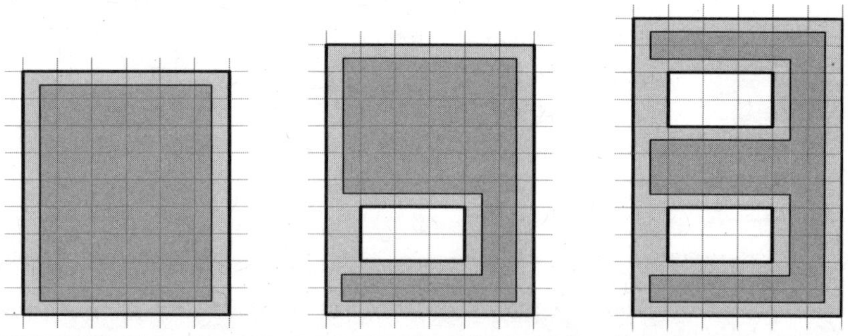

Daylit Floor Area (percentage of Area)		
25.9	38.9	51.9

9. Exemplary Performance

Projects that exceed the area requirements in Table 1 by 10 percent or more in inpatient and noninpatient areas are eligible for exemplary performance under the Innovation in Design section.

11. Operations and Maintenance Considerations

Coordinate with facilities staff pursuing parallel credits in LEED for Existing Buildings: Operations & Maintenance and/or the Green Guide for Health Care, Operations section. The Green Guide for Health Care, in particular, emphasizes the importance of providing a healing environment for patients, visitors, and staff.

12. Resources

Websites

The Impact of Light on Outcomes in Healthcare Settings, by Anjali Joseph (Center for Health Design, Issue Paper 2, 2006)
http://www.rwjf.org/files/publications/other/CHD_Issue_Paper2.pdf
A literature review of evidence-based research on the clinical outcomes associated with daylight in the healthcare setting.

Incentivizing the Daylit Hospital: The Green Guide for Health Care Approach, by Ray Pradinuk (*Health Environmental Research and Design Journal*, Sustainable Design Issue, Summer 2009)
http://www.herdjournal.com
Details on the methodology behind the Green Guide for Health Care and LEED for Healthcare Daylight and Views credits.

Integrated Lighting Tools and Resources
Betterbricks
http://www.betterbricks.com/detailPage.aspx?ID=706
This web page includes links to daylighting tools and resources, including the factsheet "Daylighting Hospital Patient Rooms," which provides findings from a joint study by the Energy Studies in Buildings Laboratory (Department of Architecture, University of Oregon) and Zimmer Gunsul Frasca Architects.

Targeting 100! Envisioning the High Performance Hospital, Implications for a New, Low Energy, High Performance Prototype, by Heather Burpee and Joel Loveland (University of Washington, 2010).
http://www.integrateddesignlab.com/Seattle/Resources/HD_Research.html
This report, from the University of Washington's Integrated Design Lab, explores the energy and cost implications of designing a hospital in compliance with Architecture 2030. It compares two building types—a typical postwar plan and an articulated layout that allows extensive access to daylight—in energy usage, construction costs, and lifecycle costs, among other design elements.

13. Definitions

biophilia the hypothesis that humans have an innate need to connect with nature.

infection control policies and procedures to minimize the risk of spreading infections through cross-contamination.

view a direct line of sight to the outdoors from a typical location in a room; in LEED for Healthcare, a view must be within an 11-degree angle from a window in both plan and section.

INNOVATION IN DESIGN

OVERVIEW

This section helps healthcare project teams maximize their designs' potential environmental and health benefits by establishing a framework for an integrated design process spanning the entire life of the project, from visioning to occupancy. It rewards teams that design innovative sustainability strategies to improve the health and well-being of building occupants, the surrounding community, and the environment. The integrated design process engages stakeholders who have not traditionally formed a part of the core design team, such as facilities engineers, infection control staff, waste management staff, and the surrounding community. These stakeholders can share important insights into the way the facility will likely be operated and the way occupants will use it. They can also act as a bridge to the team who will operate the facility, identifying design opportunities that will benefit the project should it seek certification under LEED for Existing Buildings: Operations and Maintenance.

CREDIT	TITLE	HEALTHCARE
ID Prerequisite 1	Integrated Project Planning & Design	Required
ID Credit 1	Innovation in Design	1-4 points
ID Credit 2	LEED Accredited Professional	1 point
ID Credit 3	Integrated Project Planning & Design	1 point

IMPORTANT! This reference guide supplement contains only the reference guide sections that pertain to healthcare projects. Use this supplement alongside the LEED Reference Guide for Green Building Design and Construction for complete credit information. For the omitted sections, refer to the main reference guide.

INTEGRATED PROJECT PLANNING & DESIGN

	HEALTHCARE: NC
Prerequisite	ID Prerequisite 1
Points	Required

Intent

To maximize opportunities for integrated, cost-effective adoption of green design and construction strategies, emphasizing human health as a fundamental evaluative criterion for building design, construction, and operational strategies. Utilize innovative approaches and techniques for green design and construction.

Requirements

Use cross discipline design and decision-making, beginning in the programming and pre-design phase. At a minimum, ensure the following process:

- **Owner's Project Requirements Document.** Prepare an Owner's Project Requirements document for the project. Prepare a Health Mission Statement and incorporate it in the Owner's Project Requirements. The health mission statement should address "triple bottom line" values—economic, environmental, and social—and include goals to safeguard the health of building occupants, the local community, and the global environment while creating a high performance healing environment for the building's patients, caregivers, and staff.
- **Preliminary Rating Goals.** As early as practicable and preferably before Schematic Design, conduct a Preliminary LEED meeting including a minimum of four key project team members, in addition to the Owner or Owner's representative. As part of the meeting, create a LEED® action plan that, at a minimum, includes the following:
  - The targeted LEED certification level (Certified, Silver, Gold, or Platinum);
  - The LEED credits that have been selected to meet the targeted certification level; and
  - The primary responsible party selected to meet the LEED requirements for each prerequisite and selected credit.
- **Integrated Project Team.** Assemble and involve a minimum of four of the following project team members from the list below, in addition to the Owner or Owner's representative, and as many as feasible.
  - Owner's Capital Budget Manager
  - Architect or Building Designer
  - Mechanical Engineer
  - Electrical Engineer
  - Structural Engineer
  - Energy Modeler
  - Equipment Planner
  - Acoustical Consultant
  - Telecommunications Designer

IMPORTANT! This reference guide supplement contains only the reference guide sections that pertain to healthcare projects. Use this supplement alongside the LEED Reference Guide for Green Building Design and Construction for complete credit information. For the omitted sections, refer to the main reference guide.

- Controls Designer
- Building Science or Performance Testing Agents
- Green Building or Sustainable Design Consultant
- Facility Green Teams
- Physician and Nursing Teams
- Facility Managers
- Environmental Services Staff
- Functional and Space Programmers
- Interior Designer
- Lighting Consultant/Designer
- Commissioning Agent
- Community Representatives
- Civil Engineering
- Landscape Architecture
- Habitat Restoration
- Land Planning
- Construction Management or General Contractor
- Life Cycle Cost Analysis; Construction Cost Estimating
- Other disciplines appropriate to the specific project type

Design Charrette. As early as practicable and preferably before schematic design, conduct at least one full-day integrated design charrette with the Integrated Project Team as defined above. The goal of the charrette shall be to optimize the integration of green strategies across all aspects of the building design, drawing on the expertise of all participants.

ID	
HEALTHCARE: NC	Prerequisite 1

1. Benefits and Issues to Consider

Environmental Issues

Hospitals in the United States are, on average, twice the size and consume 2.5 times the amount of energy per square foot as average commercial buildings.1 The building systems and equipment required to support modern healthcare delivery, including energy- and water-intensive medical equipment and energy-intensive data centers, impose significant environmental burdens on regional energy and water supplies and contribute to greenhouse gas emissions. Because of hospitals' size and complexity, the design and construction process for a new facility can take 10 years or more. Incorporating community members' and other stakeholders' input into the design, construction, and operations process adds yet another layer of complexity.

Following an integrated design process is particularly important for healthcare facilities because many environmental goals require sustained coordination among multiple disciplines, something that is not adequately addressed through the conventional project process. This prerequisite helps project teams maximize their designs' potential environmental and health benefits by establishing a framework for an integrated design process that spans the entire life of the project, from visioning to occupancy.

Economic Issues

The level of coordination required by an integrated design process appears to add to up-front construction costs. However, coordination among team members can actually reduce overall design and construction costs by streamlining the engineering process and avoiding change orders and other costly modifications during the construction documents and construction phases of the project.

Incorporating a health mission statement into the owner's project requirements can also help embed sustainable principles into the project's basis of design. The mission statement guides design team selection, design criteria development, and construction documents and establishes human health as a fundamental criterion for building design, construction, and operation.

2. Related Credits

This prerequisite has synergies with every prerequisite and credit in LEED for Healthcare but with these in particular:

- SS Credit 5.1, Site Development—Protect or Restore Habitat
- SS Credit 5.2, Site Development—Maximize Open Space
- SS Credit 6.1, Stormwater Design—Quantity Control
- SS Credit 6.2, Stormwater Design—Quality Control
- WE Prerequisite 1, Water Use Reduction
- WE Credit 1, Water-Efficient Landscaping—No Potable Water Use or No Irrigation
- WE Credit 3, Water Use Reduction
- EA Prerequisite 2, Minimum Energy Performance
- EA Credit 1, Optimize Energy Performance

Integrated design can inform and streamline the commissioning and measurement and verification process, contributing to the following prerequisite and credits:

- WE Credit 2, Water Use Reduction—Measurement and Verification

1 U.S. Energy Information Administration, Commercial Buildings Energy Consumption Survey (CBECS). http://www.eia.doe.gov/emeu/cbecs/contents.html (accessed October 13, 2010).

- EA Prerequisite 1, Fundamental Commissioning of Building Energy Systems
- EA Credit 3, Enhanced Commissioning
- EA Credit 5, Measurement and Verification

Designing a healing environment requires a strong integrated design process, contributing to the following credits:

- SS Credit 9.1, Connection to the Natural World—Places of Respite
- SS Credit 9.2, Connection to the Natural World—Direct Exterior Access for Patients
- IEQ Credit 2, Acoustic Environment
- IEQ Credit 8.1, Daylight and Views—Daylight
- IEQ Credit 8.2, Daylight and Views—Views

3. Summary of Referenced Standards

There are no standards referenced for this credit.

4. Implementation

Owner's Project Requirements

For information regarding development of the owner's project requirements, refer to the LEED Reference Guide for Green Building Design and Construction, EA Prerequisite 1, Fundamental Commissioning.

Incorporate a health mission statement in the environmental and sustainability section of the owner's project requirements. Its goals should include safeguarding the health of building staff, the local community, and the environment while creating a high-performance healing environment for the building's patients. It should express a commitment to these goals in present and future design, construction, and operations and reinforce any existing corporate and/or institutional commitments to environmental health and community responsibility. Use the owner's project requirements and health mission statement as a basis for design team selection, design criteria, and construction documents.

An existing healthcare mission statement of core values may be used if it meets the prerequisite requirements.

See examples of health mission statements developed by Practice Greenhealth (http://www.practicegreenhealth.org), listed in the Resources section.

Preliminary Rating Goals (Preliminary LEED Meeting)

Conduct a preliminary LEED meeting to establish sustainability goals for the project early in the design process, preferably during the visioning stage. This meeting should set the stage for the integrated design process and establish roles and responsibilities for the integrated project team, which should include at least four principal project team members in addition to the owner or owner's representative. Focus on the synergies between credit requirements to facilitate achievement of multiple credits. The meeting should determine the following:

- Targeted LEED certification level (Certified, Silver, Gold, or Platinum).
- Checklist of LEED credits targeted for achievement.
- Credit and prerequisite assignments to responsible parties on the integrated project team.
- As appropriate, metrics associated with the sustainable design goals.

Develop the overall project goals in concert with the sustainability goals to ensure that sustainability becomes part of every design and construction decision, starting in the visioning phase.

Integrated Project Team

The integrated project team members should represent the most critical disciplines involved in the project and may include representation from stakeholders not listed in the Requirements section. Engage the owner, staff, contractors, green teams, user groups, and community groups, educating them on the benefits of green design and bringing them into the design process at crucial points in the decision-making process.

The preliminary LEED meeting should establish roles and responsibilities for the integrated project team, including responsibility for specific LEED credits. Schedule regular check-in calls or meetings to assess progress toward achievement of the project's preliminary rating goals and other sustainable design metrics.

Designate an on-site party responsible for overseeing the project's environmental and health goals and implementing procedures for environmental protection.

Design Charrette

Use one or more cross-disciplinary charrettes to build a team approach to the project. Do not limit the topic of the design charrette to "green" topics. In a successful integrated design process, all design strategies are developed in a collaborative and concurrent process. Consider contracting with an outside facilitator to run the initial sustainability charrette. As an objective third party, a facilitator can be a valuable asset to early meetings, helping the integrated project team identify priorities and streamlining the assignment of roles and responsibilities.

Based on the owner's project requirements, the nature of the project, and the areas of expertise represented by the integrated project team, target the integrated design strategies to be developed during the charrette. Identify and capitalize on members' disciplinary expertise. Use the results of the charrette to inform development of the preliminary rating goals and related metrics. It is essential that the integrated design process foster an iterative cycle of team collaboration and follow-up research to move from a decision-making process based on assumptions to one grounded in evidence-based evaluation.

The goal of the design charrette is to develop a common vision for the project. A typical agenda for a full-day design charrette includes the following components:

1. Sharing information, including background research on the project objectives, stakeholders, and location.
2. Brainstorming goals and objectives by environmental category (e.g., site, water, energy, materials, indoor environmental quality).
3. Breaking out into smaller groups to identify potential design strategies and challenges and the additional research or action needed.
4. Setting the project's overarching goals, usually through consensus.
5. Assigning roles and responsibilities for additional research and development of synergistic ideas, and identifying team members with preliminary responsibility for LEED credits.

See the handbook on planning and conducting charrettes, listed in the Resources section, for additional information.

General

Consider organizing project delivery phases to align with the American Institute of Architects process for integrated project delivery. Integrated project design emphasizes collaborative teamwork, concurrent rather than linear processes, collective risk management, and performance-based compensation.

Performance-based incentives can be built into professional contracts to reward achievement of integrated design goals. Incentives may be based on reducing life-cycle costs of equipment and materials, achieving a certain level of certification in LEED for Healthcare, exceeding the performance of existing facilities, or combinations of these criteria and other benchmarks.

Participation in the charrette and follow-up meetings can be written into the contracts for design professionals. Consider allocating more design fees up front; the integration of disciplines early in the process will streamline subsequent design stages.

Consider seeking foundation support for integrated design initiatives.

Consider incorporating evidence-based design into the integrated design process. In evidence-based design, the design team works closely with the client, contractor, and specialists to make decisions based on information available from research, project evaluations, and client operations. Part of this process focuses on staff and patients' needs and on human behavioral factors (social, cultural, psychological, and physiological) in general. For more information, visit the Center for Health Design (http://www.healthdesign.org).

5. Timeline and Team

Convene the integrated project team as early in the design process as practicable, preferably before schematic design. If possible, include a representative from the contractor or construction manager so that cost and construction considerations are integrated into the development of design concepts.

Assess achievement of sustainability goals at regular meetings, corresponding at a minimum to project milestones.

Document progress toward achieving the project's sustainability goals at the conclusion of each project phase. Where applicable, consider continuing the integrated design data-gathering and documentation process for at least a year after occupancy begins. This information can be used as the foundation for a postoccupancy evaluation of the project.

6. Calculations

There are no calculations required for this prerequisite.

7. Documentation Guidance

To prepare to complete the LEED-Online documentation requirements, work through the following measures. Refer to LEED-Online for the complete descriptions of all required documentation.

- Owner's project requirements document, including a health mission statement.
- Document the preliminary LEED meeting. Document the preliminary rating goals, preliminary LEED action plan, LEED checklist, and integrated project team members present.
- Integrated project team members, professional disciplines represented, roles and responsibilities, dates of meetings, and log of participation.
- Design charrette proceedings, including a list of the decisions proposed during each charrette compared with the final design decisions.

8. Examples

Refer to the Implementation section.

9. Exemplary Performance

This prerequisite is not eligible for exemplary performance under the Innovation in Design section.

10. Regional Variations

Sustainability strategies may vary with the region's ecology, climate, planning requirements, and regulations. Project teams should use the integrated design process to develop creative, region-specific solutions to design challenges.

11. Operations and Maintenance Considerations

By including representatives of facilities and operations staff, the integrated project team can design and build a facility that is more responsive to occupants' needs and uses less energy and water. For healthcare projects on existing campuses, representatives from facilities operations can streamline integration of the new facility into existing infrastructure and operational policies, such as environmentally preferable purchasing, recycling and composting, and green cleaning.

Coordinate with facilities staff pursuing parallel credits in the Green Guide for Health Care, Operations section, such as Integrated Operations and Education Prerequisite 1, Integrated Operations and Maintenance Process.

12. Resources

Websites

Integrated Project Delivery: A Guide
American Institute of Architects
http://www.aia.org/ipdg
This guide, published in 2007, outlines a project delivery approach emphasizing collaboration and shared risk among project team members, particularly the owner, architect, and contractor.

Center for Health Design
http://www.healthdesign.org/
The Center for Health Design engages in research, education, and advocacy for evidence-based design in healthcare facilities. In evidence-based design, the design team works closely with the client, contractor, and specialists to make decisions based on the best information available from research, project evaluations, and evidence gathered from client operations.

Kaiser Permanente Position Statement on Green Buildings
http://www.healthybuilding.net/healthcare/KP_Statement.pdf
Kaiser Permanente's sample health mission statement addresses the siting, design, construction, and operation of its facilities.

A Handbook for Planning and Conducting Charrettes for High-Performance Projects, by Gail Lindsey, Joel Ann Todd, and Sheila Hayter (National Renewable Energy Laboratory, NREL/BK-710-33425, 2003)
http://www.pdc.us/pdf/sustainability/greenbuilding/Charrettes-handbook.pdf
This book provides guidance on the rationale for design charrettes and how to plan, develop, and facilitate a charrette. Sample checklists, agendas, and reports are included.

ID	
HEALTHCARE: NC	Prerequisite 1

Practice Greenhealth
http://www.practicegreenhealth.org
This membership nonprofit organization provides guidance on how to incorporate environmental sustainability into existing healthcare mission statements and offers sample health mission statements. Publications on its website include The Business Case for Greening the Healthcare Sector (Institute for Innovation in Large Organizations, 2008), which offers a sample statement of environmental principles. Sample environmental commitment statements are also available at the Practice Greenhealth website.

13. Definitions

basis of design the design information necessary to accomplish the owner's project requirements, including system descriptions, indoor environmental quality criteria, design assumptions, and references to applicable codes, standards, regulations, and guidelines.

charrette a collaborative process that draws on the expertise of participants to integrate sustainability strategies across all aspects of building design.

evidence-based design a design and evaluation process in which the design team works closely with the client, contractor, and specialists to make decisions based on the best information available from research, project evaluations, and evidence gathered from client operations.

health mission statement a broad definition of a healthcare organization's aims.

integrated design an approach that involves a project's principal stakeholders in the design process, from visioning through completion of construction, using an iterative, collaborative approach. The integrated design approach contrasts with the conventional linear approach to project delivery.

owner's project requirements a written document that details the ideas, concepts, and criteria determined by the owner to be important to the success of the project.

postoccupancy evaluation a systematic assessment, from the occupant's perspective, of a building's performance.

triple bottom line an approach to decision making that takes into account an activity's effects on the environment, society, and profit.

INNOVATION IN DESIGN

	HEALTHCARE: NC
Credit	ID Credit 1
Points	1-4 points

Intent

To provide design teams and projects the opportunity to achieve exceptional performance above the requirements set by the LEED Green Building Rating System and/or innovative performance in Green Building categories not specifically addressed by the LEED Green Building Rating System.

Requirements

Credit can be achieved through any combination of the Innovation in Design and Exemplary Performance paths as described below:

PATH 1. Innovation in Design (1-4 points)

Achieve significant, measurable environmental performance using a strategy not addressed in the LEED 2009 for Healthcare Rating System.

One point is awarded for each innovation achieved. No more than 4 points under IDc1 may be earned through PATH 1—Innovation in Design.

Identify the following in writing:

- The intent of the proposed innovation credit.
- The proposed requirement for compliance.
- The proposed submittals to demonstrate compliance.
- The design approach (strategies) used to meet the requirements.

PATH 2. Exemplary Performance (1-3 points)

Achieve exemplary performance in an existing LEED 2009 for Healthcare prerequisite or credit that allows exemplary performance as specified in the LEED Reference Guide for Green Building Design & Construction, 2010 Edition Healthcare Supplement. An exemplary performance point may be earned for achieving double the credit requirements and/or achieving the next incremental percentage threshold of an existing credit in LEED.

One point is awarded for each exemplary performance achieved. No more than 3 points under IDc1 may be earned through PATH 2— Exemplary Performance.

PATH 3. Pilot Credit (1–4 points)

Attempt a pilot credit (see the Pilot Credit Library, at www.usgbc.org/pilotcreditlibrary). Register as a pilot credit participant and complete the required documentation. A project team may pursue up to 4 pilot credits.

IMPORTANT! This reference guide supplement contains only the reference guide sections that pertain to healthcare projects. Use this supplement alongside the LEED Reference Guide for Green Building Design and Construction for complete credit information. For the omitted sections, refer to the main reference guide.

LEED ACCREDITED PROFESSIONAL

	HEALTHCARE: NC
Credit	ID Credit 2
Points	1 point

Intent

To support and encourage the design integration required by a LEED to streamline the application and certification process.

Requirements

At least 1 principal participant of the project team shall be a LEED Accredited Professional (AP).

IMPORTANT! This reference guide supplement contains only the reference guide sections that pertain to healthcare projects. Use this supplement alongside the LEED Reference Guide for Green Building Design and Construction for complete credit information. For the omitted sections, refer to the main reference guide.

INTEGRATED PROJECT PLANNING AND DESIGN

	HEALTHCARE: NC
Credit	ID Credit 3
Points	1 point

Intent

To maximize opportunities for Integrated, cost-effective adoption of green design and construction strategies, emphasizing human health as a fundamental evaluative criterion for building design, construction, and operational strategies. Utilize innovative approaches and techniques for green design and construction.

Requirements

- Assemble and involve a project team as described in IDp1
- Actively involve all team members referenced above in at least three of the following phases of project design and construction process:
  - Conceptual/schematic design
  - LEED planning
  - Preliminary design
  - Energy/envelope systems analysis or design
  - Design development
  - Final design and construction documents
  - Construction administration

Conduct regular meetings with the project team from the end of schematic design until the owner's certificate of occupancy to review project status, introduce new team members to project goals, discuss problems encountered, formulate solutions, review responsibilities, and identify next steps. These meetings can be integrated into other required project team meetings. A plan should be determined for regular integrated team coordination. At minimum, 12 meetings should be included with the integrated project team. In these meetings, utilize the process framework established by the ANSI/MTS 1.0 Whole Systems Integrated Process Guide (WSIP)-2007 for Sustainable Buildings & Communities©.

IMPORTANT! This reference guide supplement contains only the reference guide sections that pertain to healthcare projects. Use this supplement alongside the LEED Reference Guide for Green Building Design and Construction for complete credit information. For the omitted sections, refer to the main reference guide.

ID	
HEALTHCARE: NC	Credit 3

1. Benefits and Issues to Consider

Refer to the Benefits and Issues section in ID Prerequisite 1.

2. Related Credits

Refer to the Related Credits section in ID Prerequisite 1.

3. Summary of Referenced Standards

ANSI/MTS 1.0 Whole Systems Integrated Process Guide (WSIP)-2007 for Sustainable Buildings & Communities©, Whole System Integration Process (WSIP)

http://www.ansi.org/

This document provides guidance on transitioning from a linear to an integrated design process. In an integrated design process, research and analysis performed by team members representing different disciplines alternate with collaborative workshops in which the team assesses the synergies and conflicts between individual issues. This approach to project delivery emphasizes systems integration, evidence-based research, and an iterative approach to collaborative design.

4. Implementation

Use the health mission statement, preliminary rating goals, and results from the integrated design charrette (ID Prerequisite 1, Integrated Project Planning and Design) as a foundation for pursuing an enhanced integrated design process. In particular, ensure that members of the integrated design team are identified early in the design process so that they can participate in at least three phases of project design and construction process, as outlined in the credit requirements.

Establish a formal integrated design process using the ANSI framework (see the referenced standard). Document at least 12 integrated project team meetings that incorporate the components outlined in the credit requirements. Note that the specific issues addressed at each meeting will change as the project evolves. For example, an early meeting or workshop might focus on setting overall performance goals. During schematic design, the focus may shift to the site's ecological and cultural context, and during design development, to the integration of specific building systems. By the construction documents phase, the majority of systems integration will have been performed, and the team will consider how to build ongoing performance measurement and feedback loops into building operations. Incorporate value engineering into the entire process and consider the cost-effectiveness of proposed design synergies and systems integration.

5. Timeline and Team

Refer to the Timeline and Team section in ID Prerequisite 1.

6. Calculations

There are no calculations required for this credit.

7. Documentation Guidance

As a first step in preparing to complete the LEED Online documentation requirements, work through the following measure. Refer to LEED Online for the complete descriptions of all required documentation.

- Collect the minutes from at least 12 meetings of the integrated project team documenting compliance with the ANSI/MTS 1.0 Whole Systems Integrated Process Guide (WSIP)-2007 for Sustainable Buildings & Communities.

8. Examples

There are no examples for this credit.

9. Exemplary Performance

This credit is not eligible for exemplary performance under the Innovation in Design section.

10. Regional Variations

Refer to the Regional Variations section in ID Prerequisite 1.

11. Operations and Maintenance Considerations

Refer to the Operations and Maintenance section in ID Prerequisite 1.

12. Resources

Refer to the Resources section in ID Prerequisite 1.

13. Definitions

Refer to the Definitions section in ID Prerequisite 1.

REGIONAL PRIORITY

	HEALTHCARE: NC
Credit	RP Credit 1
Points	1-4 points

Intent

To provide an incentive for the achievement of credits that address geographically-specific environmental priorities.

Requirements

Earn 1, 2, 3, or 4 of the 6 Regional Priority credits identified by USGBC regional councils and chapters as having environmental importance for a project's region. A database of Regional Priority credits and regions is available on the USGBC website, www.usgbc.org.

One point is awarded for each Regional Priority credit achieved; a project team may earn up to 4 Regional Priority credits. USGBC has identified regional credits for projects in the United States, Puerto Rico, the U.S. Virgin Islands, and Guam. International projects may be eligible for certain credits and should check the database.

IMPORTANT! This reference guide supplement contains only the reference guide sections that pertain to healthcare projects. Use this supplement alongside the LEED Reference Guide for Green Building Design and Construction for complete credit information. For the omitted sections, refer to the main reference guide.

GLOSSARY

A-weighted decibel (dBA) sound pressure level measured with a conventional frequency weighting that roughly approximates how the human ear hears different frequency components of sounds at typical listening levels for speech (ANSI S12.60–2002)

added antimicrobial agent a substance added to a product (such as paint or flooring) that kills or inhibits growth of microorganisms. Some products, such as linoleum, exhibit natural antimicrobial properties. However, adding antimicrobial agents to building finishes has not been scientifically proven to reduce infection transfer more effectively than standard cleaning procedures. See U.S. EPA factsheet, Consumer Products Treated with Pesticides (http://www.epa.gov/pesticides/factsheets/treatart.htm).

articulation index (AI) a measure of the extent to which speech exceeds ambient sound levels. AI varies from 0 (absolute privacy) to 1.0 (perfect intelligibility, no privacy). (ANSI Standard S3.5)

backwash water that flows backward through a system. Backwash can be used to unplug filtration media.

biophilia the hypothesis that humans have an innate need to connect with nature

certified letter of destruction a written statement provided by a vendor (such as a licensed abatement contractor) to an owner acknowledging receipt of specified material, outlining how it will be protected prior to destruction, and verifying that it will be appropriately destroyed or abated

charrette a collaborative brainstorming session that draws on the expertise of participants to integrate sustainability strategies across all aspects of building design. Charrettes may occur repeatedly in an integrated design process.

churn the movement of workstations and people within a space

closed-loop cooling a system that acts as a heat sink for heat-rejecting building and medical equipment by recirculating water. Because the water is sealed within the system, some closed-loop cooling systems use nonpotable water (such as recycled process water harvested from an air handler's cooling coil condensate).

coal-tar sealant material used to seal parking lots and driveways, typically containing a 5% concentration of polycyclic aromatic hydrocarbons (PAHs), known carcinogens that may contaminate water bodies.

component an item that, when assembled with other elements, makes up modular furniture. Modular furniture components include panels (walls, partitions, dividers), work surfaces, storage elements, electrical and data cables, connectors, and supports.

composite sound transmission class (STC_c) the STC rating of any assembly comprising two or more subassemblies.

cycle of concentration the amount of solids in cooling tower recirculation compared with the amount of solids in make-up water. *Cycle* refers to the number of times dissolved minerals in the water are concentrated compared with makeup water, not to water flow over the tower or to on-off cycles.

dBA See **A-weighted decibel.**

demountable partition a temporary interior wall that can be easily reconfigured. In a healthcare facility, acoustical concerns and embedded equipment, as in a surgery suite, may prevent demountable partitions from being used.

GLOSSARY

departmental gross square footage (**DGSF**) the square footage of a diagnostic and treatment or clinical department, calculated from the centerline of the walls separating the department from adjacent spaces. Walls and circulation space within the department are included in the calculation.

direct access means of entering a space without having to leave the floor or pass through another patient's room, dedicated staff space, service or utility space, or major public space. Patients' and public circulation corridors, common sitting areas, and waiting and day space may be part of a direct access route.

elemental mercury pure mercury (rather than a mercury-containing compound), the vapor of which is commonly used in fluorescent and other lamp types.

engineered nanomaterial a substance designed at the molecular (nanometer) level to take advantage of its small size and novel properties that are generally not seen in its conventional bulk counterpart. See http://www.nicnas.gov.au/publications/information_sheets/general_information_sheets/nis_nanomaterials_pdf.pdf.

envelope commissioning a set of essential best practices used to ensure that the building envelope as installed separates indoors and outdoors as specified in the design documents. Practices include designating an envelope commissioning authority, performing a design review, performing field tests and inspections, and completing a summary commissioning report.

environmental quality management plan a set of measures to minimize contamination and protect human health, often applied to construction activities.

evidence-based design a strategy developed by the design team in collaboration with the client, contractor, and specialists to use the best information available from research, project evaluations, and client operations to inform design decisions.

freestanding furniture movable furnishings. Freestanding furniture may be anchored to a wall for seismic or stability requirements.

graywater untreated wastewater that has not come into contact with toilet waste. Graywater includes used water from bathtubs, showers, and bathroom washbasins, and water from clothes washers and laundry tubs. It does not include wastewater from kitchen sinks or dishwashers, unless a graywater definition established by the authority having jurisdiction in the area has precedence.

hazardous material management program a set of procedures for assessing, managing, and disposing of dangerous substances.

health mission statement a broad definition of a healthcare organization's mission.

hertz (**Hz**) the unit of frequency of sound and vibration. One Hz equals 1 cycle per second.

hot-mopped asphalt a multilayer roof consisting of asphalt, applied with a mop, between roofing membranes. Installation of this type of roofing can expose workers to asphalt fumes.

HVAC system equipment, distribution systems, and terminals that provide the processes of heating, ventilating, or air-conditioning to a building or portion of a building (ASHRAE 90.1–2007)

infection control policies and procedures to minimize the risk of spreading infections through cross-contamination.

infection control risk assessment (**ICRA**) an evaluation that anticipates the potential risks of infection transmission associated with construction and renovation projects..

integrated design an iterative, collaborative approach that involves a project's stakeholders in the design process from visioning through completion of construction, as opposed to a conventional linear design approach.

interstitial space the area between occupied floors, often used to run mechanical equipment, wiring, and other support services to the adjacent occupied floors.

lamp a device that uses electricity to produce light in any of several ways: by heating a wire for incandescence; by exciting a gas that produces ultraviolet light from a luminescent material; by generating an arc that emits visible light and some ultraviolet light; or by inducing excitation of mercury through radio frequencies. Light-emitting diodes packaged as traditional lamps also meet this definition.

lamp life the useful operating life of the sources of artificial light, such as bulbs

lead-free as defined by EPA regulations under the Safe Drinking Water Act, a label that allows small amounts of lead in solders, flux, pipes, pipe fittings, and well pumps, as opposed to 100% lead-free. (ANSI–NSF Standard 61)

length of stay the amount of time a person remains in a healthcare facility as an admitted patient.

liquid-ring pump a device that uses centrifugal acceleration to propel water into a rotating ring of liquid that can be cooled via a heat exchanger or cooling tower.

market value the amount that either was paid or would have been paid for a product; it is presumed to be less than replacement value.

modular (**movable**) **casework** shelving and cabinetry designed to be easily installed and moved or reconfigured.

net usable program area the sum of all interior areas available to house a building's functions; areas for building equipment, vertical circulation, and structure are excluded. See ANSI/BOMA Z65.1–2010, Office Buildings: Standard Methods of Measurement (http://www.boma.org).

once-through (**single-pass**) **cooling** a system in which water from any source is used to transfer heat from equipment or processes and then discharged.

persistent bioaccumulative toxic (**PBT**) **chemical** a substance that poses a long-term risk to both humans and the environment because it persists in the environment for long periods, bioaccumulates up the food chain, and can travel far from the source of contamination. See EPA's website on PBTs (http://www.epa.gov/pbt/).

place of respite an area that connects "healthcare patients, visitors, and staff to health benefits of the natural environment" (Jerry Smith, Green Guide for Health Care Places of Respite Technical Brief, http://www.gghc.org/tools.technical.php).

pollution prevention reducing or eliminating the source and proliferation of waste through modified production and purchasing practices; also called source reduction. See Pollution Prevention Act of 1990 (http://www.epa.gov/p2/pubs/p2policy/act1990.htm).

postoccupancy evaluation a systematic assessment, from the occupants' perspective, of a project's performance after completion of construction.

potable water water that meets or exceeds EPA's drinking water quality standards and is approved for human consumption by the state of local authorities having jurisdiction; it may be supplied from wells or municipal water systems.

process water water used for industrial processes and building systems such as cooling towers, boilers, and chillers. The term can also refer to water used in operational processes, such as dishwashing, clothes washing, and ice making.

product of combustion exhaust gas or flue gas that is emitted as a result of the combustion of natural gas, gasoline, diesel fuel, fuel oil, or coal.

refurbished material an item that has completed its life cycle and is refurbished for reuse without substantial alteration of its form. Refurbishing involves renovating, repairing, restoring, or generally improving the appearance, performance, quality, functionality, or value of a product.

reject heat a waste byproduct of heat exchangers, which can be found in process-intensive medical equipment.

remanufactured material an item that is made into another product. One example is concrete that is crushed and used as subbase.

replacement value the estimated cost of replacing a used product. This value may be equal to the cost of a similar new product or based on a new product with comparable features.

reverberation the repeated reflection or scattering of sound on the surfaces within an enclosed space. (ANSI S12.60–2002)

room sound absorption coefficient the sum of the room surface areas times their sound absorption coefficients divided by the room surface area. It is a dimensionless quantity that characterizes the reverberant character of the room and is related to the surface treatments and areas of those treatments in a room.

rural site (1) a settlement with fewer than 2,500 persons, (2) an area outside incorporated and census designated places, or (3) the rural portion of an extended city. See U.S. Census Bureau (http://www.census.gov/population/censusdata/urdef.txt).

salvaged material an item recovered from an existing building or construction site and reused. Common salvaged materials include structural beams and posts, flooring, doors, cabinetry, brick, and decorative items.

scrubber a device used to trap and remove pollutants from gaseous emissions.

semivolatile organic compound (**SVOC**) a pollutant that vaporizes only at high temperatures and is found mainly in dust and on indoor surfaces (such as furniture and finishes) rather than in the air. Examples include plasticizers (such as phthalates), halogenated flame retardants, and pesticides.

shell space an area designed to be fitted out for future expansion. A shell space is enclosed by the building envelope but otherwise left unfinished.

soft space an area whose functions can be easily changed. Examples include administrative offices or conference rooms adjacent to a lab with specialized equipment and infrastructure that are difficult to relocate; if the lab needs to expand, the offices or conference rooms can be moved.

sound absorption coefficient (**α**) the ability of a material to absorb sound, calculated as the ratio of sound energy absorbed by a material to the amount of sound energy incident on the material. It is frequency dependent and ranges from 0.00 (completely sound-reflecting) to 1.00 (completely sound-absorptive).

sound transmission class (**STC**) the ability of a material to prevent the transmission of sound between two spaces, expressed as a single number and determined by sound transmission loss measured in a laboratory (ASTM E90) using a method defined by standards (ASTM E413). The higher the STC rating the greater the ability of a material or system of materials in an assembly to reduce the transmission of sound between two spaces.

speech transmission index (**STI**) a measure of the extent to which speech is intelligible in the presence of ambient sound and other acoustic effects, such as reverberation. STI varies from 0 (totally unintelligible) to 1.0 (perfectly intelligible). STI is most often used to evaluate the performance of electronic sound reinforcement and paging systems. (IEC 60268-16)

STCc See **composite sound transmission class.**

submeter a device that measures amount or volume (as of water or fuel) for a specific usage rather than the facility's overall usage.

triple bottom line an approach to decision making that takes into account an activity's social, environmental, and economic effects ("people, planet, profit").

verification checks and tests carried out to determine whether components, subsystems, systems, and interfaces between systems operate in accordance with the contract documents.

view a direct line of sight to the outdoors from a typical location in a room; in LEED for Healthcare, a view must be within an 11-degree angle from a window in both plan and section.

viewshed an area of land, water, or other environmental element that is visible to the human eye from a fixed vantage point.

RECYCLED
Paper made from recycled material
FSC® C014174
FSC
www.fsc.org

This reference guide was printed on 100% postconsumer waste paper, processed chlorine free, and printed with non-toxic, soybased inks using 100% wind power. By using these materials and production processes, the U.S. Green Building Council saved the following resources:

Trees*	Solid Waste	Liquid Waste	Electricity	Greenhouse Gases	Sulfur Dioxides	Nitrogen Oxides
4 trees preserved for the future	1,748 lbs.	15,246 gallons	32 Million BTUs	5,031 lb.	36 lbs.	12 lbs.

*one harvested tree = aprox. 575 lbs

eco-ink
CARBON NEUTRAL
ecoprinted